Off the Derech

SUNY SERIES IN CONTEMPORARY JEWISH LITERATURE AND CULTURE

EZRA CAPPELL, EDITOR

Dan Shiffman, *College Bound:*
The Pursuit of Education in Jewish American Literature, 1896–1944

Eric J. Sundquist, editor, *Writing in Witness:*
A Holocaust Reader

Noam Pines, *The Infrahuman: Animality in Modern Jewish Literature*

Oded Nir, *Signatures of Struggle:*
The Figuration of Collectivity in Israeli Fiction

Zohar Weiman-Kelman, *Queer Expectations:*
A Genealogy of Jewish Women's Poetry

Richard J. Fein, translator, *The Full Pomegranate:*
Poems of Avrom Sutzkever

Victoria Aarons and Holli Levitsky, editors,
New Directions in Jewish American and
Holocaust Literatures: Reading and Teaching

Ruthie Abeliovich, *Possessed Voices:*
Aural Remains from Modernist Hebrew Theater

Jennifer Cazenave, *An Archive of the Catastrophe:*
The Unused Footage of Claude Lanzmann's Shoah

Ezra Cappell and Jessica Lang, editors,
Off the Derech: Leaving Orthodox Judaism

Off the Derech

Leaving Orthodox Judaism

Edited by

Ezra Cappell and Jessica Lang

Cover art: Tobi Kahn, *Ylai*

Published by State University of New York Press, Albany

© 2020 State University of New York

For information, contact State University of New York Press, Albany, NY
www.sunypress.edu

Library of Congress Cataloging-in-Publication Data

Names: Ezra Cappell and Jessica Lang, editors.
Title: Off the Derech: Leaving Orthodox Judaism / Cappell, Ezra and
   Lang, Jessica, editors.
Description: Albany : State University of New York Press, [2020] | Series:
   SUNY series in Contemporary Jewish Literature and Culture | Includes
   bibliographical references and index.
Identifiers: ISBN 9781438477251 (hardcover : alk. paper) | ISBN 9781438477268
   (ebook) | ISBN 9781438477244 (pbk. : alk. paper)
Further information is available at the Library of Congress.

10 9 8 7 6 5 4 3 2 1

Contents

PART II: ANALYSIS

Introduction

Jessica Lang

The term "Off the Derech" has a complex meaning and history. *Derech*, Hebrew for "path" or "way," bears a religious connotation: those on the path, those who follow the *derech*, ascribe to a rabbinic authority, both ancient and modern, which determines a way of communal and private life that leaves the individual with relatively little autonomy. The Hebrew word *halacha*, which means Jewish law, is derived from root *halach*, "to go." Taken together, committing to the legal and moral system put forward by Jewish *halacha*, Jewish law, as interpreted by certain scholars and rabbis, means that one lives by a specific code, one follows the ways (*derech*) and customs that are not only deemed necessary for belonging within certain communities but also understood as carrying with them the ultimate authority of what it means to lead a good and morally upstanding life.

The term off-the-derech originated from within ultra-Orthodox communities as a way of describing members of these communities who determined to leave it. It is a word, then, with subversive origins that carries with it a sense of stigma and difference. But, as is the case with a number of pejorative words and phrases, in an act of transgression that in some ways mirrors their original departures, many of those who self-identify as OTD, or off-the-derech, effectively re-claim it as a term that is less derisive and marginalizing and more descriptive, offering—as it does—a specific orientation. Then again, there are those who reject the label, viewing it as unnecessarily critical and derogatory. A number of the contributors to this volume address and explore the meaning of the term off-the-derech. We have chosen to use it as the title of this volume because, for better and for worse, it has become the most commonly used term to describe the act of departure from the practices and ways of living within a native religious Jewish community. It is used by those who remain within their religious communities to describe a decision that is as much a physical one—individuals who move away from family and friends—as a religious, ethical, and cultural one. It describes an abandonment of the principles held most closely by those who continue to live within their religious communities, who maintain a belief system that the "right" and "best" practices of Jewish life involve adhering to a strictly codified set of rules. For these believers, going "off-the-derech," and this is often the phrase used, describes a set of detrimental decisions that can lead that individual irrecoverably astray. It can be characterized as crazy, scandalous, weak, a betrayal, wrong, catastrophic, morally compromising, selfish, and destructive. Going off-the-derech places those individuals beyond the reach of their community and, by inference, beyond the reach of God. Often those who leave their religious communities are cut off, partly or fully, from their families—siblings, parents, spouses, and children refuse to speak or interact with their family members because doing so in many ways further contaminates them. It leaves them vulnerable to the influence of that person; it allows that person even a minimal platform within the family and, therefore, within the community; it deepens and enlarges the stain of embarrassment and difference that hold very real implications for marriage prospects for all those associated with the family. For many within religious communities, the term "off-the-derech" marks a sinner, one who is unrepentant and one who has little interest in changing course. It is a term of condemnation and exclusion, the scarlet letter of assignations. While not all of those who declare themselves to be off-the-derech are shunned by those who continue to live in their native religious communities, invariably a deep—even unscalable—sense of difference exists between those who choose to stay and those who choose to leave.

And then there are those who openly declare themselves to be off-the-derech, who embrace the term, identify with it, and determinedly re-claim it. This volume centers on them, their stories, their voices, and their presence within the larger Jewish community. Some identify with

the term "off-the-derech" precisely because of its subversive meaning—
they wish to re-define a term of stigimatization, turning it on its head,
emptying it of its pejorative meaning, and adopting it with defiance and
pride. Of course, a wide array of responses to the "off-the-derech" label
exist among the many people who have left their religious communities.
Some reject the term "off-the-derech" because of its history, its negative
valence, and its meaning in religious communities. Some reject it as a
term that gives credence to the myth of religious superiority, lending
those who are "on" the path a semblance of authority that doesn't exist
for those who are "off" of it. Some prefer the term "ex-O," short for
ex-Orthodox. "Ex-Jew" is often a term used in blogs that refers to those
who are no longer religious. "Ex-Hasidic," or "ex-Haredi," is regularly
invoked and offers a more specific indication of one's native community.
A term used by both members of religious communities and those who
have left is "Apikoros." Derived from the Greek philosopher Epicurus,
its meaning has been extended and modified since being first invoked
in rabbinic literature in the Mishnah and "is popularly used loosely for
anyone who expresses a view which is regarded not only as heretical but
even as heterodox." Over the past decade, however, the term "off-the-
derech" has become increasingly familiar, in common parlance, blogging,
journalism, and scholarship as identifying a brand of secularism born from
a lived experience within a rigidly Orthodox or ultra-Orthodox home
and community.

In fact, the gesture initiated in recent years by this movement of
leave-taking and reinvention echoes earlier movements in Jewish and
Jewish-American literature. The Haskalah, the Jewish Enlightenment in
Europe that began in the eighteenth century and effectively ran parallel to the European Enlightenment, happening at the same time, was a
determined move toward secularization that challenged rabbinic authority.
Maskilim, proponents of the Haskalah and often contributors to Haskalah
literature, embraced knowledge of the scientific, political, economic, and
intellectual world that fell outside of Jewish culture. Maskilim celebrated
secular education and culture and weakened the role of religion and the
influence of clergy in public life. In terms of literary contributions, the
Haskalah initiated the idea of a Hebrew literature largely independent
of religious influences and gave rise to the production of secular Yiddish
literature. Off-the-derech literature, among the newest directions within
the larger cannon of Jewish world literature, can trace its roots back to

the broader embrace of secularization and pushes against religious restrictions as set forth by the Haskalah.

Indeed, the single-most unifying theme across all of Jewish literature since the eighteenth century is the act of departure from the practices and cultures of native communities. More circumscribed but equally impactful reiterations of leave-taking and assimilation are seen in American literature. Early-twentieth-century Jewish immigrant stories consistently document departures within departures, with immigrants such as Mary Antin, Rose Cohen, Anzia Yezierska, Henry Roth, Abraham Cahan and others documenting first a departure from a native community usually located in Eastern Europe or Russia and, second, a departure from the religious and cultural practices that defined and dictated the very rhythm of days, weeks, and years. Because Jewish writers tend to reflect a national frame of reference in their move away from their former communities, the creation of a modern Jewish Israeli literature in many ways evolves differently as its creation of a national identity was in process at the same time as its creation of a literary identity. And yet here, too, in its very newness, in its search for definition, Israeli Jewish writers such as S. Y. Agnon, Hayim Bialik, Uri Zvi Greenberg, Yonatan Ratosh, and Natan Alterman, followed a generation later by A. B. Yehoshua, Amos Oz, Aharon Appelfeld, Mordecai Tabib, David Shahar and others, supported the creation of a new Jewish imaginary, a gesture that is explored from a range of perspectives in *Off the Derech: Leaving Orthodox Judaism*.

This volume centers on those who decide to leave their religious communities. We consider this act of departure in its broadest possible form. Some contributors have chosen modern Orthodoxy over ultra-Orthodoxy; some have chosen atheism over modern Orthodoxy. Leave-taking, and specifically choosing to adopt religious practices that distinguish the writer from his or her native community, is what binds together this group of contributors. Accordingly, we have invoked a broad conception of off-the-derech (OTD) narrative and scholarship. Because, as one might suspect, the term "off-the-derech" has political implications not only within religious communities, but also among those who identify as OTDers. While we recognize that hierarchies exist in determinations of "most religious" or "most traditional" or "most strictly observant" and that, indeed, some religious communities are more insular than others, and so less likely to have been impacted by modern secular society, our goal here is to bring together a diverse array of voices to address the growing and under-studied phenomenon of off-the-derech. We wish to present a forum by and about men and women who have either chosen to leave or were forced out of religious Jewish communities because they refused to conform to the many rules and regulations that inform daily life and so have been identified, or identify, as off the path.

Our commitment to examining this particular brand of (ir)reli-gious non-conformity extends to the volume itself. We include here a diverse set of essays written by academics, writers, journalists, social activists, and more. The writing here is in some instances personal and in others analytical; it includes interviews, stories, personal histories and scholarly essays. Our primary goal for this volume is to bring together and to recognize the diverse makeup of the OTD community and to present, collectively, an array of scholarship and perspectives that have been essential to defining this developing movement. The wide range of contributors included here document, narrate, examine, and analyze an increasingly public trend of depar-ture from ultra-Orthodoxy and the movement toward secular culture. While movement away from traditional religious practices and com-munities, and toward a lifestyle that embraces secularity has a rich tradition in Jewish and Jewish American literature, OTD literature distinguishes itself as a movement that originates in the postmodern world and moves toward, if anything, one that is post-postmodern.

The volume is divided into two sections: literature and critical analysis. The literature section includes memoirs, interviews, and personal essays by authors who identify as OTD. The critical analysis section includes the work of scholars who write about departures from ultra-Orthodoxy from literary, religious, sociological, anthropological, linguistic, gendered, and filmic perspectives.

The OTD movement is a burgeoning one. Over the past few years, the number of publications that describe lives leading up to and following these deeply personal and religious breaks has grown dramatically. Dozens of published novels, memoirs, blog entries and autobiographical accounts detail, from an insider's perspective, and with intimate knowledge of communities about which very little is known in the outside world, the many urgent reasons individuals feel the need to leave their ultra-Orthodox communities while at the same time they are often emotionally torn by an overpowering longing to stay connected to home—to the only way of life they have ever known. OTD stories tap into public interest and curiosity, not only because of what they reveal about ultra-Orthodox communities that are easily identifiable and yet mysterious to all who are not a part of them, but also because of their pathos—they encompass a profound sense of loss, displacement, and trauma. In communities predicated upon a sacred sense of conformity that is firmly established by rabbinic authority, deviation is often deemed heretical. The absence of conformity is what marks OTD authors and their stories, which collectively are stories of survival and, also, stories of adventure, stories that document a grand but deeply intimate reckoning that brings them to terms with a set of values and a lifestyle drastically—violently, even—different from those of their families and communities.

Once separated from their communities, these writers tend to describe a position of profound abandonment. Often educated in Yiddish and almost exclusively in religious Jewish texts, OTD authors document not only their search for new lives, but also the challenges of having to navigate entirely new worlds of higher public education; custodial battles over their children and other interactions with state and federal law; sexual identity; professional identity; and financial needs, in addition to struggling with the emotional aftermath of, in many cases, some form of abuse or trauma. OTD narratives in many ways mimic the last few centuries of Jewish history: displacement, rejection, and the earnest attempt to create new meaning in the absence of traditional values and practices. The history of ultra-Orthodoxy is centuries old; OTD authors are writing it a new ending. OTD literature, and this volume concentrates this impulse, breaks new ground by surveying both literature that is itself OTD and by analyzing and taking into account sociological, literary and historical trends that provide a window onto a world that has few means of egress and access, allowing readers to better understand, in more than one dimension, what it means to live off-the-derech.

The essays included in this volume reflect the sense of individuation and non-conformity that is in fact entailed by the move away from religious authority toward a more independently lived life. In the volume's opening essay, Naomi Seidman writes about the post-Holocaust home her immigrant parents built for her and her three siblings in Boro Park, Brooklyn. Her parents' strict adherence to religious practices did not preclude a sense of difference from other families in the community, one that is primarily born out of her father's appreciation and recognition of the richness that could be found in the secular, and even non-Jewish, world. Seidman, the only one of her siblings who left the religious community of her upbringing, complicates the story of leave-taking with her abiding affection and deep sense of warmth toward her father's interior and past life, the hidden pieces of him which, to this day, remain a mystery.

Joshua Halberstam and Shulem Deen address their readers directly, and focus on the challenges of self-determination for those who have left their ultra-Orthodox communities. Writing with a distinct voice, each essay effectively forms not so much a response *against* a set of practices or a doctrine, but a move *toward* an understanding of a self that is, in the immediate aftermath of leave-taking, independent to the point of being adrift, so vast is one's initial reckoning with the larger world. Speaking with the voice of experience, having left his community decades earlier, Halberstam breaks down his advice into a series of topical questions that cover the philosophical, religious, and practical. Deen speaks angrily not only of indignities he has suffered, of his challenges in claiming an authentic literary voice, but also with a sense of despair upon learning that an OTD woman and personal friend has committed suicide.

Writing about his childhood on New York's lower east side, Morris Dickstein pointedly identifies as an agnostic skeptic and writes with unvarnished criticism about his yeshiva education. And yet, like Seidman, Dickstein's criticism is blunted by a sense of nostalgia for both the community and ritual of his past. In the wake of his father's death, Morris rediscovers the songs and prayers of his youth, unexpectedly discovering an element of Orthodox Judaism that engages him, which he wishes to recapture. While recognizing that the poetry of Wordsworth, Shelley, Whitman and Dickinson is more likely to offer a sublime touch, Morris acknowledges the existence—and the possibility—of an occasional moment of rapture coming from the Tanach.

Frieda Vizel, Leah Vincent, and Frimet Goldberger document an increasing sense of alienation and difference from their native communities that inspires their respective departures. Vizel documents her transformation through ten graphic panels that trace her growing interest in the secular world from the time she was in elementary xvi | JESSICA LANG

school, eager to read and understand the words censored in her school books, through her marriage, her discovery of the Internet, her subsequent divorce, and ultimately her move to free herself from the constraints of a community where she did not belong. Similarly, Vincent traces her path as her father's favored child, a position lost to her once she hit puberty and declared her interest in attending college. Married for the second time, to a non-Jewish man, Vincent claims both her origins and her future with a biblical insistence of the rights of a first born. Having left her community with her husband and children, Goldberger addresses her post-partum depression after the birth of her second child, her reluctance to shave her head and to conform to the strict and unvarying clothing requirements for women in the community.

Offering still another perspective on gender, Leah Lax's responses to questions and comments about her published memoir, *Uncovered: How I Left Hasidic Life and Finally Came Home*, an excerpt of which follows the interview, considers the homoeroticism of the Hasidic world—a point of view which both helped Lax determine a role for herself as a young woman but became stifling as she gradually became aware of her own lesbian identity.

Unlike Lax, Vincent, and Morris, who document both their ties to their native communities as well as deeply felt moments of disconnectedness, Mark Zelcer states plainly and at the outset that at no point in his history, nor to the present day, did he share a sense of religious belief or social belonging within his community. Defining five topics to measure his departure intellectually, socially, epistemologically, religiously, and practically, Zelcer's analysis is an acknowledgment of the challenges in identifying the precise meaning behind the cognitive dissonance of not believing but living a religious life.

The volume's second half includes ten essays by a range of scholars and professionals whose focus on the OTD community, and on OTD literature, yields a richer understanding than has heretofore been available. The two opening essays are studies in contrast. Literary scholar Jessica Lang investigates acts and descriptions of intimacy in OTD memoirs authored by women. She distinguishes between the failure of more conventional understandings of physical intimacy, and the success of its imagined counterpart—intimacy through the reading of forbidden texts. From a different disciplinary vantage point, sociologist Lynn Davidman positions Jews at the center of research examining the process of leaving strictly religious groups, and contrasts Jewish exit narratives to those narratives coming out of Evangelical or Fundamentalist Christian communities.

Moshe Shenfeld and Miriam Moster examine the educational histories, prospects, and governmental policies affecting members of ultra-Orthodox communities who have left their communities. Shenfeld, raised in an Israeli Haredi family and co-founder of an Israeli advocacy organization, "Out for Change," analyzes the challenges facing ultra-Orthodox and post-ultra-Orthodox education in Israel, a state that approves and financially supports the limitations of Haredi educational institutions. Miriam Moster, looking at the American ex-Orthodox community, considers the educational attainments of individuals once they have left their ultra-Orthodox communities.

In an essay that straddles auto-ethnography and scholarly intervention, Shira Schwartz explores the ontological orientation and origins of OTD identity. Her essay provides an interesting counterpoint to the essay written by Rachel Berger, Tsivia Finman, and Lani Santo, the leadership team at Footsteps. Their essay reviews the mission and outcomes of the organization, which is headquartered in New York City, and which provides space and an array of support initiatives for individuals who are considering, or are somewhere in the process of, leaving their Jewish community.

In offering three more different disciplinary perspectives, anthropologist Jessica Roda reflects broadly on the role and impact of media on the OTD community, while sociolinguist Gabi Amramac investigates a particular community of OTDers, the Shababniks. Roda considers both the creation of the OTD community itself and its institutionalization through mediatization. Abramac's work on the Shababniks, a group of Israeli OTD-ers, some of whom have moved to Brooklyn, illustrates the diversity within the OTD community. In terms that are sociological and also journalistic, Naftuli Moster considers the transition of those leaving their religious communities from the closely scripted narratives that are intrinsic to ultra-Orthodox communal life, to the dramatically unscripted post-Orthodox world that exit-ers suddenly find themselves inhabiting. The concluding essay of the volume is by literary scholar and creative writer Ezra Cappell. At once personal and interrogative, Cappell moves between personal history, ancient Jewish text, and contemporary OTD narratives, all of which form a background to both breaking with tradition while still honoring its memory.

PART I

STORIES

My Father, Myself

Naomi Seidman

After years—decades—of problems with his heart, his kidneys, his lungs, my father was struck low not by any of these frailties but by falling down the steep, narrow stairs to his Brooklyn apartment, the hand that should have been holding the banister taken up instead with books and articles. He died the next day, but the articles kept appearing under his name in the Yiddish paper for weeks after the funeral, like the hair and nails that seem to continue to grow after death. Stating these "facts," I can hear the barely suppressed pride that colors everything I say about him. Even his death set my father apart: not for him the creeping indignities of cancer or Alzheimer's, the tubes, the smell, the expense, the toll on the family. My father died a soldier's death, with his boots on, except that the boots were Yiddish and Hebrew words, my father's stock-in-trade, his ammunition in the battles he was always fighting. When my father fell he was on his way to his grandson's bar mitzvah, climbing down the steep steps with books for the bar mitzvah boy and an envelope for the mailbox. My oldest sister was waiting outside behind the wheel of her station wagon; of course they were running late. In the ambulance the paramedic asked her if the man whose hand she held as he struggled for breath was her father or grandfather. "He's my father," answered my sister, herself a grandmother a few times over.

And then she drew herself back from the rim of panic and grief and added, with that old Seidman pride, "He's a writer. He was on his way to mail his articles to the publisher."

My sister told me this story as we sat shiva in my other sister's living room, side by side on the couch stripped of its cushions. I knew what she meant to say to the paramedic: you see a frail old man on a stretcher with his heart seizing, his face wrinkled and frightened, his neck in a brace. But that isn't who he *really* is. He isn't really old, not as old as he looks, not the way other people, ordinary people, get old. She meant that they had to do everything in their power to make sure he wouldn't die. Let no one assume that his life was over or that anyone would be relieved to see him go or resigned to his death. He was not the sort of old person about whom it would be said, "Well, he had a long, full life." Or, "He was suffering so much, it was really a blessing." My father had a lot more to say, a lot more to do. No one who knew him could ever doubt that. No one who knew him would ever be resigned to his death. Ever.

As a child, I often fought my shame at having such an old father, a father who looked like a grandfather. But I also recognized that his amazing age was one more way our family was different. Not richer, certainly, or more attractive. But we were smarter, more educated, more *interesting*. And where that came from was my father, the most educated, interesting man around. My father spoke eight or nine or eleven languages and had published in five or six of them. My father could talk brilliantly and with wit about the French Revolution, the Russian Revolution, the Ottoman Empire, the rise of anthropology, the Hebrew grammarians of Golden-Age Spain. Some of this history, actually, an amazing amount of this history, he had personally experienced. My father could tell us about the Sabbath he walked five or six miles, since using transportation was forbidden, to be present at the vote in the United Nations that would decide whether the world would recognize the State of Israel. He had shared an elevator with Elizabeth Taylor—a Jew, as he liked to remind us. He had been to a Zionist fundraising party at which Albert Einstein had said his goodbyes and gone out the door, leaving his wife behind; ten minutes later Einstein had returned, mumbling apologetically that he had forgotten his hat. Rifling through his desk drawer I found colorful currency in improbably high denominations, and from more nations than most people in the neighborhood had heard of. Lying casually among the paper clips was a black-and-white photo of my father in a light summer suit, wire-rimmed glasses on his nose, standing between two Indian women in saris. Behind him was someplace beautiful and Indian—the Taj Mahal? A foreign embassy? Had he been to India? Was that Indira Gandhi beside him? Somehow I never got around to asking him. After he died, my mother and I passed the picture back and forth, looking for clues. But the photo was unmarked. She didn't know whether he had been to India, but when it came to my father, anything was possible.

The pride we took in our father was nothing compared with the pride he took in us, the marvel he felt in having had children at all, much less the perfect beings that we were. If we survived the torrents, the oceans of love, it was because most of it washed over us unnoticed. We were wild, thoughtless American children, our minds taken up with what lay before our eyes, heedless of the horrors that gripped him. We were never chided for our thoughtlessness; both of our parents wanted it that way. When the Orthodox girls' schools my sisters and I attended—Beis Yakov of Boro Park, then Beis Yakov Academy, for high school—finally joined the American Jewish flow and decided to teach "the Holocaust," my mother was horrified to hear about what we were being subjected to in the classroom and at school assemblies. "Let the little German children look at those pictures," she said. My father was incapable of saying the word "Holocaust" without a sarcastic snort, for the laziness in spelling out the crime it implied, for the industry of "Holocausters" that had arisen, he felt, to cash in on Jewish tragedy. He kept his own grief and rage pure by refusing to convert it to American currency, to stories or "lessons to be learned," to anything abstract, pious, useful, didactic, uplifting, institutional. Like other survivors (though he never used that word), he spoke of the *daytshn*, the Germans, rather than the Nazis, or of the *roytskhim*, or murderers, rather than of genocide. American-Jewish Holocaust discourse was irredeemably corrupted for my father by sentiment and imprecision and its willingness to manipulate: everyone who had suffered was a hero; all sorts of people who had nothing to do with it were eager to claim a personal connection to Jewish suffering; Auschwitz had become a kind of catch-all existential category; the Nazis were "animals" or "bureaucrats," but in any case a group long disappeared into the black-and-white footage of European history; American Jewish children would somehow be made more loyal Jews by looking at photographs of atrocities; the non-Jewish world had learned its lessons and taken the lessons of the Holocaust to heart. It all made him furious, and sick.

The Orthodox world had its own share of *mishigas* in talking about the war. In my high school, the apocryphal tale of the ninety-three Beis Yakov girls who had killed themselves to avoid being taken into a Nazi brothel circulated religiously and lovingly, their "last will" read aloud with tears and ceremony at school assemblies, despite the articles in which my father angrily unmasked the story as grotesque fiction. He particularly hated the Hasidic miracle tales, in which a distinguished Rebbe or a group of yeshiva boys danced to the gas chambers, or was saved at the last minute by some supernatural intervention. "What? Just him? There weren't enough miracles for everyone?" he'd storm, and whoever had been telling the story would fall into stunned silence before the ferocity of this ordinarily gentle man. Among the battles my father fought, the struggle against these "Holocaust" travesties was both the longest lasting and the least effectual.

When my father died, none of us knew exactly how old he had been. His passport listed his date of birth as November 27, 1898, but it was the direct descendant of a false passport he had managed to acquire in the Warsaw Ghetto, which had saved his life. We children assumed that my mother knew when he was born, but it turned out that it was among the many things she had refrained from asking him. After my father died, I asked my mother how she had felt, in Paris after the war, about marrying a man so much older than she was. She answered, "We were all like that, our health broken, refugees that looked years older than our age. What did it matter how old your father was? Do you think I cared?" In the end, the gravestone gave no date of birth, only the date of death and a long list of the names of his murdered family, followed by the acronym H.Y.D., May God Avenge their Blood. Inscribed in the tombstone was also a rhymed Hebrew epitaph, with the first letters of each line spelling out Hillel ben Avraham Meir, composed by my mother. She had herself been a Hebrew teacher and writer before she had married my father and left the writing to him.

About ten years ago I met a young Polish-Jewish scholar, Natalia Aleksiun, at the annual conference of the Association of Jewish Studies, who was working on a dissertation on what she called "the lost generation," the graduate students who earned their degrees in Polish universities before the war and who were either killed or, like my father, never succeeded in finding an academic position in the postwar world (her book on this subject is now forthcoming). In particular she was interested in the students of the great historian, Meir Balaban, founder of the Jewish Historical Institute in Warsaw and professor of Jewish Studies at Warsaw University—my father's mentor and dissertation advisor. I had grown up hearing Balaban's name: my father loved to tell the story of how he had corresponded with Balaban about some documents related to the infamous apostate and Messianic figure, Jacob Frank, that he had discovered in the archives of his Galician hometown, Buczacz (this was the same town that gave the world not only Freud's father but also a Nobel Prize winning writer, S. Y. Agnon, and the historian Emanuel Ringelblum). Balaban, responding with interest, had addressed his letters to Professor Seidman, unaware that he was writing to a boy barely past his bar mitzvah. I sat in the lobby of the Toronto Hilton, trading what little I knew about my father's relationship with Balaban for Natalia's vast store of historical knowledge, gratified that what had seemed like a merely personal story of my father's dashed academic hopes had larger cultural resonance, could interest a scholar as lively and young as Natalia. A week later Natalia emailed me a PDF of my father's student passbook, with the year of his birth, 1907, printed under his photograph. Staring at the document on my screen, I realized that something in me preferred a father whose origins were lost in obscurity, whose date of birth, even, was mystery rather than fact. When we were young, my brother and I would look at my father at the head of the Sabbath table and giggle at a reference in one of the hymns to God as "The Ancient of Days"; it was one of our nicknames for our father, turning a merely old man (especially of such young children) into a legendary, primordial, almost theological figure. I have always preferred mystery and story to historical data, been drawn to literature over biography or history. But my father was a historian, and from that perspective it was fitting that Natalia, in this sense his spiritual daughter, had brought some of his history home to me.

Natalia's framing of my father's story in that of his academic generation reminded me that my father was not so singular a figure as he had always appeared to me. In our community, there was no one quite like him; he had an odd and idiosyncratic group of friends in the neighborhood and beyond, but no real colleagues, no cohort. But in Warsaw, he had been part of something larger: Natalia spoke of the young men (and a few women) who had come to study Polish-Jewish history with the most renowned professor of the day, some, like my father, from religious backgrounds. Balaban, the first day of class, would ask his new students where they were from, and when they mentioned the name of some god-forsaken shtetl or another, would regale the class with more fascinating details about the place than its own inhabitants could imagine. From my father I knew of Poale Agudas Yisroel, the movement of young religious Socialists, who, finding a poor evicted family surrounded by its possessions on the street, would fight the landlords on behalf of the evicted renters. My father had been active in the Agudah party, the party of Orthodox Jewry, both as the secretary of its representatives in the Polish Sejm (the Parliament) and in the Warsaw Jewish City Council. In Poland, my father's activism had brought him directly into the heart of the politics of the day. America was different. That the United States was a haven and refuge for Jews was something my father never doubted, and never forgot. On the fourth of July, an American flag hung beside the front door. My father spoke of how, on the ship to New York from Europe, an American soldier on board had fallen ill and the boat had turned back to France so he could be treated. He was unhappy about the delay, and eager to put Europe behind him, but when he heard why the boat was turning around he felt he was going to the right place.

"It was an American ship, flying under the American flag. To turn that enormous boat around," my father would say. "That was when I knew that this was a decent country."

He knew there was more work to do, that the promise of America remained unfulfilled: My father was a loyal member of the union, once he found regular employment, and we may have been the only Orthodox family that regularly marched in the Labor Day Parade. My father followed the Civil Rights Movement, if from a distance, and we owned and regularly listened to a record of the speeches of Martin Luther King. And he was certainly a well-known man in the Orthodox Jewish community of New York and beyond, particularly to the many readers of the Orthodox Yiddish press. But my sense was that in America my father was no longer at the heart of his community, which was run by American-born leaders, rabbis and political figures, the way he had been at the very heart of the now-destroyed Warsaw Jewish community. In this sense he was, and continued to be long after the war had ended, a displaced person. Among the Jewish losses of Europe's anti-Semitic campaign were also the ones Natalia was documenting—first the closing of European university doors to gifted young Jewish academics, and then the difficulty of those who survived the carnage of rebuilding an intellectual and political home elsewhere.

But meeting Natalia at the AJS conference also suggested to me another story, that of an intergenerational redemption. In uncovering Balaban's "lost generation" of students, Natalia had not only found a rich dissertation topic to propel her own career, she was also working toward a (very partial) recovery of the loss she was documenting. My father's academic career was interrupted by war and genocide, but my own path as a professor of Jewish Studies perhaps also partially redeemed this failure. This is a comforting thought, but hard to uphold. If I were Natalia, writing the history of my father and his generation, such a narrative might be easier to sustain. But I took a different path, academically and religiously and personally, and if my father's work is present in my own, it looks very different. And isn't my idea that Natalia and I, in our different ways, are "redeeming" the losses of an earlier generation a variety of the sentimentality he should have taught me to deplore? My father was boundlessly, unreservedly proud of me. It tickled him to think of his baby daughter as Professor Seidman, the title that should have first been his. But nothing I have made of my own life, nothing of what America has given me, can begin to right any of the wrongs that had been done him.

～

The truth is that my father didn't fail to find a job in a history department; he never, as far as I know, applied for such a job. My father earned a livelihood, such as it was, not in the academy but within the Jewish world to which he retreated, actively if ambivalently rejecting the values that held professorships and academic publications in esteem. In the first decades after the second world war, my father, who knew three or four operatic arias and large parts of the epics of Homer and Virgil virtually by heart, turned his back on what he called, always and only with irony, "European culture" and determined to raise his family far from its hollow promises. My father's younger life had included both the Hasidic world in which he was raised and the cosmopolitan life of interwar Warsaw. But after the war, it was only the first of these two facets of Polish-Jewish life that he worked to rebuild, watching with amazement and bitter pride as the remnant of a remnant of the old Hasidic world found its American feet.

The decision to raise his family in Boro Park was not, of course, his alone. In marrying my much-younger mother, who had managed no more than a few years of Beis Yakov teachers seminary in Czernowitz, Bukovina, before the war broke out, he accepted as well that they would carry on their married life amid the community of Hasidic and ultra-Orthodox survivors. My parents settled in Boro Park, Brooklyn, where they spoke Yiddish at home, sent their children to the strictest yeshivas, lived mostly without a television. My brother's head was close-cropped, his sidelocks long; my sisters and I wore long skirts and sleeves. My mother herself came from a distinguished family: her grandfather had been a leading rabbi in Transylvania and her father, like the man she would marry, was a journalist, a historian, and a community activist—but of the strictest Orthodoxy. Such combinations of worldliness and piety, it seemed, had not been rare in Eastern Europe. But in Boro Park, my parents were the exception. I knew no one else who had a father known as "Doctor," as my father always was. No one else's parents regularly listened to opera on the radio or hosted visiting political dignitaries in their living room.

I don't mean to suggest that the piety in our house was in any way tempered by culture or intellect. We were as religious as anyone else, as observant as my parents—both of them—had been before the war. Before Passover, as it had been in my mother's Transylvanian childhood, every book in the house was turned upside down and shaken to release any crumbs that were trapped within them, every kitchen chair taken apart and dusted—later, vacuumed—for crumbs. My father, though, stood somehow outside this frenzy of activity, either because he was a man or because (it sometimes seemed to me) he was a religious moderate and maybe even something of a skeptic. He would grumble about his papers being moved, his chair stacked high with volumes of biblical commentary. None of his grumbling made the slightest difference: he wasn't the one in charge of such matters. His role was ritual and symbolic in more ways than one. After the house had been thoroughly scoured and the white Pesach dishes brought out from the high cabinet where they lived during the year, my mother would carefully place a slice of bread on a newspaper in the exact center of the living room floor for my father to "discover" in his ritual pre-Passover search, by candlelight, for crumbs. It was my mother who took care of these details and others: The meat for our table came from butchers she had determined were reliable, and my mother made sure that my brother thoroughly checked the lettuce leaves on the Seder table for minute insects and worms. Each doorway in the house had a mezuzah and each of us knew how to raise our hands to the mezuzah and then touch fingers to lips as we crossed a threshold. The ones for the children's bedrooms were hung halfway up the door, so we could reach them. The mezuzahs were regularly checked, and subjected to a special inspection if someone fell ill. My father would murmur impatiently at what he considered his wife's superstitions, but my mother was resolute, taking the claw end of the hammer to the mezuzahs, wrapping them carefully in a kitchen towel, and carrying them off to the scribe off Eleventh Avenue. Sometimes she would return to report that one of the mezuzahs had been found to be defective, with a crucial letter partially blurred or even erased. Once she discovered the defect herself: on the door to the room where my oldest sister lay in bed wheezing and coughing with croup, the parchment scroll had been accidentally inserted upside down in its case. In short, the piety and wellbeing of the Seidman household were secure in my mother's competent hands.

If my parents sometimes seemed to practice different flavors of Judaism, they were more united in their vigilant approach to the continent that had reared, and almost killed, them both. We boycotted all things German; a gift of German-made fruit plates (but who could have given such a thing to us?) was graciously accepted but certainly never used. In this my parents were no different from others in the neighborhood: every child in Boro Park knew to spit at passing Volkswagens, maps of the world or Europe were always defaced to erase the name of Germany from under the heavens, on the soles of new shoes children would write Hitler or Nazi so they could stamp them out. During the intermediate days of Passover, 1966 or so, on the Circle Line tour of Manhattan Island, my father yanked my brother away from a conversation he had been having with an older couple with German accents; over the woman's confused and apologetic protests that he must have mistaken them, good Swiss citizens, for Germans, he sat on the boat's white bench staring stonily at the famous skyline. We children, awed and embarrassed, sat beside him in silent solidarity while my mother busied herself removing the foil from a hard-boiled egg.

For our family, it was the cultural rather than economic boycott that was pursued most vigorously, precisely because it was the culture rather than the material objects that had been the greatest attraction, and that continued to pose the greatest temptation. No German books were allowed in the house, with the exception of the first volume of the Buber-Rosenzweig Bible. *The Star of Redemption* we had in English translation. Even in French my father read only the satires of Anatole France and Moliere, who shared his scorn for European hypocrisy. The sole act of paternal violence I ever witnessed was my father throwing my fat paperback copy of Gunther Grass's *The Tin Drum* across the dining room sometime during the fall of 1974. The book sailed with surprising force and grace, just inches below the glass chandelier, and then hit and rattled the mirrored wall and slid down to the couch, where it bounced off the top and landed on its back, lying in open-leaved rebuke for the rest of the day before my mother finally picked it up with two fingers and dropped it into the garbage. I had been afraid to touch it. Later, when Grass's wartime history in the Wehrmacht was revealed, I remembered his bestseller flying through our dining room, and it occurred to me that what had seemed to me then like my father's obstinacy had finally been vindicated.

The truth was that the cultural boycott was often broken, in letter and spirit, and by my father above all—Gunter Grass aside, the European "culture" in our home was what my father himself brought to it. It made no difference that what must have been an impressive library was long gone, disappeared into that ash pit of Europe's Jewish history. My father had stored the best that Europe had to offer in his estimable brain and nothing that Europe did afterward had managed to pry it loose. My father was unable to resist what were some of his deepest loves; when he had to, he made exceptions, most of them musical: Our record collection included the cantorial records of Moishe Koussevitsky and Yossele Rosenblatt, and of course Jan Peerce and Theodore Bikel, but we also owned not only *Porgy and Bess* but *The Magic Flute* and *Aida*—my father's favorite. My father spent the last two years first interned and then in hiding in Vittel, the French Vichy government camp for Allied prisoners of war to which the false passport (Paraguayan!) had brought him; among the prisoners had been a traveling opera company, and it was in Vittel, during the last years of the war, that my father's love of opera had grown and solidified. We finally got television when I was a teenager and the only one left at home, and my parents would watch operas on the public channel. My father would cry, the tears tracing the gullies and channels of his beautiful, naked, complicated face.

It is no surprise, then, that by the time we Seidman children were ready to enter school, our worlds were much larger, stranger, and all-encompassing than that of the average Orthodox household. Along with the blessings before and after bread, or pastries, or fruit or water, vegetables, candy, wine (for of course we children drank wine), washing one's hands before a meal, after waking up, after going to the bathroom, before going to sleep, we Seidman children also heard *Der Erl-König*—in German no less—recited, from memory, by my father at the Sabbath table. We would watch my father speak the strange goyish words, the almost-but-not-quite Yiddish, the exalted rhythm and rhymes, our mouths open and eyes wide, as my father galloped over the plain with his soon-to-be-dead child in his arms. Once my mother had to interrupt: "Enough, Hillel, please, enough already. You're frightening the children."

There was no hiding the fact that we were different from other families in the neighborhood, in certain ways more "modern," the word by which the subtle differences of hairstyle and dress and headcovering and speech patterns and social behavior were gauged. (The more egregious offenses against Orthodox codes branded the offender as *frei*, "free," that is, beyond the pale.) Denim skirts were modern (denim jeans on a girl were only for the *frei*). Peanut butter sandwiches were modern (ham was *frei*). Knee socks were modern (bikinis were *frei*). Television, and Shulamith School for Girls on Forty Ninth Street, and Israeli Hebrew were modern. Yiddish, seams at the back of one's stockings, the Hasidic sects Pupa and Satmar, and a hat over a wig over a shaved head were frum (religious), or, to some, *farkhnyukt*, *too* religious, a opinion in which the disgust was expressed by the ugliness of the Yiddish word that conveyed it. We were not *farkhnyukt* (a term only applied to an "other"), but neither were we modern, and certainly not *frei*. My mother covered her close-cropped but not shaven head with a brown wig that looked very much like the wigs worn by the other women in the neighborhood, and we children were no more modern than the others in our class. But my father had a clean-shaven face, not the beards my mother's sisters' husbands wore. In certain photos, neither hidden nor displayed, we saw our father posing bareheaded with American or Israeli public figures—Abba Eban, Menachem Begin, Daniel Patrick Moynihan, Golda Meir,

Jean Kirkpatrick, Agnon (whom he had met in pre-war Buczacz); in his years covering the United Nations for the Yiddish press or on his Yiddish radio talk-show, my father had met them all.

If in certain ways, nearly all of them deriving from my father's appearance and ways, we could be perceived as more modern, in other ways we were much *less* modern than the other families in the neighborhood, with their American habits, their cars and baseball games and soft drinks. No Seidman sat behind the wheel of a car or owned an apartment or attended a baseball game, not while we lived in our parents' apartment. No peanut butter or Coca Cola ever entered our kitchen. My mother wouldn't allow us to eat at Kosher Country or other fast food restaurants, no matter how many certifications of kashrut were displayed near the door. In the Seidman dining room, an old-world courtliness reigned: No one but my father sat in the chair at the head of the table, even after his death, although my mother took to stacking it with piles of old newsprint she was sorting through for his articles, appropriately enough. On Sabbaths and holiday eves we children were kissed tenderly but ceremoniously on our heads as we stood, shifting from one foot to another. On the eve of Yom Kippur, my father would ask each of us, with absolute seriousness, to forgive him if he had ever wronged us. We were (every one of us—but I, the youngest, most of all) the treasured children of old age, and we watched politely and silently as our parents' eyes brimmed over with every kiss. More than a generation separated us from our parents, and this gap was more than ordinarily filled with mystery, formality, distance. But it was also filled with a stronger-than-usual connection, it seemed to me, just because we were the Seidman children, as if we were born older, more European, in any case different. My father never threw a ball to his son or daughters, never sat with us over our homework. We Seidmans were never spanked, and only rarely scolded. Sometimes I bitterly longed to be part of another family, a family that understood the concept of barbecue, or with a father who refrained from openly crying.

But even when I was young, and most at the mercy of that conformism of childhood, I recognized that my father had something to show for his difference. In a community in which everyone married by twenty, he had a past, possibly even in the romantic sense. There was a photo, which we discovered only after his death, of what the back of the photo identified as an engagement party in September, 1939, my father seated next to a woman none of us had ever heard him mention, ringed by family and friends. Had they managed to marry? Had there been children? Not even my mother knew. My father also had a woman friend, Gutta Sternbuch, who had been at university with him and later saved his life, more than once, in the Warsaw Ghetto and in Vittel, where they had spent the end of the war. Gutta had given the false Paraguayan passport that landed them in Vittel rather than in Treblinka. The story of the passport was a complicated and strange one: The Nazis, hoping to find the last of the hidden wealth of Warsaw's Jews, had arranged for Jewish collaborators to sell passports to Allied countries, and circulated rumors that these passports would save Jews from extermination. Gutta, a religious woman with a Beis Yakov education, had been studying at the university before the war; the passport, mailed to the Warsaw Ghetto in the last days before its destruction, had been one of three bought for this woman and her parents for an enormous sum by a Swiss-Jewish businessman, who had met Gutta once for a few hours before the war but had been so impressed that he was determined to marry her. Gutta's father was deported before the passports arrived, and she had given it to my father. Both my father and Gutta had written of this incident, of how they had combed through the undelivered mail bags in search of the passports, and having found them, deliberated about whether to approach the Gestapo with them. In the end they had, and Gutta and her mother and my father (who was, in official terms, Gutta's father) had been saved first by being taken to Vittel and then, by hiding in the camp, protected by the American and British prisoners. The passport scheme, which was known by the name of the hotel where most of the passports were distributed, "The Hotel Polski," had been a hoax, and only the first group of Jews with the passports had been taken to Vittel; others were deported to Treblinka, and even in Vittel, the Germans had returned after a few months and deported the Jewish passport-holders. Gutta had had a presentiment that this would happen, and she, my father, and her mother were hiding in an oven in Vittel, still warm from the day's baking, when the SS came into the camp. One of my father's lungs collapsed in that oven, an injury from which he never fully recovered. When the gunfire quieted and Gutta, her mother, and my father finally emerged from the oven, they came across a pile of Jewish bodies. My father had poisoned himself in despair, but an American doctor in the camp found him, revived him, and hid him in the camp until the war was over.

Gutta too had survived, married the businessman who sent her the passports, and lived in a castle on the shores of Lake Zurich. Her university research had been done in the Warsaw Ghetto, on the importance of prayer, belief, and religious observance to the traumatized children in Janusz Korczak's orphanage. What their relationship had been, why she had chosen my father's life to save, why she had nevertheless married the businessman, was not something my father discussed, though their continuing friendship and correspondence was no secret. The fact of this correspondence was astonishing enough. They were both Orthodox, raising families—she had seven, he had four children. There were spouses involved, not to mention communities, children to be decently married off. Orthodox men and women did not, generally speaking, form lifelong friendships—such friendships are unusual enough, after all, in non-Orthodox circles. That my father and Gutta had done so spoke both of their unconventionality and of the atmosphere in which their friendship had been forged. Things had been different then, before, during, and after the war, even for the most religious of young people. I knew many Orthodox girls who went to college, but the sense was that they did so mainly for *parnasah*, to make a living. Studying to be a doctor or lawyer was not uncommon. But my father and Gutta were doing something different, carrying on the life of the mind, parnasah be damned. As for what happened during the war, I could hardly picture it. Both Gutta's and my father's diaries are formal and circumspect, even while describing the most horrific of events. I had a stronger picture of what the lives of young refugees were after the war; this was a topic both of my parents discussed relatively openly. My parents had carried on a long and complicated courtship in Paris in the late 1940s, with no marriage broker, no parents or chaperones. There were photographs in the scrapbook: my mother in black and white, in stylish heels and a cinched dress that clung to her shapely hips, her waved hair uncovered; in the background, the Arc de Triomphe, Versailles, Notre Dame; by her side, my father's bald pate shone naked under the gay Parisian sky. That all of Jewish Eastern Europe would be magically reconstituted in a ten-square-block area of South Brooklyn was something they could hardly have foreseen. My father expressed his continuing amazement, walking with me down the increasingly crowded streets of his neighborhood, to see the Chernobyler *shtibl*, replanted from Ukraine to the corner apartment of a handsome brick building on the corner of Fifteenth and Fifty-First, the Novograder Yeshiva, Lithuania in Brooklyn, rubbing shoulders with the Hungarian Muncaczer Kloyz. A block away from our house, the Bobover synagogue grew without cease. My parents witnessed it all, enrolling their son in Yeshivas Karlin-Stolin and their daughters in the big Beis Yakov on Fourteenth Avenue, before the building next door was acquired and the school expanded. They jostled Jewish crowds coming out of the synagogues, walking into the luncheonette, buying a Hebrew or Yiddish paper at the newsstand. As the children grew, the neighborhood changed: The old houses, set in their gardens, were torn down to make room for oversized brick boxes built all the way out to the sidewalk. One Sunday morning, we awoke to discover a bulldozer breaking up the concrete in the driveway of our rented house. The landlord had not thought to inform us.

My father's interest in these developments sometimes seemed to me more anthropological than religious: on Sabbath mornings he made the rounds, shul-hopping from Agudah to Po'alei Agudah to Beth-El and the Sefardishe shul and Bobov. The third meal was often at Chernobyl, where my brother held the Havdalah candle and I lifted the spicebox for the ceremony. My father's Sabbath appointment, it seemed to me, was with Jews as much as with God. For outsiders, these men formed a sea of black; for my father there was an endless fascination with their variety, the tunes they sang and the hats they wore. When it came to his own children among them, in the gaggle of girls pushing into the doors of the Beis Yakov, his son glimpsed through the schoolyard fence on his way to the newsstand, he was overcome with emotion. We knew when we were just children ourselves that the children of Warsaw were always before him, as if they regularly returned in the shape of his own and others'.

Always, always, he was *doctor*. My mother referred to him that way, talking with the appointment nurse from the clinic, for instance. The neighborhood children knew it as well, and worried that one day he might give them a *needle*. In Turetzky's bungalow colony, when my father stepped off the bus with the other men coming from the city on that first Friday afternoon of the endless summer, the children retreated to a safe distance. But my father brought with him not a black doctor's bag with a set of hypodermic syringes but rather a paper bag full of Spalding balls, one for each boy and girl in the colony, and after that the afternoon bus that brought my father was always met by the children of the colony. He did not disappoint. On the last Friday of the long summer, he had with him two dozen contraptions that, when a metal lever was pushed energetically enough down a long slide (my brother helped me manage it), emitted a shower of sparks. No one had ever seen such a thing before. My mother, standing a few feet away and waiting her turn to greet him, showed her feelings in her face: a kind of worried, aggravated pride in her impossible, extravagant husband, expressed later in the privacy of our bungalow. How much had he paid for those things? What would the other mothers say about the sparks, the sharp and dangerous-looking slide? One of the boys, she could see, was already crying, and no surprise.

It could be hard on us to have such a father. Sometimes we complained to my mother that our father barely distinguished his own children from others, giving our toys away to visiting children. But of course all of us also distinguished ourselves from these other children, by virtue of being Seidmans. When the sparklers had been distributed, and when the other children had run off to try to set the grass on fire, my father bent over each of his children's heads with his customary shy ceremony and kissed us. Nobody had a father like ours.

My fascination with my father began to grow when I was a teenager, and looking for a way out of what I felt was an unbearably stifling religious community. I imagined that my own rebellion reflected his secret inclinations, a secret camaraderie that connected us as heretics out of sight of the religious family whose house we shared. The truth is I never really knew what he thought about God. There were, perhaps surprisingly, few discussions on the subject. My father put on phylacteries every morning and swayed before the dining room window, he sang "A Woman of Valor" to his wife when he came home from the synagogue on Friday nights. He sang the Sabbath hymns; there was one in particular that was from Buczacz, a Husyatiner Hasidic tune that only my father knew the melody for, and he sang it in his tuneless, cracking old voice, a hymn that seemed never to repeat itself, that rose and fell according to some principle that could never be predicted, certainly not by anyone born outside that particular town, outside that small Hasidic sect. My father told stories about the Hasidic rebbes as if he had known them personally, talked movingly about the throngs that crowded the trains and roads in Europe before the High Holy Days, Hasidim on their way to their Rebbe's courts. Who could doubt his love of Hasidism, his devotion to the world of Torah Jews? So why did I suspect him of being, as I was beginning to become, an unbeliever?

This is the scandal at the heart of this project of mine, the claim that I am in some "objective" and not only wishful sense a spiritual as well as biological descendant of my father. My sisters and brother who've stayed in the fold would no doubt scoff at the idea that I am an expression of as well as a rebel against my father's relation to Jewishness, which in his case was marked by passionate devotion and in my own by evident rejection. But my heretical thoughts, when they began to emerge, were from the start accompanied by the conviction that not only did I not believe what I was supposed to at least pretend to believe, I also believed that they were unbelievable, and thus that no one really intelligent could or would believe them. My father couldn't believe that, for instance, God was adding up our sins and good deeds on Yom Kippur and was recording our rewards and punishments for the coming year. And if these things were unbelievable, why was he nevertheless going along with these stories? There were plenty of reasons I can now imagine, though I don't know if I was able to discern them when I was younger: Because accounting for one's actions is a good idea, and ritualizing these accountings on a specific and communal day is also a good idea, and God as the face of the ideal of perfect justice is probably also a good idea. At least some Torah practices, that is, are perfectly well translatable into human terms, terms I can identify with and get behind. But I think that those "humanized" interpretations of Jewish law and practice were less important to my father than a more historical and cultural view. It was clear to me, even when I was an adolescent, that my father's Jewish practice was very closely connected to the wound of the Holocaust. To buy the best esrog, wrapped in a flossy wool we saved to use as beards on Purim, was not only a biblical injunction but the carrying on, on American soil, of the practices of the traditional Jewish masses murdered in Europe. To walk to shul, to fast on Yom Kippur, was to keep up the chain carried from generation to generation, by Jews around the world, of a deeply religious and spiritual culture, a holy people. To continue to do this in an Ashkenazic Haredi community in Brooklyn was to honor—in some small way, because so much more had been lost—Eastern European Jewry. These Jews had practiced Judaism with such piety, but also such color, such verve, such human feeling. In Hasidism and Hasidic stories, including those of the sect in which he had grown up, the Husyatiner, my father saw the best of what that world had to offer, a warmth and richness only tepidly and (I think he would say) somewhat narrowly and rigidly mirrored in the world of American Hasidism. To wrap oneself in an old tallis, as worn and broken in as a part of the body, to chant the old melodies among the remnant of the remnant of those who remembered was the fulfillment of the promise to remember, a measure of revenge against those who wished the disappearance of that earlier Jewry, a compulsive, sometimes-healing, sometimes lacerating, always necessary touch of the wounds of desolating loss and the hatred and (less visibly) guilt that accompanied it.

I think I understood this on some level even as an adolescent. And what struck me about what I imagined as my father's reasons for being religious is that for all their persuasiveness and power they didn't add up to a belief in any kind of Jewish God, in *Hashem, riboynoy shel oylem, der eybeshter*. Hashem, in these native formulations, was a folk figure, a character from the Jewish literary imaginary.

And yet, from another point of view—my own—it was hard to imagine sustaining the whole enormous and often onerous production of Orthodox Judaism, once any kind of literal belief in the Orthodox Jewish God (at least as presented to children, and in "official" theological statements) fell away. Again, I should repeat, the idea that my father was an Orthodox Jew not because he believed in the Orthodox Jewish God but because of more humanly evident factors is my own sense, to put it differently, my own invention (which would undoubtedly be contested in the circles in which he chose to live), and not something my father ever explicitly said. So my spiritual inheritance rests, at least in this regard, on a slim, invisible or imaginary thread, the notion that my father was in some unspoken, perhaps barely formulated, certainly never acted-on sense a humanist, a skeptic, something of a "secularist"—like me. I am aware that this may be a psychological ploy on my part, an attempt to claim the warmth of connection where there is only the coldness of my own betrayal, that is, to allay some of the guilt of this betrayal. But I nevertheless also feel the truth of this connection, that some aspect of my father's experience has manifested itself in a small but still important way more fully even if in more subterraneous fashion in me than in his other children. This is itself part of the folk culture my father loved—the love for the youngest, and the special connection to the one that makes problems, the trouble-maker. The other part of that story, the disowning of and broken connections with those who "left the path," is my own story, the official and visible one.

My father had a Ph.D., but I knew that his most fervent ambitions for his children were the traditional ones: Torah, the bridal canopy, and good deeds. He wanted more than anything for the Jewish chain to continue, in his own children, in the community he was helping establish. But I think he wanted something else for us, too. Not heresy or skepticism—what was the good of those?—but worldliness, culture, a rich and open life of the mind. It had been possible, in his own variety of Polish Jewish life, to have both, as he attested in every gesture of his being. Why couldn't it be possible for us, for his own children to be anything they wanted, and still Orthodox? And he did introduce the larger world to us, in the senators and ambassadors and writers who came to our dining room table for a glass of bronfn and my mother's cake.

My mother, it seemed clear to me, had a complicated and rich relationship with a God whose existence and closeness to her she felt as immediately as she knew her own house. She spoke with him constantly, kept alive the conversation in the movements of her day, as she prepared breakfast, or in the moments after she lit the candles on Friday night or, as she stood over her children's beds, muttering words she never translated for us. For all my mother's piety, she shared my father's worldliness, in a more personal form. She was too young when the war broke out to have lived in the larger world, but she sensed its presence, welcomed it without fear. There was no contradiction for her between God and the world. Both her religiosity and her tolerance saved our relationship, helped her resist the pressures of her sisters when her youngest daughter chose a different way. What her daughter was doing, she believed and said to her sisters, one day our paths awkwardly crossed in my sister's house, was between her and Hashem. My aunts, shocked at such a personal and idiosyncratic approach to widely held community standards, fell into disapproving silence. But my mother pretended not to notice.

It is simple enough to say that I am my father's daughter, in the path that my life has taken. Evidence is everywhere. My father was not only a historian but also a writer, whose attention to the craft is everywhere. I teach his Yiddish columns on "The Portion of the Week" at Torah study

Sabbath mornings at the Conservative synagogue to which I belong, and I can hear his voice strongly in these Yiddish articles: My own interest in writing was certainly sparked by the sight of him, writing, writing, writing, his attention turned inward, backward, outward (what did I know about where he was, when he was writing?) in the house full of children, no doubt helped by his being hard of hearing. Struggling with an assignment, I envy his ability to cover sheets with ink, to find focus in the push-and-pull of everyday life, to keep alive a world through the power of arranging words on the page. To be known by people more intimately and directly, it seemed to me, than mere conversation and cohabitation could accomplish.

For both of us, too, the content of what we write, what we studied, is Jewish Eastern Europe. My father turned again and again to Poland, writing about the roads being full of Hasidim going to their Rebbe's courts. Everything came down to that. Noah's sin which led to his children uncovering his private parts was not that he had drunk wine, but that he had not realized that after the flood, there was no more drinking wine innocently, as there had been before. His sin, then, was that he had forgotten that there had been a Mabul, a flood. The allegory needed no spelling out.

My own work, too, revolved around this loss, at a greater remove. Not immediately, not obviously, but ultimately and increasingly. I studied modern Hebrew and Yiddish literature of that world, reading, in my first graduate seminar at the University of California, Berkeley, Agnon's *Guest for a Night*, which my father had experienced not as literature but as history, having spent a week in 1938 with Agnon in Buczacz, where the novel was set. Shmuel Yosef Agnon had spent an evening in my house, in that first year after he had been awarded the Nobel Prize. My father had helped organize a reception for the Buczaczer Landsmanschaft. Rabbi Israel Shorr had introduced Agnon with these words: "Step aside Jerusalem, move back Rome, the holy shtetl of Buczacz has entered the world stage." Robert Alter, my professor of Hebrew literature, had taught me to focus on the text as opposed to the anecdotes I learned not to mention in class, to view Agnon's yarmulke as itself a "text" to be read, but there was no denying that what had brought me to that class, to the subject of Hebrew literature, was rooted in something much more familiar, and familial.

But I'm aware, as well, that what lies between us is as easily termed rupture as continuity. The Talmud, that belated text, memorably describes its own historical self-consciousness this way: If the earlier generations were as men, we are as donkeys. To my father's seven or nine languages, I sometimes think I barely have one.

And yet my father always expressed admiration for my writing, tempered by a kind of mocking wonder at the academic quality of the literary criticism. "I don't know if I understand it," he'd say. "I'm just a journalist. We specialize in the shallow, in the soon to be forgotten."

Closest to the bone is this. Of all my father's children, I had gone the furthest away. My two sisters lived the Orthodox lives he had chosen for us within a mile or two of the apartment in which we all grew up, raising grandchild after grandchild. My brother has married the daughter of his rosh yeshiva, the head of his Talmudic academy; they speak Yiddish with their brood of children. The world of Hasidic Eastern Europe my father never ceased to mourn continued—to the extent that it did—in their lives, not in mine. I had left that world, betrayed it, and publishing articles about it didn't change that.

Toward the end of his life, I visited him at the Israel Bonds office where he worked for years as a speechwriter. My father introduced me to one of the secretaries, proudly mentioning that I was a professor at the Pennsylvania State University (speaking with his typical formality in English), where I was teaching at the time. As he shuffled off, the secretary, an Israeli woman with a dyed-black beehive, held me back. "He's your father?" she asked, shaking her head in amazement. And then she asked the inevitable question: "How old is he?" I shrugged, unwilling to be drawn into fellowship with this woman, a fellowship that was also a conspiracy against my father. If he was old then so was I, having been born from his old body, his old soul. If he was old, then old was the best thing anyone could be. There was an era in my California life when people spoke half-seriously about their "inner child." In some sense my father had one, too—though he would never, of course, use that language. Shaving, he would raise his grizzled chin to the mirror and comment, with wonder: "Old age—what a strange thing to happen to a little boy." But if he was also a little boy, I was also an old man. To my friends who claimed they had an inner child I would joke that what I had inside was an old man, an inner old Jewish man. The old man I meant, of course, was my father.

That Long and Winding Road

Joshua Halberstam

Dear Beirish, dear Hindi,

Way up in that list of attitudes you find particularly irksome sits condescension. Understandably. You've been its targets for so long, especially of those routine remarks about how your decision to "leave the fold" must be due to some psychological problem (and here, choose from the large inventory of suspect emotional instabilities).

So I'll try hard to avoid what might seem patronizing in these remarks . . . and you can help by giving me the benefit of the doubt. This, after all, is only my take, my rambling rants, queries, suggestions, (and parenthetical posits) on a shared experience and struggle—shared, granted, only to some but, nonetheless, significant extent. This is one of the prerogatives of being an older person: we get to claim historical perspective. And, no less, I also get to assert a nonjudgmental, but wary uncertainty—an odd and oddly comforting mixture. (But, alas, maybe this, too: Older folks like to give advice; it's a way of compensating for no longer being able to set bad examples.)

On Sentimentality for Starters

Yesterday, canvassing my Jewish playlist while preparing an exam for my class, I listened to a masterful cantorial Pinchik piece—I'm a sometime devotee of *chazanus*. Not surprisingly, my mood transformed and it took some time before I could return to formulating a reasonable essay question

25

about Plato's metaphysics. Alas for my productivity, such nostalgic diversions punctuate my working hours way too often.

And so, lately I've been thinking about sentimentality. Peculiar notion, sentimentality: at once pejorative, slighting, like calling a work of art "pretty," but also appreciative, a mark of genuine connectedness. You confront steady doses of it as soon as you step "off the derech" ('scare' quotes—appropriately named in this instance—for the moment, more about the term later). A *niggun* from the old days wafts through the room and you respond reflexively with a smiling nod or furrowed brow. So, too, a Proustian bite of a well-turned potato kugel might have this effect along with hundreds of other snippets from your earlier years. Some of these holdovers surely must seem bizarre to outsiders. I still can't abide a *chumish* lying on the floor and wouldn't take a *siddur* with me into the bathroom. (In a quizzical, but, as I'll explain, not trivial transference of veneration, I also feel a pinch of discomfort reading Aristotle in the bathroom.)

These twinges from the past accost you in the form of embarrassed rebuke. Why this irrationality? Why this *mishigas*? Weren't you supposed to be freed of these discarded beliefs, these nonsensical superstitions?

In fact, these sentiments are not cheap. They are dear. Your dissonance is unwarranted. Some of these enduring sensitivities deserve not your disdain but your approbation; we need to distinguish between the surface sentiments and the ones that run deep.

I hear a scrap of an old rock song from my younger, romantically enterprising days, hum along, and am transported to a particularly mischievous, but also delectable, rendezvous I always associate with that golden oldie. The sentiment is both personal and gratuitous; a different, equally flimsy tune of the day could as easily have owned the same reminiscence. The cantorial piece, on the other hand, evokes a far more substantive reaction, neither trivial nor transient. Mind you, it's not the superior quality of the music per se, superior though it be. And, yes, you no longer take the god-beseeching, god-praising words at their word, perhaps reject the assumptions girding the very notion of *davening*. Still, what you hear is a vital human passion, a humbling cry from the guts of the Jewish soul. You can well imagine the same response to a chant from the Russian Orthodox liturgy or a Sufi Qawwali from people raised in those respective traditions.

All this might seem obvious. It is anything but.

Our attachments to the past pose a complex web of threads so difficult to untangle, some worth retaining, others deserving immediate exclusion. The ones that matter can't be replaced. It's your child's first pair of shoes you cherish, not another pair that looks just like them. You enshrine the actual ticket to that first momentous concert you attended, not another you can now buy on ebay. Simulacra won't do . . . nor will reproductions, recent covers of the melodies that moved you back when. These fabrications feel plastic and forced, while the genuine experiences burrow into your memories and visit you throughout your life.

So accept that you were bathed in a tradition with rituals and expectations some of which deserve much more than surface consideration. For example, take that business about not bringing a *sefer*, or even passages of Torah-learning into the bathroom. The underlying notion here is that a text can be sanctified, that words in-themselves demand reverence. Our unease reflects a recognition—a quaint, old-fashioned recognition—that not all objects and emotions are equivalent, that we need some oases in our lives where (if you'll allow the term) sacredness reigns. (Note: if nothing is sacred, than nothing can be de-secrated, and the ramifications of that conclusion are truly unsettling.)

Maybe the Torah-in-the-bathroom hesitation isn't yours. Maybe singing *zmiros* around a Shabbos table is too fraught with unpleasant memories, or is a pleasant enough but no more than a trivial flashback. What I am sure of is that you have and will always have some sentimental residues from your earlier frum years. You'll feel wistful and berate yourself for succumbing to a hypocritical weakness when they overtake you. Be kinder to yourself. Your sentimental response, joy or tears, is a sign that you are free to honor what you think is honorable, to delight in what you think is delightful. This is a good thing.

The Tao of Physics, the Rambam, and Our Intellectual Dishonesty

Defending sentimentality is easy compared to confronting a systemic intellectual dishonesty lurking within the OTD graduate. The attachments considered here are at once more subtle and weighty. I'm referring to the cerebral pleasure we still enjoy when scoring points in an argument we supposedly walked away from a long time ago. But here we are at it yet, dug into our trenches, flailing our arms, still in combat with them . . . and with ourselves. Let me offer an example from my own battle-scarred arena. Bear with me as I get to the point—as I say, this dishonesty has hardened roots.

A mid-1970s bestseller with the tantalizing title *The Tao of Physics: An Exploration of the Parallels Between Modern Physics and Eastern Mysticism* was eventually published in 43 editions in 23 languages. The book's central thesis was the compatibility of the Eastern mystical tradition and current science. This was a time when young Westerners (the Beats/Hippies/sitar-playing rockers) were enchanted by Eastern religions and relished the idea that theoretical physics had finally caught up with Buddhism.

One couldn't help but notice the insecurity of these newborn Buddhists. "You see, our faith turn out to be scientifically sound after all," they proclaimed, which is to say—in unarticulated acknowledgment—that it is science, not the religious belief, that counts as genuine truth. One never hears the converse: "Ah, you see, the scientific studies are consonant with what our religious claims, so the science must be accurate." We often heard this sort of self-congratulatory pronouncements from our own religious educators who boasted some acquaintance with the scientific literature—they, too, were triumphant when some empirical finding happened to be compatible with a biblical or religious tenet.

Many of us are guilty of similar subsumed priorities, namely the deference to traditional rabbinic authority. Here's an example from my own inconsistency.

I have a longstanding interest in the Rambam. I've also had a longstanding interest in Maimonides. These are not only different names for the same person, but entirely different world-views about the same person. The discussions are different, the concerns are different, and the connotations are different. Back in yeshiva, (as Beirish, you especially will attest), we spent many-an-hour threading our way through the maze of a "shverer Rambam" reconciling seemingly contradictory passages in his foundational code of law, the Mishnah Torah. "According to the Rambam," was a phrase with thunderous import. We vaguely knew of his philosophical work, the *Morah Nevukhim, The Guide to the Perplexed*, and heard hurried hints that he respected Greek thinkers and studied non-Jewish philosophy. "How was that permissible?" we wondered. The reply was always the same: "When you'll be a Rambam, you too can study philosophy." And so, duly chastened, we returned our full attention to the Code.

So the thoughts of this man who was, arguably, both the most important Halachist in Jewish history and the most important philosopher in Jewish history are analyzed in their separate domains. (These days, we can be grateful to historians of ideas who are deeply familiar with both the *Guide* and the *Mishnah Torah*, some of whom argue persuasively that you need to understand the one to understand the other.) But though I am a philosopher by profession, the views of Maimonides matter to me far less than the views of the Rambam—which is to say, I study Maimonides *because* he is the Rambam.

Why does all this matter? It matters because this preoccupation exemplifies a serious challenge to one's (my) intellectual integrity. Having grown up in the charedi universe you will understand why.

Consider the frisson we derive when we discover the Rambam's iconoclastic views. For example, in yeshiva no one told us that the Rambam didn't believe there was a hell or that you can't get into heaven merely by complying with the mitzvos without the requisite philosophical beliefs and didn't himself subscribe to all of the so-called thirteen principles associated with his name. But why should we care? Suppose the Rambam held only the most conventional belief . . . would that undermine our own non-traditional beliefs? Why then this peculiar pleasure in discovering that many of our most revered rabbinical thinkers (especially the earlier ones) espoused views that would get them booted out of Lakewood or Satmar. Are we still sitting on the backbenches of the *beis medrish* making our case with our rebbes?

Charedi teachers are certainly guilty of a purposive ignorance of the many heretical outtakes by exalted rabbis and demonstrate utter dishonesty in not mentioning that those rabbis had significant secular interests. But whether these earlier rabbis held what now counts as deviant views shouldn't matter to the OTD. Yet, as I note, so many of us are still seeking justification *within* the tradition for our decision to leave the tradition. It seems intellectually degrading.

But there is another aspect to this that is not undignified at all. For this attachment bespeaks an ongoing connection to our Jewish heritage. And that leads to a central challenge to the OTD.

So How Do You Now Do Jewish?

Perhaps you'd rather not do Jewish at all. Not just the religious part, but also the people part. You think the whole tribal affiliation bit is untenable, an anachronism, a primitive, divisive tent from which intelligent people should decamp. It's your call, and I get it. I also disagree. I find this John Lennon imagining of an untethered, generic humanity not only puerile, but also dangerous. (One recalls Cynthia Ozick's insight: Universalism is the ultimate Jewish parochialism.) And I've got to tell you; I also think that such total abandonment of your roots would amount to a significant loss for you in your life. It certainly would be a loss for the Jewish people. You might have noticed: typically, here in America, those who talk about Judaism know little about it, and those who do know Judaism don't know how to talk about it. But this might not be your concern. I readily acknowledge that the decision to be unaffiliated (if even possible) is serious and plausible and so my disagreement needs to be defended seriously and rigorously. In fact, the issue at stake here turns on key concerns of political theory, the notion of unencumbered selves whose only obligations are the ones they contract versus a competing view of humans as born into relationships with responsibilities ab initio. This topic is part of my professional métier and a larger discussion I'd love to have with you both some time. But not here, not now.

Suppose, however, as is more likely, remaining Jewish in some way is still important to you. What do you want to retain? What do you want to refurnish? All OTD'ers press this question on their fellows and ask it of themselves even as they walk out their religious door (without kissing the mezuzah, of course). The answer is never easy. And reporting here from decades on let me assure you . . . it never will be easy.

The established choices are meager and unappealing, so you will have to be inventive. This calls for some honest accounting.

Yes, charedi yeshivas provide an emaciated education, not just in secular studies (an ongoing, execrable failure), but Jewish-wise as well. You leave yeshiva ignorant of wide swaths of Jewish life and learning: scant familiarity with Navi and Ksuvim (the Prophets and Chronicles) and oblivious to non-halachik, non-traditional Jewish texts, which is to say the bulk of Jewish history, philosophy, and literature (boys more so than girls). The result is an appalling gap in one's Jewish education.

But this too: a typical twelve-year-old charedi (again, boys more so than girls) knows more Pentateuch and rabbinic commentary, certainly more Talmud, more Jewish ritual and Halacha than many (dare I say most?) practicing Reform Rabbis. And when it comes to lay members of Reform and even Conservative synagogues? It's embarrassing to even offer the comparison.

So no one should expect OTD'ers to become fervent members of non-Orthodox denominations. Some might share the social and political agenda of these congregants, but they can't help but be alienated by the Jewish illiteracy, the shameful *ahm haratzess*. They'll feel at home volunteering with these co-religionists in a soup kitchen, but not praying with them in their Temple.

Let me provide a harsh but real example. When the synagogue newsletter proclaims once more that the essence of Judaism is *tikkun olem*, OTD'ers work hard to hide their smirk. Essence of Judaism? Really? They know, (unlike the well-meaning synagogue members) that—curiously—the phrase hardly ever shows up in Jewish texts of the past millennia. It does appear a couple of times in the Talmud in very specific legal contexts—nothing about saving the world. One can offer a predictive law here: when someone extols the centrality of "tikkun olam" in Judaism, there's at least a .85 probability that he or she can't tell you the difference between the Rambam and the Ramban, and a .95 probability that he or she never studied either in any depth. The need to avoid cognitive dissonance is palpable: back in the super-traditional world the reigning attitude was "if we don't like it, it isn't Jewish," while in these modern Jewish denominations it's "if we like it, it's Jewish."

So no matter how distant you've travelled from your black-hat or long-dress yeshivas, this perspective prevails: Judaism without Torah learning—and I mean in depth, text-based, tradition-based Torah learning—ain't Judaism. Please understand me. This isn't a defense of a smug superiority toward other Jewish movements, nor, god knows, an intentional echo of your teachers' encomium to the supreme value of *talmid toyrah*. Nevertheless, we do carry deep within, however whispered in polite company, a sense of what counts, at least minimally, as authentic Judaism.

Moreover, this disaffection for established Jewish institutions isn't confined to the back pews of temples and synagogues. For example, OTD'ers can't help but wince when they read reports of statements put forth by professional "Jewish leaders." Aren't leaders supposed to have followers? "Ayn melekh b'lee ahm"—There is no king without a people." So who exactly are the followers of the heads of the ADL, AJC? You, on the other hand—for better or worse—are intimately familiar with actual Jewish leaders. Chassidische Rebbes, Roshei Yeshiva are genuine leaders with genuine followers, some in the many thousands, who adhere to their leader's judgment across the spectrum of their lives: whom to marry and when to divorce, buy a business or sell one, vote for A or vote for B, undergo an operation or rely on prayer.

And so, for better *and* worse, you're destined to stroll the alleys circling Jewish institutions without ever feeling as though you belong inside. You walked away from a robust and supportive community the likes of which few people in the contemporary, modern world experience. There was a trade-off and you traded. What's on offer as alternative Jewish communities is comparatively and disappointingly shallow; anyway, some part of you is no longer interested in submerging any part of you into a collective. You've been there, done that and are done with that. So OTD'ers who still maintain an interest in the continuation of serious Judaism in America recognize perhaps more fully than most the current dilemma of contemporary American Jewry. Only the Orthodox whom you've rejected are growing in numbers, and only the Orthodox are living, in the main, thick Jewish lives while the Judaism of the Nonorthodox dwindle in numbers and live ever-thinner Jewish lives.

You might think this is Jewry's concern, not yours. But the question of *your* Jewish life still grabs you by the collar. You've got decisions to make.

Beirish, you aren't married. Hindi, you're divorced with one very small child, age two or three, I believe. Your situations are therefore already different with regard to your Jewish options. When you have a family, all these theoretical questions about how to be Jewish morph into immediate practical choices. Do you send your children to Jewish day schools? If so, will you be comfortable with their being taught creeds and codes you worked mightily to reject? If not, will you be comfortable with your children not knowing which way to open a Talmud or how to read a verse of Torah in Hebrew? Will you have a bris for your son? Will you light candles on Friday night, celebrate Yontov and if so, how and with whom?

Here's the reality of getting off the established path. You've got infinite other paths to choose from, some stretching far into the distance from the one you left, others crisscrossing the original at various intersections. More precisely, you won't be discovering a path but creating one that suits yourself, Jewish-wise and otherwise. I always liked that line from the Kotsker Rebbe: "When you walk on a new road, you can be certain nobody has spoiled it yet." These are truly difficult determinations all OTD'ers have to make which means: (1) you'll try this, you'll try that, this works now, something else later—that it makes sense is what counts, not consistency and (2) give people lots of room for their choices . . . if you've learned anything it's that there's no one derech on which we all must trudge.

Politics, Israel and What Happened to OTD Nonconformity?

I really don't want to talk politics. I think most political discussions make people stupid. When a current issue floats across the table, dinner guests first consult the official position of their party chieftains or what they imagine that position to be and then dutifully defend that view to the end of dessert. In contemporary America that means restating the dictates of the *New Yorker*, NPR, CNBC, the editorial pages of the *NY Times* and other stalwart media of the left or, alternatively, the platform of Fox, talk radio, the *Wall Street Journal*, and other media of the right. It's all unenlightening. And boring.

The Charedi community is in many ways apolitical. Self-serving, their chief aim is protecting their own fiefdom in whose cause they happily align with any political party at its service. Of course, on social issues Charedim promote the extreme conservative flank or, to put it more plainly, the downright reactionary flank. OTDer's—not all, but a substantial majority—are delighted to scuttle away from underneath the cloak of that exclusionary Weltanschauung and wrap themselves instead in the progressive mantle of their new secular cohorts.

In truth though—and here goes my curmudgeonly diatribe—it's a bit disconcerting to find so many intrepid iconoclasts, OTD'ers who displayed such courage in defying the dominant ideology that surrounded them become so comfortable in adopting every seasonal cause, every slogan of the week of their new liberal environment. It's not the particular politics that disappoints, but the relaxation of the critical stance. Agreeing with everyone around you used to make you uneasy and it still should. But, as I say, your politics is not my business (and, anyway, we probably agree about most of it).

There is, however, one OTD political discourse that I find inexplicable and disconcerting—so please allow me to rail for a moment. It's the anti-Zionism. What's intriguing is that these OTD'ers who roundly reject nearly the entirety of their former community's politics and values retain its animosity toward Israel. Why is that?

A couple of immediate caveats: Many OTD'ers do not share this anti-Israel animus and perhaps you don't either. The many who do usually asset a discomfort with any nationalism, Jewish or otherwise, so that the well-being of Israel as a state has no more weight than does the well-being of Togo or Suriname. But, I wonder if that's truly the case: (a) if nothing else, familial ties to Israel certainly set it apart in the canvass of their concerns; (b) one wouldn't hear from them—but do—more criticism of Israel than Togo; (c) one would hear from them—but do not—equally vocal criticisms of Palestinian nationalism; (d) the easy dismissal of nationalism is too easy—as I mentioned before, this deserves a far lengthier conversation. I trust, too, we don't have to repeat the usual banality that one can love Israel and criticize its policies. Obviously. Something more interesting is at work here.

The Charedi community, as you know too well, is profoundly anti-Zionist. There are varying degrees of this hostility, from those who disparage Zionism but still support a vigorous Israeli foreign policy and do not defend the Palestinian cause to those who loudly and proudly parade their anti-Israel bombast in the marketplace.

The anti-Zionism of anti-Zionist OTD'ers is clearly not motivated by the same ideology. After all, you understand, but too many don't, how utterly risible it is when the leftist anti-Israel crowd embraces the Netura Karta as one of their own. Charedi antagonism to political Zionism has nothing to do with anti-colonialist, anti-nationalist cosmopolitanism of the left. On the contrary, for Charedim, political Zionism is not nationalistic enough! Charedim cannot abide the Zionist desire to shape Jewish history and be "a nation like all other nations." Israel, they contend, will only attain *genuine* legitimacy when it is created in Messianic days, at which time Israel will control all the land promised to her in the Bible. Jericho will be *Yericho* and part of a Jewish entity. There is no two-state solution of shared territories in this eschatology.

So why the anti-Israel talk among OTD'ers? The answer, I'm afraid, traces to wholesale adoption of the progressive agenda which espouses an aversion to present-day Likud governmental policy and, increasingly, to the Zionist enterprise more broadly. Now, of course, you might have come to your anti-Israel conclusions independently, and only after having sifted through the competing arguments.

Perhaps. But here's what I fear. I fear (and this is just a theoretical hunch) that the visceral attachment to Israel—the actual place, not the ideal—needs to be embedded early on, in one's kishkas as it were, with one's proverbial mother's milk. (Charedi *cholov Yisroel* doesn't include *cholov Medinat Yisroel*.) That's a shame. Or at least it is from the perspective of this proud Zionist.

But enough of this disagreeing, and perhaps disagreeable interlude . . . other immediate matters await.

You've Got a Story . . . Own It

They've all heard about your past but this woman is the brazen one. The one who begins the inquiry.

"So tell me, if it's okay, I don't mean to pry, but why did you leave?"

You start to answer, but she isn't finished.

"What made you, you know, stop being religious, and leave your community? I hope you don't mind my asking."

"No, it's okay," you reply. As if you have a choice. "It's fine. I'm asked the question all the time."

Damn straight you are.

"It's really kind of complicated," you say.

The others lean in, eager to hear more. The one leaning in farthest modulates his voice to sound conspiratorial:

"Was there like a specific moment, some event that triggered your escape?"

"Not really," you reply. "It was really more like a process. For some time, I felt like I didn't belong. I felt like—"

"I can imagine." It's the original questioner, reclaiming the interrogation. "I saw this movie about how they won't let divorced women keep their kids. And about the sexual abuse."

"There are real problems with the community, that's true," you say, trying not to sound as if you've repeated these lines a hundred times before, though you have. "I'm not sure, though, that there's more sexual abuse than in other communities, but, yes, the hush-up that follows is awful. But that wasn't my story. I actually had a pretty happy childhood."

The group seems disappointed. What were they expecting?

"So why then?" they press on, all eyes still fixed on you, the parade of questions to follow.

"Where did you get the courage to leave?"

"Do you still speak with your family?"

"What about your siblings? Are you the only one who left?"

"Are others in the community leaving? How many would you say?

"What was it like the first time you violated the laws, like eating non-kosher?

"Are you angry?"

"Are you not angry?"

You answer each question briefly or at length as the mood strikes. There are days when you actually savor the role of "the exotic one" and don't begrudge the curiosity. After all, you might launch a similar barrage were you to meet a former Amish, a former Mormon, a formerly religious Muslim. You, too, unlike the others in the room, are a refugee from a strange, alien world, albeit one in the wilds of Brooklyn or upstate New York. Perhaps in the recess of your wallet, Beirish, there's this picture of you with your payis down to your shoulders that you sometimes present as a dramatic exhibition of your transformation. Or Hindi, one with you wearing that smart new sheitle covering every wisp of hair. On occasion, you'll take out the photo and with a wry, drawn-out smile, you show it to them, like a magician turning over the surprising card on the table: "yes, this was me then." But on other days, you leave the picture buried in your wallet with your history. You're plain tired of the spotlight, bored by your own rehearsed vignettes, preferring that your past remain your own and not a specimen for anthropological curiosity.

OTD is a popular subject these days and you are a potential poster boy/poster girl for the inquisitive. The novelty will fade—the Jewish media is no less ADD than the national media. But this, your real life and your real history will persist . . . though the account of it will not.

Do you notice how older people, your grandparents perhaps, tell the same story over and over again? Your bristle at the repetition, having heard the tale so many times before. But old folk, especially really old folk close to their end, want to depart the world with a legacy out there. A few key pivotal stories punctuated their lives, and they will burnish those events in the telling, smoothing out the edges, removing the unpleasant callouses, adding a few (often untrue) asides. Well, having dramatically changed your life, young as you are, you're already in the storytelling business. And as you tell your tale to new audiences, new strangers, and new loved ones (and to yourself), you'll be shaping that narrative, trying out new facets, emphasizing some currently telling episode, ignoring some currently unimportant incident. The saga will change as you change. Indeed, OTD isn't only a noun, but a verb as one OTD's in different ways throughout one's life. (We should emphasize how poor we all are at judging our own pasts. Here's one way we fail. 'Tis a human condition that we mock what we're about to become. But we also mock much of what we were. Having now distanced ourselves, we find it necessary to belittle those involvements, depreciating not only the people we cared so much about, but also the ideas and emotional highs of our earlier years. Converts to religions, causes, health practices are notorious for this distortion. Otd'ers have their own stock of such earlier, now disparaged, attachments.)

So don't think you've entered the witness protection program. There's continuity here. And so the lesson of Moyshe.

Unhappy with his excessive pounds, Moyshe joins a weight-watcher group and is a diligent participant. Over the next months he sheds forty pounds. Displeased, too, with his deteriorating looks, he gets minor surgery to remove the wrinkles under his eyes and a hair transplant to cover his balding head. Upset with his feeble physique, he enrolls in a gym where he regularly visits the treadmill and pumps iron and before long is sporting bulging muscles and noticeable abs. One day, walking out of the gym, he is hit by a truck. Lying on the ground, mortally wounded, he looks up to the sky and mournfully calls out, "God how could you do this to me? I worked so hard this past year to transform myself, I was so conscientious . . . and now this?" A Heavenly voice responds: "Moyshe? Is that you? I didn't recognize you!"

We recognize you. You might no longer look like those old photos in your wallet, but they're photos of you nonetheless. Own it.

So Here's Why You Really Went OTD

I'm kidding of course. I have no idea why either of you went OTD. I suspect that you yourself may not be able to give a fully cogent reason.

The only ones who think they can are the rabbis who see themselves as psychologically keen and have you fully figured out. Charedi magazines have an article every other week on how to prevent this horrible occurrence. A few, in a self-satisfied flourish of sensitivity, call for parental attention, the need to display affection, while the more clueless just appeal to better role modeling, i.e., more Torah-learning in the house. What they will never admit is that some of their children go OTD because they actually, upon reflection, no longer subscribe to the lifestyle and attendant expectations, and that many find their charedi world stultifying, anti-intellectual, sexist, racist, intellectually and morally dishonest.

It's not surprising, however, that your Charedi parents, no less than the secular onlookers, wonder why you went AWOL. After all, remaining in one's community is the prevailing default—inertia is a natural force in human society as it is in physics. Most people believe and behave as do their parents; the charedi community, despite enormous external attractions, is particularly successful at keeping their offspring in the fold, and therefore agitated when it isn't.

But these guardians of the faith need to realize, as all should, the reasons one chooses to reject the religious demands of one's youth are manifold and not always traceable to some misguided parenting. My own case is perhaps anomalous and different from yours. I had a truly wonderful childhood. My parents loved me passionately and I loved them passionately in return. As my last name indicates, I am a scion of major Chassidic dynasties (from my mother's side as well)—both my grandfathers were Chassidic rebbes, one, the first Rebbe in Boro Park. My father, a'h, was steeped in Chassidic learning, but unlike your parents he also esteemed worldly knowledge and was a fervent Zionist. No doubt the generational difference between us matters too. I was born in the first cohort after the war. Nearly all the adults around me were recreating their lives, shell-shocked from their Shoah horrors. My own psychological response, similar to some but not all of my friends and different from my siblings, was surely shaped by that early environment. Which is to say, our choices are complex, distinctive, and certainly not amenable to the flippant "explanations" so regularly on offer.

Look, it's hard to do a life. Which means both that people ought to give you room to do yours as you see best . . . as you should others (including those who choose to remain charedi). But now on that new, bumpy, long and winding path of yours, remember: a stumble may prevent a fall. And sometimes be ready to take the big steps—You can't cross a chasm in two small jumps.

Stay in touch. There's much to talk about. I mean talk—I promise not to pontificate anymore.

Joshua

Nonetheless—

Some Final Pieces of Unsolicited Advice:

1. You're really smart. I wish my college students knew how to parse a text the way you do, ask questions the way you do, care about the answers the way you do. Goethe had it right: If you only speak one language (culture) you don't speak any. You're deeply culturally bilingual. So, educational deficits and all, don't presume you're beginning way behind the starting line. You actually have a head start.

2. Phillip Roth compared writing in Eastern Europe under communist regimes with Western countries, noting that in those dictatorships "nothing goes and everything matters," while in the West, "everything goes and nothing matters." The "nothing goes" part is familiar to you. Now, free of the constraints, it'll take work to make sure that things still matter.

3. It's really okay to be confused about stuff. Voltaire: "Doubt is not a pleasant state, but certainty is a ridiculous one."

4. You have choices, but be realistic: Perhaps you can do anything you want but you certainly can't do everything you want.

5. On finding your new derech: If you don't know where you are going any road you're on will get you there.

6. You once refused to join the chorus of those around you. That independent voice is easily subsumed. If you find yourself echoing a prevailing opinion, step back and reconsider. Make that a habit.

7. It's good that you still wonder about the point of it all. But there is also this perspective, from Isaiah Berlin: "As for the meaning of life, I do not believe that it has any, and this is a source of great comfort to me." Perhaps. But there is this other perspective from Jack Handey: "I hope life isn't a big joke, because I don't get it."

8. The challenge of part one of our lives is to decide who we want to be; the challenge of part two is to be who we are.

9. Full-time consistency is exhausting. Give yourself some slack . . . allow yourself an occasional holiday from being true to yourself.

The Law of Return

MORRIS DICKSTEIN

Growing up Orthodox on the Lower East Side of New York in the 1940s meant coming of age in a sheltered and a sheltering world regulated by sternly held notions of how to live and behave. Orthodox Judaism then had none of the political militance or millenarian zeal that would surface after the Six-Day War of 1967. No one ever talked of the Holocaust, although religious Jews felt blighted by the extinction of European Jewry and overwhelmed by the refugees who landed in the city. The will of the Almighty had never seemed harder to fathom.

A sense of helplessness pervaded the Jewish community. The conflict in Palestine felt remote, though the creation of Israel inspired tremendous excitement. For boys with the blue-and-white collection boxes of the Jewish National Fund, supporting Israel was a righteous cause, but many Jews still saw Zionism as a dubious experiment at odds with religion, devoted instead to working the land and creating a secular nation on sacred soil. The epitome of Zionism was the kibbutz, which meant tractors, socialism, and free love, with children separated from their parents and brought up in common as sun-baked young pagans. There were religious Zionists too, pioneers in khaki shorts with tiny knitted skullcaps, but Zionism scorned the passivity and otherworldliness of ghetto Judaism. Even in New York there were young men who had fought in the war and women born and educated in America who were determined to bring Orthodox Judaism up to date, to discard its parochial European trappings and give it a youthful American cast.

The Lower East Side of my childhood was no longer the bubbling cauldron of immigrant energy portrayed in novels like *Bread Givers*, *Jews Without Money*, and *Call It Sleep*, set in the heyday of the ghetto after the turn of the century. Now Yiddish was receding, a colorful ethnic English was everywhere, and echoes of the Sephardic Hebrew of Palestine were heard in the more up-to-date yeshivas. The older generation supported what survived of the Yiddish theatre, with its aging stars who toured the Catskills resorts, and there were still innumerable tiny synagogues, dairy restaurants, kosher delis, butcher shops, fragrant bakeries, and Hebrew bookstores, as well as combative daily newspapers like the *Forward*, the *Day*, the *Morning Journal*, and the Communist *Freiheit*. Yiddish remained the main language of Talmudic exegesis in the yeshiva I attended, and my parents, who had little interest in Zionism—their older brothers and sisters spoke Yiddish at home—hardly considered the new spoken Hebrew track when they enrolled me in 1945.

Second-generation Jews had begun their long march into the middle class, deserting the old neighborhood for the outer boroughs or the sub-urbs, as my parents did when they departed for Queens in 1949. Many others were too old or poor to move, or were kept in the neighborhood by family or religious bonds. Some saw America as a godless and alien place, the East Side as a haven for Jews. In our building at 131–33 Henry Street virtually everyone was Jewish and working class but only my parents were observant, which deepened their sense of gentility. On both sides of the street were rows of synagogues, each stemming from a different town in Eastern Europe, but street life itself was heathen and raucous, the scene of stick-ball games in summer and snowball fights in winter. A great annual event on our block was the return of Eddie Cantor, who had lived there in the distant past and would come to call on an ancient neighbor, a woman named Ida. It was important for those who made it to honor their humble beginnings.

My parents disliked seeing me hang out with the kids on the block; had they taken notice, they would have been outraged by the sexual games developing under the stoops, where little girls offered to show you theirs if you showed them yours. My mother frowned when I played with Leon, my closest friend, inches shorter but pounds tougher than me. At five he already had the rough hands and thick, stubby fingers of his burly father, a truck driver. My mother's father, though an unworldly man, had owned a glass business. His sons became carpenters, glaziers, in business for themselves. One day they would be substantial people, pillars of the community. Poor Leon and his family represented limited horizons.

My parents sent me to yeshiva to separate me from boys like Leon and from girls who might one day get me to drop my pants and lose my soul. There were no girls at all at our school, though there were many poor boys on scholarship, paying little or nothing. My parents didn't seem to mind that the school day stretched from nine to six, including Sundays, which left me little time on the street. (Later I would feel I missed having a childhood, though it seemed like fun at the time.) As they saw it, the choice was simple: you either became a scholar or a bum. My yeshiva schooling also shielded my parents from the disapproval of my father's eldest brother, the family patriarch. A dour and forbidding man, he was on the alert for any religious slippage in the family, any compromise with America. To my mother he represented a *Galizianer* gloom that contrasted with the zest and dignity of her Russian family. Many years later, when I grew a beard after the sixties, my uncle reached out and gave it a tug as if it were an unconvincing prop. I couldn't fool him, he said, it was "the wrong *kind* of beard." This was at the graveside where his wife was being buried.

The yeshiva curriculum was hardly designed to create observant Jews—that was simply assumed. Its goal was to produce Talmudical scholars, learned rabbis trained not to lead congregations—a suburban American impertinence—but to master the gigantic body of Jewish lore and learning, the vast commentary on the law. Other matters like the study of the Bible and the rich oral traditions, which might have gripped us as narrative, were passed through as quickly as if we were Catholics, deflected from any direct contact with the Sacred Writ. We were there to study law (*halakhah*), not legend (*aggadah*), and everything came to us already salted by a long history of interpretation.

Before I was ten we were introduced to the Talmud, and I was soon immersed in a thicket of laws pertaining to what happens when an ox gores a neighbor's cow—this in one of the world's most densely populated cities. By the age of twelve, bewildered yet soldiering on, we began studying the statutes governing marriage and divorce, including a variety of prohibited unions, and many pages dealing with "unnatural intercourse," which left us thoroughly mystified. When one boy raised his hand to ask what "unnatural intercourse" was, the clever rabbi, a

Holocaust survivor with wisply beard and a houseful of small children, said in Yiddish, "You tell me what *natural* intercourse is and I'll tell you about unnatural intercourse." Few of us had a clue except for one kid, a rabbi's son with seven or eight siblings, who would later give us a crude version of the basic facts. We learned everything by rote, whether we understood it or not, though a method of oral argument that went back hundreds of years, perhaps as far as the academy at Yavneh in the second century.

There were other day schools that offered less scholastic instruction in Judaism, and even acknowledged the time and place in which we lived. My school had a split personality. In the morning we might have been back in the *shtetl*, swaying rhythmically as we prayed, chanting in a sing-song voice as we translated from the Aramaic of the Talmud to the Yiddish of our grandfathers. But after lunch we received an up-to-date secular education which put us on the fast track toward a liberal arts university. Though some of our English and math teachers also happened to be observant Jews, the two wings of the school had distinct faculties and widely differing goals. In the morning we were in Vilna or Bialystok—time stood still; in the afternoon we were being propelled at a dizzying pace through the twentieth century.

In the end I appreciated what a yeshiva education gave me, a strong logical training, an easy familiarity with the rabbinic tradition—the mental oxygen of diaspora Judaism. But I resented the way it was forced down my throat, with little regard for how it might interest me or how the world had changed. We were swamped in a sea of minute distinctions remote from any life we knew. To this day I'm appalled at how much Jewish learning was neglected in favor of the legal and interpretive tradition. There was virtually no attention to the Hebrew Bible, Jewish history and philosophy, modern Hebrew and Yiddish literature, or the Hebrew language as a living organism rather than a blunt instrument of prayer and argument. I learned to read Hebrew without really being able to understand it. In many ways my Jewish education began only when I left the intellectual confines of the yeshiva.

At home religion was a practical thing, a matter of habit and tradition: this was the way things had always been done. In school it came with a sense of compulsion and surveillance. On the East Side I was always looking over my shoulder, since some the teachers were fond of spying on their charges in off hours, pouncing on them if their heads were uncovered or if, G-d forbid, they were caught violating the Sabbath. It seemed as if there was always someone holier than thou, ready to dole out guilt and shame by the bucketful.

There was guilt to spare at home as well, but religion came enveloped by love and softened by numerous child-centered exceptions. And at the end of the school year, we escaped from the city in long, carefree summers at the beach. Every tenement dweller, hemmed in by brick and hot cement, pined for the sight of a tree, for a mountain vista or a glimpse of open water, something my mother's family, poor as they were, had managed to locate many years before I was born. Through ads in the *New York Daily Mirror*, my mother's brothers and sisters had discovered a distant town on Long Island that became a tumultuous family compound. There, along with dozens of young working-class Italians, they had bought small parcels of land for $89.50 a lot, and built rude "bungalows" with their own hands, adding additional rooms year after year as the families grew. These houses were rustic railroad flats, with tiny bedrooms that spilled into one another and screen porches to escape the summer heat. With their picket fences, blooming hydrangeas, and meagre plots of grass, they enabled mothers and children to spend July and August at the shore while their husbands worked in the sweltering city.

There were beds everywhere, sometimes even in the kitchen. Weekends, when the extended family piled in, seemed like one long party. Except for the glorious pebbly beach facing Long Island Sound, this could have been the Catskills; but there were virtually no other Jews, no one to keep watch over me and warn me what not to do. Most of my cousins were older; sometimes I tagged along on their excursions: movies in Port Jefferson, blueberry-picking along the abandoned railroad tracks, nights at the local bowling alley. If the yeshiva was mostly superego, summer was the time for release and liberation.

This summer world was where most of the religious exceptions kicked in: swimming was healthy, even on the Sabbath, though of course one must walk the mile to the beach; ice cream was healthy too, especially on the beach, so there was no need to wait the usual six hours after a meat meal. While the school year kept telling me that religion was censorious and unbending, that heaven and hell were waiting right outside the classroom door, summer reminded me that Judaism could be lax and tolerant, all in the family, with grown-ups winking at all that solemnity. Judaism could be what you made of it, not simply what it made of you.

The Jewish tradition was flexible; it had no church, no real theology, not even a Chief Rabbi; it could adapt to almost anything, as diaspora Jews had done for centuries.

By the end of the 1940s, Jews who could afford to leave were abandoning the Lower East Side. My father, who had always worked for a salary and felt trapped by his job, opened a "dry goods" store in Flushing, just when small businesses were enjoying their last fling of prosperity. Both my parents worked twelve hours a day, six days a week, to keep the store going—including Saturday, which now became the most gigantic and embarrassing of exceptions. They sold men's wear, children's wear, and—my specialty—bras, girdles, nylons, and panties, along with just about anything else a customer would order. My mother loved the social give-and-take of the business—a new drama was always walking through the door—but my father, a shy man, fretted over every sale, and went off to buy goods in the city as often as he could.

Their hearts were still on the Lower East Side, where—between the wholesalers on Orchard Street and the bakeries near Hester Park— they still did their serious shopping. This was where most of the family still lived, and where I continued to go to school, adding almost three hours of travel onto my already interminable day. My bar mitzvah took place in an old world synagogue on East Broadway, under the eye of the most venerable Talmud scholar in America. The East Side was where my parents came from, where they still belonged; Queens was simply the place they were condemned to earn their bread. It seemed unthinkable for them to send me to school in such a *goyishe* wasteland, though my younger sister somehow received a splendid Jewish education in central Queens. But after all, there wasn't much religion that a girl really needed.

If my parents felt any guilt at seeing me set off on a twelve-hour journey—I took a bus and three trains to get to school every morning—this was soon laid to rest. Our former neighbor on Henry Street, a childless woman who had virtually adopted my sister and me, delivered me from the school cafeteria and insisted I come by regularly for lunch. As newlyweds, Esther and her husband Jack had moved into the next-door apartment a month after I was born, on the very day of my *pidyan ha-ben*, the redemption of the first-born male. They took to spoiling me in ways my parents wouldn't have dreamed of: extravagant toys, meals out at delis or dairy restaurants, sweets and chocolates always on tap. Jack was a bookie and numbers runner, a dangerous but lucrative line of work that required constant pay-offs to local detectives. But he was also a sick man with bad lungs and a racking cough who wheezed for breath after the slightest exertion.

Esther had barely escaped from Poland before the war, and never really learned to read English or speak it properly. Her English was never less than picturesque—Clinton Street was always "Clincoln Stritt"—and she got all her news from the Yiddish papers. She had largely lost contact with a few surviving relatives who had landed in London. In many ways she never left Eastern Europe, though Europe had left her. All her life she remained dependent, histrionic, and starved for affection, which was something this young prince, who played to grown-ups like a seasoned trouper, was only too willing to provide.

The operatic demands of growing up with a Jewish mother are hard to describe, though many have tried. But having *two* Jewish mothers, at opposite ends of the city, is something I despair of making credible. My real mother, who preferred the constant clamor of business to the drudgery of cooking and housework, was only too glad to palm me off, with only an occasional trace of jealousy, on a surrogate more domestic than herself, a refugee no less, whose virtuoso repertory of Jewish cooking, from lox, eggs, and onions to Borscht or blintzes, dispelled any guilt she might have felt. Esther was doting, determined, superstitious, open-hearted, and frightened of everything—a piece of the *shtetl* in a pocket of America. Thanks to Esther and my strange willingness to travel—I could read even on the most crowded subway car—I spent most of my waking hours on the Lower East Side among the Jews and slept in distant Queens among the gentiles.

On weekends at our little conservative synagogue in Flushing, my yeshiva training made me practically the deputy rabbi: before long I would be reading the Torah, leading the junior congregation, even occasionally giving a guest sermon, like some phenomenal boy-preacher in a Harlem storefront church. I rarely corrected anyone who assumed I would become a rabbi, though the thought never actually crossed my mind. At school, as my Talmud studies grew more and more oppressive, I went into deep adolescent rebellion—cutting classes, boycotting study periods, reading Shakespeare under the desk during rabbinical discourses, making fun of my unworldly teachers who rarely understood the cruel pranks I directed at them. The principal was up in arms, lecturing me for my iron resistance to what they wanted me to study, which now paled in interest compared to my English classes. But at home and in synagogue it pleased me to play the Jew, to bask in parental affection and communal pride for skills effortlessly acquired and for ambitions far from the ones that were actually shaping my life.

In our Flushing neighborhood, mainly populated by blue-collar Irish and Italians, I discovered that Jews were not the center of the world and the Lower East Side was not America. There was an Irish kid a little older than me who made it his business to advance my education. Once he walked down our street eating a bagel, a rare thing in Flushing then, and leered at me with a malevolent grin: "I'm eating *your* food." Another time he and his pals attacked a friend of mine they knew from public school, wrestling him to the ground and starting to take down his pants. My friend began whimpering as he struggled to fight back, and I was humiliated at being forced to stand by, as if this were a spectacle intended for me. Fearful of fighting and fearful of doing nothing, I began avoiding streets where I might run into my tormentor. An excess of mothering, an education that stretched the mind but stunted the body, had left me ill prepared for street fighting. I developed a mild form of the classic Jewish fear of persecution, the diaspora mentality the Zionists had tried to sweep away.

Since I hated working in my parents' store, where women invariably tittered when I reached for the "intimate apparel," my refuge was the local public library. I ran through books at an alarming rate, hurtling along from subject to subject on a quest to know everything, to pump myself up in a world where I felt clumsy and awkward. Language became mastery for a boy growing up above the store, a gawky kid who loved sports but lacked athletic grace. As if to compensate, I would shine in the citywide spelling bee, edit the student newspaper, join the debate team to thrash out the urgent issues of the day: Should wiretapping be banned? (Mr. Justice Holmes said it was a "dirty business.") Should "Red China" be admitted to the UN? Should we build the St. Lawrence Seaway?

Competing with debaters from other yeshivas—I remember Alan Dershowitz from one of the opposing teams—we were the high school descendants of those legendary contrarians, the School of Hillel and the School of Shammai. We were living out the heritage of the dialectic that had repelled me in its Talmudical form. Who knows how much my life as a literary scholar grew out of the religious studies I struggled to escape, how much my love of books was simply a secular modern form of the Jewish love of the Book. Just as Jews held on to their identity by clinging to rabbinical traditions during their dispersion, I shaped my twentieth-century identity by grasping at secular knowledge and endowing it with personal power and moral gravity.

Perhaps culture became my religion, as teaching would later serve as a form of lay preaching, of rabbinical *pilpul*. Certainly my calling as a critic stemmed in part from the kind of Midrashic and textual commentary long pursued by the sages of Israel. Even my rebellion against orthodoxy belonged to a modern tradition of Jewish intellectual life. Modernism breaks out when the Jews leave the ghetto, when the late Victorian sons begin doubting the faith of the high Victorian fathers. Even the socialism of the ghetto and the liberal politics of the second generation can be traced back, if we wish, to the abrasive teachings of the Hebrew prophets. Their willingness to denounce kings and merchant princes, their warnings against oppressing the poor and performing empty ritual, would later evolve into a social gospel, a religion of the heart.

I became an agnostic, a skeptical Jew, yet was never able to leave religion behind. As a Columbia undergraduate I began taking courses at the Jewish Theological Seminary, which horrified one of my pious cousins, who told my father he would rather send his children to church. At the seminary I encountered not only the learning and Hebrew culture left out of my yeshiva education but a laissez-faire version of the traditional prayer service—the synagogue of my childhood stripped of coercion and surveillance, with no one to tell me I was doing it wrong. If the legendary scholars at the seminary lacked anything, it was passion. They were children of the *Haskalah*, the rationalism of the Hebrew Enlightenment.

When my father died late in 1992, I tried to say *kaddish* for him as often as I could, and looked for a daily service that would give meaning to the act of remembrance, which in turn became a remembrance of my own childhood. My parents' permissive brand of orthodoxy had left me with a well of affection for Judaism rather than a hard nut of resentment. On the Upper West Side, I found a *minyan* descended from the *Havurah*—the commune-like prayer groups from the late sixties and seventies that linked an emotional return to Judaism with a feeling for social justice. The service was traditional yet women played an equal role. On the Sabbath children spilled out everywhere. As the post-sixties generation began raising families, passion returned to Judaism by way of the counterculture.

It moved me to rediscover the prayers and melodies I knew so well, to see the Jewish holidays celebrated with energy and fervor, not as moribund routine but as family occasions which strengthened the bonds of community. Unexpectedly, I found something in Orthodox Judaism I wanted to recapture, a part of my childhood that still resonated for me. In the past I had known moments of rapture, when the prayers took on an electric power, when meaning seemed to flow through me and I felt in touch with life under the sign of eternity. In later years I felt this cosmic shudder more in reading Wordsworth or Shelley, Whitman or Dickinson, than in reciting familiar prayers. Being a literary intellectual had become another way of being a Jew. But occasionally a biblical text, usually one of the Psalms, or a passage from the prophets, would move me to the edge of tears, as if it contained a fragment of the meaning of life.

Despite such moments, religion for me remained in the realm of the familiar rather than the sublime. Unlike the world-despising faiths that look to a future free of all contingency, Judaism hallows everyday life and connects the present to the historical past, as it connected me with my own past and past generations. Complete assimilation is unimaginable to me. Nothing seems more natural, more consoling, than to greet the Sabbath with song, to fast on the Day of Atonement, to suffer through eight days of eating matzoh on Passover. I do this haphazardly, as a secular Jew's selective memory of religious observance. I cannot conceive of returning to the study of the Talmud, but I cherish the annual readings of the Book of Esther, the Book of Ruth, the Book of Lamentations, the Book of Jonah, or the story of the binding of Isaac, which carry such a weight of history and myth. The death of my father left centuries of tradition in my hands. For some reason, not faith, I feel the need to pass it on.

Today's Orthodox Judaism, whether in Brooklyn or Israel, has been undermined by a tribalism that condones violence, fears peace, and demonizes the other. This was not the Judaism of my childhood, a diaspora Judaism, wary of nationalism, fragmented and beleaguered rather than triumphalist. It was devoted perhaps too narrowly to learning and moral scruple rather than Messianic redemption—a Judaism of dailiness and ritual rather than the grand fulfilment of Biblical prophecies. I once found orthodox Judaism a burden but also a quiet joy; now, for some, it is a source of righteous hatred, the ground for a swaggering, gun-toting xenophobia that puts Jews in danger and treats Arabs as less than human. I no longer recognize it.

Tuesdays with Facebook

Shulem Deen

Edited selections from my "Overshare Tuesday" series, a set of Facebook posts written between July 2015 and March 2016, following publication of my book, "All Who Go Do Not Return."

Tuesday, July 7, 2015

Tell me that my book moved you. Tell me that it made you think. That it made you cry, that it made you laugh, that you learned something new. Tell me that you liked the writing, or that you hated it; that you think the structure was well done, or wasn't. Tell me it's a shit piece of work, that it mentions too many unkempt beards, that it's just another work in a stale genre. Tell me that it infuriated you, or stirred you to action. Tell me that it put you to sleep.

But please, for the love of Zeus, don't tell me how sorry you feel for me.

∾

My Overshares often feel like downers, and many people don't like downers. They like uppers. Happy endings. Bouquets of roses. Raspberries in creamy Greek yogurt. Because that's what their lives have always been like, and they don't like to complicate it with the sadness of others. So here's some happy info for the happy people:

I had a great birthday party the other week. I ended up hammered, and a highball glass crashed to the floor, and the bar people weren't too happy, but I had more fun in one night than I had in the entire four years prior.

❧

I am working on a novel. A novel I have been working on for more than a decade, but had put on hold in order to write my memoir. Now I'm back at it. I'm also writing the outlines of a new non-fiction, memoiristic project. I'm working on a bunch of shorter pieces, too. You will like them. I think. I hope. Please pretend, at least.

The big problem is how to finance your writing life. You need wide open stretches of time to think and create, but no one's paying you for that time, and so the wide open stretches get narrower and narrower as you squeeze in a gig here and a gig there, until all you have is a sliver of exhausted evenings, and the occasional weekend after resolutely telling the people you love that you will *not* go to the beach with them because you have to write. And there goes your social life too.

This was supposed to be the upper.

❧

WANTED:
A place to live for September. Preferably without rats. My budget is small, but there are ways to stretch it. Tell me your secrets, I'll tell you mine.

Tuesday, July 14, 2015

When you tell me you are an Orthodox Jew, do I suggest it is because of some childhood trauma?

When you tell me you are Catholic, do I challenge you on whether you've read enough on the subject?

When you tell me you are Buddhist, do I ask how you think your beliefs logically possible?

When you tell me you are Hindu, do I suggest that you would be more appealing if you didn't announce it so proudly?

When you tell me you are Episcopalian, do I suggest it is a result of some psychological imbalance?

When you tell me you are Muslim, do I challenge you immediately to a debate on medieval philosophy?

When you tell me you are Sikh, do I insist that you have a bad understanding of science?

When you tell me that you are a Protestant Christian, do I question your ability to be a moral and ethical person?

No, I do none of those things.

Why then do you do them when I tell you I'm an atheist?

I respect you, regardless of your beliefs. Respect me too, even if I don't share them.

Tuesday, July 28, 2015

I really wanted that Breadloaf fellowship. *They* invited me to apply—I was nominated, they told me. And so I thought it was in the bag.

The other day, the email came, after four months of waiting:

"Thank you for applying, yada yada yada, we get lots of applicants, blah blah blah. We can only award 6% of X and 20% of Y, and sorry you didn't make the cut but we just think you're a crap writer, and you should go flip hamburgers for a living."

Fine. You're probably not such a great writer's retreat anyway.

Then, a writer I know from Twitter tweets about getting her Breadloaf fellowship.

Then again, she went to Iowa. I knew I should've gone to Iowa.

Why am I so angry? I wish I weren't so angry. Maybe it's because my therapist was out last week. Therapists, too, need vacations, I am told. Their voicemails say, "If this is an emergency, please hang up and call 9-1-1." Is being angry an emergency? I think not. Probably more a 3-1-1 type thing. Does 3-1-1 handle anger problems? Does anyone know?

"Stop with the stories," a friend said to me recently. "Have an opinion!"

And I thought: You kidding me?! What if someone disagrees with me?

Speaking of opinions: last week I had one. I'll say only: Eh, opinions are overrated.

Cheers, all. Til next week.

Tuesday, August 4, 2015

My therapist's back. Thought you'd want to know.

～

This morning I made a pot of coffee that was way too light. I poured it all down the sink and made a new pot.

That's what life feels like sometimes. You might be wasting some coffee, but the rich dark stuff comes only on the second try

～

I find one of the most difficult things to talk about is money. A couple months ago, I was asked to give a talk at a convention of rationalists in the Smokey Mountains, Tennessee, over the July 4th weekend. They call it the Annual Freethinkers Advance. (It's a retreat, really, but freethinkers don't "retreat," they "advance." Get it?)

I mentioned this invite to a friend.

"Are they paying?" he asked.

"Yes."

"And how much *do things like that* pay?"

"You're asking like a Jew," I said.

What is the functional difference between "How much are they paying you?" and "How much do things like that pay?"

None. But I don't know how to answer either without saying: It's none of your goddamn business.

I think different cultures have different attitudes towards money.

Israelis probably ask outright: "How much dey pay you?"

WASPs probably don't mention money at all. They just know, by the cut of your trousers.

My point is: Talk of money triggers me. Money has always disappointed me—and what I do for it, you wouldn't believe.

～

Like I said, some days you just have to pour out the coffee and make a new pot.

Tuesday, June 30, 2015

There's nothing like the feeling of working on an essay, rearranging a paragraph, cutting a sentence, adding a word, and then realizing: This baby is *done!*

Until the editor asks for a complete rewrite. That feeling is not good at all.

❧

One of the questions I get asked a lot is: How did you learn to write?

More particularly, how did you learn to write English, if you grew up in a Yiddish-speaking world?

It's usually asked with a kind of puzzled look. Like something doesn't fit. And it fills me with dread, like they're trying to expose me. I hear an accusation, like I'm withholding a secret: Spill it, kid. What aren't you tellin' us? And every time I answer, it's like I'm confirming something they already know. There's a raised eyebrow and a slow nod. Ah, I knew you were hiding something.

Some of my answers:

The language in my childhood home was English. My parents weren't fluent in Yiddish, so there was a lot of mixing with English.

Ah, people's eyes light up. *Now* they understand.

Also, I lived in Borough Park as a kid, where there was lots of English. A kind of frummie, non-standard English, with lots of Yiddish and Hebrew mixed in. Some call it Yinglish, or Yeshivish. We just called it English. Also, we had two hours at the end of the school day during which we learned English and math, and I took it pretty seriously.

I see, they say. So two hours. Not so bad.

Also, I tell them, I was a big reader as a kid. I read mail order catalogs, the fine print on the sweepstakes coupons, the Tzivos Hashem newsletter, and my mother's books on macrobiotic cooking.

Um hmm, they go. So that must've helped.

Also, I add, I actually did one semester in community college back in 2008. Since I had no high school diploma, I was officially required to take English Composition 101. The instructor spent a lot of time teaching us how to indent and double-space in Microsoft Word, but I don't remember much else.

Oh, they go. So you *did* go to college. I thought you were self-taught! Now I see it in their eyes: every bit of mystique gone.

Fraud!

FRAUD! FRAUD! FRAUD!

No, they don't say fraud. But their eyes say it. Or my mind says it. Or just that something in their previously adoring expression goes limp. They're heading for the door, beckoning to their friends and spouses, they're leaving, going to find some other wunderkind (why are there no wunder-40-year-olds?) to adore.

Wait!

I worked really hard to learn how to write!

Believe me, Borough Park people can't write for shit! My school taught me some basic words, and some really atrocious grammar! And that college semester was worthless! My girlfriend even says I sound "so frummie" to this very day!

Come back! Love me! Adore me! Ask me more questions! I've got so much more to say!

But they're all gone.

Tuesday, July 21, 2015

Not a day for oversharing. RIP Faigy.

Wednesday, July 30, 2015

It's been a very intense week. Faigy Mayer—a beloved member of our OTD community—committed suicide and the aftermath has been pretty dismal.

First there was grief. Then there was finger pointing. Then finger pointing at the finger pointers. Then anger that everyone is finger pointing and would people just shut up—yes, you, I'm pointing at you—would you stop pointing?

There have been hurtful things said. As a community, I feel like we're struggling. Maybe it's just me. Sometimes my name gets thrown out there, either explicitly or obliquely, and I don't usually mind, even when something unkind is said, but it hurts when it comes from friends. I'm not sure I know how to deal with it. Ignore it? But they're friends.

Tomorrow. Tomorrow will be a better day.

∽

I didn't write yesterday, because I wanted to write from a lighter, brighter place. Mentally. Emotionally. And so I thought I'd wait a day.

Nothing's changed.

But maybe tomorrow. Maybe next week.

In the meantime, easy on the whiskey, friends. And keep taking your meds.

Tuesday, August 5, 2015

Have you noticed? Man buns. They're everywhere.

∽

I sometimes fantasize about unplugging from social media, deactivating Facebook, closing my Twittter account, and generally avoiding the rabbit warrens of this hyperlinked world. I imagine reading the print editions of the *New York Times*, the *New Yorker*, and *Harper's*, as well as the *Forward* for my tribal fix, and maybe a handful of other print magazines, just to mix things up.

This I fantasize. Then I panic. I think about missing out on the videos of cops shooting unarmed black people, on the debates about race and privilege and Obama and fundamentalism and Bernie Sanders and Cecil the lion. I would miss the video of some crazy Russian guy driving a nail through his scrotum. The Buzzfeed listicles, with the Number Six that will make you laugh/cry/blow your mind/you just won't believe. I'd feel so 1990. Could I live like that? I don't know. I really just don't know.

∽

Faigy Mayer is still on my mind.

Deb Tambor is still on my mind.

Suicide is complicated, and we may never know the real reasons behind it, but I feel like it should move us to action, even if imperfectly.

When Deb died, there was a push to help parents survive the hell of custody battles, and a lot's been accomplished since.

Now, after Faigy's death, there's a lot of talk about essential needs, and the lack of a safety net for OTD folks. I've been hearing so many stories; I don't think I was ever aware of just how many people in our community suffer debilitating anxiety over housing and food and having a decent outfit for a job interview. And the feelings of helplessness that can wreck even the sanest person's emotional stability, with sometimes devastating long term effects.

How do we best help those who lack the basics? How do we keep our community growing and thriving, while also reaching out to those stuck in a rut?

How do we ensure that everyone in our community has, at minimum, housing, food, and clothes? How do we help maintain the dignity of those we help, while also being mindful not to foster dependency? How do we distinguish between acute crises and chronic ones, and what are the different ways to help each?

I don't know the answers, but those of us who feel strongly about community should be thinking about this. We may have left Borough Park and Williamsburg and Monsey, along with their many charities and support organizations, but maybe that's the obligation we now face, of setting up our own vital support networks. It's true: as a community we're small, we're young, we're not overly abundant in material and institutional resources, but maybe that's no excuse. And maybe we're not as lacking as we think.

This is what's on my mind now.

Tuesday, August 25, 2015

Matisyahu took a stand.

Natalie Portman had an opinion.

Jonathan Franzen shared some things about himself.

I feel like it's such a brave thing these days to express an honest thought. It seems so fraught, like there's some unspoken consensus on what views one may hold, and if you don't have the correct one, you will be pounced upon by the social media hordes and renounced by your friends and family, including your BFF from college who spent so many fucked up nights with you that she knows your grossest parts—she's smelled your sweat and your vomit and your shit, and covered for you when you needed covering, but now she won't stand for your opinions, because they're problematic and that's not ok and she can't even. Social justice, bitches.

∾

I've found a place. A decent place. Not nearly as good as where I am now; the new place is tiny, fucking Lilliputian. In a basement. But it's clean and fresh, and the price is good, and it's in a decent neighborhood. I'm feeling ok about it. Not thrilled, but ok.

Now I need help moving, and I'm willing to pay. If you're a man with a van, or a gal with a truck, or a Martian with a spaceship with room enough to transport the small amount of shit that's left over after my many wanderings, and the medium amount of shit accumulated since, please, be a pal and HMU.

Back when I was a Hasid, when moving into a new place, we threw what we called a Chanukas Habayis. There were stale Ostreicher's chocolate chip cookies, and Gordon's vodka, and we sang 'Borei olam bekinyan, hashlem zeh habinyan,' and received wishes for raising large broods of children, and having many happy celebrations, and always having dirty floors—from the muddy boots of guests tramping in.

Sometimes I'm nostalgic for those things.

Others call it a Housewarming Party. But that's just not the same.

Tuesday, September 1, 2015

Leon Wieseltier once wrote: "I hear it said of somebody that he is leading a double life. I think to myself: Just two? "

∾

I'm all moved; in my new place now, still unpacking, settling in. Moving's a bitch, but it could've been worse.

I've done some exploring. My new neighborhood, Crown Heights, has a restaurant with a sign "artisanal burger lab." So I've found Ridiculous Brooklyn, it seems.

Previously, I lived in the Brooklyn boondocks.

"Gravesend?" people would ask. "Where's that?"

I'd say, it's just beyond Bensonhurst, which some people have heard of. But usually I'd say, it's the last neighborhood before Coney Island, which gave it a sense of desolate remoteness with the promise of excitement just beyond, like the vast expanse of Nevada desert before the Vegas lights.

I really liked Gravesend, with it's original Dutch name—Grahve's Zahnd, The Count's Beach—and which was the name of one of Brooklyn's original six towns. I liked that King's Highway, which I lived right off of, was one of Brooklyn's first roads, and which originally ran all the way from Bushwick, cutting across Flatbush, and ending at Bay Ridge. It's been considerably shortened, but Kings Highway still has something of that *derech hamelech* aura, grandly cutting through the otherwise orderly Brooklyn grids.

I loved the Homestretch bar half a block down—the diviest of all dive bars, a Brooklyn gem of which I was originally (stupidly) wary, until my friend Joshua literally dragged me in there, and where the bartender makes up the prices as she goes and as often as not the drink's on the house.

Gravesend was remote, but more importantly, it made no claims about itself; it wasn't gentrified, it wasn't crime-ridden, it wasn't quaint. In a certain world, it would be thought lacking in character. In a world in which almost every neighborhood stakes some claim to being the-new-last-year's-trendy-neighborhood, genuine character is hard to find, and the very absence of it has its own appeal.

Alas, now I've come to a place so brimming with character and charm, it's overwhelming. Lubavitchers to my right. Island culture to my left. Overprivileged gentrifiers all around.

So much charm, it's like gorging on pie at Thanksgiving dinner, and you never want to see a fucking pie again. You just want back at the bar where the sixty-something bartender with the big blonde hair can't remember the price for a Jameson-on-the-rocks, and is just, like, "Don't worry about it, hon."

Tuesday, September 16, 2015

On a recent Friday evening, I met a Russian man in Union Square who claimed to have discovered the meaning of life.

"I have unique logical formula," he said. He wanted me to help him get word out. "You can be Saint Paul to my Jesus. You will become very, very famous. Most famous in world."

I said that if I wanted fame, I'd want to be my own Jesus.

"That is clever," he said. "But Jesus died on cross."

∾

Crown Heights is an extraordinary place.

So many thoughts, on Chabad, on Island culture (West Indian Day parade was unfrickinbelievable), on gentrification. On the sheer beauty of the ordinary row houses here.

More on this to come.

EREV YOM KIPPUR—Tuesday, September 22, 2015

Today, I share a memory.

(There is some Hebrew; translation at end.)

I was 15, a yeshiva student in New Square, NY, in the days between Rosh Hashana and Yom Kippur. A sign on the yeshiva door said that Reb Chaim Brim, an elderly Hasid from Jerusalem, will give a talk at noon.

The tables in the study hall were rearranged, pushed closely together to allow a large open space in the middle of the room, and students sat in circles around them, five, six rows deep.

Reb Chaim sat within the first circle, just one Hasid among many.

I don't remember how he began—it wasn't a speech, just off-the-cuff remarks, a 'shmuez,' a conversation. At one point, he said, "The shachris haftorah on Yom Kippur says it all." And then he began to speak it, word for word, really slowly, entirely from memory.

הן לריב ומצה תצומו, ולהכות באגרף רשע . . . .
הכזה יהיה צום אבחרהו, יום ענות אדם נפשו?!
הלכף כאגמן ראשו ושק ואפר יציע,
הלזה תקרא צום ויום רצון ליהוה?!

He offered no translation, no interpretation, no commentary. Only the words, not reciting them as scripture, but speaking them naturally.

הלוא זה צום אבחרהו:
פתח חרצבות רשע, התר אגדות מוטה,
ושלח רצוצים חפשים וכל מוטה תנתקו.

I thought he was going to end, but he kept going. He spoke not angrily, or harshly, but with a half-smile, as if revealing a secret, good-naturedly, as if to say, "I know it looks complicated, but it isn't. Here's all you really need."

הלוא פרס לרעב לחמך, ועניים מרודים תביא בית.
כי תראה ערם וכסיתו, ומבשרך לא תתעלם.
אז יבקע כשחר אורך, וארכתך מהרה תצמח,
והלך לפניך צדקך כבוד יהוה יאספך.
אז תקרא ויהוה יענה, תשוע ויאמר הנני.

אם תסיר מתוכך מוטה, שלח אצבע ודבר און.
ותפק לרעב נפשך, ונפש נענה תשביע.
וזרח בחשך אורך ואפלתך כצהרים.
ונחך יהוה תמיד, והשביע בצחצחות נפשך,
ועצמתיך יחליץ, והיית כגן רוה, וכמוצא מים אשר לא יכזבו מימיו.

I'd read the words many times, but I'd never heard them before, never listened. In Reb Chaim's soft-spoken recitation there was an effect that I've seen only from very few speakers, those who offer the skillful oration not of dynamism, not of thundering cries, but only a still small voice, more electrifying than a thousand fist-pounders.

Today I am a non-believer. I believe in no god, no prophets, no saints. I do not fast on Yom Kippur. I do not pray. But the words of Isaiah, as spoken in that yeshiva study hall by Reb Chaim Brim, still cut today as deeply as they did then. Because even secularists, without God, without religion, still have orthodoxies; so often, we expect proper thought, proper practice, and we're so quick to judge, to condemn, to hurt. We wage Twitter wars, we rip each other to shreds in Facebook comments, we write op-eds about what's wrong with the world (yes, looking at self here), but we pass one homeless person after another on the street, and don't even *see* them. We feel so fucking self-righteous, and by we, I mean me. I don't mean to sound preachy.

We think we're tolerant but sometimes I wonder. Tolerance would mean accepting people we disagree with. But how far? Racists? Homophobes? Rush Limbaugh?

But yes, sometimes it feels like we have more understanding for convicted killers than for people who hold a wrong political view. That can't be just.

When will secularism produce its own Pope Francis? It seems almost inconceivable.

I don't generally go to shul on Yom Kippur; I haven't yet found a way to tune out the nonsense and to focus on the purely human. But I might go this year, maybe tonight, maybe tomorrow. If I do, it will be my first Yom Kippur in shul since 2007—that's eight years. If I do, it will be to find within myself greater acceptance for people with good intentions even if they disagree with me. The Donald Trump fans. The anti-vaxxers. The *kapparos-shluggers* and the anti-*kapparos shluggers*.

I might hate their ideas, and sometimes their practices, but I will try not to hate *them*. And if and when I feel it coming on, I might just go read some more Isaiah. Really, really slowly.

English translation of Isaiah 58 (NLT version), which is read in the synagogue on the morning of Yom Kippur:

> Tell my people Israel of their sins! Yet they act so pious!
> They come to the Temple every day, and seem delighted to
>   learn all about me.
> They act like a righteous nation that would never abandon
>   the laws of its God.
> They ask me to take action on their behalf, pretending
>   they want to be near me.
> 'We have fasted before you!' they say. 'Why aren't you impressed?
> We have been very hard on ourselves, and you don't even
>   notice it!'
>
> "I will tell you why!" I respond. "It's because you are
>   fasting to please yourselves.

Even while you fast, you keep oppressing your workers.
What good is fasting, when you keep on fighting and
  quarreling?
This kind of fasting will never get you anywhere with me.
You humble yourselves by going through the motions of
  penance,
bowing your heads like reeds bending in the wind.
You dress in burlap and cover yourselves with ashes.
Is this what you call fasting? Do you really think this will
  please the Lord?

No, this is the kind of fasting I want:
Free those who are wrongly imprisoned; lighten the burden
  of those who work for you.
Let the oppressed go free, and remove the chains that bind
  people.
Share your food with the hungry, and give shelter to the
  homeless.
Give clothes to those who need them, and do not hide
  from relatives who need your help.

Remove the heavy yoke of oppression.
Stop pointing your finger and spreading vicious rumors!
Feed the hungry, and help those in trouble.
Then your light will shine out from the darkness, and the
  darkness around you will be as bright as noon.
The Lord will guide you continually, giving you water
  when you are dry, and restoring your strength.
You will be like a well-watered garden, like an ever-flowing
  spring.

Tuesday, October 20, 2015

The other week, during the Sukkos holiday, I overheard a woman yelling at her son in the sukkah next door: "BEREL! GET OFF YOUR—" she paused, then, somewhat lacking conviction, said: "—lower region."

∾

We had a visitor the other night, a friend of my roommate's. She looked to be in her upper 20s. She brought mango juice and put it on the table.

"Can't go wrong with mango juice," she said.

She took off her shoes, and sat across from me, one leg over the other, her gray pantyhose hanging loose in the toe. She seemed pleasant enough, and we sat around chatting and drinking a bit. I had the last of a bottle of Jameson, and they were drinking some kind of tequila. She told me she'd focused on gender studies in college, though she never graduated—she didn't say why.

At some point she told me where she worked—for Hasidic employers—and I told her that I knew her employer's family. I'd gone to yeshiva with some of them.

In any case, she learned I was ex-Hasidic, and, somewhat abruptly, her manner changed.

It's hard to describe—the attitude was subtle. It's possible she wasn't even aware of it, but there was suddenly this tone, this underhanded condescension, along with a kind of combativeness.

One particular exchange was about Yiddish. I made some remark about it, and she waved her hand dismissively: "It's a dying language." She'd heard so from a college professor, or something.

"I have five children," I said, "all of whom speak Yiddish almost exclusively. And their world is growing, not dying."

I feel like it makes me something of an authority on the subject.

She disagreed, saying something about the majority of Ashkenazi Jews no longer speaking Yiddish, "ergo" (she actually said "ergo") Yiddish is a dying language.

I thought that was pretty solipsistic (she was Ashkenazi, raised Reform), but I let it go.

Let it go, I've been telling myself when arguments and debates boil up—with friends, lovers, strangers. Let it go.

A few minutes later, I said something else, on a different topic—I forget what—and she contradicted me. I wanted to say: If you're going to be an asshole, get the fuck out of my home. But I stayed silent. She was my roommate's guest, and I didn't want to be rude.

Then, out of nowhere, maybe because she was getting tipsy, she came over and put her arms around me. I felt angry, revolted. I can't explain it. I wanted to say, get your fucking hands off me. Instead, I hugged her back—aww!—and patted her on the back like we were chums.

Some years ago, I had a friend—call her Jenny—who would often hang out with our group of friends. Jenny wasn't Jewish, but was somehow attracted to our small gang of ex-Hasidim. This was around '08–'09, not long after I'd left, and we were a tight group. We'd get together every Thursday night at Franklin Park Bar before it was popular, and bring chulent and kishke and potato kugel from Grill on Lee, and stay until last call at 2 a.m., and make friends with hipsters and the occasional group of Chabad women.

One day I made a point about something, and Jenny declared, matter-of-factly, that my facts were wrong. I told her that I was quite sure about my facts, and she said: "You're arguing with *me*? You're an ex-Hasid who's never been to school."

It was one of those moments that stick with you, that reveal something about a person's character.

We were talking about a medical issue, and I pulled up the CDC website, and showed her. My facts were correct. She looked away and said nothing.

I don't think she meant much by it; she was, for the most part, sweet and kind and a good friend, but there were a number of such incidents, and I realized that Jenny liked our group because she lacked some essential feeling of self-worth, and needed our group to occasionally condescend to in order to feel validated. And so I let our friendship drift apart, and decided to stop hanging out with her. Over the years Jenny tried reaching out a couple times, and we had coffee once, sometime in 2012, but I resisted real reconnection. Something had changed; hard as I tried, I could no longer see her as a friend.

This has been a real challenge—and not easy to explain. The difficulty is the uncertainty about your right to your own feelings. "Jeez, don't be so sensitive." "It's in your head, dude." But when it happens continually, you recognize a pattern. "It's unintended," some will say. But can I call you an idiot, and say I was just stating the facts, didn't mean it as an insult?

Maybe this is what the kids today call micro-aggressions, although the last thing I want is to give it a hashtag and form an outrage brigade on Twitter.

I guess what I'm saying is: You *can* go wrong with mango juice.

Tuesday, November 3, 2015

Grant me please a sentimental moment.

Today I return to Rockland—bland, colorless, charmless Rockland, which I had actually loved so much until it spit me out but kept dragging me back for another and another flogging.

Rockland was my home for so long that I almost forgot my roots were in Brooklyn. From age 13, when, one early winter eve, a yellow school bus brought me to New Square and I felt so enraptured, it was as if my childhood in Brooklyn was nearly erased and my life began from that point. That's how it felt, for years, so thoroughly had my life been transformed.

Granted, New Square is to Rockland what a flock of pooping Canada geese might be to a pristine front lawn in Pearl River or like a diesel truck on the Palisades Parkway, or the dirty picnic tables in Haverstraw Park at the end of a Chol Hamoed day.

But still. It's Rockland.

As much as I loved Rockland, though, it did not love me back.

My last visits to Rockland were from Brooklyn, where I moved back to in 2009. For years I'd take three subways and two NJ transit trains to Suffern, then pray that my friend, whose car I'd borrow for a couple hours, would be there so that I could make the 30-minute drive to pick up my boys, boys who didn't want to see me but it was a small privilege I had gotten after torturous months of battle. Six times a year, for a couple hours—goddammit, I was going to exercise that right even if it took me six hours travel time for a two-hour visit. That's what Rockland became to me—the place I shlepped to every other month, my emotions mountains of anxiety, only its faraway peaks offering the faint white glimmer of hope that my boys would still know I was their father.

Prior to that, Rockland was all those trips to New City, that accursed corner of Main Street and New Hempstead Road, that imposing facade of justice fronting one of the most justly-despised institutions on earth, the Rockland Family Court, its judges issuing rulings with no moral mandate, its "officers of the court" making a living off the destruction of homes and families, representatives of a state so oblivious to human suffering that its inhumane bureaucratic functions would give George Orwell or Franz Kafka a whole new world of inspiration for describing the deviousness of humanity. Where else can a sinister and morally corrupt Norwegian Gentile collude with a Satmar Hasidic rabbi to rip children from their parents all in service to the gods of mammon and religious fanaticism?

But Rockland is also the place I first knew freedom, from that noblest of institutions, the Finkelstein Memorial Library, where children of Haitian immigrants and grandchildren of Holocaust survivors would sit side by side at the computer banks—granted, exchanging few words, but together nonetheless; where I read still-memorable biographies of figures ranging from Charlie Chaplin to Isaac Herzog, where I borrowed Beatles audiocassettes and *NOW* music CDs; where I discovered Yossi Klein Halevi's "Entrance to the Garden of Eden," and Amy Dockser Marcus's "View from Mount Nebo"—each revelatory and transformative in its own way.

Prior to all that was life in New Square, which had a grip on me in ways still inexplicable, a place that exerts so much power over its adherents that it is loved as only an abusive lover can be both adored and hated. Those who throw around words like "cult" clearly don't understand the complexity of the place, with its men and women of true piety, its masses of ordinary folk just trying to get through the day, and its second-tier leaders who operate in the service of its figurehead but who are also the ones who placed him there and keep him there and brutalize all who dare oppose him or them.

The last time I was in the New Square synagogue, I was spat at, literally. When I finally left Rockland, in September 2009, I was broken. So truly broken. But as the old Hasidic saying goes: "There is nothing so whole as a broken heart," and in many ways that was true for me. As difficult as it was to endure it all, pain is a great motivator, and the drive to keep going is often greatest when one feels lost.

I write this now from the car, on my way to tonight's event, and I can't help feeling like a conquering hero. Tickets to this event have been sold out for days. Tomorrow I leave for St. Louis, and from there on to at least three dozen more appearances, and the invites keep coming. I know it doesn't sound very humble, but it isn't boastfulness either. It's a recognition of my own perseverance, an acknowledgment that bushwhacking through the wild to make your own path can leave you bruised and pricked and stabbed and oh so tired, but at the end of that path is a closeup view of those shimmering white mountain peaks—still far away but so vivid and bright that you need no light, no sun, no star, nothing else but that beautiful glowing whiteness to guide you.

Tuesday, November 11, 2015

I'm at this Halloween party, and a guy introduces himself. Sam or Joe or Mike, or some such, unmemorable.

"I read your book," he says. "It's really good." I'm about to thank him when he adds, "I know you didn't write it, but still."

Huh? "What do you mean I didn't write it?"

"Didn't you have an editor?"

"I did."

"So . . . the editor does the real writing, no?"

DA FUCK?! Is this what people actually think? That's depressing in so many ways. It was I who wrote my damn book, goddammit.

∽

Calm down, Shulem, calm down. Not everyone knows everything about book-writing. Don't get so offended. Also, stop speaking in the third person. It's unbecoming.

∽

Man, am I tired. Five plane rides, four talks, different hotel rooms every night, and what feels like a million faces. Very good turnout at each of the venues. Books sold out everywhere. Now I'm back in NYC for a couple local events, and Monday I'm off to Cleveland for another whirlwind round.

Most memorable evening: One night, at one of the hotels, I went downstairs to the bar and two dudes showed up—one from North England and the other from Belfast. Tattooed, muscled, straight out of Clockwork Orange kinda guys, but charming in their own way. They both looked to be 30-ish.

I mentioned to the Irish guy that I have kids. Five.

"I've got kids, too," he said. "Thirteen." With four different women. He rattled off their names—Timmy, Andy, Veronica, Sean, Britney, etc. etc.—and said that he loved each one of them, but wasn't sure where they all were. I tried not to have my mind blown, but I think it blew anyway.

He was also a fighter for some terrorist group; not the IRA, the opposite side, I forget what they were called. He was protestant.

"Did you kill people?" I asked.

"No comment," he said, his face as straight as straight gets.

"What are you guys doing in Detroit?" I asked.

"We're training to install Wi-Fi on airplanes."

Then he and his friend suggested a bar thirty minutes away. They said it was worth it.

"We're not going anyplace fancy," the Irish guy warned me before we got into the cab.

It turned out to be a strip club. And was just closing when we got there.

Tuesday, November 24, 2015

"What is your greatest fear?" A friend asked me recently.

"Irrelevance," I said. The fear of living without impact. It's very real.

∽

Last night in Cleveland, my event competed with the Israeli Philharmonic Orchestra. Also, a man called to protest my appearance.

Still, 300 of the loveliest people turned up. Afterward, one of the organizers said, "Thank you for sharing with such vulnerability." I know what she meant, and I get such comments frequently. For some reason, it never feels like a compliment. In my head, I go: *Are you saying it was weird?* To me, expressing myself with vulnerability comes naturally, but maybe we live in a society that expects more emotional restraint.

My roommate, Joel, thinks it has to do with expectations we have of men in contemporary society. I don't know if he's right, but maybe. Do we see women's vulnerability as ordinary, and male vulnerability as unusual? Something to think about.

Tuesday, March 29, 2016

The other day, some Chabad dude came over to me at Chocolatte, the local kosher coffee shop. "Did you put on tefillin today?"

"Thanks," I said, "but I don't need tefillin."

"You don't *need* or you don't *want?*" He looked very annoyed. "Because those are two different things."

He was wearing an open parka and underneath it a Tzivos Hashem t-shirt, which I found hilarious.

"I don't need," I said. It's the truth.

Dude wouldn't let up—he had to make his point.

"Need and want are different things. You can say you don't want, but you can't say you don't need."

Now he was being obnoxious, and I felt like kicking him in his Tzivos Hashem balls. Can't I just sip my americano and play 2048 in peace? Do I ask you to put a colander on your head and mumble praise to the FSM, blessed be He? No, I don't, because I don't ask people to do things they find meaningless and ridiculous.

So knock it off, Chabad tefillin people.

❧

A guy from Lakewood emailed me to say that he marvels at the "difference in the intelligence level" between New Square and Lakewood, which, he claims, is "beyond immense," and he "blames the stupidity of New Square" for any troubles I might've had—Lakewood being a bastion of good sense and moderation and all.

Then this gem, for the real purpose of his email:

"What I would like specifically will sound weird but so what! Let me first be clear that I am absolutely straight! Although I have never physically interacted with anyone but my wife, I have engaged in phonesex on anonymous lines and email chats with women . . . I have some unusual fantasies based on my frum background & would love to interact with a woman from a similar background, any ideas?"

Is this the "Lakewood intelligence" he speaks of? And do frum people actually think us heathens have all the secrets for illicit sex?

If only. Alas.

Tuesday, October 28, 2015

A friend wrote to me recently: "I'm annoyed by your ability to be insincere for the sake of *kuvid* or cash or chicks." (How to translate "*kuvid*"? Honor? Respect? Esteem?)

The "cash or chicks" part was a little odd, because he was clearly overestimating what I was getting in either, but I took his point. He knows me for some time, believes he knows the real me, and thinks I put on a different persona to appeal to the masses, such as they are. He insists I just want to be liked. And I think to myself: *Nu*, so what's wrong with *that*?

I'm not sure, but it made me all the more pleased with my latest column for the *Forward*, in which I confessed to a decade-old incident of semi-accidental shoplifting from a hotel gift shop in Washington DC, many years earlier. This brought some interesting responses, and some interesting *dis*like to mix things up.

One woman, whom I know to be very Orthodox, wrote: "I've liked everything you've ever written, but cannot agree with you here."

What bothered me was not that she disagreed, but that until then she'd agreed with *everything*. I mean, I'm a non-believing, treyf-eating, sex-on-yom-kippur-having, obscenities-loving shaygetz. And she is a sheitel-wearing, Hashem-loving Orthodox woman, who likes to daven and to hear a nice Dvar Torah and sends her children to fine Orthodox yeshivas, etcetera etcetera. How does she agree with *everything* I've written until this point? Am I so nauseatingly inoffensive that even devout Orthodox women can agree with me on *everything*?

Good lord, I thought, I'm glad I wrote something she finally disagreed with.

❧

Just as I was pondering all this, I got an email from a stranger, a man by the name of Bernard. (Signed, "Orthodox/NOT-Hasidic." Caps his.) He said he had sympathized with my wanting to "divest from Skver" (thanks for the sympathy, sir), because of course, no one should be one of those fanatics, but my shoplifting confession struck his righteous haunches badly. He called me a man of "warped logic." I was, he declared, among other things, "a yiddishe gonif," and "just a confused man."

I thought it was nice that someone was taking a stand, and I emailed back my warmest regards, and I also called him a judgmental prick and mindless scum.

He wrote back immediately to call me a sick gonif and a loser.

I called him a fat fucking superstitious pig.

He responded that I was an angry depressed vulgar lowlife.

I told him he had sawdust for brains. (One of the favorite insults of one of my cheder rebbes.)

He called me an embarrassment to society, then I called him a twisted fuck, and then he called me a jerk.

We went a few more rounds, the last of which brought a long shrill screed from him about my cowardice, with repeated calls for me to "be a man and name the hotel." Like he was going to call the place and tell on me.

I wrote back, "Capitol Skyline," which was the truth.

I wondered if it still existed. I hoped he would call them. I imagined a dramatic postscript to my story, in which I confessed my sin to that fancy corporate hotel, and promised to mail a $35 check for that grossly overpriced souvenir.

Instead, Bernard went completely silent. I waited and waited, but "Orthodox/NOT Hasidic" Bernard did not follow through. If I was hoping for a more exciting ending to the story, I got none.

And still I'm left with very little "kuvid, cash, or chicks."

Black Hat, Combat Helmet, Thinking Cap

A Mostly Philosophical Memoir

Mark Zelcer

People often assume that if one is a professional philosopher, like I am, then one is a deep thinker, and if one is a deep thinker, one thinks deeply about everything. In my case, at least, this involves at least two problematic inferences. I think deeply about some philosophical topics, or so I like to believe. But for the most part, I am not particularly deep, I do not deduce reasons for my actions from first principles, and I am no more an expert on most things than anyone else. I generally follow my instincts, and when my decisions are questioned, I concoct reasons on the spot; I offer post-hoc rationalizations. We all do.

I guess I became a philosopher because I enjoy reading and thinking about philosophical problems. I never pondered my commitment to the search for Truth or entertained the prospect of discovering the secret to life, the universe, and everything. Similarly, when I joined the U.S. Army, I woke up one morning and joined. I was not seeking adventure, discipline, or money, nor was I running away from anything. Similarly, my religious life just (d)evolved to where it is now. No planning. No deliberation. Like others whose work appears in this volume, I was raised insularly Orthodox, in my case very Orthodox, and that changed for no reason I can articulate, no fancy philosophical analysis, no complex argument.

One may, or perhaps should, expect of a philosopher in my position an erudite defense of "Why I am not Orthodox" or an essay along the lines of Bertrand Russell's famous "Why I am not a Christian." But I do not offer that. I have no philosophical reasons to promote, I am not quite sure I even understand my own psychological reasons. Sometimes I speculate. I have considered that religion was the greatest source of anguish for me from around my Bar Mitzvah through my early-twenties. Everything I seemed to want to do was prohibited, and this was an endless fount of strife between myself, my family, schools, and friends. Otherwise I have few complaints about my life of that time. I (I almost wrote *baruch Hashem*) was not abused, I have no serious health issues——mental or otherwise, my family was stable, I lacked for little. But religion pricked at every turn. I wanted X and religion demanded *not-X*. If I did not want Z, religion was right there imposing it. I needed autonomy and control. Religion allowed none. Being a kid, I always lost, religion always won, and it hurt every time. *Frumkeit* is relentless. I gave up.

If I was bitter, I would point to the yeshivas that made big deals of things that, at the time and in retrospect, are trivialities (Torah Temimah, The Mirrer Yeshiva, and Chofetz Chaim, if you must know, all expelled me). Their *rabbeim* further ruined my impression of religious leadership. I would point to unheeded cries of despair when I needed to exert some control over my own destiny or just be understood. I could point to those religious people I encountered who I neither liked nor for whom was I ever able to muster any respect. I could point so many fingers in so many directions, but I would just be speculating about the causes of my life's trajectory.

Eventually I grew up. No one interferes with my life choices anymore, the *agmas nefesh* stopped. So why not just revert to my default state, move to Borough Park, discover the latest trend in 1930s era headwear, and whittle away *Shabbos* afternoons talking to neighbors about which rabbis supervise the newest kosher restaurants?

The reason I never reverted is because there is nothing to revert to. First, I never *believed* and second, I never *belonged*. I was never interested in the rules, lifestyle, causes, food, politics, heroes, clothes, or social hierarchy. I do not find the life or community beautiful, charming, quaint, pragmatic, meaningful, romantic, or true. I always felt like I was excluded more than that I left.

Because of all that, I feel no need to do what one might expect philosophers to do when confronted with the weighty metaphysics of God and Ultimate Truth. I defend no decision, nor offer apology or apologetics.

Instead this essay articulates a series of philosophico-phenomenological pictures, which is a fancy way of saying that I give a range of accounts of inner mental experiences to shed light on what it is like to leave Orthodox Judaism, from the perspective of someone who spends too much time thinking about philosophy. The essay, I am afraid, will reflect an abundance of confusion about how I view such a transition.

Although I never believed the same things many Orthodox Jews believe, I certainly thought in the same way many of them think. Orthodox Jews have a unique worldview that encompasses patterns and habits of thought that stem from prolonged exposure to the social dynamics, religious conceptual scheme, and embodied practice of a halakhic outlook, and particular societal structure that emerges from the contingencies of the Orthodox Jewish lifestyle.

Being religious extends beyond its routine, its lifestyle, and belief system. It is a culture, a *weltanschauung*, a commitment to a unique set of objects, practices, and community, inhabiting its own understanding of space, time, matter, self, and society. Cumulatively this makes for a distinct experience, and abandoning it is interesting in a number of ways that are important to philosophical thinkers. Each of the following models is a way to organize the experience, each of which deserves far more *shakla ve-tarya* (give and take) than is given here.

Leaving as an Intellectual Decision

Consider reason and belief. Many people believe in God. Some people believe and then stop believing. Some people don't believe and then start. Some claim their belief is grounded in reasons and arguments. Jewish philosophers, and many other Western thinkers, have been giving arguments for God's existence for over two millennia. They have been refuting reasons for abandoning religion even longer.

Four significant arguments and one counter argument linger in the philosophical canon. The youngest, by a thousand years, is the ontological argument, which (paraphrasing all these considerably) claims that God is a necessarily existent being and therefore by definition, must exist. The cosmological argument dates at least to Aristotle and argues that it is necessary to postulate a God in order to explain the existence of the cosmos. The teleological argument, perhaps the most famous, at least as old as Socrates, argues that the world is so well designed that it must have been deliberately fashioned by a Creator. Finally, one argument claims the occurrence of miracles proves God exists. There are also literally hundreds of variations and additional arguments that have been discussed by countless philosophers and theologians over the past two millennia.

Though religious Jews do not engage in much philosophical speculation, at some point in yeshiva one encounters Maimonides's retelling of Aristotle's cosmological argument or Judah Halevi's argument for the accuracy of the transmission of the Torah and consequently the truth of its miraculous content. One is also told that the obviousness of the conclusions follows from careful study of the arguments, which is however completely unnecessary, as the great thinkers have already done that for us.

There are fewer counterarguments against the existence of God than proofs in favor. Perhaps the most famous—the problem of evil—is at least as old as the biblical book of *Job*. If God exists, and He is good, all powerful, and all knowing, why is there so much evil and suffering in the world? Why does He not prevent it? Is He unable? Is He wicked? Is He oblivious?

Growing up, we were mostly grandchildren of Holocaust survivors, so this question could not hide. Some rabbis blamed Zionists, others blamed non-religious Jews for engendering God's wrath. It was nonetheless a mystery why religious Jews were punished for sins of the non-religious, or anti-Zionists were punished for Zionists' sins. Moreover, we wondered, who can blame Jews for abandoning God when it was so apparent that historically God has little problem abandoning us. In any case, we were told, one can read the book of *Job* (which few respectable *yeshiva bochurim* did), or any other text dealing with the problem of *tzadik ve'ra lo*, and get a satisfactory answer. We assumed that because the question has a canonical name—*tzadik ve'ra lo*—it also has a canonical answer that would suffice if we only knew it.

But frum Jews don't dwell on such things. There is always Talmud waiting to be studied. Philosophy is for such time as when one's mind is not fresh and there is no energy for *real* learning. But many of us left that world and became philosophers, or at least started thinking seriously about philosophy, and looked into these arguments with some care. Some were initially convinced that close scrutiny of the philosophical arguments would reveal satisfactory answers that would ease our mental itches. Some probed further than medieval arguments. Thus one finds a respectable-sized literature dedicated to refuting arguments for God's existence and expounding on the problem of evil, written by people who spent much of their youth in yeshiva.[1]

The philosophical literature on God's existence is enormous. It spans thousands of books and essays written over centuries. I teach some of it to college classes every year. Students find it interesting. Philosophers find the arguments very interesting. Many *yeshiva bochurim*, who became philosophers and ceased to believe, did so because the supposed proofs do not hold up to scrutiny. More broadly, many who quit religion did so for intellectual reasons. Perhaps the arguments for God's existence could not withstand forceful philosophical prodding. Perhaps theodicies that are supposed to resolve the problem of evil are unsatisfying. Perhaps, extending the scope of this paradigm, religious Judaism fails to meet the standards of morality,[2] rationality, or scientific rigor that one took on at some point. If so, we can say that *such people left religious Judaism for intellectual reasons.*

I did not. Moreover, I am skeptical that many people really do. But let us not focus on many people, just on my experience. I never changed my mind. I do not think that the supposed proofs prove anything and I also don't think that undermining proofs for God's existence undermines my view of religion or my moral commitments, even if these are the best possible proofs. I think that for proofs to be compelling or the problems problematic, one has to at least consider religious belief a "live hypothesis." One must at least acknowledge that it is possible that religion has an accurate version of the truth. If one cannot do that, if one thinks, as I did, that there is no way to think of religion as True, one is in the position that, of necessity, there must be something wrong with the proof. In the jargon of modern philosophers, religious incredulity always struck me as a "Moorean fact," a fact whose truth is more compelling than the premises of any argument against it could be. One only bothers to prove something if she believes that the premises of the proof can be more compelling than the simple fact of the falsity of the conclusion. G. E. Moore argued that this is common sense.[3] I agree. I take it to be more rational to hold on to disbelief in the literalness of talking about God than to accept the premises and logic of academic arguments that support God's existence.

I sometimes see it this way: I am somewhat colorblind. So, when people would say "the leaves change color in the fall," when I was a child, I did not believe them. I thought leaves were green and stayed green until they fell off the tree. "Why would leaves change color?" thought my seven-year-old-self. People were not lying, I simply thought they were using a figure of speech or a metaphor. I use it myself.

Looking out in the Brooklyn night sky (and how often does one really do that?), I saw, maybe, twenty or thirty stars on a clear night. When God promises Abraham in *Genesis* that his children will be as numerous as the stars in the sky, my childhood self understood that to be a metaphor for "lots of offspring," though I did not see the relation between "many offspring" and "stars in the sky." I did not think that God promised Abraham a mere twenty or thirty descendants.

I also did not think people were speaking literally about God making promises or even existing. Leaves changing color is a metaphor I did not understand for "it's fall"; "as numerous as the stars in the heavens" is a metaphor I did not understand for "many offspring"; and "God" is just a metaphor, for some force of nature that explains the universe.

Of course, now I know that people believe that leaves literally change color, that there are far more than 30 stars in the universe, and people really do believe that there is a being out there who answers to God's description. With experience, I realized that the reason people used those "metaphors" is because, in the first case, they experience them, and in the second case, people outside contemporary big cities always see lots of stars and I could verify this by just getting out a bit more. Indeed both are literally true. But I have still not figured out the last one. That's the way the cookie crumbles, I suppose, to use another metaphor I do not understand. I have no idea why people take "God" literally; I just know they do. And I know I never did. It has to be a metaphor. Right? In what sense can "God" be literal?

I never believed; I never stopped believing. Reason did not lead me (or most other people) into belief nor did I reason my way out of believing.[4] Talking about the problem of evil, hypocrisy of scripture, political commitments in conflict with rabbinic law, or anything else is beside the point. None of those issues ever struck me as problematic, as I never took any aspect of religion literally enough to be concerned with things within it with which I disagreed.

While some thinkers may present their intellectual evolution and ultimately their religious development in terms of becoming disillusioned with arguments that supposedly undergirded evidence for God's existence, I find it hard to understand that stance. It is possible that with loss of religion comes a shift in what one finds plausible: initially the poorly understood premises in arguments for God's existence, then later incredulity toward talk about God as a philosophical conclusion. But for me, there was never any shift in belief. I grew up religious, not taking anything about the underlying nature of religion literally. The latter fact never changed. So though some claim that leaving religion is a matter of ceasing to see the truth of theism, or that one ought to stop believing because the best arguments for theism fail, I never experienced that. I suspect that for many observant Jews, belief in an omnipotent deity is not all that relevant to their world outlook either.

The arguments for God's existence seem independent of the way we lived our lives. So I reject this as an account of how my internal worldview shifted. Let us then explore a second way of thinking about leaving religion.

Leaving as a Transformative Experience

The philosophical problem of "transformative experiences" is gaining traction among epistemologists and decision theorists. Here is why. We typically make decisions, or at least we think we do, based on the expected consequences of the outcome. We certainly believe that when we carefully plan, and decide to do something based on that planning, we are doing so out of concern to achieve the desired outcome. We don't always get it right, but we try. Thus, for example, if we are deciding between purchasing a house and renting one, we decide based on what we think the outcome of each option is. Renting may be cheaper. Owning builds equity. Renting makes the landlord responsible for repairs. Buying confers a sense of permanence, etc. When we make a decision, we are thus doing so on the assumption that we have an idea of what the outcome will be and how we believe we will feel about the consequences of our decision.

Some decisions, however, seem to defy this model. Consider what L. A. Paul has called "transformative experiences,"[5] events that give rise to significant identity transformations. These experiences are characterized by the fact that although one can predict the outcome of the decision, one cannot predict how she will feel once the outcome occurs, and hence cannot evaluate the outcome in the same way. This is due to the individual *being* a different person, in the sense that the experience itself will cause her to change her overall attitudes, beliefs, priorities, dispositions, and emotions. They change one's phenomenological outlook, they change the way the world appears. They do not merely add information, they change how all the information appears. As Shulem Deen puts it, it is "not like realizing you got an arithmetic problem wrong. It's more like discovering your entire mathematical system is flawed, that every calculation you've ever made was incorrect."[6]

To use Paul's example, the decision to have a child is transformative. One knows the outcome of going through with the decision to have a child: a baby will likely be born; however, prior to actually having a first child, one could not predict what one will feel like as a new parent (most any parent can verify this). Current feelings and dispositions cannot be reliable guides to how one will feel after the baby arrives. Any decision made based on the assumption that one can predict how one will feel after a transformative experience is thus not a rational decision. It may not be irrational, but was not arrived at via accepted canons of rational utility theory.

There are a few paradigmatic cases of transformative experiences beside parenthood. Fictionally, consider (again, Paul's example) what it would be like to become a vampire. One can intellectually know what that would entail (desire to drink blood, be nocturnal, etc.), but one cannot know what it will feel like and what it is like to evaluate every experience as a vampire. More realistically, experiencing war is transformative. People do not leave war the same way they went in. As cliché as this sounds, war changes people. It changes the way the world looks in a way that makes it disconcerting to try to recall what your world looked like before. I spent a year at war in Iraq, I know this first hand and any soldier will verify this. Religious conversion is similarly thought of as a paradigm case. If one has the appropriate kind of spiritual experience that causes one to undergo a religious conversion, that person is in a similar position vis-à-vis their former selves. Such converts and *baalei teshuva* (though not necessarily all of them) are new people in the same sense as parents or veterans.

We can quibble over some of the cases or some of the individuals in some of the cases, but the account seems onto something, if not more-or-less correct. So let's talk symmetry. Is losing a child, (now I'll say it) *rachmana litzlan*, transformative in the same way as having one? I just don't know. Probably. Someone would have to collect empirical data, see if it meets the criteria, and let us know. I would bet the answer is yes.

Is there a symmetrical case for war? It is unclear how to even make sense of the concept of un-going to war or going to not-war. There is no obvious symmetrical anti-case. Not going to war is not transformative, by definition. But, while some cultures have rituals to purge combatants of the baggage of war,[7] there is no opposite, in the relevant sense, of being deployed to combat.

Is there an opposite and symmetrical case to religious conversion? On its face, *leaving* Orthodoxy can have all the hallmarks of joining it (in the *baal teshuva* sense above). Modern Hebrew uses *hozer b'tshuva* and *hozer b'sheela* as opposites. This expression is a modern play on words, but the fact that the words can be so easily played with suggests there is a two-way street. One becomes Orthodox, and one leaves Orthodoxy. Sounds symmetric.

If becoming religious is transformative, what follows from the fact that leaving is? If someone leaves because she made a decision that she thinks will make her happier, she did not make a rational decision, just as the *ba'alat teshuva* does not make a rational decision. But the rationality of the decision is hardly at issue and I am anyway comfortable with the fact that like parenthood, the decision to leave religion is not one that falls under the purview of rational decision theory. More importantly for us, rather, are the phenomenological consequences of such a transformation.

War is transformative as it rewires one's epistemic stance, reorients one's moral compass, and changes one's attitude toward his fellow man. War re-prioritizes one's emotions, decision procedures, and ways of knowing. War gives an individual different ethical priorities, bringing to awareness a new spectrum of suffering, the salience of death, the fragility of life, and a heightened skepticism of the goodness of others. (I could go on.)

A transformative experience divides lives into before and after the transformation, like the death of Socrates must have for Plato. One undergoes a Kuhnian paradigm shift wherein one's previous vocabulary is no longer meaningful to one's current self. Former interpretations of social or scientific events no longer resonate; new ones must be offered. One can hardly imagine having a meaningful interaction with their former self. They would not recognize themselves in you, nor you in them.

But upon reflection, I wonder. I doubt I would easily recognize myself in the yeshiva bochur who was excited to put on tefillin and was so *makpid* on a variety of *mitzvas*. And I suppose I do, in some way, divide life into now and then. But has my epistemic stance really so fundamentally changed? Certainly some priorities shifted, but could I not reflect on the contrasts between then and now and make genuine meaningful comparisons? I think I may be sufficiently similar to my former self that this analysis may not be exactly relevant. War was worse. I hardly think I am incommensurate with my former religious self. The fact that so many memoirists write so cogently about their past selves suggests that others in this position have little problem understanding their former selves. (To be fair, it may suggest that all memoirs are problematic in certain ways.)

Like religious conversion or *hazara be-teshuva*, some people's experiences of leaving are not transformative. Those that are may be the result of epiphanies, experiences, realizations or some other psychic shift. I assume that one can have an epiphany that causes one to realize that there is nothing wrong with flipping a light switch on *shabbos*. I would think however that it is rarer for one to have a mystical spiritual experience that gets one to *stop* worshipping God. So if there are symmetrical cases to religious conversion, there are fewer, and fewer kinds, of them. Moreover, it seems like one who leaves has better access to their former mindset than one who joins. One can more easily understand and evaluate their former religious priorities and compare their wellbeing with their current self. I rarely ask myself "what was I thinking?" I know very well what I was thinking. I was religious. Religious things made sense.[8] Further, once you leave, it is generally possible to return. One can go back and forth and evaluate the decision and reverse it if desired. One cannot do so with war, parenthood, or the consequences of a profound mystical vision. Abandoning Orthodoxy might not be a great example of a transformative experience after all.[9]

Leaving as Adding a Worldview

Another way to think of what goes on in the mind of someone who leaves religion is to think of him, not as swapping one worldview for another, but as taking on an additional one. For many, just because they are no longer "in the religious world," does not mean they are out of it. One does not simply shed an identity.

To be religious is to see the world in a certain way, to have a unique ontology, and to instinctively think certain thoughts in certain circumstances. To stop being Orthodox is sometimes not to abandon one's worldview, but to add a new one. One still takes seriously their original ontology (e.g., *succas*, *shofars*, and *mikvas*), their penchant for thinking in Talmudic terms, their sense of right and wrong (*mutar*, *assur*), of propriety (*pas*, *pas nisht*), and their sense of time (e.g., *yontif*). But in addition, they may come to accept a scientific ontology and worldview (e.g., evolutionary theory), additional canons of reasoning (e.g., feminist standpoint theory), and an additional layer of temporal awareness (e.g., Sunday is "the day off").

One way this can manifest itself resembles linguistic "code switching"; one goes back and forth between thinking like a *yeshiva bochur* or *Bais Yaakov maidel* on the one hand, and a secular person, on the other.

I live in a number of worlds. I interact with religious friends and family often enough. I almost effortlessly converse with them using familiar jargon of the yeshiva world in which they still live. Amongst religious people, I can blend in effortlessly. I use a Jewish name, I dress to fit in. This is not atypical. I do the same thing in the Army Reserves. When I go in for my monthly training weekends or month-long exercises, I look and sound like I am in the Army. Army jargon is as replete with military acronyms as yeshivish jargon is with Yiddishisms.[10] Have you ever listened to military people talk about their clothing? The greenest private can recite from memory long stretches of AR 670-1 like it is his Bar Mitzvah parsha. AR 670-1 is the manual that dictates the wear and appearance of the military uniform. The amount of hermeneutical interpretation surrounding that document that Soldiers routinely engage in is enough to make any Talmudist envious. In the Reserves, it is typical for Soldiers to come out of their civilian lives and into their Army lives and switch identity, clothing, and language.

Don't try to understand philosophers when they talk either. It is all *a priori* this and supererogatory that. It took me years to figure out what two-dimensionalism, fictionalism, reliabilism, modal realism, and transcendental deductions are. It is said that philosophy, of all academic disciplines, has the most jokes, but even those are incomprehensible to non-philosophers.[11] But I can now joke with the best of them.

As an academic I am known by the "English name" my parents gave me for use "in business." In the Army I go by rank and last name. Among family and friends I use my Hebrew name.[12]

It often seems to me like I use different outfits and "languages" in different contexts. I talk about Xerxes when I speak to my ancient philosophy classes and Achashverosh when I speak with religious people (they are believed to be the same person). Herodotus comes to mind when thinking about Ancient philosophy and *Megillat Esther* comes to mind when thinking about Purim. More than that, I speak about the relationship between the Persians and Greeks in my philosophy classes, the relationship between the Persians and the Jews when speaking to religious friends, and in the Army I have had occasion to talk about the insider threat that allowed the Persian Army to exploit a new attack vector when Xerxes turned Ephialtes at Thermopylae. I often feel like I am channeling Akira Kurosawa's movie *Rashomon* wherein I experience the same conversation from multiple perspectives.

But code-switching hardly seems adequate to describe what is going on in my head. Everything there is impacted by everything else in it. I may say Achashverosh, but I am also thinking Xerxes. It does not seem correct to think that one just switches between worldviews in the way a bilingual switches between languages.

It may be more plausible to think of the adoption of an additional worldview in an integrative way. Do our worldviews fashion a *modus vivendi*? Are the various identities inextricably entangled? Pearl Gluck writes that "Just because I strayed from one world and could never live in it again doesn't mean I feel its presence any less. Even at moments when I am surrounded by Bulgarian sailors at a late-night joint, the little Hasidic rebbe inside of me seems to pop out and sit staring at me across the bar."[13] I experience this frequently. When I teach philosophy I struggle mightily to find words to substitute for Talmudic phrases like *nafka mina* or *mima nafshach* that come naturally.[14] I recently participated in a military wedding in a church. A religious service was part of the ceremony. When the time came, I could not help but think that I should probably be kneeling with a *shinuy*, so as to make it not quite count as technical kneeling. I administered an oath to a Soldier who was reenlisting in the Army and when he skipped a word my mind immediately went to "is he *yotze?*" is his reenlistment valid? Should I do it again just in case? (All nonsensical questions in these contexts, but they would certainly have occupied the rabbis of the Talmud for many pages.)

Joseph Soloveitchik argues that authentic Halakhic Jews are perpetually conflicted because they cannot accept just one worldview. His model considers two idealized individuals: *homo religiosus* and cognitive man. The former is a prototypical spiritual religious person, the latter a strict scientific thinker. His essay "Halakhic Man" is a defense of the idea that the ideal Halakhic individual is one who is neither of those, but rather a concatenated individual who takes the best of both, in a very particular way. Soloveitchik understands the ideal Jewish individual as one possessing opposing sets of intellectual virtues and oscillating between fully seeing the world according to one set, and then, just as that approach begins to overwhelm his consciousness, has the mental experience of starting to understand, and then fully embracing, the opposing, incompatible, worldview. He then delves into the mental world of this new view and takes that as far as he can until lured back by the original one. This inner dialectic goes back and forth indefinitely. Though this view shapes his conceptual landscape, the inner dialectic is not resolved in the way Hegel or Marx (allegedly) speak of the reconciliation of a thesis and antithesis in a synthesis. The worldviews never harmonize. The Halakhic man simply lives life feeling uncomfortable with both worldviews.

The philosopher Hilary Putnam examined[15] what he takes to be a Wittgensteinian theme that runs through the thought of the Jewish philosophers Franz Rosenzweig, Martin Buber, and Emmanuel Levinas. Wittgenstein treats religious thinking as a "form of life." As such, there is no set of propositions that can be discussed and debated with outsiders. Consequently, when believers and non-believers attempt to communicate about matters of faith, they talk past each other because they are playing different "language games," as Wittgenstein calls it. This sentiment should resonate with close observers of debates in the philosophy of religion. What biblical stories mean to believers is not what they mean to non-believers and often they appear to be talking at each other rather than conversing.

Putnam's Jewish thinkers cannot appreciate Soloveitchik's dialectic. For them there is no reconciling, only a mutual lack of comprehension between different forms of life. Soloveitchik's model seems closer to our concern as leaving is not a process whereby one begins to talk past their former self.[16] I have a number of worldviews inside me. They can communicate with one another. I have no internal believer and non-believer, but I do possess multiple worldviews that can be called forms of life that manage to work together in an unusual kind of way.

Soloveitchik's analysis is better than Putnam's for our purposes, but still inadequate. Leaving Orthodoxy presupposes at least a partial rejection of its form of life while retaining some of the thought processes that it presupposes. It also allows for some reconciliation or interpenetration that makes for a novel outlook. Perhaps, then, we are looking in the wrong place for a theoretical perspective.

Leaving as Doing Different Things

Let us look away from the mind and toward the body. Sometimes leaving Orthodoxy takes on the form of just practicing differently. One may change practice as a result of conscious deliberation or historical happenstance. It may be accompanied by a change of mind, disillusionment, or anything else; or not. It may be the result of pragmatic concerns involving working on the Sabbath, falling in love, and eating what is available. This is probably common. After all, non-religious people all have ancestors who were religious. It is likely that people often do what they must rather than take principled philosophical stances about leaving. How does cessation of religious practice impact one's phenomenology? How does changing one's behavior change who one is inside?

Let us borrow another idea prominent in Soloveitchik's work, this time from his essay "The Halakhic Mind" (a work in the neo-Kantian tradition). Soloveitchik articulates a philosophy of religion that sees a *halakhic* mind as generated from a *halakhic* outlook, ontology, and practice. Put simply, he understands the complex *halakhic* mind described above as emerging from the study and practice of Jewish law and life. Sounds plausible enough. But consider just how embodied Jewish ritual is and how consequential each action comes to be.[17] Most accounts of leaving include something about the rituals the author stops practicing, the bodily activities she stops engaging in, or the new physical habits she undertook. How can they not? Bodily ritual is ubiquitous in Jewish law and life. So much of everyday life is saturated with deliberation because of its embodiment that a change, radical or subtle, cannot but have phenomenological consequences. May I eat this? Is it time to put on tefillin? Is this *muktza*; can I touch it? May we have sex? May I say this? May I look at this? Women worry about covering their hair, collarbones, elbows, and knees. Men worry about their *tzitzis*, *payos*, *tchup*, and headgear. And on it goes from the first to last page of the written and unwritten codes of Jewish law.

A different set of practices, as Soloveitchik has it, will give rise as an epiphenomenon (i.e., an emergent byproduct), to a different phenomenological outlook. This new outlook arises from the new material objects one handles, [types of] people one interacts with, and actions one's body performs. One consequently experiences a new set of emotions, realizations, and intellectual connections. Indeed, as in many religions, some rituals, especially in more "spiritual" branches of ultra-Orthodoxy, serve no other function but to provoke emotional experiences.

Moreover, because so many commandments are sex-linked, a religious life ties a particular gender consciousness to one's religious identity. Further, the behaviors linked to the particular contemporary sociological exigencies of, e.g., the *frum shidduch* world (marriage market) give rise to their own emergent bits of identity. Thus, much of our mental experience arises from the embodied ritual of Jewish religious life that has consequences for one's core identity.

A change in practice, however little it is accompanied by a deliberate change in thought, will impact one's inner life. Thus, where Soloveitchik believes that we can look to the *halakha*—its ontology and practice—and reconstruct the inner world of the Halakhic individual, we argue similarly that we should be able to look to the non-halakhic practice to reconstruct anyone's worldview. The lesson then is that we should consider, along the lines of the famous James-Lange theory (i.e., that actions cause emotions), that we think differently when we do differently; not the reverse. Phenomenological change arises from change in practice.[18]

I find this plausible because I cannot recall any long period of deliberation before I started acting differently. Without the impossible task of recalling which particular observances fell away at what point in my thinking, it is hard to conceive of a substantial amount of time where I was acting *frum* (broadly construed) and not feeling *frum*. I can however understand that many have imposing constraints preventing them from acting according to the way they feel. Undoubtedly this is a source of significant and debilitating cognitive dissonance which is but one of the reasons this an imperfect model for understanding leaving Orthodoxy. Let us consider one final approach.

Leaving as a Change of Social Identity

Our final phenomenological picture moves from the perspective of the body to the body politic, and examines leaving as a change in social identity. Humans identify with their societies. They also expect other members of their society to identify strongly with them and each other. Why? Humans are a cooperative bunch. We evolved to cooperate. We couldn't survive as a species otherwise. But apparently we did not evolve to cooperate with one another simpliciter. We evolved to be especially cooperative with our ingroup. An ingroup is the relatively small subgroup with which one identifies.

Nature does not issue us ingroups. We create them and are socialized to think of ourselves as "one of us" as opposed to "one of them." This socialization comes in linguistic habits, living arrangements, education, shared lives, and so much more in our culture and subcultures. Socialization partly also comes from without as we tend to be molded by what we believe "they" (the outgroup) think of us. (Recall Sartre's argument that anti-Semites define Jews.) Self-perception and ingroup identity, for religious Jews, is reinforced constantly, in every action and gesture.

The rigors of Jewish education cannot easily be met absent a community. When Jews went into exile, the rabbis instituted communal prayer thereby guaranteeing that Jews would live in close proximity to one another to fulfill their basic religious needs. Jews have to live close enough together to pray, get kosher food, build communal *mikvaot*, and obtain material ritual objects, like *etrogim*, *tefillin*, and *matzoh*. As much as Orthodox Judaism is a way of life, it is simultaneously a community of people who regularly congregate, interact, gossip, share meals, create entertainment, and rear children. An Orthodox Jewish identity is inextricably tied to a community of Orthodox Jews and is constantly reinforced at all levels of religious education. Some communities are incredibly insular and others less so. Regardless, the community and its education determines so much of the identity of its constituent individuals.

Religious communities foster a sense of collective responsibility and collective intentionality. *Kol Yisrael arevim zeh la-zeh*, we are told we are all responsible for one another. When someone makes a *chillul hashem*, the shame is collective. The community also breeds many kinds of homogeneity which synergistically further strengthens ingroup cohesion. Most religious Jews, for example, vote for the same candidates in political elections, have similar beliefs about how everyone else should act, and in many ways, act as if they were part of a similar economic class. (Rich or poor, there are a limited number of schools, shuls, kosher shops, clothing options, and neighborhoods to live in.)

Imagine one is no longer a part of the social fabric, either by choice or compulsion. When one leaves, religion no longer determines which business transactions are permitted, which clothing one may wear, with whom one may associate, when to be in shul, how to eat, where to live, or anything else. The rituals that serve so well to perpetuate ingroup cohesion become so much a part of one's identity that losing them can be traumatic and jarring. The affiliation that one exclusively held must now be exchanged for a foreign one.

Thus our last analysis sees the transition from religious to secular as a change of ingroup affiliation. My own primary sense of group identity is as a Jew, despite my Yeshivas' best efforts to make it a *frum* Jew. I never identified with any other racial or ethnic category and I suspect that few religious Jews do either.[19] But for many, their primary identification is as a *chosid*, a *heimishe Yid*, or as a *haredi*. For people who leave, one formerly "belongs" in shul, then one does not. One had an extensive social and economic safety net, now one does not. One does the same thing as everyone else, now one must find new people to emulate. Hence the anxiety reported by the formerly Orthodox about things as simple as talking to people unlike themselves. I still lack many skills that people are expected to have in general society: I cannot do things like dance or comprehend menus in *treif* restaurants.

There is much here worthy of empirical scholarship.[20] Armchair sociology suggests that there is something genetically hyper-cooperative about Jews. When religious Jews leave the small ingroup of whatever sect they belonged to, they find another group to identify strongly with, or a more collectivist ideology to take seriously. They often make some larger group their ingroup. Hence polling data showing Orthodox Jews in the United States vote right-of-center and non-Orthodox Jews vote left-of-center. It would be interesting to see which social and political affiliations change among those who leave. Do the formerly religious vote with their religious upbringing or do they reject that, too, and vote with their new communities? Seeing what kinds of affiliations change, and how, can tell us much about the nature of ingroup identity and cooperations in humans and those who leave in particular. Understanding changes in social and political self-identification can go some way to helping us understand the extent to which an individual who leaves Orthodoxy both felt connected to his or her identity as a religious Jew and now feels connected to new communities.[21]

Meaning in life is often derived from a community or entity larger than oneself. When one leaves a community that provides that meaning (whether one realizes it or not) one is often compelled to embrace a new family or group.

But a community provides more than meaning and finding meaning in a new community may not be enough. One must also integrate. Switching communities may not be the most significant part of one's transition, it may not be what motivates it, but it is certainly the most traumatic and hardest part. It is where those who leave require the most assistance. Most people need no help learning how to be *mechalel shabbos* or eat a cheeseburger. But it is not easy to become fluent in new rituals and learn new styles of human interaction. Much behavior, angst, and attitude accompanying one's transition from religious to secular can be accounted for when we consider that one is leaving a familiar, pervasive, and unique communal experience and joining a new unfamiliar community with as many rules, but whose mysterious and unwritten nature one is forced to infer. Because of the jarring reality of new communities, this should also be considered when we are in search of a theoretical framework to understand the process of transitioning from Orthodoxy.

Conclusion

People leave Orthodoxy for reasons they cannot articulate. We sketched a few ways of thinking about leaving Orthodoxy. In some cases it is how I have seen my world, in others I sympathize with the fact that it is how others organize theirs. Some of these have been successfully used in studies of ex-Orthodox Jews, some have been used as part of autobiographical reconstructions.[22] I do not know how to refute any of these models, nor am I sure how to argue for them. I know that they all resonate with my experience to an extent, but none completely. I hope that they provide useful jumping-off points for further exploration.

Notes

1. Rebecca Goldstein's work, for example, often fuses fiction, memoir, and philosophy in examining God's existence (see e.g., *Betraying Spinoza: The Renegade Jew Who Gave Us Modernity* [New York: Nextbook/Schocken, 2006] or her *Thirty-Six Arguments for the Existence of God: A Work of Fiction* [New York: Vintage, 2011]). See also Stewart Shapiro's essay "Faith and Reason, the Perpetual War: Ruminations of a fool," in *Philosophers Without Gods*, ed. Louise M. Antony (New York: Oxford University Press, 2007), 3–16.

2. See e.g., Joseph Levine "From Yeshiva Bochur to Secular Humanist" in *Philosophers Without Gods*, loc cit, 17–31.

3. G. E. Moore, "A Defense of Common Sense," in *Contemporary British Philosophy* (2nd series), ed. J. H. Muirhead (London: George Allen and Unwin, 1925), 192–233.

4. Cf. Pascal Boyer, *Religion Explained* (New York: Basic Books, 2001).

5. L. A. Paul, *Transformative Experience* (New York: Oxford, 2016).

6. Shulem Deen, *All Who Go do not Return* (Minneapolis, MN: Graywolf Press, 2015), 185.

7. See Sebastian Junger, *Tribe* (New York: Twelve, 2016).

8. It would be interesting to compare accounts of people who stopped practicing with those who started. Who better articulates the views of their former selves?

9. Thanks to Robert Card for discussion.

10. To get a feel for military jargon, I challenge any civilian to make sense of Phil Klay's short story "OIF" in his collection *Redeployment* (New York: Penguin Press, 2014), 73–76.

11. Robert Martin, *There are Two Errors in the the Title of this Book* (New York: Broadview Press, 1992), 108–09.

12. These examples are significant for religious Jews. An oft-quoted pseudo-rabbinic expression reports that what preserved Israelite identity in Egypt was that they did not change their language, their dress, or their names.

13. Pearl Gluck, "Shtreimel Envy," in *The Modern Jewish Girl's Guide to Guilt*, ed. Andrew Ellenson (New York: Penguin Books, 2005), 291.

14. Unlike the legendary Sidney Morgenbesser, I cannot pull off using Yiddish in philosophy classes. See the obituary by David Shatz (http://www.tabletmag.com/jewish-arts-and-culture/books/177249/sidney-morgenbesser).

15. Hilary Putnam, *Jewish Philosophy as a Way of Life* (Indianapolis: Indiana University Press, 2008).

16. In another context Soloveitchik argues that religions are incommensurable and interfaith dialog is impossible.

17. For the discussion of embodiment, I am indebted to Lynn Davidman's *Becoming Un-Orthodox* (New York: Oxford University Press, 2015), esp. chapter 1 and appendix 1.

18. Orthodoxy's focus on practice over belief makes this approach more salient than it would be for other religions.

19. One of the most perplexing and disappointing moments in my life came when I first heard about an ethnic hierarchy among Israeli Jews, separating Ashkenazim and Mizrahim. It was hard for me to process why, outside the religious/secular divide, there are ethnic prejudices among Jews.

20. Some research has been done in Israel, but because of the nature of Israeli society, conclusions would not generalize.

21. Just as people once spoke of homosexuals as individuals who engage in homosexual behavior and it is now commonplace to speak of a "gay community," what was once spoken of as people who "went off the derech" is now being thought of as a nascent OTD community, with organizations and activities for mutual support. It will be interesting to observe this development and see in what way, if any, this identity persists and retains social taboos and loyalties and enforces collective values or political loyalties.

22. I have drawn inspiration from the memoirs mentioned in the notes as well as the works about Baruch Spinoza and Solomon Maimon, by Shalom Auslander, Hella Winston, and the accounts in Shimon Lev's *ve-She'Yodea Lishol* (Tel Aviv: Hargol, 1998).

How I Lost My Innocence

FRIEDA VIZEL

I grew up in the insular Hasidic village in Kiryas Joel—a Satmar village in the New York Hudson Valley and one of the most sheltered Hasidic enclaves. I was raised in a bubble; barely aware of anything beyond my *shtetle*. We had no television, movies, secular books, we didn't know of the radios that came with our cassette players—even English was spoken poorly. And yet, at twenty-five, I left the Hasidic sect. I am often asked: what single event, what person, place or thing, corrupted me so that it led to my abandoning the faith? What was the moment that peeled away the curtain? I've been on a quest to find this First Cause that made me see the light, and have managed to narrow it down to ten:

1. In middle school, I erased the black-crayoned censoring of texts and images and found depictions of strange, unkosher animals and naughty but tingly words like "pregnancy."

2. In high school, I discovered that the *Merriam Webster Dictionary* that was required for school had wild secrets in it if you knew how to look, although even then you could only look, not quite understand. Some gleeful girls rushed from the page for SEX and INTERCOURSE to the one for PENIS and VAGINA and on and on in confusion, delight, horror.

3. After September 11, when I was a girl of marriageable age, I figured out that my Sony Walkman could play the radio on seven-seventy from my bedroom closet. Rush Limbaugh was a wild and devious creature to me, freedom-minded and uninhibited and passionately against those communist liberals who hated freedom and wanted to be like Russia. I was (briefly) a closeted die-hard right-winger, with a covert picture of Bush in my possession.

4. Two years later, my marriage was arranged to a pious, awkward boy, and soon after tying the knot I discovered that—huzza!—there were mass sins to be had with a husband as wide-eyed about movies as me. We devoured all eighties TV-show box sets from Walmart. I felt worldly!

5. Sometime later, I discovered that the phone line could become Internet and the computer could become much more interesting. I began dialing up—trying to anyhow—and looking at all the celebrity links on MSN.com. Meanwhile, anyone who tried to call our home phone got a busy signal.

6. Then the moment, even later, when I was twenty-one and holding a little babe at the breast, that I found the blogs of other Hasidim. It was a personal earthquake. Who else had secrets!?

7. There were many moments over many days afterwards, as I found out that these online blogging atheists believed that the Torah was not true and that humans came from monkeys!

8. Many, many days of Internet obsession later (plus the consumption of basic science books) came one day, one random, ordinary, housework oriented day, when all the monkey business clicked. It made sense! I got it! I understood how history and science explained the world!

9. There was that moment when I looked around at all my Hasidic
   friends, all the other women, and felt awfully weird. I realized I was
   odd. I didn't fit in.

10. Finally, there was the moment my husband left because I'd become too difficult. The moment I began to feel shamed and shunned and shut out. The moment I realized I could plan for my own journey. The moment I decided I needed to go, to move on, to leave the small shtetl, to live with many more moments of delicious curiosity.

The Trickster Bride

LEAH VINCENT

When I was a Yeshivish girl, every day of my life was a love story. I was devoted to four great romances: with my father, with my father's God, with the messiah, and with my husband-to-be. There was a fifth great love in Yeshivish life: the love between men, *chavrusas*, who spent long days sitting in pairs, studying Talmudic texts. But this passion was forbidden to me. Girls were not allowed to learn Talmud.

My family lived in Pittsburgh. My father, a stern, sad man, was the Rabbi of a palatial synagogue with stained-glass windows. A crown topped the building's domed roof. Inside, the pews were smooth wood and the Torah arks were draped in velvet. Like others stationed in small cities around the country, my father worked to entice Jews into the Yeshivish community. At this, he was successful. People swarmed to the romance that flashed within Yeshivish life. Boys raised on baseball and prom attended *bring close* lectures, enthralled. Girls fluent in Steinem and Elmo bathed in love bombs at Sabbath meals. The Yeshivish God promised endless ardor at a price high enough to seem trustworthy. *We are never so defenseless against suffering as when we love.*[1]

I was a dark, skinny child, elfin, and quick to tears. At school, I mimicked my father's work, trying to convince my non-Yeshivish classmates to adopt our way of life. I was as passionate and as unlikable as any middle-aged missionary. I had few friends. My hair grew in a thicket of curls. My oldest sister, Goldy, kept it manageable until she left home at sixteen, but once she was gone, no one reminded me to brush my hair. When Goldy returned for Passover she tried to comb out my mass of knots but the brush got trapped in the clumps at the base of my neck and she had to hack it free with scissors.

In my young mind, my father, his God, the messiah, and my husband-to-be merged into a single entity. They were all male. All potent. All residents of mysterious realms forbidden to me. When my father strode through the dining room, the scent of his mouthwash trailed behind him like Paul Bunyan's axe, opening a geological cleft in my heart.

I filled my loneliness with fantasies of my wedding day, spending long Sunday afternoons sketching my bridal gown. It would have sleeves like hot air balloons. I prayed daily for the messiah, and raised my face from my prayer book whenever tears came, not above boasting my devotion. Any day now, the messiah would fly us to Israel on the wings of eagles and the Sanctified House would fall from heaven, fully furnished. These stories were more real to me than Cheerios, Barbies, or pavement. I knew the Sanctified House, with its altar, candelabra, and table of twelve breads, like I knew my own home. In the windowless back room of the inner sanctuary, two naked cherubim faced each other, their gilded spines gleaming in the pale light. The air between them was thick with the odor of God. And what, I wonder now, if one were to reach for the other? The back room was forbidden to the people filling the Temple's courtyard. Would they hear one naked body shatter under the other's touch? *And there I will meet with thee, and I will speak with thee . . . from between the two cherubim which are upon the ark of testimony* (Exodus 25:22).

At eighteen, after a handful of chaste meetings, my sister Goldy got engaged to the second young man whom the matchmaker had set her up with. This decision was the result of a pragmatic calculation that compared the reputation, wealth, and spiritual assets of our family and the family of her date. Love was supposed to be the product of this kind of lifelong arrangement, not the instigator. Yeshivish culture viewed this as a mature approach to romance. Bolstered somewhat by a strict cultural taboo against divorce, our system produced lasting marriages, of which we were very proud.

I was twelve years old when Goldy married. At her wedding, I fantasized about marrying her groom's younger brother. He was a thin boy, with a pale face hidden under the brim of his black Borsalino. By then, I had learned from playground chatter that non-Jewish couples lay naked together. I hoped Yeshivish Jews got some kind of special exemption from such immodesty. Perhaps God sent them babies when they kissed.

Goldy and her husband had a child every year. My new brother-in-law, trained only in Talmud, had a hard time holding down a job. I lived with them one summer and often saw him snap at Goldy. I don't think they were ever happy, but I'm in no position to know. Happiness is capacious enough to be felt in a plethora of contradictory ways. I expected that I would marry at eighteen, just like Goldy. I hoped for twelve children, one more than my mother.

I knew that there were a handful of Yeshivish people who went *off the derech*, OTD, leaving Yeshivish life. They became drug addicts, prostitutes. Many died. It was a prophesy told in songs and confirmed by stories. Who would be so perverse as to choose a broken life? These were my thoughts when I was still under the illusion that I was whole. Like many ultra-Orthodox children, I had already been touched by older children in ways that broke me far more deeply than I understood. In the Yeshivish community, autonomy over one's body is an alien idea, masturbation is outlawed, and healthy contact between the sexes is prohibited. Communal spaces teem with poorly supervised children. It is a perfect Petri dish for molestation to spread and mutate. But as a Yeshivish girl, it would have been immodest for me even to look for words to describe what had happened to me. *The truth of our bodies and our minds has been mystified to us.*[2]

The path of a Yeshivish girl's life is narrow and the pace along it predetermined. I knew what my future would look like: I would love my father and his God and I would one day serve the messiah and my husband. It was all decided.

Man tracht uhn Gott lacht, as the rabbis often said—man plans and God laughs. At sixteen, seventeen, I went *off the derech*. Fourteen years later, I wrote a memoir about my experience. After it was published, I gave lectures at libraries and colleges. I wore a black blazer over a sleeveless blouse and a large diamond on my finger. In violation of the OTD prophesy, I was alive and married to a good man, a Chasid-turned-atheist who bragged that he'd never had a spiritual moment in his life. I had the child I had always dreamed of. I owned an apartment in Manhattan. I had earned a graduate degree from Harvard in public policy. Reviewers of my book said that I was articulate. They said that I was inspiring. They said that I was brave. I was often tempted to step out from behind the lectern, leaving my notes. To peel off my jacket. To stand in front of my audience and sink a blade into my arm, again and again, like a hungry jaw. To shit my pants. To vomit. *This is my story*, I wanted to say. *This. I have lost the great loves of my life: my father, my God, my religious husband, my messiah.* My heart has been torn from my chest. A coronary amputation never heals. You just learn to live with the pain. I didn't know how to explain that in words. I didn't know how to say that it was all worth it anyhow. That a love devoid of freedom can only offer the illusory pleasure of an addict's high.

They say my people come from a family of two sisters. The younger has a slim body and sparkling eyes with long, dark lashes. Her laughter breaks your heart. The older has a dead man's gaze. It is the younger girl's wedding night. The desert quiet is broken by the crackle of the fire, the clink of cups. *Behold you are consecrated to me.* The groom, Jacob, is a pious man with an intelligent face. He shakes his father-in-law's hand with a wet palm. He is besotted with his bride. In the tent, her body is warm. She is as still as a sheep beneath him. He had planned to be tender, but he enters her in one jagged motion and the moment bursts open in a violent spasm.

Jacob wakes. A woman lies beside him in the tent, her shoulders glowing in the light of morning. It is not the younger but the older girl, snuck in under cover of the wedding veil. Now, consecrated to him, his wife. It was her father's doing, but they say that she wanted it. She had cried her whole life until then, praying for a man like Jacob. She looks up from the pillow, her face dark with fear.

I am named for this woman, Leah. The trickster bride who is never loved by her husband, the romantic dreamer whose dreams come true, but with bitter consequence. As a child, I hated my namesake. Jacob marries Rachel, the younger sister, a week later, but most Jews descend from his mythic union with the older, unloved Leah. Our blood is steeped in passion, but our arteries twist in on themselves in disappointment. These are only stories, but I know more than most how we are bound to the stories of our lives.

And the Lord saw Leah was hated, and he opened her womb, but Rachel was barren (Genesis 29:31).

Fertility is a Yeshivish women's goal and central occupation. Leah, unloved, gives Jacob six sons. The other matriarchs, Sarah, Rachel, and

Rebecca, three of the four women foundational to the Yeshivish woman's notion of femininity, the women adored by the patriarchs, are barren.

And Isaac entreated the Lord for his wife, because she was barren (Genesis 25:21).

And it was that Sarai was barren (Genesis 11:30).

It's a great joke. The meaning changes, depending who's telling it.

My own mother was pregnant every two years. When I was young, she wore a wig that fell like waves of dark water over her shoulders. I never saw her own hair. She was born in Scotland and called the shoe-maker a *cobbler*. Whenever she said that word our stolid middle-class neighborhood shimmered with the sudden magic of a fairy tale. Only sitting on the couch, with a baby at her breast, did she seem calm. Her tension was worst around my father. Like a chipmunk, my mother stored laughter in her mouth, always ready for my father's jokes. She scurried around his back, serving him meals. When I was twenty and still somewhat religious, a man I almost married, a man who had left Yeshivish life to sell blowjobs for speedballs before repenting, taught me what clinical anxiety was. Before then, I hadn't realized anxiety could be a disorder. The conditions of our mothers melt into the fabric of reality. They become the texture of the sky.

My mother often said, always without a trace of irony: *I am an enabler*. Her life's work, as she understood it, was to enable her husband and children. She embraced the *raison d'etre* discarded by the housewives of the sixties and elevated it to a sacred calling. As a child, I wanted to be just like her. Still, it bothered me when I heard her say: *I am an enabler*. I recognized the way that word, *enabler*, rounded by the last traces of her Scottish accent, correlated with the puzzling phenomena of my mother's ever-eroding spirit. She was like a cliff crumbling year by year before the waves of her life.

My mother's father had been a fiery man, a Scottish zealot who wore a red goatee and a top hat. They said my grandmother worshiped him like a planet orbiting a star. When my mother was twelve, my grandfather keeled over with a heart attack and died. My grandmother sank into darkness. My mother almost never spoke of her childhood, but once, when I was grown, she told me, *I couldn't say the word father for years. The pain was so great.* Me, too, I wanted to say. I also lost my father. We have more in common than you know. Trauma echoes across time. But she would only have heard this as an attack.

I knew my mother's mother as a small, dusty woman who visited us every few years. I couldn't understand why the spirits of old Yeshivish women, even the ones with living husbands, always seemed shriveled like raisins, empty and desiccated. My grandmother perched on our couch with crossed ankles, tense as a china figurine. We called her *Bubba* Miriam. She snapped at us to sit like ladies.

> *Grace is false, and beauty is nothingness, a woman who fears God should be praised!* (Proverbs 31:10–31, "A Woman of Valor")

Other Yeshivish men sang this classic love song every Friday night to honor their wives, but my father only sang it when *Bubba* Miriam visited. He explained that King Solomon had written it for his mother, not his wife. When it came to matters of the heart, my father was a stickler for the rules.

I know only one story about my father's courtship of my mother. He took her out to eat at a restaurant, but she ate very little, insisted she wasn't hungry. After they parted ways, my father spied my mother entering a bakery. He always retold this anecdote laughingly, lovingly. The hot nucleus of this family tale contained some message about a woman's hunger. Some message about an all-knowing man.

One afternoon when I was playing at a Yeshivish friend's house, the girl's father snapped at her mother, who responded in kind. A crack appeared in the surface of my mind. I hadn't known that Yeshivish couples fought. My parents never did. My mother agreed with everything my father said. He was a holy man, she told us. Only once, I overheard my father waylay my mother beside the pantry and hiss at her for not smiling enough at Sabbath lunch. There were less-religious guests at the table and it was important to demonstrate to them the superiority of our way of life.

It was well-known in my family that I was my father's favorite, before the onset of puberty made such intimacy impossible. At the

Sabbath table, when he posed religious fables to the children, he always asked for my guess at the moral of his story. They said it was because I was the most like my mother—I had her hooked nose and soft heart. But this logic puzzled me. It was not clear to me that my father loved my mother. They never made contact in front of us. My mother's emotions were unintelligible. My father seemed lonely. He had an aura of depression. Occasionally, he would collapse with back pain. I remember him lying on the carpet, reciting the ritual that ended the Sabbath, a cup of grape juice awkwardly extended in his hand, the children gathered nervously by his body. His weakness disoriented us. My mother hovered, frantic as a one-winged bee.

As a girl, I never sat in my father's chair. I listened in awe when he spoke at the Sabbath table. I was glad to be a thin child, because he said that an unmarried girl ought to be thin. On Friday nights, when he rested his hand on the top of my head to bless me, my skull felt as soft as paper. Then adolescence arrived. I started chafing at my exclusion from the men's conversation. I told my mother that I wanted to go to college. I began a friendship with a boy. My father stopped talking to me and I was pushed out of my family.

In my early twenties, I wrote to my father to ask why he had abandoned me.

"I am not a therapist," he wrote back, "but I have enough experience with addictions to know that what you have sought from me over the years is my approval to "feed your habit"—is the term co-dependency? This I refuse to you, because I love you."

If I had remained Yeshivish, my desire—my "addiction"—for my father's approval would have earned me no reprimand. It would have been expected. But I was a Yeshivish girl in the secular world. My heart, still devoted to love, now appeared crippled and deformed.

To my surprise and dismay, I found secular life devoid of romance. Commercials and magazines dripped with sex, men on payphones barked *fuck* into the receiver with abandon, belly button piercings flashed in the summer sun, but beneath these empty signifiers, people's lives were bare. They worked, they ate, they watched TV. Secular life was a wasteland of freedom. In books and pop music and movies I found a trail of breadcrumbs to sustain me: Roxette. Jack Dawson. Hermia. I listened to my heart when he called for me. I believed that my heart would go on. I told myself that the *course of true love never does run smooth*.[3] Then I was raped by a man I met in a park, a marijuana dealer whose Rastafarianism matched up just enough with the religious attitudes I was familiar with for me to trust him. I called this man *Nasi*, prince, tried to convince him to love me, and spent all of my money on him when he didn't.

I was as dumb and gasping as a goldfish, raised in liquid devotion to men, then scooped out of the bowl. After the Rastafarian left me, I met men on the subway and fucked them with the anxious passion of a virginal bride. One night I sold my body to a man I met online. The pain was often unbearable. I cut my body to stay sane. On first dates, I spilled my story like a dump truck upending a load of trash. One of these men was going to cook me a feast from the scraps of my life. He'd be my husband, my father, my god, and my messiah. I was sure of it.

I sought passion not only in the bodies of men but also in houses of prayer. After a brief stint as a Buddhist, I became a Sufi. Sometimes I thought my soul was in my cunt. I would orgasm as I spun on the rug of the mosque, my arm lifted to heaven, the chants of *All-ah, All-ah* pounding against my skin. Back home, in my bed, I would kiss yet another man's skin as if it covered God Himself.

By the time I was twenty-five years old, I was ready for comfort. Perhaps this is a natural stage in the life of all Yeshivish girls, when they move from the idea of romance to its actuality. For of course, Yeshivish life cannot fulfill all of its romantic promises. *Marriage*, one of my sisters told me, *should feel like a pair of broken-in slippers*. In a neat bait-and-switch, a girl goes from daydreams of a white-cloaked scholar-prince to a marriage with an alien body, raw with fresh acne, a bramble of hair crowning its butt crack. A body that smells of onions and sweat. A body that *shuckles* in prayer, rocking violently back and forth in union with God. A body that spends its days with a male partner, a respected *chavrusah*, who is valued for his ideas and inspiration, whose intricacies of mind and soul are explored as the two work together to digest the ancient words of the rabbis. A body that asks what's for dinner, fills your bathroom with its detritus, lies beside you in bed, pulls down his pajama pants and rolls over your body. *If it hurts or you're scared, don't scream,* I once overheard one Chasidish girl telling another before her wedding night. *It scares the men when you scream.* With devotion and obedience a girl must make the man she marries into royalty. Her very force of will must transmogrify the physical facts. I knew all this, somehow, even though I left Yeshivish life before I married. I enacted it with the non-Jewish men I encountered. It was encoded in my DNA.

After I left ultra-Orthodoxy, I avoided other OTD people. My brain was still a minefield of Yeshivish ideas. I liked myself well enough, but I assumed that other men and women who went OTD were what I had been taught to expect: losers, drug addicts, reckless hedonists. Finally, a friend persuaded me to attend a meeting at Footsteps, an organization that helped the OTD community. I was startled to discover that the members of Footsteps were good people, beautiful in their courage, startlingly similar to me in their passions and pains. At Footsteps I met Zeke, a kind and intelligent man with bright blue eyes and enormous dreams.

By then, I had abandoned Sufism for atheism, giving up on romance with men and God alike. The pursuit of love had left me exhausted. I was done. Or so I told myself. It was true that the heat of spiritual ecstasy infused my mind every time I learned something new about evolution or looked at maps of the cosmos. Removing God and the puppeteers who had built Him did not quench that-which-inspired-awe, still burning in the heart of the world. But Zeke was a committed atheist. Together, we went to an atheism conference. I laughed along with everyone else at the foolishness of believers. I was determined to stay cold.

I told my therapist that I had met a man whom I might marry, but I wasn't sure if I liked him. My brain was making Yeshivish calculations. Zeke came from a good family. We shared the same ambition. He admired me. But there was a problem. I had already married once, briefly and platonically, to a roommate whose visa was expiring, exchanging the promise of a green card for the gift of a last name other than my father's. Entering a second marriage with Zeke worried me. My father had asked my mother not to read non-Jewish books, but we children were allowed them, and I had spent my childhood devouring stacks of fairytales. I feared that a second marriage to Zeke couldn't last because all happy endings came in threes. Still, in the end we decided to marry.

For me and Zeke, as for many secular couples, marriage was a vehicle for happiness. We wanted to be together because we enjoyed our life together. We saw no virtue in unhappy matrimony. In my twenties, I'd had many relationships with married men and I was terrified that marrying might turn me into someone like their wives: used, jealous, betrayed. Zeke and I promised each other that we would divorce when we became unhappy. I clung to this promise, hoping that it would ensure our marriage would always be happy. I wanted our relationship to last forever.

I was a different kind of wife than my mother. Zeke and I were honest with each other about everything and fought often, especially in the first years. I exploded in great tantrums and sank into deep sulks. He withdrew and pursued me in turns. When inevitable problems arose, we went to couples therapy. I read dozens of books about relationships.

How did a marriage last in the secular world? There seemed a bewildering absence of helpful instruction on matters of love. The women I knew were delighted to talk about weddings, but said little about the hours and decades that followed. Perhaps other secular couples knew some secret that I didn't. I thought often of my parents' formal system, the system adhered to by every Yeshivish couple: breaking off all physical contact when a woman has her period and for seven days afterward. This practice was supposed to keep a couple's passion fresh and communication strong. In practice, it involved a woman sticking a cloth up her vagina twice a day to check for blood and occasionally, if an inconclusive stain appeared on the cloth, handing this scrap of cotton, now soaked in her scent and fluid, to a rabbi, for the verdict on whether or not she was allowed to her husband. Despite this humiliation, or perhaps because of it, I remained strangely seduced by the practice. In one of our many efforts to overcome our problems, Zeke and I rented an apartment with two bedrooms and slept apart. I hoped that this distance might amplify our passion just as marital purity laws promised. Instead, trouble grew in the space between us. In our next apartment we again shared a bed.

Zeke and I were married for seven years before we gave up. He was a good man, but ultimately, we wanted different lives. *If you see a thing whole . . . it seems that it's always beautiful. Planets, lives. But up close a world's all dirt and rocks. And day to day, life's a hard job, you get tired, you lose the pattern.*[4]

Shortly after I left Zeke, I took a brief trip to Milan, Italy. I needed to catch my breath. I wandered the streets of that glamorous city all day long, reviewing the hard-won lessons of my life. For too long, I had been caught in some other woman's dream, the dream of the woman I had thought I would become. I knew that I could no longer idealize men. I could no longer build my life around a relationship. As I walked, it became clear to me that I had asked too much from love. If I couldn't sustain a nourishing relationship either with the boyfriends I had worshipped with blind passion or with the husband I had chosen rationally, I couldn't with anyone. My problems were my own. My pain belonged to me. No man was going to make me better without also making me a whole lot worse. I made myself a promise: I would never again fall in love. I would never again enter a long-term relationship.

I wasn't negating my need for love, I told myself, I was merely accepting that no man could satisfy my hunger for it. The more I thought about it, the more I found myself drawn back to the promise of God's massive love. I did not believe in Him, but I wanted to find a way to bring His love back into my life. It was a confusing paradox, but if I was truly committed to never again having a partner, maybe I no longer had to maintain a consistent persona for anyone. As a woman on her own I could pursue my most contradictory desires.

Dusk fell across the city of Milan, covering the stone buildings with a pale purple glow. Fortune tellers called out to the tourists. I stopped at one of them. *What next* I asked the fortune teller. *Who will I be after all of this?* I could not admit, even to myself, that I was afraid to be a woman without a man. The old woman looked into my eyes. Her face was like a brown leather bag. She looked away. She told me that in 2015 I would meet the love of my life.

The next morning, walking again through the streets, I stopped short in front of a shop window crowded with the same distinctive black fedora hats worn by my father, my brothers, and the groom of my childhood dreams. Yeshivish hats are made by an Italian manufacturer, Borsalino. I went inside the store and bought a Borsalino of my own.

Back home, I moved from man to man, like a dog sniffing lampposts. A German artist with a bald head and big white muscles asked if I'd be his girlfriend. I borrowed his pants. The first time he canceled plans with me, I sent the pants by messenger to his studio and blocked him on Facebook. I found a musician with soft blonde hair, a psychologist with a low voice and an interest in Buddhism. My heart was finally impenetrable, but my body had needs.

Now that I had given up on loving men, I began to wonder why anyone ever fell for these creatures. Yeshivish men now appeared to me as troglodytes, sealed off in musty caverns of text, but hipster men had their own problems. I developed a theory: after the sexual revolution unhitched sex from marriage and family, young secular men became solitary creatures. But no one can survive alone, so they repopulated their personal homesteads with their inner children, whom they now protected as fiercely as their fathers and grandfathers had once guarded their real-life progeny. I appreciated vulnerability in a man, but there was nothing more boring than taking off a man's clothes and finding that he was composed of a gaggle of posturing, selfish little boys. I told myself that at least I brought warmth and maturity to my erotic encounters, no matter how brief they were. It was hard to admit that my primary concern was for the needs of my own personal gaggle.

But men were just a diversion. My sights were now set on God. I began writing essays interrogating my experiences as an ultra-Orthodox Jew, a Buddhist, a dervish, and an atheist. I was determined to construct a personal spirituality that did not succumb to the toxicity of religion or the navel-gazing consumerism of too many New Age movements.

One evening in September of 2015, I got a message on a hookup app from a guy named Ben. After a brief text conversation, Ben and I met for tea in the back garden of a Williamsburg cafe. In a reversal of the cardinal rule of online dating, he was more handsome than his photo had promised, with a close beard, high cheekbones and beautiful olive eyes. We plunged into a meaty and meandering conversation, leaping from ape behavioral patterns to feminism to free will. He name-dropped Maimonides. I was startled to learn that he wasn't Jewish.

A midwestern boy, Ben had been a math prodigy raised without religion. He'd given up his academic career in artificial intelligence to write a labyrinthine psychological analysis of how his cousin, an Army Ranger, had come to participate in an armed bank robbery. Ben may have been the only secular thirty-something in a five-mile radius as obsessed as I was with conceptions of morality. I soon discovered that we shared a voracious hunger for reexamining our deepest beliefs, a hunger that most adults in their thirties, satisfied with their worldviews or bored by the whole project, have long abandoned. Both Ben and I were desperate to build a life big enough to contain our unruly minds.

Together, we enrolled in classes on Kant and Freud. We talked incessantly, careening from Rousseau to scale-invariant phase transitions, from gaslighting to schismogenesis trickster figures, from the amygdala to the evolutionary origins of God. We kept a joint notebook of our ideas. There were dozens, then hundreds of notes, a freewheeling index of what was quickly becoming a hybrid mind. Ben explained entropy, authophagy, and the neocortex to me. I taught him about *kaparos, shema,* and *kvetching*. His mind seemed to stretch endlessly, enticingly, in every direction. He reminded me of my father, whom I had once called the smartest man I knew. Now, though, I was measuring a man's intelligence by the parameters of my own. For the first time in my life I had a true intellectual partner.

Ben was more than that too, of course. The first time we fucked, I burst into laughter. It did not seem possible that this too could be good between us. The love we built was as carnal as it was ethereal, as emotional as it was intellectual. In conversation and in sexual role-play we began to unpick the knots of our past traumas. We were mother and father to each other, ally and confidante—even, at times, messiah and devotee. But I saved Ben as much as he saved me. We took turns. *The messiah will come only when he is no longer necessary; he will come only on the day after his arrival; he will come, not on the last day, but on the very last.*[5]

A little more than a year after we first met, Ben and I married. By then, like the shifting fragments of colored glass in a kaleidoscope, all the lessons of my life had rearranged and come to mean new things. I had once believed that I had loved too much, that the four great romances of my Yeshivish childhood—for my father, his God, my husband-to-be, and the messiah—had enlarged my developing heart to an unsustainable size. But I now came to believe the opposite: the problem was that I did not love enough. In my quest for a love large enough to match my childhood passions, I had neglected the fifth and vital romance: for one's *chavrusah.*

Modern self-help books urge couples to foster independence. Monogamy itself comes to seem like a slavish adherence to tradition at the expense of personal growth. My father once accused me of co-dependence. Dependence comes from the root *to hang down.* I don't swing from Ben like a baby clinging to its mother, nor does he swing from me. But we don't hang separately, either. We swing together from the underbelly of the ever-mysterious universe. We are creating an audacious monogamy.

We're still in the early days. In contrast to my deliberately conditional marriage to Zeke, Ben and I have committed to a permanent marriage, but who knows how life will unfold. Two months after our wedding, I became bedridden with a serious disease. We lost the home we had bought together to corrupt developers and mold. But these troubles only became fuel for our marriage. With each blow, Ben and I traced the long nerves of history that carried pain deep into our spirits. We asked how our private suffering mapped to larger knots of trauma in society. We read. We talked. We dove into narrative therapy, *Familienaufstellung*, somatic therapy, adaptive leadership, Kabbalah, feminist theories of science, neural retraining, Dionysian sex rituals, and exacting rubrics of moral analysis and accountability. Our life is a strange and wondrous one, built on an ever-evolving array of ideas and speculations.

We have hard days. Brutal days. Like all passionate lovers, we trigger each other's unprocessed trauma with exquisite precision. But we regard each small explosion as a mining opportunity, exposing new places of each other's psyche to learn about, to love, to heal. My heart has grown to unimaginable size.

Human beings need love. Capitalism offers a flood of products designed to induce a feeling almost like love: sleek new cars, smartphones, Twitter feeds. The Yeshivish community presents a scarecrow Prince Charming, stuffing the clothes of Divinity with oppression, hypocrisy, and falsehood. I want the best of both worlds and none of the bad.

I have an older brother who has always been kind to me. Once, explaining why my parents were quick to take communications from me as attacks, my brother said matter-of-factly, as if we both understood it, that I was a *sonei Yisroel*, a hater of Israel. Because I rail against the ultra-Orthodox community's evils, claim women are endowed with the same rights and responsibilities as men, and wrote a memoir about leaving the community, my brother thought that I wanted to destroy Yeshivish life. He couldn't have been more wrong. Our forefather Jacob, the husband of my namesake Leah, was granted the epithet *Yisroel*, Israel, after he tussled with an angel. Yisroel is my father's name, too. In her prayerbook, the theologian Rabbi Jill Hammer suggests that in English we might use Yisroel's literal translation: God Wrestler. How could I be a *Sonei Yisroel*, a hater of those who wrestle with notions of the Divine? I am one of them myself, forever struggling to recover spiritual truth from Yeshivish dogma. I have no choice. We are born into stories that start long before we do and ensnare us well before we have a chance to protest. To discard the story of how I came to be would only be one way of continuing it. Instead, I choose to wander back and forth across the narratives of my life, hunting for truth, and in the process creating myself. I am Leah. I am the daughter of my mother and I am the daughter of Yisroel. I will invent the story that permits my existence and it will be a story of love.

Notes

1. Sigmund Freud, *Civilization and Its Discontents* (New York: W. W. Norton & Company, 2010).

2. Adrienne Rich, *Women and Honor: Some Notes on Lying* (Pittsburgh, PA: Motheroot Publications, 1979).

3. William Shakespeare, *A Midsummer Night's Dream* (New York: W. W. Norton & Company, 2018).

4. Ursula K. Le Guin, *The Dispossessed* (New York: Harper Voyager, 1994).

5. Franz Kafka, "The Coming of the Messiah," in *Parables and Paradoxes* (New York: Schocken Books, 1961).

A Stranger among Familiar Faces

Navigating Complicated Familial Relationships when Leaving the Hasidic Community

Frimet Goldberger

I often wonder, especially when I'm nestled in the company of family, if leaving my community was the right decision. When I sit with them at a niece's wedding, slurping vegetable soup, I am reminded of my childhood dinners and this thought flits through my mind, searing holes in the confidence that has rooted within me for over a decade. My mother would chop the half-rotten vegetables, which she had bargained to $5 a box from Feder's Grocery, then cook them in her twelve-quart pot, by far not the largest in her collection. Its savory warmth wafting through tightly-sealed windows greeted me as I bounded up the concrete stairs after school, famished. There, on the stovetop, annealed by decades of heavy use, rested a pot of soup and *ibergetzuygene beilik* (breaded chicken breast) with mashed potatoes.

Mommy's pots looked like they were rescued from a collapsed building after an earthquake: the *cholent* pot that used to be a smooth red now bore witness to years of steel wool scrubbing; the enormous oval *fish tup*, or fish pot, had so many dents it could be mistaken for an artifact displayed at the MET. Lids scarcely covered the pots, their shapes contoured a million times with overuse. Two attributes distinguished her cauldrons from others: they were always immaculately scrubbed, and they contained the most simple, delicious, and hearty foods.

"How are your children, Frimet?"

It's the one safe question I get asked repeatedly at these occasions. I know what they want to hear, or I think I do.

"Good," I answer, grabbing a chunk of challah to mop the soup bowl. "They're growing up."

Pshee. Keneina hora. "Did you bring them?"

I find an excuse: they have school tomorrow; they don't like to stay out late on school nights; they have too many exams coming up. But I don't dare mention the real reason my children aren't present at some of their cousins' weddings. They are bored out of their minds. Though my daughter has become friends with a few of her many female cousins who speak English and are intrigued by her life and the co-ed school she attends, my son cannot communicate with his male cousins, who barely understand English.

Their cousins inhabit an entirely different planet—no, universe— where Yiddish is spoken almost exclusively, where the Internet and secular books are banned, and where anyone who sports a slightly different look than the locals is perceived as an alien.

I say none of this. I am polite and cordial, and I keep reminding myself where I come from and that I was one of the wedding goers a mere ten years ago.

❧

I was born and bred in Kiryas Joel, an insular, self-sufficient, and self-contained village in upstate New York, established exclusively for Hasidim of the Satmar sect. The late Satmar Rabbi, or, as Hasidim refer to him, Rebbe, Yoel Teitelbaum, hailed from a city in Romania called Satu Mare, from which the Satmar Hasidic sect derives its name. A fierce and passionate advocate for adherence to the most stringent Hasidic ways, Rebbe Teitelbaum was the sect's revered founder and leader who came over to the *treifena medina*—this unkosher, anything-goes country—after the Holocaust.

He settled in Williamsburg with a small group of disciples, and, thanks to his charisma and uncompromising ways, his movement quickly gained momentum. The Satmar community of the 1950s attracted a tremendous and diverse following from all over the religious spectrum. Despondent souls who lost family and faith in the German inferno discovered a doting father in Reb Yoel. His zealotry was admired by many, and his ability to transplant the *shtetl* life to this deeply profane place called New York seemed nothing short of miraculous.

Yet he also wished for a community to call his own, one that would be completely isolated from its neighbors—unlike Williamsburg, where Jews and gentiles of all stripes coexisted. When he discovered a vast land deep in the quiet hills of upstate New York, far away from the immoral temptations of Manhattan, Hasidic Jews followed him in droves.

The isolation allowed for rigidity to rule and radicalism to prosper. Gone was the Hasidic community of Chaim Potok's *The Chosen*, where boys still enjoyed the all-American pastime of baseball. The establishment of Kiryas Joel marked a new era of Hasidic isolationism and extremism. The community grew at an exponential rate. The village boasts separate boys' and girls' schools, supermarkets, *mikvehs*, or ritual baths, for both men and women, and bustling streets filled with thousands of children. Birth rates in Kiryas Joel are among the highest in the country. Boys and girls marry young, ideally at the age of eighteen, through arranged marriages, and rear eight to ten children, on average. Movies, television, and now the Internet are strictly banned, thereby effectively keeping secular influences out.

∼

My mother birthed and raised a dozen, practically unassisted. The four boys came first in quick succession, setting the tone for the family dynamics. Here was a young woman running after four rambunctious boys, each less than two years apart from his older sibling. Having a girl is *always* a big deal in Hasidic families, despite the fact that their lives are not celebrated with the same grandeur as boys. Other than the initial naming ritual, the *Kiddush* on the first Shabbos after the baby's birth, girls do not have many rites-of-passage ceremonies. Bat Mitzvahs, widely celebrated in the non-Hasidic world, do not exist. Girls are viewed as the weaker, less-learned gender—a discrimination that is certainly not exclusive to Hasidim—and thus do not need to abide by the Torah's mitzvahs and commands in the same rigid vein as boys do. Still, the birth of a girl, especially when there are a few boys ahead of her, is a joyous occasion.

"Did you hear that so and so had a girl after five boys? She will have so many outfits and be so spoiled!"

And so it came to be that after four boys, my mother, somewhere in her mid-to-late-twenties, brought home a pink bundle from the hospital one winter. My oldest sister was followed by another girl, then another, then a boy who, much like his placement in the family's pecking order, was always the odd one out. Then came another girl.

Baby Frimet arrived on Shabbos. She was a bubbly little girl who intuited her place in the family, the stressors her caretaker was under, and always behaved like a little angel. Or so I am told. When my mother nursed her dying mother, I was right there with her. When Bubby Weiss took her last breath in her small Williamsburg apartment, I was wailing in the other room. I toilet-trained in a day, an oft-repeated compliment. I was the family darling baby.

Until, one day, I wasn't.

My childhood was not much different from all the girls I knew growing up. Daily life revolved around school, family, holidays, friends, neighbors, and gossip. Family is everything in the Hasidic community. From cradle to grave, your siblings, parents, and extended family are your life. Families multiply like colonies of ants. They celebrate babies' births, bar mitzvahs, engagements, weddings, more babies, more bar mitzvahs, more engagements—and on the cycle goes—a copious continuum of God and tradition based around family. There is joy and laughter, and though love is not always an effervescent presence, family festivities often make up for its absence. Everyone is involved in everything; the secular ideal of the nuclear family is non-existent. Cousins and nieces and aunts, though a bit removed, are as much an integral part of the family as one's siblings.

I grew up in the shadows of my older sisters. Being the youngest girl of the five, they were my role models. I'd sit on the floor outside the bathroom and admire Tzurty's dexterity as she straightened her frizzy red hair into a perfectly straight bob. She would lift a few hairs from her forehead and tease the underside of it with Mommy's blue *sheitel* (wig) comb. Spray, neatly tuck the valley behind the mountain under a velvet headband, or what we called "rife," and voila! There goes the *kallah mod*, the girl who looks ripe for a *shidduch*.

Malka was my favorite sister. She was kind, compassionate, and always had a joke at the ready. "Can I count the freckles on your face?"

she asked, in Yiddish, one evening as she bent over the tub ledge to wash my body. I must have been four or five. "One, two, three, four . . . ten thousand." I giggled and splashed water up the immaculate tiled wall that my mother or sisters scrubbed with Soft Scrub on Friday afternoons. We both knew there was no way to count the pigmented spots on my befreckled face.

I'd spend hours with my sisters in the kitchen listening to English songs about Hashem and Shabbos and Jerusalem. At first, I'd admire their creations: three-tiered, elaborate meringues that Rivky labored over to sell to friends and neighbors and village people for engagement parties. As a teenager, I'd join their adventures in the kitchen. And once they left the house to feed their new husbands, I'd toil away at the kitchen counter with a *rife* on my short, straightened hair, listening to Yeshiva Boys Choir—an Orthodox boys band that was strictly verboten by my father, but whose cassettes we listened to anyway when he wasn't home.

I watched my sisters leave for their first *beshow*, a short meeting between a prospective bride and groom that typically ends with an engagement. Their hair styled to perfection and their faces featuring a dab of blush on the cheeks, a swipe of mascara on the lashes and a coating of Clinique neutral lipstick, I'd behold the impeccable aura that seemed to follow, and I'd imagine being them. I danced at their weddings in navy and gold lacy dresses and white patent shoes. I peered through the blinds as they climbed the concrete stairs with their new husbands, their heads bedecked in a brand-spanking-new *sheitel*, wig, and hat. They'd turn their new crowns with timidity to admire their husbands. I watched their bellies grow and their babies brought home from the hospital, tightly wrapped in pink or blue. I spent countless hours babysitting my nieces and nephews, dreaming of one day owning a clean house like theirs, with potpourri-infused linen closets, and polished mahogany furniture. I fantasized being like them—there was no other way to be. This was the ideal life: mother, wife, daughter, *aishes chayil*, a Jewish woman of valor.

∽

At 16, I discovered the big, bad secular world beyond the proverbial walls of our village. Raizel, a dear friend and neighbor, had surreptitiously brought home a *Reader's Digest* from her more modern aunt's house. We devoured it. The following day, we hopped on a minibus to Walmart outside the village to purchase more *goyish* books. We were insatiable.

My world made an about face. I no longer cared to abide by my promise to never, *ever*, wear mascara like my sisters did—a promise I made in a heated moment of piety. I adopted Nora Roberts as my family and her salacious novels as my best friends. Here was a world in which men did all kinds of delicious things to women. I was at once scandalized and intrigued.

We quickly graduated to movies. We pooled together our meager paychecks, or whatever was left after we gave them to our parents, and purchased a 2X2 DVD player and five movies. I watched *How to Lose a Guy in Ten Days* about five-thousand times in my bed, under the dark, dependable confines of my blanket. I developed a cosmic crush on Matthew McConaughey, before I understood male/female sexual dynamics.

But then there was the matter outside my bedroom doors—my flesh family. For the first time in my life, I didn't have to share a room with a sibling. They had all married, but for me and my two younger brothers. I could no longer relate to my surroundings in the way I did before. I kept this dirty secret wrapped in a gift box, niftily tucked beneath blankets in the closet. I had these other profane paperbacks positioned one next to another under my mattress. I could not betray my new family for the one outside the bedroom door—the people who were too busy spinning the wheels of monotony. I unwittingly began the process of untying the knots that kept me bound to my family.

I was a defiled girl. The change within me was so sudden, yet so subtle. My parents knew; no one else did. They saw me scrub the floors with headphones cemented to my ears. My father, in a fit of rage, lifted my mattress and discovered the stack of romance novels. He stormed off to the Satmar Rebbe and put my name on the radar of the village's *Vaad Hatznius*, the mysterious group of men tasked with maintaining the highest standards of modesty in the village, and granted the freedom to do as they please with those who dare defy the rules.

I must have kept up the facade well, because my secret transgressions were not known on the streets. My *shidduch* status was still altogether acceptable. My mother was going to look for an innocent eighteen-year-old boy who studied in yeshiva all day and could recite pages of Talmud, verbatim, on cue. When I overheard her rejecting the matchmaker's offer of a twenty-one-year-old boy who socialized in iffy circles, my interest was piqued. I set out to inquire about this strange man who had been proposed to me, learned he was not ignorant to everything secular, and relentlessly pressured my mother to pursue the match.

What good Hasidic boy would want an *oifgeklerte*, secularly informed, girl like me? It didn't matter. If an average boy who never experienced the joys of *goyishe* movies wanted me, I didn't want him. I needed a good boy who also appreciated the thrill of breaking rules and loosening shackles. I wanted a boy—any boy. I ached to leave my parents' home and, thanks to Nora Roberts, into the arms of a man.

I was seventeen, two months shy of my eighteenth birthday, when I first met my husband. He walked into the foyer of my parents' home, his black leather shoes reflecting on the sparkling wood floor I had washed earlier that day, and wheeled his head around to me. My first impression was of a beet-red face. The redness, I later discovered, was the consequence of an afternoon spent covertly playing baseball with his buddies in a deserted field far away from prying eyes.

A good Hasidic yeshiva boy does not indulge in a pastime like baseball, but he was not your exemplary yeshiva boy. He did not bounce his sidelocks like a metal slinky and sway over a Talmud all day. His interests were varied. He was an *alte bucher*, an older boy, twenty-one years of age, holding up the marriage assembly line of siblings who were "of age," eighteen and above. He no longer sat in yeshiva full time; he worked odd jobs when the opportunity presented itself, smoked cigarettes, and drove with his friends to theaters outside the borders of our holy village.

I had discovered all this about him through Raizel, whose brother-in-law was this *alte bucher's* age. This was enough to get me into my *shabbosdig* blue and white sweater set to meet him for a *beshow*. I was, yet again, different than my other siblings—setting myself apart in subtle yet significant ways. I lusted after what they never dreamed of—longings I didn't dare share with them.

He followed his parents into the dining room where I sat, flanked on either side by my mother and father. I observed as he lifted his long, checked, navy-blue *reckel*, the Hasidic suit jacket, folded it around his hips, and settled facing me. Our mothers made small talk about the merits of the Wall of China embroidered tablecloth versus the knockoffs that some families now bought their newly-married daughters. They knew each other well, our mothers, and this meeting felt like the formality that it was. Occasionally, our eyes would meet, and I—ever the perceptive one—could discern a slight smirk rising on his lips.

After fifteen minutes, they ushered us into my childhood playroom. We took a seat across from each other, a table and awkwardness between us. They left the door slightly ajar, a requirement for unmarried couples. We listened to our mothers chitchat, and while we were supposed to talk about something—anything—silence reigned for the first five minutes. I felt as nervous as when my school's matronly secretary ordered me to lead the morning prayers. I was with a stranger of the opposite sex whose bashful focus was on me, and it was terrifying.

I asked about his family—how many kids they were, how many grandchildren, are there any great-grandchildren?—even though I already knew about them from my classmate, his younger sister. But someone had to break the ice, and this was *the* way to start a *beshow*.

And there we were, facing each other and toying with the taupe embroidered cherries of the starched white tablecloth.

"Are you a Republican or Democrat?" I asked. I *had* to gauge his interest of the outside world, and politics was a safe, vanilla topic. He had been to the theatre, I knew that much. I assumed his knowledge of politics, and maybe, just maybe, he listened to the radio shows I was devouring as a young idealist whose worldview meshed with Republican talking heads.

He was a Republican, he answered.

Check.

"*Hust gehert fin Sean Hannity?*" Did you hear of Sean Hannity? I continued boldly.

He did. Check.

After thirty minutes that felt longer than my seventeen years, my mother poked her head in, a sign that we are to wrap up the *beshow* and answer the anxiously awaiting circle in the know.

"So, *vus zugste?*" My mother asked. So, what do you say? Do you agree to this match when all the trays of cakes and delicacies are already lined up on the kitchen counter, awaiting your affirmative answer, and when all your sisters are dressed in their everyday finest, ready to come over at a moment's notice?

I wanted out of my parents grip and into the arms of a man. I ached with a teenager's lust for sex and romance. If he listened to talk radio and frequented the theatre, he was different—a pariah just like me. There was something forbidden and thrilling about our short and clumsy conversation, and I thought it a divine determination that we were meant to be together.

Yes, I said, while clutching the edge of my knit sweater. Yes, I'll marry him and raise a family with him. Yes.

∼

By the time I entered the third decade of my life, barely eligible to vote and definitely not old enough to have a glass of wine, everything had changed. I entered the decade with a baby in my arms and the last remnants of baby fat on my cheeks.

Life was simple. I worked six hours a day fielding phone calls and fulfilling coffee orders for municipal officials in the Kiryas Joel Village Office. I made some great friends in that place—women who, like me, fretted over dinner options and socks to match to their babies' sweater sets. I stopped into Landau's Supermarket on the way home to buy chicken and potatoes or at my sister Malky's house on the way home to say hi to my nieces and nephews and to drop off a bag of veggies or a bottle of milk. I'd pick up the baby from the babysitter down the block, cook *ibergetzuygene beilik* (schnitzel) and mashed potatoes, feed and bathe him and clean the house.

I repeated the same routine the following day.

On Shabbos, we'd walk to my mom's or his mom's to eat gefilte fish and *kotchenyu* (jellied fish sauce), chicken soup and *kneidlach*, *cholent* and *lokshen kugel*. The menu rarely changed.

I knew my place in life—to be a mother and a fine housewife—like my sisters and sisters-in-law, mother, and friends. I didn't have to think about who I was or what I could be. Aspirations, shmasperations. I didn't know what the word meant, anyway. Everything was predetermined and I didn't mind it at all. We snuck into Blockbuster and made a dash for the library door. Life was comfortable.

About a month after we celebrated my son's first birthday with a homemade cheesecake smothered in caramel buttercream—because who bought bakery stuff, let alone birthday cakes?—I peed on a stick and two bright blue lines appeared, smiling sardonically. I was pregnant. Again. What a blessing, *ka'h*, may the evil eye not curse you. Except, I didn't want it. Not yet anyway. And yet, she happened. All ten toes and ten fingers and eight pounds and three ounces came kicking out of me on that cold January evening. I was twenty-one; she was another tiny soul to care for.

Life became one confusing blur of misery. I don't know who cried more in that first year of my daughter's life—the newborn or the adult. I didn't sleep for days. I got hooked on sleeping pills and descended into a cycle of depression.

I tried talking to my mother, but how do you explain postpartum depression to a woman who birthed twelve children and never shed a tear in front of them? Depression? *Phech*. Get up, wash your face, and go cook *paprigash* and iron some shirts. I lost a piece of her during those sleepless nights and dark days. I realized how far this apple fell from the tree.

I called my sister. She empathized, as she herself had suffered through many a postpartum. But there was an impalpable distinction—her being the *geshikte* (efficient) balabusta, and I, well, I was falling apart and contemplating a silent departure.

Yet another family knot came undone.

A year later I was told by the *Vaad Hatznius*, the modesty police, that my three-year-old son could not return to *cheder*, the only boys' school in town, because I didn't shave my hair—the hair I went to great and painful lengths to cover every last trace of. Most Hasidic sects require married women to shave their heads and don a wig or kerchief on top of their shorn heads, a tradition that goes back centuries but whose direct origin no one can trace. I shaved my head that night, all of it, down to a stubble, as I did for the first three years of our marriage. The *Vaad* was going to send someone to check if I had *bei hur*—the Yiddish name for hair on a married woman. My mother would find out. So would my sisters and my next door neighbor. The whole damn village would know before I even got a chance to pack my bags and run.

I could kiss goodbye to my security blanket, my life, my everything: family.

I stared at my reflection in the vanity mirror, resolutely. This was going to be the last time that godforsaken shaver stripped my scalp.

The next morning, as the sun circled around to my Zenta Road kitchen window, we made a decision to leave. Three freshly-shorn heads and one little girl with baby curls. I was twenty-three.

We moved into a ramshackle house. The walls were coated in feces and the floors were covered in dirt from the Middle Ages. We made it into a home, a haven for two broken souls who barely knew each other despite being married and producing two offspring. We lived and loved, cooked and baked, fought and cried—and grew.

We grew in love. We grew so much as a couple and family, the story merits its own essay—or book.

It took another three years and too many hair-raising run-ins with Hasidic authorities to wake us up to the reality that the Hasidic community did not want us, adamant as we were to hold on. One school, a "modern" Hasidic haven, expelled my five-year-old son three times— THREE!—because his mother's skirt was too short, her wig showed a little hair in the front, and she was going off the deep end where short sleeves and thin stockings transformed all womankind into whores. They ordered me to bring my wig in a bag to the principal of this school. And I did. Because where else were we going to go?

At twenty-six, we said goodbye. Adios. Ciao. *Zei gezunt in shtark, Chasidishville*—stay healthy and strong.

I never looked back. Yet as I entered my fourth decade and observed other families around me say goodbye, adios, ciao, *zei gezunt in shtark, Chasidishville*, I contemplated our loss—the simple, predestined life, a family-centered existence, and above all, our own families. I could never recapture that which is a mere feeling of nostalgia.

Family. Oh, I didn't exactly lose them. They're still here. But the strong ties are coming undone. The ability to relate to one another is gone. They are no longer the center of my universe. I no longer pick up the phone and dial my mother's number to ask for advice, to wish her good morning, and ask about the weather—a tradition my sisters still keep to, since my mother listens to the radio for weather updates. I don't take my kids for sleepovers with their seventy-plus cousins on my side, and equal, if not greater, number from their father's side.

We might as well be living on two different planets. My life is that of a Martian in their eyes, and their lives, much as I try to go back in time and remember what it was like, are those of Martians, too.

◆

Nothing could prepare me for this change.

I became a stranger among once familiar faces.

It was hard, and it hurt. It was harder than I thought it would be when we packed our bags and enthusiastically skipped town to live a more self-determined life. I was like an immigrant in my own country whose family is still ensconced in my mother country.

The move complicated the relationships I had with my family members. What are they to make of all these changes when they wholeheartedly believe their way is *the right* way to be a Jew? I am a pox on their house—a thorn among the roses on the family branch. I will never hear it directly from them, but I know it. I know it from the stares when I walk into a wedding hall, the awkwardness when I mention something culturally curious.

My relationship with my mother was always tenuous at best. She's a stoic woman who lived a practical life, did what she had to do to raise her brood, but never showed much affection. Yet I always admired her and lived to please her, if only to make her life a tad easier and to give her some much-deserved *nachas*—pride, especially from one's children. My siblings and I would bend over backwards to bring joy to my mother's world. She is the family's ineffable everything—the tie that binds us—yet I never felt comfortable sharing intimate details of my life with her.

For years after we left, I avoided talking to her too often. I did not wish to hurt her any more than she was already hurting. The stories emanating from the rumor mill invariably involved my poor, poor mother who was heartbroken by me and my new lifestyle. "*She cries every week at lecht bentchen*—candle lighting on Shabbos—a cousin told a cousin who told a friend who told a neighbor who repeated it to me.

I am certainly not alone in this. My fellow travelers, of whom there are many, struggle to reconcile with family whilst forging their independence and finding their footing in the non-Hasidic world. When my mother showed up one day a few years back to grandparents' day at my children's school, I was so deeply moved by her presence that I posted a short update on social media to share my joy with friends. The reactions was overwhelming. Those who left the community and lost family in the process found hope, and those who maintained relationships were heartened.

This is what I wrote:

"Today I am a daughter.
Today my children have a grandmother who loves them unconditionally.

Today I understand the phrase 'blood runs thicker than
water.'
Today I feel whole again."

My mother, bless her beautiful heart, got up early to catch the 8:10
Monsey Trails bus together with my wonderful sister. They came to
us—to my children—to participate in Grandparents Day. She came to
see her grandchildren, whom she loves dearly, in their natural habitat.

I was predictably nervous, unsure of how she will respond. Their
school is, after all, a far cry from the *cheders* and schools her other
grandchildren attend. It is coed; it is "modern"; the curriculum includes
modern Hebrew and other un-Satmar-like subjects. Yet we chose to invite
her because she deserves to be a part of her grandchildren's lives, and
my precious ones deserve to have an involved *bubbe* (grandmother).

My mother came. With a big smile plastered on her face and an
open mind and heart, she came to show her love and support. She put
her hands on the metallic sheet for the kids to trace, playfully helped
them cut and paste on the canvas, and sat in on their Ivrit and language arts classes. She gave copious amounts of hugs and kisses, pro-
fusely thanked the staff and teachers, and *shepped nachas*—oh so much
nachas.

After having lunch and driving my mom and sister around to shopping malls, I dropped them off at the bus stop. Later, as I was reveling in
the success of the day, I got a call from my sister. She said my mother
was full of praises on the bus ride home, and that my respect for her
goes a long way. "She loves you," she said.

I hung up and cried. How could I not?

Today marks a pivotal point in my adult life and in my relationship
with my family. Today I feel whole again."

But, alas, relationships are never static, and what inspired me at one
point to continue to work on the connection or to drop it altogether,
lost its meaning eventually. Life isn't static either. We change. We grow.
And as we continued to evolve in our new lifestyle, our relationship
with family deteriorated.

I am not one to complain about family and their lack of acknowledgement or respect for my lifestyle. They accept me, or the facade I present when I'm with them. I love them, and I can tell they love me. But it's a disingenuous love for the woman I once was.

They haven't disowned me. They want to see me and my children. On many occasions, my mother and sisters have shown tremendous love and tolerance far beyond what I have witnessed with other families. I cannot in good conscience speak ill of them. My love for the female members of my family runs deep and eternal.

But here's where it gets complicated: I have no one to talk to and little to talk about when we meet. I sit at my niece's wedding and discuss my siblings' lives, rarely my own. Time and all its infinite healing powers can also create widening and seemingly unbridgeable gaps. The distance served me well for many years; it helped move our transition along so much more smoothly and painlessly than if we had kept our semi-close ties with family. We needed distance.

I felt this change most acutely at the past few weddings we attended. I sit there at the table—the odd one out, the rebel, the *shiksah*—non-Jewish woman—silent. I ask about their lives, their children, their *shidduchim*, but when they ask "how are you?" I say "good, *burech hashem*—thank God" and avoid elaborating. They don't care to know. They won't understand. What can I share with them anyway? That my son is acing his honors classes and is in the 99th percentile in standardized testing? That my daughter is excelling in her enrichment courses and is on the honors track for middle school? That I'm not confident with my approach to electronics and concerned about their access to inappropriate content? That my son is being a teenager and calling his sister names and his parents TERRIBLE, HORRIBLE HUMANS—and how do you deal with teens anyway? Or that I really, badly want to travel the world once my kids are in college? That we even need a college fund! That OMG, Donald Trump—how did this happen?!?!

Nothing. I can tell them about The Babka Lady, my fledgling babka business, or in the past, about the struggles of attending classes while rushing home to make the kids' busses. It is almost always a one-sided conversation. In years past, I could still pretend to be someone I'm not. But I find that with time, I can no longer give them what they want, or pretend to be who I'm not—a Frimet who's "modern" but still lives a "normal" life.

The ties are disentangling. The blood is being diluted. Of course, this doesn't negate the fact that I love and admire my mother and my sisters and the large families they're raising while managing to keep a clean home and delicious food on the table. Where do they get the strength, anyway? It doesn't taint the memories of my childhood—of Friday nights curled up on the couch with mommy and my sisters, sharing a box of M&M's; of Shabbos meals with my sisters and their children, dipping mommy's homemade challah into her gelatin-ed fish sauce. Of the copious hours spent with them in the kitchen, on the street, worshipping their hair, and Ferragamo heels. Of the days of yore when I aspired to be like them.

The memories are there, a constant reminder of what I lost and what I miss dearly. In bleak moments I wonder if the tradeoff was worth it. Wouldn't life be simpler back there where decisions are made for us? Wouldn't we be happier with a larger family and a neighbor outside every window?

These doubts appear out of nowhere, chipping away at my confidence for my life choices. On most days, I am certain that leaving my community of birth and the stringent, stifling lifestyle was the right move. But I also acknowledge that this new secular world I've come to embrace is no panacea; it brings its own set of unique challenges, stress, and heartache.

I rarely share anything substantive about my life with my mother, yet she cares. I know she does. She is incapable of understanding—I get it, and I don't blame her for it.

Other than one brother who joined me on the other side, I see my sisters once every few months at weddings or during a short visit on a holiday. I talk to them whenever one of us remembers the other, which isn't very often, sadly.

Whose fault is it? No one's. I can't blame my family in good conscience for not understanding a life that is so foreign to them, that they believe to be an abomination of everything they subscribe to. I don't blame myself either; I am entitled to my choices. It's no one's fault. It just is.

ᕔ

For ten years, we deliberately distanced ourselves—to maintain our sanity and to avoid unnecessary discomfort on both sides. It took us a decade to feel wholly settled in our new lives and satisfied with the choices we've made.

Since I wrote the first draft of this memoir, my family and I have grown closer. Perhaps it's my comfort in the skin I'm wearing that prompted this shift, or my realization that, cliché as it may be, life is too short to waste precious time on resentment. Or it's thanks to my mother's now unconditional acceptance, and her ineffable joy in my company.

I have grown quite adept at separating my everyday life from the one I carry with me to visit family. I am a writer and speaker who sometimes exposes the grimy underbelly of the community my family lives in, and when I'm with them, I feel like a fraud. But I've tapped into their 'don't ask, don't tell' ways, and it seems to be working well for all of us.

In March 2018, we threw an elaborate party in our home for our families to celebrate our son's bar mitzvah. In-between hors d'oeuvres, the guitarist crooning familiar Yiddish tunes, my mother glowing and pinching the bar mitzvah boy's cheeks, repeatedly, and our son buoyantly dancing with his grandfathers and over twenty-five uncles, I had an epiphany: My children are learning invaluable lessons in coexistence. They can glide in and out of seemingly disparate worlds quite seamlessly—and they do it with such love.

Family is family. Blood is blood. Perhaps they are no longer an integral part of my life, but they will always hold a place deep in the recesses of my heart and memory.

Uncovered

An Interview with Leah Lax

JESSICA LANG AND EZRA CAPPELL

About gender and religion: *Toward the end of the first chapter of your memoir* Uncovered: How I Left Hasidic Life and Finally Came Home, *your husband-to-be Levi approaches you to lower a veil over your face before your wedding. But first, he looks at you. You write that in that moment, he sees Leah, not Lisa, "daughter of Rita and Herb, the girl who once climbed rooftops and dreamed she was a boy" (23). In this memoir that presents religion through the lens of the ultra-Orthodoxy of the Lubavitcher movement, this is the first indication that the book will explore notions of femininity, queerness, and particularly gender. Later, in Chapter Eight, you imagine yourself as "one of those young men sneaking through the dangerous religion-hating Soviet Union to clandestine yeshivas in basements and abandoned buildings, always hungry, ever alert for evil authorities, feeling noble and driven by the Cause" (111)—an early point of access to that exploration and one you return to many times. In the narrative, you seem un-conflicted about being female, and apparently smitten with your girlfriend, and yet you seem to have often imagined yourself a boy or young man. Coming from a secular environment as you did, what did gender mean to you?*

First, I want to point out how huge it is for adolescents today that the media, their world, is rife with language and prototypes for varieties of gender and sexuality. You note that I came from a secular environment, but I came of age in the early seventies when the word "gender" wasn't widely used and the word "gay" or any of the various synonyms, all of which were epithets, was only whispered, so that young people trying to figure themselves out had little language for such things. In *Uncovered*, I tried to show you a girl who is moving forward intuitively without the language that might have pointed her toward understanding herself. As a healthy normal person she has no awareness of being somewhat outside of the mainstream, and no sense of need to seek a label of understanding for dreams and desires that felt quite normal, since such labeling tends to designate an aberration or object of concern. As a result, she sets herself on a collision course unaware and walks straight into the binary Hasidic world.

Ironically, most young, ultra-Orthodox non-heterosexuals labor under the same innocence and lack of language for themselves I had back then in the secular world and find themselves thrust into similar conflicts with their environment. Those that survive into an honest life usually do so because they dare to access the Internet, where they can find language and respectable prototypes for who they are.

Personally, I have never understood the masculine/feminine binary. What does masculine even mean? To me, any attempt to define the word rings of stereotype. The strongest, gruffest man might exhibit true tenderness for a child, or delicacy with a flower or a paintbrush, or be moved to tears by music. To say that those genuine gestures are not masculine is to rob him of some of his finest attributes and also robs him of the natural contradictions and breadth of qualities within a single person that make him human. If I were a man, I would insist I own those as well, as a man.

But then, in my mind, "masculine" and "feminine" have always flowed together into a single complex whole. I dream equally as often that I'm male as female, and I tend to interchange pronouns so unconsciously that even when my wife hears my error and corrects me I have no recollection of having said it. "Her," she'll correct me, rolling her eyes. "What?" I say. "You referred to that woman as "him," she says. "No I didn't!" I say. But somewhere inside me, the two are almost interchangeable, and this has nothing to do with my body, which is electrified only by women.

Today I think some would call me a genderqueer lesbian. But back then, this fluidity of "gender" was so deep within my psyche, so raw and baseline and unarticulated, that I could not begin to parse its meaning. I therefore saw no reason to keep myself from wanting the full Hasidic experience. I loved the rustling, feminine lighting of the Sabbath candles and the sense that women, like God, can create a day, *and* the sweating men-arm-in-arm in ecstatic dance-as-prayer. I had never seen a reason to exclusively identify with my male or female peers, but this was at least partially responsible for my loneliness. Who was I? Ultimately, the Hasidim addressed this unspoken question by giving me a clear label as (their definition of) a Woman, with specific appearance, dress, demeanor, and role. It was a relief in a way. I could follow a bulleted list specified by Jewish Law and then I'd *belong*.

Could you then say that religion taught you a version of femininity that wasn't otherwise available to you?

It taught me a rigid and fairly stereotyped version, but yes. I don't think otherwise any version was fully available to me, although I will always wonder whether that would have mattered. You have to wonder about the road not taken . . .

In what way did that single-gendered experience of ultra-Orthodox Judaism resonate for you when you first entered that life?

Lacking language for my fluid self, Orthodoxy not only gave me a definition and a clear label that meant a place where I could feel I belonged, as long as I followed the rules. Just trim those little corners of yourself and you'll fit right in the box.

But those little corners can be stubborn. And the Hasidic world is so homoerotic! They group men only with men, women with women, ignoring any other possibility. The men would kiss one another, dance with one another, and stay up late at intimate alcohol-laden private *farbrengens* baring their souls and sharing spiritual longing as love, uniting voices as one in yearning for God, while the women cluster as well, whispering in one another's ears and dancing together, always offering a hand and a hug in support of one another in that challenging woman's life. I found these intimate gatherings, these expressions of same-sex love, pure, and beautiful, and freeing.

What did the Hasidic definition of gender mean to you later as a young mother and Lubavitcher woman?

I worked hard to fit their mold, innocent of how essential it is that one's inner and outer life, psyche and construct remain more or less in sync. As that constructed identity took form, cognitive dissonance grew along with it, until long-term insomnia, panic attacks in my sleep, and stress-related ailments like asthma set in—all of which disappeared after I took back my life.

What does gender mean to you now as an openly gay woman, artist, and advocate?

Today, I'm as matter-of-fact about my gender and sexuality as is the average heterosexual. I shake my head at why that had to be so hard earned.

I didn't write *Uncovered* as an advocate for anything, but because I was already established as an artist and my story was getting in the way of other creative work. I struck a bargain with myself. But all writing that sounds genuine is an act of free speech, so that the very act makes me an advocate for that freedom. Creativity and spontaneity have to go hand in hand, in spite of rules, including religious rules.

Gradually, I saw that *Uncovered* was being perceived in the Lubavitch community as a threat. It's been wonderful hearing how much my book has been read among them as a result. I had dreamed of covered women reading it everywhere, covered in brown paper, under the blanket at night, hidden in bathrooms. Sometimes, you write a memoir and find you've become a voice others wish they had. Today, I will drop everything to reply to the Hasidim who secretly contact me.

I was very much struck by the wish you frequently expressed in your book to participate in precisely the parts of Hasidic life that were off limits to women. After you explore that fantasy you once had of saving Soviet Jewry, in Chapter 9, you attend a farbrengen, *a public gathering with the Rebbe who leads the Lubavitch sect, and look down from the women's gallery upon the thousands of men who have gathered, longing "to be one of them, one with them" while "breathing in the man air, the air of the presence of God" (127; 125–26). Can you explore this tension and this conflict?*

Although the rigid Hasidic definition of womanhood drew me with relief into the fold, it was the ecstatic spirit of the men's spiritual life that most exemplified Hasidic life as a whole that had the deepest pull. I wanted what the men had, or what they said they had, and since I related to them just as naturally, at first I didn't see the barriers and let myself slip to go there. I dreamed of immersing in heady study and group prayer, wanting to achieve a transcendence reserved for men, which would help me rise above my troubling self, utterly accepted in the arms of God. I tried to show you that irony, how the very desires that brought me into that world walled me off quite literally, as a woman, from the experiences I sought there. I feel, in a way, that I backed right into that situation.

Somehow faith often seems masculine, as well, in your writing.

I don't see that piece as specific to me since the Hasidic language of faith is entirely masculine. That's a loss, isn't it, for all Hasidic and Orthodox women? Not to mention the examples of the masculine appropriation of the feminine throughout the religion, in the same way that God's feminine presence, the Shechinah, is folded into a God we address as Him. In one scene, I tried to capture how the bris ritual allows the men to appropriate birth: the father bears the infant into the congregation as if into the world, then names that child into existence and only then his son's Godly soul, life itself, truly enters his being. The mother is not present among them, erased.

Do you really think your religious transformation was a reflection of your desire to experiment with gender, or was it a cutoff of that part of yourself?

I had no conscious desire to experiment. Rather, I was naturally attuned to both "roles," as the Hasidic world refers to those gendered delineated lives. Then, in becoming Hasidic I forced a whole vital portion of my identity underground, a cutoff indeed. And yet, I believe that that repression also saved me, since eventually it drove my forays into literature, poetry, and questioning of faith that led me to look into forbidden books for my lost self, for a place where I might *be.*

As I gradually exchanged Hasidic Woman for the real me, I was shocked to find my faith, Her faith, waning exactly at the same rate that I was becoming real. I grieved that.

Do you think it is possible to remain Orthodox while embracing feminism?

There are many women who say they can, and who am I to say otherwise? I think of my Hasidic daughter, who sees feminism as simply a belief that women should have work opportunities and compensation equal to men, coupled with a recognition that this is yet to happen. She considers herself a feminist, although I wonder if she's freer to embrace that because she's single and doesn't have a mother's pitiable drive to construct a world of clarity and rules to soothe her children and keep them safe.

Your departure from ultra-Orthodoxy is closely tied to both a personal and public coming out. Part of that coming out seems to be your finally acknowledging a flexible gender identification. In one very moving description, you write about donning a talit, *a prayer shawl traditionally reserved for men. On the one hand, you note that, "it is anachronous to appropriate this male attire. Why not do something uniquely feminine?" But then you discover the light-filled refuge created by the* talit *when you pulled it down over your head and face, which you describe in a way that seems like the ultimate finding of home—long the province of women. Can you address this shift in spiritual practice and its connection to your departure from Lubavitch life?*

For me, donning a *talit* that day was fraught with fear, long imbued, of defying Jewish Law, but particularly by crossing the Law's gendered-boundaries, but the compulsion to do so was great. I knew that once I took that step I could never go back. Standing there that day in that little library synagogue in Los Angeles, I had to ask myself, "But what does gender have to do with human need?"

Thus I began taking back my life. Then I put the wig back on and flew home. I went grocery shopping, cooked for *Shabbos*, served my family, and sat at the table with my husband at the head in his long black coat, beard, and hat, our children seated around us in their *Shabbos* best. In that setting I told my family that I had put my woman's hands on the Torah before the congregation and sung out the blessings, and prayed aloud among men while wearing a *talis*. I tried to describe the religious families that dared to show up to join us, men in beards and women in scarves and modest dress, and the female *baalas korei* who sang the Torah portion.

If their lives were built of cubicles, I was dissolving all of those walls. I was met with a line of eyes. Only then I began to understand what I had done, the beginning of destruction they were witnessing, in a way for us all.

In an epilogue you write: "To my covered sisters: To get the best from religion, you have to sift. Allow yourself to do that, no matter what people say. Stand up to the guilt or shame some use as a tool of religion (it's a dishonest tool), and reserve the right to think and judge for yourself . . ." (347) You write this knowing that there have to be others who live as you once did, covered women who struggle both with faith and with sexual orientation. And yet you have just documented how isolating this struggle is. Have you found any emerging or existing communities of Orthodox or ultra-Orthodox men and women who identify as non-heterosexual but remain committed to their on-the-derech life? Is that even possible?

Of course there are many individuals who stay, or stay for a time. But even for those who are headed out, there are many points on the path. Besides, we know to what extent observant women are trained in self-sacrifice. They often have many children, and all too often their coming out would mean utter rejection by family and community—the specter of loss can be staggering, keeping them firmly in place.

Some of those women enter secret relationships and risk getting caught. A few tell their husbands and some even find them understanding, which can ironically strengthen their tie to home and family. Some wind up harming themselves.

But you asked if there are communities, not isolated individuals. Thanks to the Internet, a number of secret groups have sprung up with names like LGBT Off The Derech, and LGBTQ Chabad, as well as a number of general OTD groups. Although each group has volunteers that carefully monitor for zealots and trolls, many still join under pseudonyms. I've found these groups wonderfully eclectic and ecumenical, with a tolerant mutually supportive array of Orthodox and ex-Orthodox people and those in various agonized states between the two. Conversations can be wry, often hilariously full of inside jokes, or supportive and practical, or philosophical, with only occasional cries of despair, as members try to thresh out an identity that feels newborn or as they try to individuate from family expectations with minimal loss. Too many have been exiled from everything they know and they can be terrified. But here people share the journey. They applaud one another on getting a job, an apartment, or into a university, and also when all too frequently someone checks into a psych ward to avoid self-harm or mourns the loss of a fellow traveler. Still, reflecting the trauma of exile, the rates of depression, drug use, homelessness, promiscuity, and, particularly, suicide are high.

Uncovered was used as a rallying cry to form the LGBTQ Chabad group. I stay on the periphery, but there are always moments when I feel downright motherly and offer a word and a verbal hug to these young, struggling, beautiful people, particularly when their own parents have rejected them.

About family and religion: *At your marriage to Levi, in order to mark your assuming a new identity as Hasidic wife, you take on a new first name, moving from "Lisa" to the Hebrew "Leah." Before the ritual veiling of the bride (which seems to presage all the other "coverings" of an Orthodox woman), your misty-eyed mother pins the veil on you and we get a glimpse of the dysfunction you are leaving behind: "I think of the secret of her hoarded clutter, how her elegant mother refuses to walk into our home, how we were left alone in it growing up, how often she forgets to make meals. I think, Put the veil on me, Mom? Now you care? Fortunate for you, this gown isn't the dirty gray of our life together. The white dress covers all that, and now here you are, offering to help me disappear." You seem to reject your mother in these lines—"the gown isn't the dirty gray of our life"—and also hold her responsible for your decision to become religious: she helps you to disappear. Was part of the appeal of Orthodoxy a rejection of the environment in which you had been raised?*

Oh, yes. When I was first falling in love with the beauty and philosophy and idealism in Orthodoxy (hugely augmented by the too-eager welcome I found there) the more my liberal artist mother railed against what she called their "mind control" the more I moved toward my new friends. Her opposition sealed the deal in the exact same way that complimenting your teenaged daughter's outfit is a good way to guarantee that she'll immediately go upstairs and change her clothes.

I was moving from the unstructured chaos of her sixties liberal home into soothing predictability, order, and authority, from her relative values into (overly) reassuring absolutes. At one point, I retorted to her that in Orthodoxy, "mothers are Mothers and fathers are Fathers." This reduced her to tears.

In spite of the many ways I held my mother responsible for everything I was fleeing, I did not forget that she was a passionate, talented artist, and how she had once inspired me. She put a paintbrush in my hand when I was four, and thereafter took me to the painting classes she taught, where she took my childish work as seriously as she did that of her students, on into my teens. She fostered my music through years of piano lessons and then harpsichord and cello, all of which thrilled her. Our mess of a home was also filled with classical music, piles of art books, and her large, brilliant canvases stacked against the walls, the smell of painter's turpentine ever wafting in from her studio. Until I found the Hasidim I had long thought my art would be my tool of escape and dreamed of the artist I would become.

After my marriage, I abandoned all that. I wove the sound of the cello into my book as the sound of a certain unbidden consciousness of self, no matter how hard I worked to suppress it. When I finally left, I took the cello with me. Today, I've worked with several major composers and consider the role of music in my life one of my chief joys. *Uncovered* is dedicated to my mother, to her memory.

I found it quite compelling that in spite of the way your writing is deeply revealing, you weave a theme of hiding and disappearance. Niglah and nister, the hidden versus the revealed, seems to dictate so much in Orthodox Jewish life. You seem to have made an artistic decision to document this push/pull. For example, you reveal the very personal events leading to your abortion, and then we read that the rabbi commanded you never to speak of it. Can you talk about the relation, for you, between religious revelation (and secrecy) and the openness that writing demands?

Nigleh and nistar was our constant dialectic. We were to exemplify God in the world and God was hidden by definition, hidden in all things, His invisible feminine presence ever hovering with protective arms. Our rituals were a means of bringing God out of hiding, and yet we women were supposed to hide ourselves in so many ways. But then I started writing, and everything I wrote sounded prescribed and polemical. I found I had not been able to hear how my own voice had also been covered, as if hidden, until I read my poor efforts and it didn't sound like me.

So I started paying attention while writing to those tiny voices and odd little ideas that pop up in all of us from an unknown place, the very impulses our mothers and teachers and rabbis train out of us and call it self-control. Those voices and impulses became my most precious guide on the page. Which is why I think genuine writing has to be utterly free speech that is only filtered through, not defined by, rules . . . of craft, and then leaps beyond them. Meaning, after a life of hard rules, learning to write retrained my mind. The process un-socialized me, encouraged me to choose my rules and then use them only as a springboard. It seems I followed a perfect guide called *How To Become A Subversive*. Writers are dangerous.

As to the abortion, that moment in the book when I/she stood ready to overrule a rabbi in order to get what I needed, and then decided I would never submit my body to such control again, was the key turning point for everything that followed. The rabbi's admonishment never to speak of having had the abortion or of his support of it created enormous tension that then drove my journey. *Nigleh* versus *nistar* indeed. Secrecy pushed me toward revelation. Today, I have told and retold that story because the rabbi said not to.

What aspects of your religious life did feel real and authentic?

Although mikvah immersion is meant to purify a woman from her fearsome fluids so that her husband can dare touch her, in spite of this misogyny, the mikvah became a refuge, a woman's sanctum. I could linger there in a hot bath, then pad naked but for a towel to go immerse in the sauna-hot pool with a prayer on my lips. In the mikvah, the very body that we covered and were ashamed of, whose urges I suppressed, became the agency of prayer. A body prayer. Mikvah was the one place where I couldn't hide from myself, where I could hand God my secret self. Hovering beneath the surface, I imagined the water resonating with thousands of generations of women's hope and devotion and need.

What role does Judaism and faith play in your life today?

I do not, will not subject myself to any of Judaism's demands or that of any religion, and yet, after my years of being cut off as a woman specifically from the rituals that were the great heart of the religion, I'm fierce about my right of ownership. That's my inheritance: a wisdom legacy for each subsequent generation to peruse as they see fit, although I believe no one should so much as toy with sacrificing their own will in the process.

Regarding the body: *Your memoir spends a great deal of time depicting your very physical life among the Hasidim: we watch you getting dressed in a wig and modest clothes, bathing, immersing nude in the mikvah, inserting a diaphragm, having sex, in labor, bearing children, scrubbing, cleaning, cooking, comforting, mothering, writing—you are a single body in constant motion. And yet my sense at the end of the book is one of stillness. Can you look back and share your thoughts about the sheer physicality of it all? How has that changed?*

I think the success of the world's great religions is tied to their common demand on women—cover your body and hair (that is, suppress your individuality and creativity), marry young and have many children whether or not you are suited to the task, and live in service of perpetuating the religion into the next generation. We Hasidic women were both the healing and survival of a tortured people. "Rabbi Frumen" used to tell us that every diaper we changed was a holy act. Our endless work was supposedly our *shacharis*, our *tefilin*, our Torah study.

A key moment for me in the book was when Levi, who was undergoing chemo, stepped out of the shower without his beard. "It's just hair," he said. But it wasn't just hair. His beard was a symbol of our life for which he had sacrificed. I thought, what if these clothes and wig were just . . . clothes and a wig, and not a soul-saving gesture of obedience to God? What if all kosher food isn't the saving of the Jewish soul? What if it is just food? When symbols broke for us, I could finally see the sheer physicality, and the banality, of my life.

Before my book came out, I did a search and found almost no memoirs from any religion by formerly covered women who had given their lives over for years as religious wives and mothers as I had. I imagined the millions of them around the world who had also had their innate desire for the life of the spirit relentlessly redirected to dishes and laundry, that is, to sacrifice and self-effacement. That is a traditional woman's language of prayer. We tried to fill the gaps of loneliness or emptiness by absorbing the message as a mantra, clinging to those promises of God. It is that woman's life, and that self-delusion, that I tried to depict, and why my book is dedicated in part "to my covered sisters."

As to stillness, I'm happiest today when I get to stop my charge to absorb the physicality of the world. After years of Hasidic assertions of grandiosity: "God created the world for us. We alone can make Him manifest. Our every ritual changes the world. Light a candle and create a day. . . ." I treasure smallness, inconsequence, and mystery, without delusions. No one today can tell me that we never die.

Two sequences in your book come very close together. The abortion and then your sister's revelation that your father sexually abused her and probably you, as well. Both seem strangely self-determinative. Am I reading that right?

Yes. After the abortion, I became determined to own my body. Until I did so, I did not own my life. Those should be one and the same, my body, my life, but like women the world over it took a rebellious sort of courage to embrace this simple fact. Then I understood that my safety and my future had to remain in my hands—a strange notion for a Hasidic woman.

As a result, I was approaching middle age with the budding self-awareness of an adolescent, newly attuned to self-honesty, when my sister sat me down and told me about Daddy. When she did, she somehow sounded more real than any of the Hasidic aphorisms or mystical teachings or pithy stories meant to shape us that filled my days. I had tried to replace my family with the Hasidim. Now I was looking straight at the love that I had thrown out as well. After all those lonely years, I heard my sister saying *I am this story. You, too, are this story.*

Now I both owned my body and had begun to face and reclaim my past, thorns and all, as an irrevocable part of myself.

We have remained very close.

About the genre: Uncovered *is very different from other Off-the-Derech memoirs. Most of the others, for example, turn on the experience of victimization, while yours doesn't do that at all. Can you list in what ways your book is unique in the genre?*

- As far I've been able to ascertain, Uncovered is the first and so far the only non-heterosexual OTD memoir.

- Rather than in New York, the story is set in Texas, in one of the thousands of communities of acolytes led by Chabad emissaries around the globe.

- Uncovered is not a coming-of-age story; it turns in middle age. I remained in my Hasidic marriage nearly thirty years and had become a respected teacher and a formative presence in our community.

- I wasn't born among the Hasidim. I was a mid-continent public school girl. My book takes on a larger social and historical context, as I completed my move into right-wing religion on a college campus as part of a wave of young people doing the same across the country at the time. We were rebelling against our sixties liberal parents, incubating our country's political future.

- Since I wasn't born among them, it isn't written from the standpoint of an alien in American secular society, someone forced into exile.

- The narrative doesn't seem encapsulated in a Jewish milieu. The larger society is always there despite our efforts to isolate—the Challenger explodes, the Berlin wall falls, we are attacked on 9/11. These events tended to jerk us back into the American family.

- Although the story is sad at times, the book isn't pervaded with loss or with a sense of having been victimized. After all, I reasoned, I *chose* to be there, and there were reasons for that choice. The journey itself was formative.

- Like the others, my community rejected me when I left, but I wasn't alone. My mother and extended family were waiting with open arms. The ending of *Uncovered* is joyous.

- The book received significant attention in the secular press and praise from noted writers and award committees, garnering several awards.

- It was praised by Gloria Steinem and deemed a feminist memoir, bringing it to academic attention in Women's and Gender Studies departments.

- It had limited attention from Jewish book fairs and publications.

- Readership for *Uncovered* has been broad, across genders and faiths. It seems to be read as oddly universal, as a cautionary tale. The long-term consequences of my move toward right-wing religion took on powerful resonance as I traveled on book tour throughout most of the 2016 presidential campaign.

How do these differences relate to you as a writer?

As a child, I watched the magic of my mother's making her art, but I also had to find words on my own for all that she left wordless. That is, she made me a writer. Which is why, in the first few pages, I put a scene of watching her paint as a small child. To me, in every aspect of the book, *Uncovered* tells of my becoming a writer.

Emunah, the Hebrew word for faith, has the same letters as *amanut*, art, and *umanut*, craftsmanship, faith born of creative imagination. But the Hasidim understand the wayward power of that imagination. And they certainly know the impact of the written word. We were warned away from secular art, music, and literature. My first act of rebellion was to go to a public library, where I reached for, not comparative religion or its criticism, but poetry by women in searing voices that shocked me awake. Then I filled my children's lives with books, hoping to save them.

Excerpts from *Uncovered: How I Left Hasidic Life and Finally Came Home*

Leah Lax

18.

One by one as their eleven children enter adolescence, Rabbi Frumen and his wife have been sending them away to yeshivas, and of course the community is following their lead, at enormous financial strain. To be "exiled to a place of Torah," *goleh lemakom torah*, and experience displacement and sacrifice for the sake of Torah knowledge, is important for building Hasidic character. Rabbi Frumen insists he will never make a Hasidic high school in Houston.

Libby has grown up expecting to go away and now she is fourteen. Several of her best friends have already departed. She is eager to embark on this rite of passage. The yeshiva boarding school for girls will neatly skip her over that questioning, searching, rule-challenging age called adolescence. They will shave away the parts of her that don't fit their mold, seal her on the proper path. They will keep her away from boys and fill her with Hasidic philosophy, Hebrew, Yiddish, Torah, and prophets. Her secular education will be kept to a censored minimum. The teachers will glorify marriage and childbearing and a covered life, assuring her that by humbly conforming she will be granting the entire Jewish people a future.

"Let her go," a Hasidic neighbor tells me, "so that she'll come back to you." I imagine today that this advice might apply better to a

153

young adult than to a fourteen year old. But I don't want to confuse my daughter. In the end, I don't know how to do anything other than what we are supposed to do.

Teaching others to sin is a sin for which one cannot atone. I point the way for my daughter into a woman's covered silence. I lay out the path of self-sacrifice and send her on her way. This, then, is who she will be, who she will become. I send her. I do that.

∽

December, and another package arrives from Rosellen—*Writing Fiction: a Guide to Narrative Craft* by Janet Burroway. I dive in, but there is so much I can't grasp.

"Conflict" is a simple word, but when Burroway says one should write about conflict, she emphasizes unresolved conflict as most true-to-life. My sense of story was formed by Hasidic stories we tell at Sabbath tables and at rites of passage. In those, the hero stands up to forces against God, but in the course of the story, the conflict, inner or outer, is always resolved. Also in the texts we study, Truth is a clear singular ideal that one must work to discover by wading through contradictory notions until each is proven right or wrong. All contradictions and conflicts then evaporate, and that moment of clarification is Revelation. Which means that in the fiction stories from the library that I'm now reading, when I come across what Burroway defines as conflict, I tend to go back assuming I must have read something wrong. I don't understand unresolved conflict on the page or resolutions that aren't really resolutions.

On Rosellen's recommendation, I check out a book of stories by Alice Munro, only to find that every time I think I understand a character, he or she does the opposite of what I've come to expect. Munro's characters twist and turn, flip-flop with their feelings, and rarely resolve their conflicts, just live through them, and yes, change somehow, and move on. And yet, the stories captivate me. I think, but the people seem so real.

∽

Nineteen ninety-two. The Rebbe has had a stroke. All of Lubavitch is shaken. He's in a hospital in Manhattan with tubes and monitors and the sound of labored breathing. Groups of the faithful cluster on the sidewalk below his window reciting psalms. I go to Crown Heights to visit Leibl.

The annual Women's Convention is going on. Remembering the convention I once attended in Chicago, I make my way over worn red carpeting into the main session in the Oholei Torah ballroom, studded with yellowed chandeliers, to find myself once again in an enormous crowd of bewigged and faithful women. I take my place inconspicuous among them, as one woman after another ascends the podium to exhort and inspire us. And then the keynote: Rabbi Bentzion Teitel. A murmur spreads across the room. Rabbi Teitel is a highly respected figure, a thunderous voice in the movement

Standing above us, his sweeping gaze seems intent on exposing every truth, every sin. His monologue gradually rises in pitch, and then suddenly he shouts into the microphone. "Anyone here," he says in a loud accusing tone, leaving the phrase hanging.

Female humility before a rabbi grows huge. No one can hide. We wait.

"ANYone, who so much as imagines for a moment that the Rebbe cannot and WILL NOT stand up out of his hospital bed ON HIS OWN when he chooses, pull the tubes out of his body with his own hands and lead us AS THE MESSIAH to Jerusalem is *chaser emunah!*"

We have been accused with a nasty epithet for someone lacking faith. We have been shamed. The shame is palpable, choking us.

And finally, I'm furious. I want to jump up, open my woman's mouth in public and call out, "You are no prophet! I believe in God, not in you! Only God knows the future. The Rebbe is an old, sick man who has lived out his years!" But I don't. No one moves. We women don't move, save sideways glances. I wait, like the other women, clap, like the others, leave politely, like the others. I walk out invisible in the crowd, sick with myself.

I can't yet see the leaps in logic in the Rebbe's talks that kept us willing to submit ourselves, but when I leave Crown Heights, after hugging Leibl and bidding him good-bye, I leave behind the Rebbe as larger-than-life scholar and miracle worker and take with me only the picture of him as an old but very real man—blue eyes he once trained on me as a girl, white plastic reading glasses low on his nose, overdue for a haircut, his well-known habits of abundant cups of tea and too much salt on his food. A brilliant man, a scholar, but just a man. Soon, I think, he will die. So will we all.

∾

On the evening of June 12, 1994, the third day of Tammuz, the children bathed and in their pajamas, the year of mourning for my father
ends. I go to the soul candle I've kept burning through this past year,
take a used plate from the sink and cover the glass cylinder. I watch
as the flame chokes and shrinks down to an orange ember then slowly
flicks out. I lift the plate and a languid gray line ribbons upward from
the dead ember. Memories of my father have caught me at the oddest
times through the year. It's a relief to move on. "Now we can have
music!" I announce, and soon lively klezmer fills the house. Itzik and
Shalom and Avrami dance on the blue carpet sea to laughing clarinets,
and I dance with them while Mendel and Sarah watch and chatter and
laugh. Shalom breaks loose, runs in circles, jumps on the couch. Late
that night, as I sleep a rare deep sleep, the Rebbe dies.

All of the men of our community fly to New York, so that many
overlapping accounts will filter back through our community. Levi meets
Leibl on the street in Crown Heights, and they join the mourners,
10,000 strong, walking behind the hearse performing final kindness of
accompanying the Rebbe's dead body to the grave. Wives and sisters
and young children look down from brownstone windows as a vast field
of black hats blocks Eastern Parkway for miles.

And yet, many whole families walk in the crowd, women and
children as well. They plod, heads down, solemn. Men openly cry, tears
glistening beards and falling on black coats. Levi and Leibl pass clusters
of followers in frantic celebratory song and dance, arms on shoulders,
around and around. They have brought musical instruments to announce
the Rebbe's resurrection. The Messiah is here! They sing and play. Long
live the Rebbe, the King! He died for our sins. Long live Our Master,
our Teacher, our Rebbe, King Messiah forever! He will rise again! The
music glitters over the flowing somber crowd as aloof policemen watch
from the sidelines.

∾

The *yahrzeit* anniversary of my father's death bleeds into the Rebbe's.
Now they are both gone, and the dancing Hasidim sicken me.

∾

I continue my fevered nighttime writing, but I'm beginning to notice how I tend to slip into polemics, that religious voice implanted in me long ago. Late one night, I stop and print out what I've written, then read it out loud in the dim light. Levi moans a sleepy protest and turns over in his bed. The writing sounds contrived, insincere. I crumple the pages and pitch them into the trash. "The real truth is," I write Rosellen the next day, "I rage silently at the boring details that use my every minute and keep me from what I really want to do. I rage at housework and shopping and standing in lines. Then I swing to the opposite and submerge myself in family and home, where I find the daily sameness peaceful and reassuring—for a while. Until a niggling nervousness takes hold again." Admitting discontent is enormous new territory. "All those Hasidic women who feel important to God because they are bringing order to their families—I'd like to be like them, but I can't. Order is holiness, they teach us. But I need to form my own image and not just find it reflected in their eyes." I have written real unresolved conflict into a character that feels true for the first time. I print out the letter and put it in the mail.

∽

Another year passes, and tall, now-bearded Leibl transfers to yeshiva in Tzfat, Israel, ancient town of mystics. Libby is settled in a Chicago yeshiva, and now Mendel is going away. Itzik, Shalom, Avrami, and Sarah come to the airport, and we watch the plane pull back from the terminal. There's Mendel's soft face at one of the windows in contrast with the masculine thrusting power of revving motors, that inexorable mechanical drive. The jet way separates and folds in on itself like a discarded umbilical.

At the window, Avrami puts a hand on Shalom's shoulder. Each in turn is getting to be the oldest at home. Sarah is impatient to leave. She's satisfied to see her active, contentious brother depart, but I can't stop watching Mendel's childhood pulling away before it's over. The plane turns and heads down the tarmac. We stay until it is a speck in the sky.

At night, as my diminishing family sleeps, I wander into the den. I know Mendel won't become a Talmud scholar, that's not him, but I tell myself that he can plunge into a rowdy group there and at least still get to be a teen. There will be forays to the dorm rooftop at night for secret cigarettes, raiding the kitchen, fringes and yarmulkes flying in pickup basketball games, and in a couple of years, secret stashes of beer in the dorm, even clandestine calls to the kinds of girls who speak to boys. So why do I worry that this life robs my children of their adolescence?

Because he's not officially allowed to question. They won't foster questioning, or train him to formulate questions. And those he comes up with on his own he'll only get to pose to someone he respects if he is seeking clarification of the Law, not if he questions the Law itself.

I wonder if we are all frozen in some kind of pre-adolescence. Most of us never learned how to rebel or explore. Look at us, like children young enough to think their parents, the Law and the Rebbe, omnipotent. But I want to form questions, argue and sift, choose what I want in and leave the rest, like I once planned to do when I was a teen. Now I have to watch my children equally robbed.

I write Rosellen and describe the God I first met at Rabbi Rakovsky's Sabbath table—as multi-faceted as the human spirit, embedded in all things, nurturing and all-gendered, including the *shechinah*, the gentle ever-present Mother. It is this God, not the Law's stern authority, who fed my young dreams. So why is this very Jewish mystical God barely present in our masculine world of the Law? It wasn't supposed to be like this.

And yet, something is setting me more squarely in the present:

Dear Rosellen,

Itzik's biggest wish for his seventh birthday was a new bicycle and a turkey dinner. I located a refurbished all-but-new bike while he was still in school, drove out to the bike shop after I got the turkey in the oven and spent an hour in the crowded shop while they lowered the seat and handle bars, changed out the wheels for pedal brakes, put on better tires, and added a kickstand. You're not charging me more for this, are you? I dashed home with the little red bike in the back of the mom van. Just as the kids turned up the walk from school, I pulled up, and they came running.

Why did it take until the sixth child to be able to see this? It's the joy, pure and simple; no preaching, nothing sublime. Just a new red bike and the house filled with the smell of turkey dinner, Levi home early to share it with us.

You had to see Itzik dance. Three siblings to dance around him, ooh over the turkey, and take turns racing on the bike. Itzik throwing his arms around me again and again. Avrami, Sarah and Itzik in helmets and coats racing ahead on their bikes after dinner, helmets bobbing in the dark, the children glowing under the streetlamp where they stop to chatter and wait for me at each corner while I catch up on foot with little Shalom's sweet hand in mine. I've been moved all week by how simple it all is.

If I could, my birthday gift would be for Itzik to keep his joy in little things, and if that's not possible, to someday have a child like him to give him joy like I have.

Love,

Leah der Oysher (the Rich One)

But I lied. Levi didn't come home for dinner.

∾

Leibl calls from a pay phone in Tzfat where he's been in yeshiva for around six weeks. He talks about hiking the valley beneath his dorm with friends and about their trip south to the Dead Sea. Somehow he has made the transition to modern Hebrew, so very different from ancient texts—he laughs about a radio program and reports a conversation he overheard on a bus. But there's a loudspeaker and raucous singing in the background, some noisy march. Long live our Rebbe, King Messiah forever. "What is that?" I say.

"Guys get together and march around here," he says.

"Do they, like, carry posters?"

"Yeah, and there are bumper stickers and billboards around town." Pictures of the Rebbe's face next to 'The King Shall Live!' on sides of buildings, shop windows, car windows, telephone poles, in entries to buildings and private homes and yes, held high in impromptu parades by shouting young men. "I'm getting sick of that song," Leibl says. The noise only grows as the marchers pass. Our Master lives forever!

∾

November 4, 1995. For weeks, the Israeli right has been demonstrating against the peace accord that Primate Minister Rabin signed at Oslo. They were spurred on after he was awarded the Nobel Prize. Recently, a right wing organization named Eyal disseminated an image of Rabin in a Nazi uniform: Rabin's troubled eyes, his lined Jewish face and bushy gray hair, with a swastika on his chest. The posters appeared mysteriously across the country, then around the world. This is the climate in which Yitzchak Rabin arrives at Kings of Israel Plaza in largely secular Tel Aviv to give a speech at a peace rally. When he's done, amid applause and cheers, he descends the steps with his security detail toward a waiting car. A young bearded man in a yarmulke steps up and guns him down.

That night, in Tzfat, Leibl's dorm mates, study partners, hiking buddies, friends, with whom he floated in the Dead Sea and laughingly smeared mud on one another, gather and march in wild celebration. My son watches from the window of his dorm room. The boys march over the cobbled streets under street lamps, under the stars, mountains as a backdrop, singing, shouting, passing bottles of vodka. A single huge moving shadow follows them, and then on to the yeshiva where they force open the door to the study hall. Inside, they pass more bottles, jump on tables and dance. "The Nazi is dead!" they cry. "He slept with our enemies! The messiah is coming! The Rebbe is coming back to us. Long live the Rebbe!"

The heavy door opens. In walks the Rosh Yeshiva, rabbi director, in his grave, long beard, black coat, deep voice. "Get down," he says. "Leave. NOW."

The next day, all is decorum again in the study hall. The boys are grouped around a long table over open books, quiet, some a little hung over, the rabbi holding forth. Leibl is among them. The murderer, Yigal Amir, member of Eyal, is in jail. His trial will be quick and superfluous, but that is irrelevant; time is stopped here. In the study hall, there is no Rabin, no politics, no world. God's Word is justice. The rabbi unravels the Talmudic logic one thread at a time. One of the boys rubs the back of his neck. Another twiddles his ritual strings. Brows furrow. The low buzz of a lazy fly. Three policemen enter.

One of them announces the name of the boy sitting next to Leibl. The boy stands slowly on shaking legs. He is sixteen. "You made the poster," the policeman says.

"Do you have a warrant?" the rabbi says. "Proof?"

The policeman speaks to the boy. "We have your father. We'll release him when you give yourself up."

❧

"You think this is a democracy?" Leibl shouts into the phone to me the next day. "You can get picked up for what you think here. They're arresting religious Jews all over the country."

"Had that boy's father done anything?" I say.

"Nothing," he says. "They took him without a warrant, then used him as a trap."

"Those boys were wrong, celebrating like that," I say.

The yeshiva director found his car vandalized the next day. "The kids here are not who I am," he says. "Get me out of here!"

❧

Now it's a year and a half later, April, 1997, on the last day of Passover. The sky is streaked near sunset, flocks of northern birds pausing for the night on their migration back home. Leibl dropped out of rabbinical training and transferred to a yeshiva in New York that grants a high school diploma. He reads secular books and follows politics and wants to leave yeshiva. In Houston, our neighborhood has also changed. Dollar stores have replaced boutique shops. The nearby shopping center is strewn with trash and sullen teens loiter around signs that warn against shoplifting. The same tense Hasidic/black schism I once saw in Crown Heights is evolving here.

I've also changed, mostly through reading and writing to Rosellen, who has moved away to Chicago, but I hold on for the kids, in spite of the long, slow-growing split in me. But nothing has changed in the synagogue, and today, Avrami is exultant. Today is the last day of Passover, and this is his thirteenth birthday. We'll make a feast next Sabbath to celebrate his bar mitzvah, but today in the open hall we've set out tables laden with piles of handmade matzohs—uneven rounds with acrid, burnt edges, and many bottles of kosher wine, nothing more. This is the Meal of the Messiah. We flew Leibl, Libby, and Mendel home for this and for the bar mitzvah—Avrami sits with his father and brothers. The men of the community gather and take seats at the tables with

Rabbi Frumen presiding. Levi presented Avrami with his first black hat in honor of this arrival into manhood. It is new and big for his boy face.

I sit behind a partition with Levi's mother, Libby, and Sarah, the only females here—Mrs. Frumen and all the other women are busy at home with Passover work. Besides, the community views this special final Passover gathering as a ritual for men.

At a signal from Rabbi Frumen, the men begin the seven *nigun*, wordless songs of the Alter Rebbe. Each is another rung on a ladder to heaven. Rabbis, professionals, laborers, doctors, young, old—the song rises in its rich minor key. Community, family, and God form a kind of silent harmony. Avrami closes his eyes, grips the front of his chair and rocks as he sings. A cup of wine, a bite of matzoh, another song, another cup. The group is lost in the winding heart of the melody, bodies and hearts open, heads back in song. Rabbi Frumen gestures to our son.

Quiet. Eyes open. Avrami begins reciting the impossibly complex bar mitzvah discourse, from memory, in a singsong. "*Isa bemedrash tilim*," he chants in his boy voice.

Usually when a bar mitzvah boy recites this difficult discourse, the group soon interrupts with cries of mazal tov to give the boy a break, but Avrami continues without pause. For twenty-five minutes there's no other sound in the room, his young voice a new note in harmony with their lingering song. When he finishes, he is breathless with triumph. There are cries of mazal tov, and then a new jubilant tune. Praise God that He chose us as His alone! The men laugh and clop the table to the dancing rhythm. Amid that, Avrami suddenly launches out of his seat, runs over behind the partition to us and throws his arms around his grandmother and then around me. In my arms, he says in my ear, "This is my real bar mitzvah." Just wine, rough handmade matzoh burnt on the edges, song, and arrival.

༄

"We will stand by Leibl," I say to Levi, "or lose him." I just stopped my husband in the living room and demanded he listen.

"What are you saying?"

"Leibl is not staying in yeshiva. He's not becoming a rabbi. He says he's going to college."

Leibl purchased books and studied on his own for months, then took the SAT and achievement tests and did very well.

Levi says little, but he acquiesces.

In May, Leibl is accepted to Rice University in Houston. After years away, Leibl, our glorious new rebel, is coming home.

Another day, after he's moved back in, I find Leibl and his father deep in conversation in the den, Levi reminiscing about his happy years studying math and physics at the University of Pennsylvania. Levi is nostalgic, his face open. Leibl leans forward, eager to hear.

Avrami, too, leaves for yeshiva in Chicago. I keep thinking I will round a corner in the house and find him—on his stomach, head propped on his fists playing a board game with Itzik, flashing his smile and the dimples that embarrass him. Tearing down the street on his too-small bicycle. Cracking one of his wry jokes at the Sabbath table.

Although only the three youngest are at home now, it is still easy to stay caught up in kids' growth and drama, easy to avoid the mirror, easy to pour myself into writing at night to avoid quite existing during the day. I could let more years pass this way. Then one day Mendel calls from a pay phone and mentions the latest gossip: a teenaged boy at the Lubavitcher yeshiva in Manchester, England, committed suicide by jumping off his dorm roof. There is no official word, but the gossip has spread through the web of boys in Lubavitcher yeshivas. They say the boy was gay. He killed himself because he was gay.

I hang up and double over. Can't breathe. I feel his overwhelming despair at a world that rejects what he is. I see him going up those lonely stairs and walking out on the roof; I squeeze my eyes shut, but can't shut out the image.

I don't sleep. I carry that boy with me into the next day and the next. I don't understand why I do that. I do and I don't, but the boy haunts me. He had nowhere to turn, no way to be himself without destroying his life. He was forced to choose between rejecting his life as he knew it, or ending it. He chose.

I am a 'we.' The community. We made his tragedy inevitable. He killed himself because he believed what we teach and so he couldn't bear his own heartbeat.

He is my children. He was forced into soldier-like "adulthood" that tries to kill parts of his soul.

Then, a deep enigmatic empathy whispers to me that I know that boy from the inside. I know him. I dream him. I dream I am him: Someone forces me into a gilded cage where I live day after day. Finally, I escape and climb to the roof. In the dream, my final jump is one of wild abandon. I am weightless at last against a forgiving sky.

～

Late June. I take Itzik and Shalom for free tennis lessons at a city tennis center nearby. I convince another family to send their two boys along. The four jump out of the car and dash off to the courts impervious to steam and sun and deafening cicadas, oblivious as well of their yarmulkes and closely cropped skulls, or of the fact that they are the only white kids in the class. I settle in to wait for them on a cracked vinyl sofa in the tennis house with my new secondhand laptop, grateful for the frigid air conditioning. Of course the gay boy in England comes back to me. He's a frequent companion. I sit back, sigh. But there's gossip in the community every year about yet another boy "like that" expelled from a yeshiva, always followed by appalled comments about how the family will be marked now and the siblings will pay. I think, what does it mean that I feel I know something I've never experienced? I want to write what life was like for that boy day-to-day.

Every morning the boys in Hasidic yeshivahs are bused to a mikvah where they strip and jump in together as spiritual preparation for morning prayers. Afterwards, they shower all at once, locker room style. Among all that male flesh, the boy who jumped from the roof must have felt like any other young man would feel if asked to socialize, nonchalant, among a group of milling naked women. Day and night, the boys share intimacies, eating, drinking, dressing, learning together. They dance arm in arm.

My shadow yeshiva boy is awash in hormones. Forbidden thoughts and fantasies plague him. He is painfully self-conscious about where he puts his gaze and terrified of betraying himself with a glance at a boy. But he loves yeshiva life. He loves deciphering cryptic holy texts, loves the sense of God at his sleeve, loves the camaraderie, and feeling certain of what is good and right. And he loves his father, hopelessly. He treasures his father's support and approval.

Sitting there on the vinyl sofa, an old air-conditioning window unit as clattering backdrop, I wander through the boy's conflicted life, the intensity of his young devotion, his confusion as he comes to know himself. I feel what that boy feels. I want what he wants. A lump of empathy sits in my throat. A fictional young man takes form. I name him Berkeh.

At the mikvah, Berkeh won't get undressed with the others. He stays in the waiting area, but the boys wander through, naked or half-dressed, youthful sinewy bodies shining with droplets in glistening wet hair. Sitting there, Berkeh's hand clenches as if grasping something. He tries to train his eyes on the white floor tiles, wishing the same blankness on his mind.

When the boys finish their tennis lesson, they pile back into the car smelling of sweat, red-faced and chattering about the teacher, scores, and other boys at the lesson, particularly the ones they envy. I drive home immersed in Berkeh yet unaware of parallels between our lives.

On another day on the vinyl sofa in the tennis house, I meet Berkeh's study partner, Shlomo. Shlomo is his friend since their days in summer camp, and Shlomo is in love with him. Berkeh is deeply attached to Shlomo, but Berkeh is an admired scholar at the yeshiva. He works hard to resist Shlomo's attention. Then the principal/rabbi recommends Berkeh to the chief benefactor of the yeshivah to go on a date with the man's daughter as a candidate for marriage. This is an enormous honor, and Berkeh is thrilled. He knows his father will be proud. Berkeh will be celebrated by his community. He will be everything he has been raised to be.

He goes out with the girl. "You're different from the others," she says. She leans close to him. She reaches her hand to his face and holds it there a whisper beyond the forbidden touch, her fingers trembling.

When the whole yeshiva is invited to the wedding of a former student, Berkeh throws himself into the celebration, imagining his own forthcoming arrival as a full-fledged community member—a married man, finally able to take his adult place among them. He sees the girl he dated dancing on the other side of the partition and jumps into the men's circular dance. Tiny cups of vodka shots are passed as they dance and Berkeh downs each one with abandon. Soon there are circles within circles of dancing men. Berkeh is reeling from alcohol, loud music beating in his head. But each time he sights Shlomo he moves closer to the innermost group until he is thrown into the center to dance with the groom. The two then dance, around and around, surrounded by men singing, stomping, cheering them on. Then the groom lets go to honor another and Berkeh nearly falls. He staggers away—into Shlomo, who seems to have been waiting. The two then begin to dance, slowly, then faster, whirling to the music, gripping forearms, and it seems to Berkeh that the men have formed a circle around them instead of around the groom. The laughing music deafens him, fills him. He sees boys laughing and pointing at them, and he laughs, too. There is nothing left but the pulse beat of Shlomo's arms on his palms and the music beating in his head as they dance. The room flies, blurred laughing faces rush past as tears course down Berkeh's cheeks.

I don't notice that Berkeh is the same age I was when I married, although I do know, if I were to let the story continue, that Berkeh would marry the girl who almost touched his face. I also know, and shudder, that the story is best ended where I've stopped, that if I were to let the story go on, he might kill himself.

I drop off my children's friends at their home and then turn into our driveway. Itzik and Shalom run into the house, the very walls quivering from their boyish energy as they inhale sandwiches and apple juice and then rush out to their bicycles. I step outside as they charge down the street. Watching them, I feel certain that, for Berkeh, there is no resolution.

∼

Rosellen drops postcards, notes, a thoughtful line, but rarely writes me back with the real engagement I continue to invite. I am unaware of the deluge I have made her withstand with all of my letters—four years'-worth now—have had no thought of the raw need that must leap out at her when she opens one of them. I've grown impatient with our one-sided correspondence, don't recognize that she has continued to proffer exactly what I want and need: honest connection, mutuality, rare freedom to speak my mind.

One day, dishrag thrown over my shoulder, I wipe wet hands on my apron and go outside to collect the mail. There in the blazing heat, I pluck out an envelope in Rosellen's confident script. In it, she apologizes for not holding up her end of the correspondence. I wipe sweat from my face. My mentor is tired, urging me to go on without her. "Sometimes," she says, "I drop your letter on the 'Leah' pile as if I've touched fire. It's very hard for me to feel I can respond to your self doubt when I think of the book you should be writing." I laugh to imagine myself in the secular world as a published author. But my laugh has an empty sound.

~

Along with studies in computers and math at Rice, Leibl dives into classes in psychology of the brain, art history, and fencing. He explores cultural programs, student groups, sports, political causes, finds friends that will last for years. Gradually his beard and yarmulke disappear and he blends exuberantly into the world—as I hold even tighter to the outward scrim of my life, now a thin brittle thing. I tell myself I do it for the children, afraid if I change I will bring down the walls of their home. Meanwhile, Leibl disappears for days at a time, sleeps on couches in friends' dorm rooms, studies in the common room of his college through whole nights, only to burst thrillingly through the front door at odd times with a load of laundry, calling out, "Is there food?"

There are still moments in my Jewish days that hold true: when my flaming match touches the wick of the Sabbath candles—the fizz, catch, rising fire—and the moment my head slips beneath mikvah water when I float under the surface and see bubbles, a weightless hand, a blue veil over everything. In that underwater passageway, I think, so many have come through here hoping to emerge into a different life. A different self.

That Sabbath not long ago—when I closed the book of Torah for the last time only to find myself aroused by lesbian poetry as children piled toys on the carpet—that Sabbath began a dance of intertwined desire and religious doubts. I drift into hilarious fantasies of making love to Adrienne Rich. And I no longer tell myself I just dreamed I was a man; in those dreams I am a woman making love to a woman. I still shudder at the word 'lesbian,' but I know myself now.

After a hiatus of many months, I write helplessly to Rosellen. I tell her not to think my letter demands she respond, but that I need to write, need to talk, out of "a kind of desperation."

~

"When I do read Torah now I find (dare I say this?) a web of party lines. I've denied for so long that a life in Torah is artificial. Is it part of aging, to realize that the structures we build around us are artificial even though we still see beauty in them?

Maybe it's okay that my children will inherit my ambivalence. If I hand them only conviction, they could turn away from our ways with the same strength I once turned *toward* the faith. With ambivalence, there's nothing clear to rebel against—maybe that's the ironic key to Jewish survival."

And then, discovery:

"Doubts and the need to critically assess must be part of the human condition. But a big part of our faith is to deny those doubts. Do we as Hasidim deny our humanity?

I have begun to smell pretense in our communal gatherings, and the Jewish observance in our home feels like a fragile old shell. I now understand how denial creates a false self. Am I teaching my children a lie?"

❧

"I am bereaved," Rosellen writes, "to think that you feel the need to join me in the land of skepticism."

"Perhaps," I write back, "a small part of my soul never left."

But our faith had written so much of my mothering. Did you say a blessing over that apple? Straighten your yarmulke. That skirt's getting short. Thank God—don't forget to do that. And in the face of their disappointments and childish frustrations: It was meant to be. This also is for good. You are my little soldier. Now, I hardly know what to say. I become tongue-tied, inept with them. It shouldn't be this way. I'm still their mother. I still start the day with lists, hunt down each one to report on comings and goings, make sure each has eaten and done homework. I settle arguments, or not, take one at a time to sit down so that I can listen to their day. It's not right that I feel like a sham just because I wear this skirt and wig while a different more real person struggles to emerge.

I want to tell my children that I don't believe so much about our life anymore, but I don't dare. If I could, I'd say: It isn't important to me if you recite the right prayer or wear the right clothing. Just know yourself. Don't go forward without that, like I did. Don't be dishonest with yourself and with people you love, or with God, like I have been.

If I change, if I get honest, will you know me?

∽

Early spring, months after writing Berkeh. Our suburban neighborhood is abloom with azaleas, hibiscus coming into bud, magnolias opening plate-sized grandiosity, and the sun is warm and still benign in a clear sky. Vee lines of Canada geese are like arrows pointed home. I pull out of a grocery store parking lot thinking about necessary losses. Then, I have a moment of impulsive insanity, telling myself I better move faster than I can think. I turn the opposite direction from home and speed across town to the University of Houston. I park illegally, stop two book-laden students for directions, and lift my skirt to climb the stairs of Cullen Hall to the cluttered office of the graduate Creative Writing Program. "You want an application?" the clerk asks. "The deadline is in two days."

At home, I pull out one of my stories, this one about Munya, an old Russian immigrant woman who works nights as a mikvah attendant. One night an unmarried woman arrives in pants and uncovered hair wanting to immerse. She is hoping the mikvah will cleanse her of her secret that she was raped as a child. Munya feels so compelled to help her she steps outside the Law for the first time. When the woman stands before her naked in the water she speaks her own prayer, in her own words: "Today I will allow myself to be a woman."

I attach the story to the application. But the second page of the application says, "List Here All of Your Awards and Publications." I leave it blank. Rosellen faxes a letter of recommendation hours before the deadline. Then, I tell Levi. I don't ask him. I tell him.

Incredulous, he sweeps his arm outward, taking in the house, the kids. "What about us?" he says.

"I won't get in," I say, "but if I do, we'll manage."

In May, there's a letter with official letterhead. "We are very sorry to inform you . . ." it says. I don't read the rest. I tear the page up, let the pieces fall, walk away.

And here is Levi—it has been months since we touched—rising from his chair, picking up the torn pieces from the floor.

"It's no use," I say. "Don't bother."

He fits the pieces together, then reads what he can. "Wait," he says. "It's not so bad."

"I don't care," I say.

"No. Look," he says. "You're on the waiting list." He reads out loud: "Please contact us so we may know how best to reach you."

I turn back, stepping close to the heat and weight of him. I take what is left of the letter from his hands, and my fingers brush his—they are cool, rough, dry. I look up into his eyes. Where have you been, I think. "Oh," I say. "Oh."

∼

Late August, and I'm running up the stairs of the Roy Cullen Building at the University of Houston. My foot catches in the skirt and I almost fall. I am so nervous. And then I'm on the landing. It's a little dingy around here. But I have arrived. Where are the trumpets?

An older man approaches; dark hair clipped short, sagging cheeks, small dark eyes, sharp, and intent. He's holding a briefcase and a sheaf of unruly papers. "You're a new face," he says.

"Yes," I say, and I freely offer my hand to a man perhaps for the first time as an adult. But of course his hands are occupied. There's an awkward moment.

"Name?" he says.

"Leah Lax."

"Oh, I have your short story right here somewhere," he says, glancing at the papers about to fall. "We have a new mentorship program. I'm to be yours." He is author Daniel Stern.

I start graduate classes, including Dan Stern's Fiction Writing Seminar, and the Hasidic community seems to drift away. I stop going to the synagogue or community gatherings. When I do run into any of the women, they seem proud of me, but there is a clear expectation that I will extract from university only the knowledge I need to develop my skills without succumbing to unkosher ideas. I am to show the world how Hasidim can be educated without compromising our religion. I expect this is what Levi also trusts, hopes, expects of me.

Oh, but it is stunning to see the quality of thought and creativity that happens when nothing is censored. But this place is outrageous in its freedom. I had wanted to rise above my life to a place without stricture, but this is the stratosphere.

One night, I sit working on a critique of a fellow student's story for Dan Stern's class—we have to critique one another's work each week—but the story disturbs me. The character cuts himself and then sinks into a dream state of pain that is ecstasy. This is the fourth story with self-mutilation in it this semester. I can't understand someone using pain to fight pain, can't imagine perverting oneself into becoming your own enemy, can't see my own life.

The next day, I go in early to class like a gremlin, take out a blank sheet of paper and write out in large capitals, "WELCOME TO DAN STERN'S SELF-MUTILATION WORKSHOP." I post the sign on the outside of the door. I'm secretly reprimanding the students, sure, but I am also having a hard time adjusting to no censorship at all. The air is too rarified and I've been getting the bends. Later, I won't be proud of posting that sign, censoring them like that. The students arrive, laugh at the sign and take their places. Dan comes in last. He looks angry and rips it down. "Who did this?" he says. No one says a word. I think, at least I made them laugh at themselves. Cutting scenes disappear from future stories.

The program includes extensive studies in literature and criticism. I'm an eager greenhorn in skirt and scarf. I read fifty books the first year and keep a log. I fill notebooks with scribbles in the margins: Read Foucault! Look up: hegemony, *sui generis*, epistemology. Sometimes I withdraw, chagrined by my puppy enthusiasm, but that doesn't last, not with so much to learn.

I take a fiction seminar with author Robert Boswell (we call him Boz), who talks weekly about the importance of irony in our writing. The first time I hear him say that word, I go home and stare uncomprehending at an apparently simple definition in a dictionary wondering why can't I get this? Why can't I ever recognize irony on the page or imagine how to write it? Boz hammers the issue week after week and my problem with irony becomes a little secret crisis. He says irony is a clash of opposites, when someone says one thing but means another, or an event occurs in direct contradiction to the tone already set—a comic event at a funeral, stolid lethargy in the middle of a rushing crowd, an expression of hatred spoken in a tender voice. I am stymied by that, by the way he's asking me to embrace two opposites at the same time.

This is when I begin to understand that my mind has been trained to squelch contradictory ideas or feelings, so that now it's difficult to acknowledge or write about such conflict. As a Hasidic woman, if choice 'a' is true, choice 'b' must be false. One path. Everything is right OR wrong. Good OR evil. And I have to label it as such. I think could both be true at once, without resolution, or judgment, or labels? Can I acknowledge that, write that?

Trying to understand all of this feels like my mind is being punched into three dimensions, like a cartoon character that has been steamrolled, then, toddling away into the world, pops into herself. Pop. Pop. Pop.

With this new vision, the world changes. People become fascinating bundles of contradictions without labels or judgment. Events are the same. I no longer need to draw conclusions; I just want to get close and examine all the strands and colors and surprises.

There are so many new rules in writing. True to form, I work to learn and follow the rules. And yet, gradually I begin to understand that I own these rules for my writing self, and they don't own me. That's when I become a writer. And an adult.

I'm changing. Maybe it's reading all those books, each with a different standpoint or philosophy, each with a different heart, forming in my mind a new collection of voices that aren't a Group in lockstep. Maybe it's all the time I'm spending outside of Hasidic land in heady academic freedom. I don't know. But now I can see that religious life had filled me with grandiose convictions, made me believe I knew God's words and thoughts and that I truly changed the world with the strike of a match or the proper tying of shoes, and now I just feel small and ineffective. I think, is this what the world out there is? No clear path. Just an enormous jumble of conflicting beliefs, events, personalities, desires, and nothing I do will change it? I'll die, a blip, and leave no mark at all. And it doesn't matter how I tie my shoes.

∽

Yet, after all the years in black and white, I still don't even quite know what color is.

And although I now see paradox and irony everywhere I turn, I'm little prepared to deal with it. I'm a child in the secular world, or a new immigrant, without insight or reference points. In class and in the student lounge, I sidle up to conversations but they talk about movies and television shows and politics and I don't know most of what they're talking about. Students meet and hang out in bars and coffee shops and restaurants where I wouldn't know what to order or how to figure tax and a tip.

~

I throw myself into schoolwork while trying to keep up with house and children, too often coaching one of the older ones over the phone. Find two packages of hot dogs in the freezer. Set the oven on three fifty. Keep an eye on it! At home, I do housework as if it is vital, but I do it as if I have been robbed.

Conversation that never happened, with the Group— Greek Chorus with a Yiddish Accent: in which I finally talk back

Me (pointing an accusing finger): Now I know you showed me only what you wanted me to see of the world. You said the world was full of filth and lies. You made me miss living.

GCYA: We told you, we told you, about the pig that shows its cloven hoof to fool us into believing it is kosher. In the world, nothing is as it seems. Be careful, we said. Evil is mixed with good, good with evil. Don't claim we said otherwise.

Me: Then you consoled me by claiming reality was just a bad dream, and your dream of perfection was reality. You did that to make me turn my back on the world and accept your Torah. Now the world has passed me by.

GCYA: But we did say truth has many facets. Don't accuse us of simplistic ideas.

Me: That never helped. You warped my mind, pressed it flat.

(group fades away)

~

I read Robert Lowell's poetry and note his despair when he lost his faith. I write Rosellen. "Someone should have warned Lowell that developing himself as a writer would demand such brutal self-honesty that he would never be able to embrace religion wholeheartedly again" I write, "I wish I could have warned him. I would have told him that the analysis writing requires of you is going to break down all of your illusions, your props against the wind. Stop! I want to tell him, because faith is our most precious illusion, impossibly fragile when the screen obscuring the world is removed. Stop! Because you can't stay happy if you don't stay blind. Lowell didn't stop believing in God," I write her. "He lost his ability to find Him."

In class and out, I try to engage fellow students in conversation, but there is a wall between us I can't breech. They aren't forthcoming, never available for coffee, and I don't realize it could be how I look. Then one day I find real live gay students congregating in the student lounge, full of ease and brazen humor. I sit down on the periphery of that golden group in my long skirt and scarf. They fall silent, and then quietly disperse.

I switch to shorter skirts. The scarf slips back on my head. I lose the pantyhose. When I run into one of the Hasidic women at the grocery store, she looks at my exposed hair and bare legs and drops her eyes. No one calls me any more to supervise a mikvah immersion or teach a class.

I dream I am walking through a watery universe that is actually a giant mikvah. All of the group is here under the water, Mira, my old mikvah buddy who barely speaks to me now, Shterna, who brushes past when we meet, no more late night chats, Rabbi Frumen and his angry righteous wife, even Levi. There are children everywhere in this watery world, ours included, playing, jumping, and no one seems to notice that no one can breathe or that the water is contaminated with human waste. But I'm just a visitor, soon to leave.

And yet, in waking life I continue going to the mikvah each month. I do it with dismay, with spiritual greed. I go in spite of new awareness of misogyny and primal fear of a bleeding woman that informed these laws and now stains the process for me. For seven days after my period ends, I perform the internal inspections to make sure I've stopped bleeding. I formally count the days, and take care not to touch Levi. But that moment when I emerge from the chest-high water, stand back up and turn toward the damp tiled wall to mouth ancient words is the only time left when I can pray. Naked in the mikvah, I know who I am. Rabbis and their books are gone. I wonder, what will happen to me now?

PART II

ANALYSIS

Between Us

Intimacy in Women's Off-the-Derech Memoirs

Jessica Lang

Memoirs and other forms of life writing that range from the more formal—autobiography—to the informal—personal blogging—are often identified as sites where authors excavate and lay bare a version of themselves that is not otherwise available. These revelations are accompanied by emotional affect (e.g., shame, despair, triumph) all of which work to create an aura of intimacy for readers. Janet Mason Ellery, in her powerful personal essay in which she publicly acknowledges for the first time her pregnancy, at the age of sixteen, and the forced adoption of her newborn daughter, creates sustained moments of narrative intimacy—we learn of her grief, her pain, all of which are tied to physical experiences—that feed an intimacy with her reader. Joan Didion's *The Year of Magical Thinking* offers intimacy in a different form: in spare, simple, repetitive prose that is startlingly without affect, Didion emphasizes subjectivity—"I"—inviting her readers to occupy her position as their own. This forms yet another means of intimacy. The fact that memoir is often criticized, both by readers and by their authors, for inauthenticity, for being more caught up with narrative than history, does little to change the author's attempt and desire to establish a specific and "open" relationship with her reader and the reader's understanding that he or she will encounter personal, private, and intimate revelations over the course of the reading encounter. Indeed, the outrage incurred by the revelation of false memoir is at least in part tied to a sense of betrayal on the part of the reader that the moment of revelation, a moment of truth-telling and identity-formation, in short, a moment of closeness between author and reader, has been falsified and rendered inauthentic.

In contrast to Ellery and Didion's memoirs, and to those written by many other authors, off-the-derech (OTD) memoirs, memoirs that explore departures from the strict religious practices, or path ("derech" means "path" in Hebrew), of ultra-Orthodox Judaism, document and centralize a struggle with intimacy. While integral to memoir writing more generally, intimacy plays a heightened role in OTD memoir because of the tension it carries. Intimacy offers a particular vantage point, a lens through which authors explore not only personal experiences about themselves but also the sharing of these experiences, their telling, which is, in short, the production (in the case of OTD memoir a mitigated one) of an intimate reading encounter. In other words, memoir as a genre typically reflects narrative intimacy—a closeness and familiarity that is encapsulated in the text—and engenders intimacy with its readers. I make the case here that the struggle to produce textual intimacy, and ultimately its failure, is, in fact, a central feature of OTD memoir, one that sets this particular brand of life-writing apart from other types of memoir. While most memoirs attend to intimacy through confession, illness, deformity, or a personal experience that has left a permanent marker, and this element is often where the center and the power of the text is located, OTD memoirs treat intimacy differently, unable to employ the range of narrative techniques that create or build intimate descriptions or intimate reading encounters. Indeed, in many OTD memoirs, narrative and reading intimacy is achieved during unsuspecting moments that have little connection or relationship to more typical representations of intimacy.

This essay focuses specifically on intimacy in OTD memoirs written by women. There are a number of reasons behind this narrower focus. First, while the complexity around intimacy plays a significant role in all OTD memoirs, those written by women tend to dwell more substantively and explore more deeply moments of physical intimacy and longing. In many ways this makes sense because of the expectation in ultra-Orthodox communities that women will devote themselves to child-bearing, child-rearing, and maintaining in all respects a kosher home—points I will explore at greater length in short order. Furthermore, not only is physical intimacy one of the most obvious forms of personal revelation in life-writing, and not only is it often used to explore, both literally and figuratively the subject of intimacy, but rumors around physical intimacy and sexual practices within the ultra-Orthodox community are rife in the secular world.[1] It is both surprising and telling that OTD women memoirists spend a good deal of time exploring sexual intimacy in their work. Within their communities, young women are typically educated about sexual intercourse only shortly before marriage and only in the briefest possible terms. Some women supplement this education by talking to friends, sisters, and reading books, usually forbidden, about the subject. In choosing to write openly and at length about their sexual histories, identities, and former and current practices, OTD women memoirists reject one of many practices that informed their upbringing.

A second reason that I focus here on OTD women memoirsists is because gender determines so much of one's existence within ultra-Orthodox communities. Women's voices and decisions within these communities are largely controlled by rabbinic (read: male) authority. I am especially interested in analyzing and considering forms of expression and narration by women because historically women occupy less public and less visible positions. This element of privacy and concealment, which is in part dictated, acknowledged, and enforced by husbands, fathers, and rabbis, leads to a complicated exploration of intimacy when women are outside of their native community. Finally, it seems to me clear that women authors of OTD memoirs are unabashedly feminist—that part of the memoir writing process for them has been a process of discovering their individuality, their voice, their presence in a culture—indeed, in an ancient tradition—that makes them feel invisible and mute. The vast majority of published OTD memoirs are written by women. One reason behind this gendered discrepancy may well be the symbolism that exists for women who not only leave their native communities but also insist on speaking about it, effectively becoming an authority figure of their own past. It is in many ways the ultimate rejection of their upbringing which positions authority in the hands of men who are strictly Torah-observant and learned in ancient Jewish text, law, and practice.

In keeping with my objective of a feminist literary critique of OTD memoir, I aim here to resist the formal traditional boundaries and hierarchies that so often define academic rhetoric. I take as my model here the work of literary scholars such as Carol Ascher, Janet Ellerby, Cheryl

Torsney and others who agree with Jane Tompkins's assessment that there "are two voices inside me . . . One is the voice of a critic who wants to correct a mistake . . . The other is the voice of a person who wants to write about her feelings (I have wanted to do this for a long time but have felt too embarrassed)."[2] Tompkins goes on to identify the limitations and problems with what she calls the "public-private dichotomy," the segregation of professional discourse, in this case epistemology, from personal feelings, even feelings about epistemology.[3] "The public-private dichotomy, Tompkins writes, "which is to say, the public-private *hierarchy*, is a founding condition of female oppression. I say to hell with it. The reason I feel embarrassed at my own attempts to speak personally in a professional context is that I have been conditioned to feel that way. That's all there is to it."[4] OTD memoirs, particularly those written by women, reflect Tompkins's gesture here. These writers, too, in ways that are complex and often excruciating, relinquish a cultural insistence that separates public from private. Women OTD narrators offer readers a story that many from within the ultra-Orthodox community believe is not theirs to tell. I mean this both in terms of the meaning the story conveys—it speaks out about feelings, practices and experiences that reveal details of a culture that is deeply insular, protective, and cut off from view. But I also mean, quite literally, that the telling itself is viewed as transgressive. Women's voices, especially in song and prayer but also, and by extension, in speech and narrative, are viewed as dangerously alluring and as such are forbidden. Like Maxine Hong Kingston, whose wrenching story of her aunt she describes in "No-Name Woman" is a determined gesture to go public with a story that has been declared a taboo family secret for decades, women OTD memoirists also raise their voices to share their vision of Jewish ultra-Orthodoxy, its legacy, and their view of it in a—and most certainly their—post-Orthodox world.

All OTD memoirs must, necessarily, invest a great deal in describing and explaining a world that for the vast majority of readers, even those with some familiarity of Jewish culture, remains largely unknown. The history of separation between public and private, and its attendant implications for men and women, remains a feature of the ultra-Orthodox landscape that is at once among its most visible and its most submerged.

On the surface, this separation seems quite simple and resonates with historical practices that place women largely in a domestic space that is often defined as "private" and men in more accessible, more visible spaces that are labeled "public."[5] But in fact, and as revealed in OTD literature, among other genres, this separation, both historically and in its evolution, is a great deal more complex in ultra-Orthodox society than a simple equation that identifies women with the private sphere and men with the public one. Sociologist Orna Blumen explores the more recent evolution of intersectionality between public life and the privacy of the home among ultra-Orthodox Jews who reside in an Israeli neighborhood. She notes that prior to the 1960s "Jewish ultra-Orthodox public space was almost entirely a masculine construct" but that in the past decade and a half, as women have in increasing numbers joined the paid work force to support their husbands' religious scholarship, they have introduced a "new definition of femininity," one that "legitimize[s] daily excursions and demarcate[s] the new ultra-Orthodox intersection of femininity, work and space."[6] Her conclusion, however, pierces any appearance of progressiveness: "[A]lthough the façade of the ultra-Orthodox public space has changed dramatically, this study has shown that neither women nor paid work have been accepted into the social negotiation as co-equals; rather, the restructuring of the public space scene has become more sophisticated so as to secure and re-encode the old ultra-Orthodox hierarchies within the modified façade . . . Consequently, men's presence and authority in the public space and the social negotiation are naturalized, while women, who obtained a license to enter the public space by virtue of their non-religious work, retain their lower-rank status."[7]

This is chiefly because any conception of "private" or "privacy" must take into account the observations of fellow occupants of that same space, their supervision, and the reporting structure that endorses this system. Furthermore, it is these complicated interactions between public and private that are, I believe, determinative in expressions of intimacy in OTD memoirs. There are several reasons for this: first, separation (both between genders and, in coordination with this, between public and private) resonates with feminist theoretical concerns insofar as it determines all aspects of presentation of the self in public arenas and, also, in private settings. And, second, because control over private space in ultra-Orthodoxy is nearly as determinative as that over public space, a condition that I will explore at greater length below. Therefore, the distinction of public and private for women and girls in ultra-Orthodoxy in many ways does not meet the conditions one might assume to be in place otherwise. That is, even in private spaces activities, behaviors and practices are watched, monitored and, if deemed necessary, reported. And while inner circles within private spaces may be limited to a single gender, in the space of the home it will be limited to women, ultimately the reporting structure is such that delinquent or transgressive behaviors are referred to rabbinic—i.e., male—authority.

To present one of the most telling examples of the complex interactions between public and private and its gendered implications, take the rituals around *niddah* and *mikvah* (sometimes spelled *mikveh*), which inform conjugal relations within the Orthodox community. Deborah Feldman opens chapter 6 of her OTD memoir, *Unorthodox*, provocatively: "*Niddah*, says my marriage teacher, literally translates as 'kicked aside,' but it doesn't really mean that, she rushes to assure me. It's just the word used to refer to a woman's 'time,' the two weeks out of the month when she is considered impure according to Judaic law . . . A woman becomes *niddah* or 'kicked aside' as soon as one drop of blood exists her womb. When a woman is *niddah*, her husband cannot touch her, not even to hand her a plate of food. He cannot see any part of her body. He cannot hear her sing. She is forbidden to him."[8] If questions arise as to whether a vaginal secretion is in fact blood, one's husband is expected to bring evidence of the spot, usually on a pair of underwear, to a rabbinic authority for evaluation. Shulem Deen points to evidence of just this in his OTD memoir *All Who Go Do Not Return*, seeing a "pair of women's underwear" in a plastic bag that is hanging from the doorknob of a rabbi's basement study. Deen has gone to meet with this rabbi, who has a reputation for leniency, to request permission to practice birth control after the birth of his fifth child.[9] The scene implies that another husband, perhaps also seeking a lenient determination, has brought evidence of a possible impurity that the rabbi needs to evaluate.

Leah Lax, author of the OTD memoir *Uncovered*, refuses to go to the *mikvah* for an extended period of time in order to end the possibility of marital relations with her husband. Her decision not to go to the *mikvah* is born out of a sense of increasing awareness of her emerging sexual identity as a lesbian and, with that, sexual power. If she does not go to the *mikvah*, she is not available for sexual relations with her husband. After this abstention, she describes going to the *mikvah* "one last time, so that my touch won't be forbidden to Levi [her husband] . . . I follow all the rules. I count the Seven Clean Days after my period. Each day, I take a white square of cloth and swab inside to check for lingering blood, protecting Levi [her husband] from this ultimate impurity."[10] Her decision to go "one last time," to follow all the rules in order to see if she and her husband can achieve the kind of physical and emotional intimacy she longs for, doesn't lead to physical intimacy—but then, as Lax has repeatedly illustrated, they never had real physical intimacy. Knowing that this would be the final time she would try to meet her husband on what she grows to consider his terms, Lax chooses speech over action, and in his arms, her head against his chest, breaks "years of mutual silence" (338).

Sarah, a subject in Lynn Davidman's study *Becoming Un-Orthodox: Stories of Ex-Hasidic Jews*, is subjected to closer observation and tighter control by her husband. He "carefully kept track of the days of her period and the ensuing seven days during which she was still considered ritually impure and physical contact between them was forbidden. It felt to Sarah as if her husband had an internal clock; he was always aware of where she stood in her menstrual cycle. On the appropriate day . . . he would ask Sarah to prepare herself to immerse in the *mikveh*."[11] Davidman notes that, as with other women, Sarah recognized that she "had minimal control over her own body." The laws regarding intimacy required rabbinic supervision and so the separation between what can be considered "private" and "not private" become blurred.

Feldman finds the practice of *niddah* "a form of psychological torment," a pattern that leaves her "feeling perpetually unsettled" because it swings so regularly from "forced intimacy" to "feeling discarded and unwanted."[12] Her description of her experience of sex and all of its attendant practices and conditions—*niddah*; *mikvah*; the pressure to start a family—are marked by external pressure exerted by her husband, her extended family, the rabbis of her community, and even lay members of the community. These layers of communication and pressure are exposed because of the newlywed's failed attempts to consummate their marriage following the ceremony. Feldman is taken aback—"mortified"—by her mother-in-law's intervention: " 'My husband [Feldman's father-in-law] tells me it wasn't finished' " (170). The train of communication regarding the wedding night goes like this: Feldman's new father-in-law asked his son if he has consummated his marriage. The father-in-law tells his wife what his son has communicated, namely that the bride and groom have not yet had sexual intercourse. The wife tells the female members of her own and Feldman's family and also confronts Feldman directly. By the end of their first week of marriage, the rabbis, presumably the *beis din*, a board of legal judges, too, are aware of the "problem": "At the end of the week the rabbis say to call it quits because I am bleeding from all the irritation, and technically speaking there's no way to tell if that blood is coming from splitting the hymen, therefore rendering me impure. They rule that I am now *niddah* and must proceed like any other married woman to count seven clean days, or fourteen cloths, before immersing myself in the *mikvah*."[13] Sexual intimacy, as Feldman, Lax, Deen and others declare, is not the sole province of any one couple or any one person. It is adjudicated by rabbinic authority; family members weigh in with advice and admonitions; pregnancy, the sought after and highly visible consequence of intercourse, serves as public confirmation of a commitment to adhering to and strengthening the community through the birth of the next generation.

It is important to note that it is not only OTD memoirs that document resistance to the intrusiveness that inform the practice of *niddah* and *mikvah*. As social scientists Tova Hartman and Naomi Marmon reveal in their study of these issues among a small pool of Orthodox women in Israel, a range of responses emerged. "There were those who felt vehemently that the regulatory aspect of *niddah* itself impinged on their psychological and emotional well-being in ways damaging and profound. They felt subjugated, harassed, and in some cases abused by a rabbinic authority that intruded in the most private aspect of their lives, put their excretory functions on display, and exposed their sexuality for patriarchal supervision and control. Others also described the regulatory element of *niddah* as oppressive but seemed to mean it as a term of inconvenience rather than the more penetrating and severe connotations implied by the systemic critique."[14] Still others conducted themselves as Leah Lax did, using the laws around *niddah* and *mikvah* as a means to control their sex lives: "Because women are the arbiters of *niddah* observance, it also functions as a locus of women's power. By, for example, refusing to go to the *mikveh* or delaying their immersion, they command the *halakhically*—that is, legally—sanctioned authority to withhold sex from their husbands . . . Because Orthodox women are conscious of the potential to delay immersion and thereby halt sexual relations, this awareness serves as an instrument of power even when they choose not to act on it."[15] Importantly, women who are deeply committed to the practice of Jewish law, as well as many who identify as OTD, share a range of responses regarding the practices of *niddah* and *mikvah*, often identifying them as deeply burdensome, intrusive, and abusive. One Orthodox woman reports feeling "that it is the long hands of the rabbis of hundreds of years literally entering my body to check me."[16] Others use it as a means of self-empowerment and still others, among those who commit to its practice, celebrate it.

But no matter individual women's feelings regarding the practices around marital relations in the Orthodox and ultra-Orthodox communities, the *halakhic* (i.e., legal) standard directing *niddah* and *mikvah* ensure that sexual practices are not private activities. Sociologist Samuel Heilman confirms this in his study *Defenders of the Faith*. While recognizing that "the pleasures of sex" are among the "bodily pleasures that all people inevitably experience," Heilman notes that for contemporary haredim "one of the most difficult struggles of life is not to be overcome by the charm and seduction of these pleasures."[17] Heilman continues: "Among the haredim . . . sex 'is not perceived as a personal matter, an intimacy that occurs between man and women.' It is a religious obligation."[18] As a religious obligation, or mitzvah, sex and its attendant practices are subjected to a level of scrutiny and surveillance from many directions: the *mikvah* lady who inspects a woman's body before and as she immerses herself; the rabbi who evaluates stains on cloths or underwear; the family members who inquire about sexual intimacy during the early days of a marriage; the rabbinic counsel that rules on larger questions and issues, both deeply private and otherwise; community members who offer advice, interventions, counsel, and judgment. Thus even what most consider to be deeply intimate habits, practices, and bodily functions, those that are more conventionally associated with privacy—and, as such, serve as a reflection of some sense of personal autonomy—are in ultra-Orthodox communities not even relegated to a single-gendered space. Rather, they are presented and adjudicated in order to meet the *halakhic* standards established by the community.

∽

One trait shared by narrators of women's OTD memoirs is a recognition of the absence of boundaries delineating public and private. This recognition is shared with readers at different moments and with different voices. In moments of reflection, in which the author writes with all of her authority of standing outside the community, they are often embittered. Feldman's description of "psychological torment" and being "mortified" at her mother-in-law's intervention in her sex life are a product, in part, of her departure from the community and her consequent ability to voice the feelings she was unable to publicize as a newlywed. Talia Lavin's description of the pleasures of leaving "the path," including "shrimp and pork and other satisfactions of the flesh," are tempered by hearing, in her head, "the songs of the Sabbath meals I wasn't attending" and the feeling that "the food I ate on fast days burned in my gut."[19] Like Feldman, she writes from a position of authority, only being able to identify her emotional response in retrospect. But while living through their actual experiences, OTD narrators write accordingly of their acceptance of these practices, of absorbing and practicing what was expected of them. Jane Tompkins refers to "the public-private *hierarchy*" as the "founding condition of female oppression," suggesting that such a system is an either-or proposition, that the public hierarchy that oppresses women cannot be in place in private, where they retain control. Women authors of OTD memoirs, however, document a hierarchy they recognize as perpetually in place—the rabbinic authority that asserts itself in public is just as powerful in private. Their resistance to this authority is both deliberate and instinctual.

Women OTD memoirists regularly document this resistance as realting to language, reading, and intellectual development, areas that are closely controlled. Feldman hides her English-language books from her grandparents by tucking them under her mattress or in her underwear drawer. When her grandfather does a thorough search for *chametz*, leavened products, in preparation for Passover, Feldman tries to deter him from rifling through those drawers by claiming that they contain "private female stuff"—which they indeed do! (25) Feldman's grandfather, known for his piety and breadth of Talmudic knowledge, shouts his objections when he hears his granddaughter speaking to her cousins in English: "An impure language, Zeidy says, acts like a poison to the soul. Reading an English book is even worse; it leaves my soul vulnerable, a welcome mat put out for the devil" (26).

Lax, after her youngest—and seventh—child is weaned, finds herself "often pulled to the computer at night," trying "to pull words out of years of silence" (210). She turns to reading fiction and poetry for the first time in nearly two decades: "I wonder how I can make up for all the years of having not read . . . I read in the bathtub as the water grows cold and children bang on the door. I read in bed, only to find the book splayed on the floor, pages bent, when I wake before morning (240)." All but abandoned by her family but still living on the fringe of the Orthodox Jewish community, Leah Vincent discovers a college reading list at her local library: "I had given up all hope of going to college, but there was nobody to stop me from checking out all the books on that list and devouring them."[20] While books were not forbidden to Chaya Deitsch, she too recognized the "rich fantasy existence" they provided that were more typically made unavailable to ultra-Orthodox students: "Books . . . provided entrée into all sorts of different worlds, allowing me to freely try on alternative lives."[21] Sociologist Lynn Davidman, in her study *Becoming Un-Orthodox*, notes that one of her subjects, Abby, whose questions about menstruation and sexuality went unanswered by her mother, "discovered a place where she could seek information about what was happening to her body: the library . . . Reading gave access to material that offered doubters tools and a language for questioning the Hasidic world."[22] Goldy Landau describes how, as a teenager, she discovered a public library and "secretly practiced reading and writing in English. I discovered the Internet, and spent hours devouring books . . . When my forbidden visits to the public library were reported to the Va'ad Hatznius—the Hasidic Modesty Police—I was expelled from school immediately, and quickly shipped off to a religious boot-camp in Israel. . . ."[23] Reading what Feldman's grandfather calls "'Der tumeneh shpràch!'"—the impure language—OTD women narrators recognize that books, and the private act of reading and imagining, present one powerful respite from rabbinic authority (26).

Reading in OTD womens' memoirs is both an act of rebellion and, simultaneously, illustrates a rare exploration of intimacy on the part of the narrator. Feldman explicitly acknowledges how "extraordinarily happy and free" she feels when she reads; she is convinced that "everything else in my life [could be] bearable, if only I could have books all the time" (20). She also delights in doing the forbidden, such as reading an English translation of the Talmud, a secret purchase that is hidden under the mattress in between reading sessions. It is not just the fact that she peruses English words in this instance, but that the holiest of languages,

Hebrew, and the holiest of texts, the Talmud, has been translated and accessed through a secular language that makes this such a transgressive act. The first secular book that Leah Lax turns to is a volume of poetry by Adrienne Rich and, as her children play and nap and place their demands around her, she recognizes the erotic play of words that begin "to seep into a half-conscious place like the slow, deep spread of spilled ink . . . Something is waking me up, as if I've been cold and dead a long time" (257–58). Similarly, after fighting her way into Brooklyn College, Leah Vincent discovers the real meaning of reading: "I read Kant til the philosophical mumbo-jumbo phrases fell apart and the meanings became clear. Ah, so our minds shape the information we process. Our realities are limited by our perceptions. Got it" (123). Here Vincent pushes against the authority that structured her childhood, a system built on communal acceptance of ancient text and rabbinic decree.

If reading provides OTD women writers with a means of both access and egress, writing about oneself, the ultimate form of personal and public discovery, a form of revelation deemed emphatically immodest by those within ultra-Orthodox communities, serves as its even more scandalous counterpart. This is only compounded by the overwhelmingly consistent decision of OTD women authors to address topics such as sexuality—not only *niddah* and *mikvah*, but the act of intercourse, sexual preferences, and sexual identity, that are quite literally kept under wraps until one's wedding and even beyond. The specific challenge women writers face in writing an OTD memoir lies in the necessary trespassing between two worlds that are held apart by the distinctions that knowledge and experience create. OTD authors write of the religious fundamentalism of their youth as both an insider—they lived it—and an outsider, a figure who has separated (sometimes forcibly) from their native community. They write as subjects of an authority they were always subjected to and could never claim themselves. Their writing is often defiant and determinedly revealing; it is also earnest and at times simplistic. The vast majority of published OTD writing is written by women. Among many possible reasons why is this one: departure from one's native community and the discovery of one's narrative voice inscribe and re-inscribe expressions of self-definition that are—alternately and simultaneously—explorations of the public and private self.

Women's OTD narrations are peppered with the language of their community, the rhythm of Yiddish accompanied by an often uneasy English, and descriptions of religious and cultural practices all of which need to be, in some way or another, explained and clarified for the general reading public to understand. In a presentation she gave at Baruch College in May 2016, OTD author Judy Brown reviewed the challenges of effectively having to translate back and forth—and forth and back—from her thoughts to her writing to her audience and back again. In her first book, *Hush*, her publisher convinced her to include a glossary at the end of the work in order to make the work of translation take place outside of the immediate context of the story. The glossary not only defines words Brown invokes in her writing, but also gives a phonetic explanation of Yiddish consonants that is accompanied by a warning: "Please keep in mind that certain sounds in Yiddish are unusual for native English speakers."[24] The warning itself—charming; unusual—is worth reflecting upon: it brings together familiarity and foreignness that in effect personalizes the act of translation for each reader. Brown suggests with this note that not only she, a native Yiddish speaker from an ultra-Orthodox community suffers from a quality of 'lost-in-translation'; her readers, too, will face a sense of the "unusual," and the foreign, in short, the un-translatable, in reading her work. In her second more autobiographical work, *This Is Not a Love Story*, Brown chooses to forgo the glossary, instead offering translations that are built into the text, ready for readers to grab onto: "I needed this ancient omen to work so that Hashem, our one true God, would get me new heart-shaped earrings."[25] "Hashem," a name for God that is permitted to be uttered (as opposed to alternatives printed in Jewish liturgy that are not allowed to be uttered or can only be spoken during prayer), is defined within the text rather than referenced formally in an appendix. Having grown up speaking Yiddish, Brown reveals the challenges of writing in English in a way that would prove meaningful to a popular audience, many of whom would have little or no exposure to the culture of ultra-Orthodox Jewry.[26]

And then there is the vocabulary itself—together with, even more fundamentally, the very concept of language. Feldman relates her disbelief in being told shortly before her marriage about the basic mechanics of sex: "She tries to tell me about the passageway . . . I can't see where that spot, that entryway, can exist on my own body" (153). It is a discovery that divides her life in two: knowing that her body "had been designed for sex" (153). Davidman confirms that most OTD women grow up "with no knowledge of their body parts and having no language with which to discuss them . . . [T]hey were not taught the word vagina, and so, when they suddenly found themselves bleeding 'down there,' thought something horrible was happening to them" (13). The combination of, on the one hand, ignorance, and, on the other, subjectivity to communal authority that ultimately rested with rabbinic control, imbues OTD women's memoir with a sense of detachment and foreignness when it comes to describing and reflecting on precisely the most intimate moments available to them.

The sense of standing as an outsider looking into a window of the ultra-Orthodox community serves women OTD narrators well. It positions them alongside many of their readers, demanding that they survey a scene, a practice, an episode, and define its place and meaning, positioning it within a specific context. This same necessary distance, however, also imposes a sense of remoteness that impacts the narration. The duality of this position, of being both insider and outsider, works in parallel with the constant interplay between public and private that these same women have experienced the entirety of the time they have lived within ultra-Orthodox communities. And here is where the crux of women OTD authors' relationships with intimacy is often exposed: the rare moments it is achieved feature an isolated narrator engaged in some moment of introspection, often powered by a curiosity or interest in an element outside of the narrow spectrum readily available to them. Secular literature is the most regularly documented outlet that is at once sought after and hidden from view. The moments that feature what might be more conventionally considered "intimate" scenes, because they involve descriptions more typically considered private or autonomous, such as sexual interactions, even between committed partners, in fact are surprisingly impersonal and narrated in a detached, often powerless, voice.

In the memoir *Cut Me Loose: Sin and Salvation after My Ultra-Orthodox Girlhood*, by Leah Vincent, the author's first experience with sex is described using a strange narrative disconnect. Vincent, all of 18 years old and effectively abandoned by her family, is supporting herself and painfully alone. She meets up with a casual acquaintance at a seedy mid-town club. Seated side by side on a dirty couch, with little warning, he leans on top of her, pulls her underwear to one side and, as Vincent notes, "pushed into me"(97). Unsure if those few moments qualify as sexual intercourse, Leah rides back to her Brooklyn apartment "replaying the touch of Nicholas's skin on mine, picturing his sparkling eyes, the hunger for me on his face and in his body. I kept my legs crossed, applying pressure to the spot where the burn still emanated as the echoes of the evening flashed across my weary mind. That was sex, a voice in my head tried to tell me" (98). Vincent returns to the episode in the book's Afterword: "I was [raped] in the encounter with Nicholas that I describe in this book" (228). In narrating her story the first time, Vincent tells her readers a story that describes the act of sexual intercourse in terms that are a combination of plain-spoken, even reductive—"that was sex"—and romanticized—she pictures "his sparkling eyes, the hunger for me" (228). Only in reflecting back on the scene, in a tone that is analytical and carrying with it a sense of certainty, experience, and authority does Vincent offer her ultimate conclusions about her interaction with Nicholas, namely that it was a violent and non-consensual encounter. Tellingly, in none of these explorations is there a sense of deliberative and cultivated reader/writer intimacy. Rather, Vincent, intent on describing her feelings "in the moment" and then analyzing them as she looks back, refuses to imbue them with intimacy precisely because physical interactions, even illicit ones—and by "illicit" I mean both what her family regards as illicit, the scandal of her having sex out of wedlock and with a non-Jewish black man, and her own understanding of "illicit," the fact that she was raped—still rely on an understanding of the female body as subject to male jurisdiction. And what, Vincent implicitly and rhetorically asks, is intimate about that?

The same holds true for Leah Lax's experience of intimacy with her husband, Levi. She describes herself entering a "passive, obedient mode," feeling "flat, dispassionate," and approaching her husband with "little physical desire" (46; 53). Sex becomes "a once-monthly act of obedience to the Law" (165). In contrast, Lax leads readers closer and closer to her own self-realization and self-understanding, namely, that she feels most alive, most present, most intimate with herself and her readers, only when she celebrates her love of women. "Today," Lax narrates her thoughts to the reader, giving us access to the ultimate interiority, "is my bar mitzvah. Today I am a woman—the person my mother birthed, and not some artificially molded and silenced shadow standing behind the men. I am me: a lesbian" (320).

❧

Women's OTD memoirs lay bare much of what is considered "private" in their native communities. The irony is that the preservation of privacy does not extend to their families, the community rabbis, or their social circles. It does, however, extend to those outside of their community, which includes most readers and, indeed, the writers themselves. Off-the-derech writers in general, and women even more so, come from insular and intensely private communities, places where acts of intimacy are both curtained from view but also, as with every aspect of ultra-Orthodox life, subject to rabbinic oversight and control. And while twentieth- and twenty-first-century literature has dramatically loosened the reins of social rules and mores, the reality for off-the-derech authors is quite different. They come from a social environment that is emphatically and deliberately not up to contemporary standards or times. The consequence is that OTD women's memoirs abandon the more typical features of memoir and do so with a great deal of un-self-consciousness. Descriptions of intimacy in OTD women's memoir, with its physical and emotional aspects, illuminate a struggle on the part of the narrator, one born of experience—that is, the experience of intimacy itself is sufficiently noteworthy that it is explored within their stories of departure—but also one of narration—telling the story of intimacy to readers and, relatedly, establishing a relationship with the reader. Off-the-derech memoirs center on the act of revelation, with all the resonance, religious and secular, which the word carries. And intimacy has a fraught relationship with revelation whereby the one both tempers and inspires the other. Women authors of OTD memoirs, where the act of belonging involves adherence to laws that cover every aspect, no matter how minute, of one's life, recognize that intimacy is a product of the deeply communal and highly regulated lives led within the insular communities in which off-the-derech authors once lived. Their declaration of independence from these communities includes a production of intimate reading that, at its core, centers on the deeply personal nature of individualism.

Notes

1. Here are just a few popular websites that take on some of the rumors about sex and related practices among religious Jews: http://www.snopes.com/religion/sheet.asp; http://www.cbc.ca/firsthand/m/features/answers-questions-hasidic-love-and-sex-that-you-were-afraid-to-ask; http://www.huffingtonpost.com/2015/02/14/orthodox-judaism-sex_n_6661068.html For a scholarly article that examines a number of myths about sexuality and Judaism, their origins and their (in)accuracies, please see: David S. Ribner and Peggy J. Kleinplatz,

"The hole in the sheet and other myths about sexuality and Judaism," *Sexual and Relationship Therapy* 22 (2007): 445–56.

2. Jane Tompkins, "Me and My Shadow" in *The Intimate Critique: Autobiographical Literary Criticism*, ed. Diane P. Freedman, Olivia Frey, and Frances Murphy Zauhar (Durham, NC: Duke University Press, 1993), 24.

3. Ibid., 25.

4. Ibid.

5. I rely here in part on Hannah Arendt's well-known depiction of the distinction between public and private spheres in the classical (secular) world, the household was the center of the private sphere and its distinctive trait—its "necessity"—ensured that it "was the center of the strictest inequality," namely, the space belonging to women, children and slaves. The realm of the *polis*, in contrast, "was the sphere of freedom." Citizens of the *polis* were, by definition, men and landowners, freed from household labor done by non-citizens. Hannah Arendt, *The Human Condition*, 2nd ed. (Chicago: University of Chicago Press, 1998), 32.

6. Orna Blumen, "The Gendered Display of Work: The Midday Scene in an Ultra-Orthodox Street in Israel," *Nashim: A Journal of Jewish Women's Studies & Gender Issues* 13(2007): 145.

7. Blumen, "The Gendered Display of Work," 146.

8. Deborah Feldman, *Unorthodox: The Scandalous Rejection of My Hasidic Roots* (New York: Simon and Schuster, 2012), 139–40.

9. Shulem Deen, *All Who Go Do Not Return* (Minneapolis, MN: Graywolf Press, 2015), Chapter 16.

10. Leah Lax, *Uncovered: How I Left Hasidic Life and Finally Came Home* (New York: She Writes Press, 2015), 336.

11. Lynn Davidman, *Becoming Un-Orthodox: Stories of Ex-Hasidic Jews* (New York: Oxford University Press, 2015), 169.

12. Feldman, *Unorthodox*, 178.

13. Ibid., 172.

14. Tova Hartman and Naomi Marmon, "Lived Regulations, Systemic Attributions: Menstrual Separation and Ritual Immersion in the Experience of Orthodox Jewish Women," *Gender and Society*, 18, no. 3 (2004): 389–408.

15. Ibid., 403.

16. Ibid., 396.

17. Samuel Heilman, *Defenders of the Faith: Inside Ultra-Orthodox Jewry* (New York: Schocken Books, 1992), 316.

18. Ibid., 317.

19. Talia Lavin, "Off the Path of Orthodoxy," *The New Yorker*, 31 July 2015, https://www.newyorker.com/news/news-desk/off-the-path-of-orthodoxy.

20. Leah Vincent, *Cut Me Loose: Sin and Salvation after My Ultra-Orthodox Girlhood* (New York: Penguin Books, 2014), 73.

21. Chaya Deitsch, *Here and There: Leaving Hasidism, Keeping My Family* (New York: Schocken Books, 2015), 56.

22. Davidman, *Becoming Un-Orthodox*, 38.

23. Goldy Landau, "The Day My Hasidic Father Visited Me At Wellesley," *The Forward*, August 9, 2017, http://forward.com/opinion/379538/the-day-my-hasidic-father-visited-me-at-wellesley/.

24. Judy Brown [initially published under the pseudonym Eishes Chayil], *Hush* (New York: Walker & Company), 346.

25. Judy Brown, *This Is Not a Love Story: A Memoir* (New York: Little, Brown and Company, 2015), first page of ch. 1.

26. These comments were made at the conference "Dissent and Dissension," Baruch College, May 2016.

Bibliography

Arendt, Hannah. *The Human Condition*, 2nd ed. Chicago: University of Chicago Press, 1998.

Brown, Judy. *Hush*. New York: Walker & Company, 2012. [Originally published under the pseudonym Eishes Chayil.]

Brown, Judy. *This Is Not a Love Story: A Memoir*. New York: Little, Brown and Company, 2015.

Davidman, Lynn. *Becoming Un-Orthodox: Stories of Ex-Hasidic Jews*. New York: Oxford University Press, 2015.

Deen, Shulem. *All Who Go Do Not Return*. Minneapolis: Graywolf Press, 2015.

Deitsch, Chaya. *Here and There: Leaving Hasidism, Keeping My Family*. New York: Schocken Books, 2015.

Feldman, Deborah. *Unorthodox: The Scandalous Rejection of My Hasidic Roots*. New York: Simon and Schuster, 2012.

Hartman, Tova, and Naomi Marmon. "Lived Regulations, Systemic Attributions: Menstrual Separation and Ritual Immersion in the Experience of Orthodox Jewish Women." *Gender and Society* 18, no. 3 (2004): 389–408.

Heilman, Samuel. *Defenders of the Faith: Inside Ultra-Orthodox Jewry*. New York: Schocken Books, 1992.

Landau, Goldy. "The Day My Hasidic Father Visited Me At Wellesley." *The Forward*. August 9, 2017. http://forward.com/opinion/379538/the-day-my-hasidic-father-visited-me-at-wellesley/.

Lavin, Talia. "Off the Path of Orthodoxy." *The New Yorker*. July 31, 2015. https://www.newyorker.com/news/news-desk/off-the-path-of-orthodoxy.

Lax, Leah. *Uncovered: How I Left Hasidic Life and Finally Came Home*. New York: She Writes Press, 2015.

Ribner, David S., and Peggy J. Kleinplatz. "The Hole in the Sheet and Other Myths about Sexuality and Judaism." *Sexual and Relationship Therapy* 22 (2007): 445–56.

Tompkins, Jane. "Me and My Shadow" in *The Intimate Critique: Autobiographical Literary Criticism*, ed. Diane P. Freedman, Olivia Frey, and Frances Murphy Zauhar. Durham, NC: Duke University Press, 1993.

Vincent, Leah. *Cut Me Loose: Sin and Salvation after My Ultra-Orthodox Girlhood.* New York: Penguin Books, 2014.

The Embodied Process of *Haredi* Defection[1]

Lynn Davidman

OFF THE DERECH: *I am writing an essay for this volume in response to the editors' request. I object to this title, however; it carries within it the assumption that those who leave Orthodoxy have left the righteous path, suggesting there is one true path. OTD is an expression used by Orthodox Jews to describe someone who intentionally stops practicing the tenets of Orthodox Judaism. As a secular Jew who grew up Orthodox, I have found in contemporary Jewish pluralism fresh ways of constructing my Jewish identity through participation in a vigorous Jewish culture, including secular communities, new rituals, fresh interpretations of ancient texts, and the flowering of new forms of Jewish literature, music, and social justice activism.*

In this paper I ask what might we learn about the process of leaving strict religious groups if we put Jews at the center of the research? There is a large body of literature about those who leave Evangelical or Fundamentalist Christianity but there are few studies on Jews who leave Haredi Judaism. My goal here is to analyze how the study of Jews expands our cultural assumptions about religious exiting and, more basically, about the nature of religion in general. Judaism emphasizes religious rituals and practices rather than faith and beliefs, which are central to Christian religions.

Studying the exit narratives of ultra-Orthodox Jews and comparing them with those of people who leave fundamentalist Christianity, reveals that research on those who leave has generally rested upon Protestant models and conceptions of religion. Christian defection[2] narratives, and scholarly research about them, all tell of struggles with belief; in contrast, the exit stories of ultra-Orthodox Jews highlight the difficulties of ceasing to perform the hundreds of embedded, habitual rituals that are so central to their lives. Bringing Jews into the study of religious exiting reveals dimensions of the leaving process that had not been considered before, because they were not central to Christian models of religion and thus were not seen as important in studies of Christian defection. These contrasts further show the need to expand how we study and develop our analyses of religious exiting, and thus of religion in general.

Narratives of Religious Exit: Loss of Faith

In the Christian understanding of religion, statements of faith are the foremost symbols of religious commitment; a person can still be considered a devout Christian (in many sects), even if he/she does not often pray or attend church, for instance. The equation of religion with faith is apparent in the scholarly literature, as well as in memoirs, Internet sites, and blogs. This nearly exclusive attention to Christianity has led to an overall bias in the study of religion. The assumptions of those who study religion are based on what is central to Christianity: professing faith, attending church, and following moral rules based on Scripture. Scholars who study religion ask questions, use research methods, and develop theories that are rooted in the conventions and traditions of Protestantism in the United States.

Protestants place a large emphasis on the subjective experience of faith as essential for religious identity. This predisposition is present even in research on those who *leave* the strictly controlled Christian communities in which they grew up. Nearly all the research on religious exiters has focused on Christians, particularly on people who leave Evangelical and Fundamentalist Christian (Protestant) sects. Not surprisingly, they have found that among those who left, all recounted struggles with their beliefs and values.

The research on defectors has overwhelmingly focused on a loss of faith as central to the decision to leave the religion in which they were raised. In his research, Phil Zuckerman, a prominent scholar in this field, profiled the stories of people who left a wide variety of religious groups, including Mormonism, evangelical Christianity, and Jehovah's Witnesses. His book is *Faith No More: Why People Reject Religion*[3]; others are: *Falling from the Faith: The Causes and Consequences of Religious Apostasy;*[4] *Losing Faith in Faith: From Preacher to Atheist;*[5] and *Finding Faith, Losing Faith: Stories of Conversion and Apostacy.*[6] The accounts of defection in these books focused on events that led respondents to question the existence of God, and to doubt their religious beliefs. John Barbour has written that his foregrounding of faith in his memoir is an outcome of his studying Christian apostates.[7] He found that those who left their religious communities did so when they began to question their belief in God's existence; these moments of grappling with serious doubts were represented by the defectors as the most difficult and isolating aspects of their transitions out of religion. In this body of research, little attention has been paid to other processes involved in leaving such as its impact on relations within their family, their practice of religious rituals, or changes in their daily lives.

In contrast to those who left their strict Christian religious communities, the accounts of my Haredi respondents reflected the differences between the two religions. For Jews, proper performance of rituals is the sine qua non of religious commitment whereas faith is central to *Christian* religious communities. These distinctions are apparent in the defection narratives told by the forty ex-Haredim in the United States, whom I interviewed for my recent book, *Becoming Un-Orthodox: Stories of ex-*Hasidic *Jews.*[8]

The Worlds of *Haredi* Jews

Before presenting my analysis of the extent to which Jewish defection differs from Christian, I need to introduce you to the life worlds of *Haredim*, who in English are referred to as the "ultra-Orthodox." *Haredim* live in a world where the cosmic and ethical worldview seeps through the most banal of daily activities. Piety is defined "more in terms of practice than belief," as put by Phillips and Kelner.[9] Their exacting performance of bodily rituals, as opposed to professing belief in God, is the means through which ultra-Orthodox Jews learn, deepen, and demonstrate their religious commitment. The 613 rules and commandments that Haredim

seek to follow precisely are rooted in the Hebrew scriptures, as interpreted by leading rabbis throughout the millennia, and across the globe.
Hasidic Jews' bodily practices are extensive. They are all-consuming, and
punctuate every day of their lives with rituals performed to acknowledge
the importance of God's blessings and presence in their lives. Hasidim
are required to engage in a variety of bodily practices—rituals performed
by and enacted upon the body—that create, maintain, and display
membership in the group. As children are socialized into this religious
community, they learn and internalize the group's norms, beliefs, and
values and how to perform the group's rituals, including the corporeal
rites through which the religion becomes embodied.

The body of religious laws followed by Haredim includes commandments about how to observe the Shabbat, how to avoid taboo places,
how to follow a kosher diet, how to dress, how to treat facial hair for
men and head hair for married women, and how community members
must always comport themselves. For instance, upon arising, Hasidic
Jews may walk only three steps from their beds before they ritually
rinse their hands in a prepared two-handled bowl of *nagel vasser* [a Yiddish word meaning nail water], an embodied ritual intended to sanctify
each person in God's holiness. As they wash their hands, they must
say a *bracha* (blessing to God), thanking him for returning their souls
to them after sleep. There are blessings that accompany most actions
of the *Haredim* and serve to remind them of God's constant presence
in their lives. These bodily rituals, whose performance is at the center
of Haredi identity, create, maintain and display individuals' piety even
as they serve to create boundaries between their communities and the
polluting outside world.

Haredi ritual practices are performed by, and upon, the bodies of
members of these strictly religious sects. Beginning in childhood, Haredim are taught to internalize the community's ritual behaviors that, over
years of practice, become automatic, habitual, and taken for granted.
The sociologist Emile Durkheim, who was brought up in an observant
Jewish home, asserted that religious ideas and myths, the stories groups
tell about themselves, cannot be understood or sustained if they are not
embedded in a system of ritual practices and techniques of the body.
Extending his argument beyond group members to those who choose to
leave their religious groups, suggests that Haredim can only leave the
group by ceasing to observe its ritual practices and techniques of the body.

In my interviews with forty defectors in the United States,[10] we mutually sought to create narratives about the processes involved in their journeys out of their religious enclaves. I had not thought to ask questions about bodies, and the potential disruptions to bodily processes that might have been important in their exiting process. My interview guide had no questions about the bodily rituals observed by Haredi Jews, or the embodied nature of leaving a Haredi community. As we spoke, however, all my interviewees themselves raised the topic of Haredi bodily routines and told me how challenging it was to stop practicing their internalized, habitual, bodily rituals. As I read each of my transcripts several times, the theme of embodiment emerged as the central focus of my research. Haredim provided an exemplary case for highlighting the need to consider bodily practices as central not only to leaving religion, but as an essential aspect of all religions.

The former Haredim I met in this study all spoke of some incident or contradiction they experienced in childhood that might have predisposed them to question their religious lives. As some Haredi Jews began to feel uncomfortable continuing their ritual practices, they had gone to famous rabbis to seek solutions that would help them reconcile their internal daily struggles about following the religious laws. My respondents told me when they did not receive answers that eased their painful internal battles, they became tempted to break a commandment just to see what would happen.[11] When they did so, they unknowingly put themselves at the top of the slippery slope that might be headed toward their defection.

During our conversations, my respondents described in detail how they conducted their first transgressive acts. I classified these first violations into three central types of embodied practices, essential to living a Hasidic life that they chose to transgress. Included in these experimental transgressions are: altering their dress, demeanor and comportment, breaking the dietary laws of kashrut (eating only kosher foods), and entering places that were taboo to members of their communities. It was scary for them to break a commandment from God; all their lives they had been told they would be swiftly punished by God for violating His commandments. As I spoke with formerly Haredi defectors, they described how, when they first disrupted or detached from their everyday routines of observing God's commandments and deliberately broke a sacred religious commandment, it was a moment of great drama and significance.

Right then, they became aware that their very identities could be at stake, a profound realization that led many to go very slowly and make only gradual changes in bodily rituals.

There was a common pattern in the way exiters approached transformations of their bodily practices. As my respondents thought about violating a commandment, they sought to do so in a "private" place, meaning outside the boundaries of their enclave, where no one in their community could see them and report their transgressive behavior. Many of the places in which these acts of resistance were first done were actually "public" places such as restaurants, dance clubs, shops, and city streets. From the point of view of the speaker, however, they were considered "private" because they were places where they would not be observed by anyone else in their religious community. To explicate this notion of private and public, I draw on Erving Goffman's terminology of "backstage" and "front stage" performances: "A back region or backstage may be defined as a place, *relative to a given performance* (emphasis mine) where the impression fostered by the [front stage] performance is knowingly contradicted."[12] First experiments took place backstage, beyond the community's gaze, so that transgressors can maintain their front stage performances without being accused of deviance or risking their reputation and those of their family members within their tightly-knit communities.

In the next section, I will provide excerpts from my conversation partners' stories that show the various religious practices my respondents experimented with; their first religious lapses.

Experimenting with Transgressive Acts

Changing Comportment, Dress, and Appearance

Sima was in her early thirties when we met. She had grown up in a Haredi community whose religious regulations, dating back to the Hebrew Bible, forbade men to wear articles of women's clothing and did not allow women to wear men's garments. Even pants cut and made for women were taboo. In response to my question about her first experiment with breaking commandments, she told me the story of the first time she bought and tried on a pair of women's pants. At this stage of experimenting she only wore the pants in a backstage, private setting. She knew she would wear them publicly only after she had made the momentous decision to leave her former way of life.

Sima reported her first experience breaking the rules concerning gendered embodied practices was a decisive moment in her life, as she said:

> For me, putting on pants was the equivalent of taking off your *kippah*, (the skullcap worn by observant Jewish men), or stopping to put on *tefillin* (leather boxes containing Torah passages worn by Orthodox males). It was like the, the most. And really when I wore pants for a few hours at a friend's house, I felt lots of things. First, I felt like I was sort of naked, like I was really exposed. But on the other hand, I was very, very happy.

Linking her process with male disinscription of significant Haredi markers, such as removing their yarmulkes or ceasing to put on *tefillin* when they prayed, underscored Sima's perception of the gravity of her actions. She could have related her transgression to women's ways of enacting bodily resistance. Her choice to equate her transgressive bodily behavior with those of men, however, reveals her awareness that men's deeds were considered more important in her community. Sima's choice of the words "exposure" and "nakedness," indicated how deeply she had internalized the tenets of modesty required of women in all spheres of life. Her language indicated how Haredi norms are deeply inscribed as appropriate habitual behavior. Her language of vulnerability and exposure suggest she experienced a sense of shame along with happiness and liberation. The intense pleasure Sima found in experimenting with wearing pants signaled her resistance to remaining in the Haredi world forever. Her combined expression of vulnerability—"exposure"—and happiness is understandable: She had grown accustomed to hiding her individual thoughts and desires by conforming to the norms of group. Transgressing the norms thus produced an unnerving combination of feelings: embarrassment along with liberation.

Eating Forbidden Foods

Several of my respondents' first experiment was eating *treyf*, non-kosher food. As did the other experimenters, they did so in places outside their community's gaze, which is to say, in private. Even if they were in a "public" place, such as a restaurant, they chose one at a great distance from their communities, so they could avoid the risk of being caught and punished. These actions were their very first step in the process of breaking away from Hasidic understandings of the body's orientation to the divine. The popular American adage, "you are what you eat," is relevant here: if you eat only kosher foods, you are a "kosher" person, meaning one who is ritually pure and follows all the laws. But if you transgress and eat *treyf* food, you, yourself, become *treyf*, defiled. By eating forbidden foods, the defectors had opened their bodies up to any number of polluting elements from the secular world.

Ehud, a professor in his early fifties, looked anguished as we spoke; he bent over and kept his hand over his forehead as he told a fascinating story about the first time he ate un-kosher food. He began this story with this first sentence: "Then the chicken thing happened . . . the first time the chicken happened I can tell you exactly, because I remember the day so well."

In recalling his first transgression, Ehud used passive language as if to suggest that the incident did not reflect deliberation or conscious agency on his part:

> I was sitting there with this piece of *treyf* chicken on my plate, and I thought to myself, "I'm going to eat this?" I felt so conflicted and this battle was going on through my mind, and of course these two non-Jewish people who sat across from me, this guy and this woman, had no idea what I was going through. None whatsoever. I just remember it was a big deal for me. But the irony of it was that when I first tasted it, it tasted just the same as my family's Friday night chickens!! It wasn't all that different (he laughed heartily, as did I).

When I asked him if he was afraid to take his first bite, he told me he did not fear that God's punishment would immediately follow his transgressive activity, despite what he had been taught since birth. He expressed confidence that God was not going to strike him down:

> I didn't believe Haredi rationales for following religious law. So, it was "just" [he made apostrophes in the air] the act

of transgressing. You know, it's just, there's this invisible line that you're stepping over, this is the first time in your life that you're doing it. I was twenty-two or so when this happened. It is one thing to do it when you're sixteen and it's another when you're in your twenties. It's a little harder probably, because teenagers' behavior can be seen as a passing phase, whereas for an adult, this decision could shake the very foundation of my identity. It was complicated, despite my age of 22; because at that time, I had not yet ever gone out with a woman, so in some ways I knew I was still pretty much like a kid.

Ehud's language of stepping over an invisible line was a powerful metaphor for his understanding that eating *treyf* put him outside the boundaries of the Hasidic world. The enclave's distinctive borders were designed to keep non-members out and insiders in. Ehud's transgressive act made it clear to him that he was in danger of leaving the safety of his community and might not return. His account of eating *treyf* vividly illustrates the embodied nature of Hasidic religious practice. Although Ehud had, by this time, decided not to follow the commandments, he still agonized about changing even one ritual bodily habit.

Entering Taboo Spaces

Shlomo, a male ex-Hasid, was clearly excited to tell me about his first religious transgression, which involved entering taboo spaces as well as temporarily changing his appearance; the story of the time when he was fifteen years of age and he, along with a couple of his Hasidic friends, snuck into a mixed gender dancing club.

> Now I think when I was fifteen years old, I, and two or three other guys, first went to a club, a dancing club. I did not feel entirely comfortable there because I still had the curls that people were starin' at instead of starin' at the girls dancing. I decided to put my *peyos*, (curly sidelocks), behind my ears, trying to hide them. And my friends started to make fun of me like, "oh now you're not Jewish because I can't see your curls." Like I am like, listen I'm going to try to hide it because

I don't want people staring at me instead of looking at the girls. One night we went bar hoppin' and we just bumped into one bar . . . We got to meet the owner, and she took us around, introducing us to the bartender and showing us what was at the bar. She was so different from the girls in our community. So, we thought, "Wow, this is really cool. This is our place. We're going to try to come back here."

Shlomo's friends' comments reveal how each communities' set of laws is taken as essential to Jewish identity. His friends equated Shlomo's hiding his *peyos*—so they would not be visible and embarrass him—with his being no longer Jewish.

It made a great impression upon those I interviewed that when they broke religious laws they were not immediately punished by God. This empowered them to repeat their transgressions or perhaps try a new one.[13] As respondents continued to transgress community rules concerning appropriate dress, diet, and staying away from prohibited, polluting places, they slid into a phase of passing betwixt and between their increasingly dual identities: that of their lives in the enclave and that of their emerging selves in the secular world.

Passing

In the last section, we saw how the respondents spoke of the intensity and strong feelings they had the first time they violated one of their community's norms. As we talked, I could sense a tone of triumph: they had dared to risk God's wrath and punishment—which they had been taught would swiftly follow all violations of religious norms—and nothing had happened at all! Their first "sins" were against one of the hundreds of ultra-Orthodox bodily rituals that had been inscribed upon them through socialization, and continued to shape their repertoires of automatic, taken-for-granted behaviors. Finding that their first violations did not have any undesirable consequences, they became more daring and began to repeat their transgressions and to violate other commandments, but still in settings far outside their community boundaries.

There is a Talmudic expression stating that once a person has broken a commandment, it feels to that individual as if this transgressive behavior is now permissible. This saying describes the attitudes of Shlomo, whose story continues in the next section. Once he saw there had been no negative consequences the first time he and his friends went to the bar, they became regulars. He and his friends spoke of this bar/dance club they frequented as their "special place."

Here he could hide his hair and yarmulke (skullcap) that marked him as an observant Jew and engage in the forbidden pleasures of mixed dancing. The dance club provided an opportunity for these teenage Haredim to see and explore alternative worlds they liked better than their own. For Shlomo, manipulation of the placement of his *peyos* was one of his passing strategies. When he had his *peyos* visible, it was clear that he was a member of a Hasidic group; as he repeatedly traveled between his native community in Monsey, New York, and the secular world of what he called "dance clubs" he manipulated the visibility of his *peyos*. When Shlomo hid his *peyos* beneath a cap, he could pass as a secular person and not stand out in the clubs. He liked that feeling of getting increasingly comfortable in negotiating the world outside their enclave.

Many Haredim told similar stories of using the strategy of manipulating their appearance as they moved back and forth between their secular and religious worlds. For example, another man, Aryeh, told me that as he grew increasingly confident about his desire to leave, he tested the boundaries between his Haredi world and the secular one he was increasingly attracted to by removing his skullcap when he left the Hasidic neighborhood, only to replace it on his head when he came closer to home again. He explained that over time he became bolder, and decreased the distance from home when he re-placed his kippah.

Shlomo and Aryeh kept testing the religious boundaries in which they were raised by continually decreasing the actual or perceived distance between their Hasidic community and the increasingly familiar secular world. All my conversation partners told me how much pleasure they took in discovering their new freedom to continue violating Haredi rules such as eating non-kosher food, dressing and comporting themselves inappropriately, and other transgressive acts. When these deeds were done, they reassembled their Haredi faces and bodies back into place before returning home. Over time they developed a routine of passing between the mutually exclusive realms of their enclave communities, where they publicly performed the embodied routines of Hasidic daily life, and the larger, more open society, where they continued to transgress freely, ignoring religious strictures and experimenting with new ways of being in the world.

One Taboo Space with Multiple Violations

Leah was an outspoken, professional, articulate, and strong feminist in her forties when we met. I had asked Leah to detail for me her process of exiting and her story began with her discovering a bar at the edge of her community. She enjoyed the experience so much she went increasingly often. Her narrative was different from those of other Haredi women; none of them included stories of regularly going to bars as a stage in their exiting process. Leah's narrative was fascinating and dramatic; it provided such a powerful model of the stage of passing that I am reproducing our conversation here in some detail:

> LD: When did you start violating commandments, such as those of Shabbes?
>
> LEAH: Well, Shabbes . . . I don't know how I stopped observing Shabbes, but at some point, I did.
>
> LD: Can you try to remember some of that?
>
> LEAH: At some point, *Shabbes* became claustrophobic, and I couldn't stand it anymore. I just hated it. I *hated*, you know, the way we frenetically raced around to get everything done by Friday afternoon, so it would all be ready for *Shabbes*, which started on Friday at sundown until it became dark on Saturday. I couldn't stand just being locked up like that for 25 hours. I just would go nuts. At the edge of the Brooklyn neighborhood where I lived there was a bar and I would just sit there at home on *Shabbes*, and have this fantasy I should go to a bar. Like I'm an international adventuress or something. I have no idea where I got this, but I thought I should be able to walk into a bar, have a drink, you know, like the women in the movies [that she watched when she

snuck out to Greenwich Village], Bette Davis or something. That's who I was. Lauren Bacall. Yeah, that was me. You know, Katherine Hepburn. And they would walk into a bar and say, "Give me a drink."

So I started to sneak out of my house, carrying money (forbidden on the Sabbath), wearing my pants under my skirt, and I would hide the skirt outside of the bar. When I walked in there were all these men I didn't know and I was so afraid one of them would talk to me because I had no idea what I would say. So, I would do this, you know, on a Friday night sometimes. I would do this on a Saturday afternoon. I was trying to be a woman of assertion, and I'd smoke cigarettes . . .

LD: How did you know what to order?

LEAH: Oh, a martini of course, just like the women in the movies. I just had to get out of there [her parents' home]. I don't know. I had to have a cigarette. I had to watch TV. I had to be in the world. It just was too restrictive. There were more activities that were forbidden on *Shabbes* than were allowed and those few were so limiting and boring to me at some point.

Leah's story began with a Friday evening in which she violated multiple commandments by entering a bar at the edge of her community. Her pleasure at being there was so enticing she began to move back and forth between her Hasidic home and a paradigmatically taboo place, a bar. Her account revealed that her passage between these places involved breaking several religious laws at once: entering taboo places, wearing pants, and carrying money. She passed back and forth—in the space of a few hours—between a bar, a secular space, where she dressed and comported herself as a secular person, and the world of her parents' Hasidic enclave, where she still lived, publicly fulfilling the duties and practices of a young Haredi woman.

Leah went into the bar wearing her pants; when she left she put her skirt back on to return home. She enjoyed the mystery and hint of danger of the bar and began to go there regularly. Leah's breaking the laws of "modesty" demanded of women by wearing what was considered men's clothing was a critical step in her exiting process, as was her breaking the laws of Sabbath by carrying money and going to bars.

At this point Leah was no longer experimenting with a few transgressive acts; she was becoming bolder in her rebellion and began to eat non-kosher food. She had entered the stage of "*passing*," of moving back and forth between two radically different worlds and trying to maintain credibility in each. Leah and my other informants described passing as a difficult stage; it was a liminal state in which they were caught betwixt and between their communities and the freer outside world, uncertain of why they were or might become. Flipping their behaviors and the identities they performed between two realms led to an increasingly uncomfortable sense of cognitive dissonance, which eventually they sought to resolve in one way or another.

Leah and others came to see how much they wanted to defect from their Haredi worlds, but they were aware it was a fearsome and daunting move. Many spent several years in the unnerving stage of passing because they had nowhere to go, did not have jobs, and did not want to risk the loss of their families. They also feared all the dangers they had been taught that were lurking in the larger *goyishe* (non-Jewish) world.

Over a period of time that varied, but generally lasted for several years, my respondents became less frightened of, and increasingly more comfortable in, the secular world. They sought to end the emotional torment of their deepening feelings of cognitive dissonance, so they began to leave their Haredi enclaves and step out into the larger world outside.

Stepping Out

My conversation partners' accounts of stepping out of the enclave highlight the interwoven motifs of emancipation and ontological vulnerability. These feelings illustrated how difficult it was for defectors to move beyond their feelings of insecurity and helplessness and toward a stronger sense of liberation, empowerment, and independence. In contrast to the few who left and had role models or other forms of support in leaving, such as getting married and defecting as a couple, Sam, a secular Talmud scholar—he was a brilliant student when he was young and what he had learned stayed with him—was completely alone when he decided to finally leave. As he said,

> When I finally did walk out, I felt really lost. I had nowhere to go and I lost literally every friend I'd ever had. They were all gone in one day . . . in one minute. I will never again in my life live in that world . . . On the one hand it was just the most profoundly life-giving, moving, rooted kind of place. And I knew leaving it would be like going into exile. It was like finding yourself washed upon a foreign shore. Robinson Crusoe. That how I thought of it. There's nobody there. Literally, I had to start everything over.

Not only did Sam face the fears and anxiety of leaving described by all my other informants, he was further devastated by the hypocrisy of his friends who shunned him. They themselves were also transgressing and passing, however, they chose the safety and familiarity of remaining in the only world they had known.

In contrast, Leah sought to meet people who could help her shed her old automatic habits and teach her new social and cultural skills. She told me about her new friend who served as her model and guide to behavior in the secular world:

> I remember I met this one woman where I was working, and she was just like very forward. She would be sexually forward with people, such as saying to a man at the bar: "Hello. Come here. Let me take a look at you." I was so shocked, it was like my jaw just dropped right down. This woman was just sort of like *Sex in the City*. So even though in my mind I wanted to be free and cool, I still acted like yeshiva girl. And it was . . . I'd be like dumbfounded.
>
> Once she took me to a bar and we went around talking to the people there. She was a much older woman than me, but she said to me, "I like you," and so she took me on as her project. I thought it was great, because I didn't have to say very much. And so, we went to bars together. And

cigarettes came in useful there while you're sitting there. And she taught me to smoke, and how to hold my cigarette in one hand and a cocktail in the other.

It was clear that Leah's guide played a critical role in helping her adapt to the world outside of the Haredi enclave by being her guide to the secular world.

Others were not lucky enough to find guides to teach them the norms of behavior and comportment appropriate for living in a secular world. For example, Sarah, who had already left the community and was working at an upper-end women's clothing store, still struggled to lose the mannerisms, dress, comportment, and interactional styles, which, as she saw, were less polite and genteel than those of people she met outside: "I felt like an immigrant who did not know anything about the new society I had just entered." Sarah confided to me that her boss occasionally chided her for being *rude* to customers, an adverb she had never heard before.

As Sarah continued to work in the store, she learned there were basic assumptions about comportment and behavioral skills shared by the customers and other shop workers, which she clearly lacked. She had not been raised with the cultural and social knowledge that would have provided her with the social graces needed to interact politely with those shoppers who had such different ways of comporting themselves. In the Haredi world, she had not learned delicate ways of approaching strangers. To her, the customers' ways of asking for items in the store and their mannerisms were strange. Sarah could tell these others had been raised in communities that were quite different from the one in which she was raised. She observed their behaviors and interactions and decided to learn this new way of being in the world.

In defecting, formerly Orthodox Jews who change their diet, hair, shaving practices, and clothing as they exit their enclave religious communities perform a sort of identity negotiation by beginning to play out personal, religious, social, and political questions of self on the bodily canvas. They reject the divine origins of the rules and regulations of their homogeneous enclave rituals and instead adopt the notion that fluidity in appearance is acceptable.

These accounts of ex-Haredim who defected from their strictly observant enclave communities showed there was more to defection than losing faith or religious beliefs. The defectors I met described how their process of identity transformation involved a negotiation between the corporeal performances that sustained and reflected their religious identities and the new, extensive range of bodily practices available in the wider society. Leaving successfully required them to root out and shed the embodied practices of their former lives, even as they simultaneously learned the bodily routines and practices of the world beyond their enclaves.

This essay, and *Becoming Un-Orthodox*, the book on which it is based, uses a case study of Hasidic defectors to highlight the critical role of the body in the processes of identity transformations, including those religious in nature. Comparing Christian religious exiters—whose narratives focused on losing religious ideas and beliefs—to the case of Hasidic Jewish defectors, whose exiting stories focused s on their learning to shed the habitual, embodied observance of all the bodily practices that they took-for-granted in their Haredi lives—shows us an under-appreciated, but essential component of religion: it is embedded within us and our daily practices. If is my hope that studies such as this one, and research on non-Western religions, will expand the fundamental assumptions and research methods of scholars of religion.

Notes

1. The term "Haredi" is an adjective describing Jews who call themselves "Haredim." Members of these strictly Orthodox communities prefer this term over the English expression, "ultra-Orthodox"; a term they feel suggests they are going above and beyond the requirements of Jewish law, whereas they see themselves as simply strictly adhering to the laws and commandments of God. There is no English term that captures the precise meanings and nuances as the word "Haredim." For simplicity's sake, I use the two interchangeably in this essay.

2. There are a variety of verbs used to refer to the process of people's breaking away from their native religion: exiting, de-converting, leaving, and defecting. I do not use the term "de-converting" because it suggests people leaving a religious tradition they converted into earlier. My preferred term is defection, although I am aware it is highly charged. I choose this term deliberately because it most accurately depicts the major, agonizing decision to abandon their religious worlds, knowing that their defection puts them at risk of losing everything and everyone in their prior lives. My respondents did not make a simple or casual choice to leave the religious worlds in which they had been

ensconced their entire lives. Rather, they were self-reflective apostates who denounced their former religious lives.

3. Phil Zuckerman, *Faith No More: Why People Reject Religion* (New York: Oxford University Press, 2012).

4. David G. Bromley, *Falling From the Faith: Causes and Consequences of Religious Apostasy* (Newbury Park, CA: Sage Publications).

5. Dan Barker, *Losing Faith in Faith: From Preacher to Atheist* (Madison, WI: FFRF, Inc., 1992).

6. Scot McKnight and Hauna Ondrey, *Finding Faith, Losing Faith: Stories of Conversion and Apostasy* (Waco, TX: Baylor University Press, 2008).

7. John D. Barbour, *Versions of Deconversion: Autobiography and the Loss of Faith* (Charlottesville: University Press of Virginia, 1994).

8. Lynn Davidman, *Becoming Un-Orthodox: Stories of Ex-Hasidic Jews* (New York and Oxford: Oxford University Press, 2015).

9. Benjamin T. Phillips and Shaul Kelner, "Reconceptualizing Religious Change: Ethno-Apostasy and Change in Religion Among American Jews," *Sociology of Religion* 67, no. 4 (2006): 509.

10. A detailed description and analysis of the methodologies used in this book can be found in *Becoming Un-Orthodox*.

11. Davidman, "Becoming Un-Orthodox," 65.

12. Erving Goffman, *The Presentation of Self in Everyday Life* (Garden City, NY: Doubleday, 1959).

13. Davidman, "Becoming Un-Orthodox," 67.

Bibliography

Andrews, Seth. *Deconverted: A Journey from Religion to Reason.* Denver: Outskirt Press, 2013.

Barbour, John D. *Versions of Deconversion: Autobiography and the Loss of Faith.* Charlottesville: University Press of Virginia, 1994.

Barker, Dan. *Losing Faith in Faith: From Preacher to Atheist.* Madison, WI: FFRF, Inc., 1992.

Bromley, David G. *Falling From the Faith: Causes and Consequences of Religious Apostasy.* Newbury Park, CA: Sage Publications, 1988.

Bromley, David G. "Linking Social Structure and the Exit Process in Religious Organizations: Defectors, Whistle-Blowers, and Apostates." *Journal for the Scientific Study of Religion* 37, no. 1 (March 1998): 145–60.

Davidman, Lynn. *Becoming Un-Orthodox: Stories of Ex-Hasidic Jews.* New York and Oxford: Oxford University Press, 2015.

Ebaugh, Helen Rose Fuchs. *Becoming an Ex: The Process of Role Exit.* Chicago: The University of Chicago Press, 1988.

Feldman, Deborah. *Unorthodox: The Scandalous Rejection of My Hasidic Roots.* New York: Simon and Schuster, 2012.

Goffman, Erving. *The Presentation of Self in Everyday Life.* Garden City, NY: Doubleday, 1959.

Hoge, Dean R. *Converts, Dropouts, and Returnees: A Study of Religious Change among Catholics.* New York: The Pilgrim Press, 1981.

Lobdell, William. *Losing My Religion: How I Lost My Faith Reporting on Religion in America—and Found Unexpected Peace.* New York: Collins, 2009.

McKnight, Scot, and Hauna Ondrey. *Finding Faith, Losing Faith: Stories of Conversion and Apostasy.* Waco, TX: Baylor University Press, 2008.

Phillips, Benjamin T., and Shaul Kelner. "Reconceptualizing Religious Change: Ethno-Apostacy and Change in Religion Among American Jews." *Sociology of Religion* 67, no. 4 (2006): 507–24.

Rambo, Lewis R. *Understanding Religious Conversion.* New Haven, CT: Yale University Press, 1993.

Roozen, David A. "Church Dropouts: Changing Patterns of Disengagement and Re-Entry." *Review of Religious Research* 21, no. 4 (1980): 427–50.

Streib, Heinz, Ralph W. Hood Jr., Barbara Keller, Rosina-Martha Csöff, and Christopher F. Silver. *Deconversion: Qualitative and Quantitative Results from Cross-Cultural Research in Germany and the United States of America.* Göttingen, Germany: Vandenhoeck & Ruprecht, 2009.

Winston, Hella. *Unchosen: The Hidden Lives of Hasidic Rebels.* Boston: Beacon Press, 2005.

Zuckerman, Phil. *Faith No More: Why People Reject Religion.* New York: Oxford University Press, 2012.

The Right to Education

Israeli OTD People and Their Struggle for a Fair Chance

MOSHE SHENFELD

Translation: Penny (Pinny) Gold

Introduction: Why Specifically Israel?

Ever since the destruction of the Temple, the Jewish nation has been known for its widespread geographic distribution. In most countries where there is a significant Jewish population today, Haredi[1] communities can also be found; and in almost every place where there is a Haredi society, there are also individuals who leave it. This article will deal with *Off The Derech* (OTD) people—those who grew up in the Haredi society and chose to leave it or were forced out of it—the challenges they face, and the question of the State's responsibility toward them. Specifically, this article will focus on OTD people in Israel in recent decades.

In many ways, the challenges which OTD individuals in Israel face are similar to the ones facing those who leave the Haredi society in other countries. The emotional turmoil that results from the loss of faith, the partial or full separation from the family, community, and social network, lack of familiarity with the general culture, and various levels of educational gaps affect most OTD people around the world. At the same time, "going OTD" in Israel is unique in a number of ways. One issue is that the Haredi educational system in Israel is focused

217

on religious studies and does not provide most of its students with a marketable education in the modern labor market. This fact does not prevent the State of Israel from approving, and even partially funding, the Haredi educational institutions, while simultaneously not setting the curricula therein, and hardly monitoring these religious institutions. Second, considering the size of the Haredi society, currently accounting for more than 10 percent of the entire Israeli population, not only does the low educational level and employment rate of its members, and of those who leave it, affect them, but it also impacts well beyond the boundaries of the Haredi sector thus affecting the overall Israeli economy. A third issue is composed of the decision of the State of Israel to fund various educational tracks to bridge knowledge gaps for Haredim, which until recently remained closed to those who grew up in the Haredi society but chose to leave it. These three characteristics—OTD people's educational gaps which accumulated with the State's approval, their exclusion from the gap-closing programs, and the possible effects they will have on Israel's economic future—distinguish the OTD community in Israel from its counterparts around the world.

In 2013, I had the honor to found, together with some of my colleagues, the *Out for Change* Association and serve as its chairman until recently. Since its founding, the Association stands at the forefront of the battle to ensure the rights of the OTD community, demanding that the State of Israel take responsibility for the challenges OTD people face due to the educational gaps they have accumulated and assist them in closing these gaps. In this article, I will: characterize the Haredi society and those who leave it, describe the discrimination this group faces, explain why the State of Israel is responsible for this discrimination, will review the battle to end this discrimination, and detail our achievements in this struggle.[2]

Haredim

The Haredi Society in Israel and Its Characteristics

The Israeli population includes a number of ethnic and religious minority groups, among them are Haredim, a sub-group of Orthodox Judaism, which positions its ideology and lifestyle as a counterculture to the society around it.[3] From an ideological perspective, Haredi society is characterized by the requirement for men to study Torah (which earned it the nickname "Society of Scholars"). Its members must fully commit to Jewish tradition, adhere to Halacha (Jewish Law) in its most stringent and rigorous interpretation, and adopt an anti-Zionist stance, or at least a reserved attitude regarding the Zionist enterprise and the State of Israel.[4] From a sociological-anthropological perspective, it is characterized by: its members' attire, the behavior of the society, its institutions individuals, its educational system, and its perception of representing an ideal Jewish life.[5] Haredi society insists on seclusion from general society and has successfully created a framework which almost completely disconnects most of its members from any information of what is happening in the outside world, especially regarding matters that contradict its religious lifestyle.[6] Beyond the difficulty of defining this society, there is also the problem of identifying it, and the Central Bureau of Statistics (CBS) in Israel has proposed no less than four different methods to identify Haredim, on the basis of one or more of the following indices: the educational institution they attended, those of their children, their residential area, and lastly, their self-identity.[7]

Two characteristics of the Haredi society are specifically important for the subject of this article. The first characteristic is its growth rate. In the years 2012–2014, a Haredi woman had an average of 6.9 children, compared to 3.1 in the rest of the population. As a result, the age distribution in the Haredi society is substantially different than that of the rest of the Israeli population. In 2015, Haredim constituted about 11% of the entire Israeli population, but their share among 0 to 19-year-olds was 18%.[8] In addition to its natural population growth, Haredi society benefits also from non-Haredi families who send their children to Haredi educational institutions, which contributed to the fact that in 2014, 29% of all Jewish students in kindergarten went to a Haredi institution.[9]

The second characteristic is the curriculum in the Haredi educational system and its implications on its graduates' employment. The prevailing worldview in Haredi society is that Torah study exempts the men from the burden of working for a living.[10] Accordingly, in the Haredi educational system for boys, there is almost no place for general studies, and their knowledge of mathematics, English, and other general subjects is very limited.[11] As part of the Haredi society's objection to the State meddling with its curricula, most Haredi educational institutions refuse to allow any outside monitoring by the State of their curricula and they even avoid participating in comparative testing that take place in all other Israeli educational institutions. As such, the available information on the curricula and study levels in these institutions is only partial.[12] A substantial difference exists between boys and girls regarding curricula and the level of studies taught. Almost all boys complete their general education in 7th or 8th grade, and thereafter the students focus exclusively on Torah studies.[13] Even in the lower grades, the extent of general studies is very limited. In 2013, 42% of Haredi boys studied in Exempt Institutions,[14] which are required to devote only 6 to 8 weekly hours for general studies (which are often pushed to the end of the school day), and do not teach English and science at all.[15] Even the subjects that are included in the curriculum are taught at a very low level that does not provide the tools that are required for future integration into the general labor market. Thus, for example, instruction of mathematics usually ends at the level of the multiplication table and simple fractions; and English, even when taught, is comprised only of reading and writing simple sentences.[16] Recently published data show that the average grade of Haredi educational system students that are tested in the national comparative tests in mathematics and English is about 25 out of 100, compared to about 60 out of 100 in the rest of the Jewish educational systems.[17] In contrast, girls receive a more extensive general education. Almost all girls study general subjects at a level close to that of the State schools, but most of them do not take the *Bagrut* (matriculation) exams.[18] About 60% of them are tested by a private institution, and receive a certificate not recognized by the universities. This policy is due to the desire of the management of the Haredi girls' schools to prevent female students from going on to academic studies in the universities, rather than continuing on the accepted Haredi path of learning for girls, which is only teaching studies for two additional years of study.[19]

The instruction level in the Haredi educational system also affects the eligibility rate of its students qualifying for a *Bagrut* Certificate. In the 2011–2012 academic year, only 38% of girls and 14% of boys in the Haredi institutions took the *Bagrut* exam, only 17% of girls and 2% of boys earned a full *Bagrut* Certificate, and only 9% of girls and 1% of boys received a certificate that allows them to get admitted to university. In comparison, the average *Bagrut* test takers among the Jews in Israel is 93%, where 71% are eligible for a full *Bagrut* Certificate and 61% are eligible for a certificate that allows admission to university.[20] The low general studies level also affects the proficiency of male Haredi youth, which is significantly lower than that of the other Jews in all types of proficiencies that were tested, especially when it comes to problem-solving in an eLearning environment. The situation is similar among women as well, but the gap is about half the size as that of the men.[21] Additionally, there are large gaps between Haredi men and other Jewish men regarding English language proficiency: only about 23% of Haredi men aged 20 to 34 report English language proficiency, less than 50% of whom report fluent speaking and reading on a very good level, compared to 83% of Jewish non-Haredi men who report language proficiency, 90% of which are on a very good level.[22]

The low education level of Haredim also affects their employment rates and the quality of their employment should they enter the workforce. In recent years, the percentage of employment among Haredi men is about 50%, which is significantly lower than that of other Jewish men, where the rate reaches 87%.[23] In 2015, the average monthly income of a Haredi household from work was lower by about 45% than that of other Jewish households, and the tax payment was lower by about 67% than that of other Jews. Combining these data points with the high number of persons in an average Haredi household makes these educational gaps even more significant; the end result is that the Haredi society is one of the poorest sectors in Israel.[24]

There are a number of causes for the low employment level in the Haredi society, which include, among others, the Haredi ideology and lack of incentives by the State.[25] At the same time, surveys and assessment studies that were conducted in the various gap-closing tracks show that the main causes for dropping out of the programs and for Haredi men's difficulties in finding a quality profession are the educational gaps and lack of learning habits.[26] Another indication for this is the similarity between the employment rate of Haredi men and of other men in Israel with 0 to 4 years of education during the past forty years.[27]

The combination of the aforementioned two characteristics—the low education level in the Haredi society and its high birth rate—has led over the past few years to the growth of the Haredi employment problem in Israel and its continued drain on the overall Israeli economy. According to a CBS prediction, without transfers between population groups, the percentage of Haredim in primary working ages will rise from 7.5% at the end of 2015 to 26% at the end of 2065.[28] This change will dramatically affect the Israeli economy and, according to a Ministry of Finance estimate, without a significant change in the employment percentages of Haredim and Arabs, the State of Israel will arrive at a debt-to-GDP ratio that will lead to bankruptcy by 2059.[29]

The State's Conduct in Light of Lack of Teaching Core Subjects in the Haredi Educational System

For many years, the academic research regarding the Haredi society was focused on sociological aspects, while the implications of the Haredi life-style on the economy were mainly ignored.[30] During the second half of the 1990s, a number of studies showed for the first time the low Haredi employment rate, the causes thereof, and the danger that it poses to the Israeli economy. In the early 2000s, the governmental research bodies, first the Bank of Israel, the National Insurance Institute, and the CBS, also began to deal with the subject.[31] Alongside the increased awareness of these data points in the general population and policymakers, various bodies began to debate the question: How is it appropriate to deal with the risk that the Haredi lifestyle poses to the Israeli economy?

The first attempt to solve the economic problem was focused on changing the contents being taught in the Haredi educational system. The question of the autonomy of the Haredi educational system is as old as the State of Israel—it even predates the establishment of Israel in 1948. The Status Quo Letter that David Ben Gurion, then the Chairman of the Jewish Agency Executive, sent to Agudath Israel, which represented the Haredim, promised to the Haredi educational system full autonomy, subject to a defined minimum of mandatory studies (later nicknamed "Core Subjects") by the State.[32] Accordingly, some Knesset Members and various organizations demanded that the Ministry of Education enforce the requirement to teach Core Subjects in the Haredi educational sys-tem, or at least cut the funding of educational institutions that do not teach them. The battle took place partly in the legal arena, by filing petitions with the High Court of Justice, and partly in the political arena by attempts to change the laws and/or the regulations of the Ministry of Education, so as to prevent the continued funding of institutions that do not teach Core Subjects.

During the years 1999–2008, a number of petitions were filed with the High Court, demanding the enforcement of the requirement to teach Core Subjects in the Haredi educational system, but the Ministry of

Education opposed every attempt and even avoided complying with the court's instructions several times. In 2008, the Knesset passed the Unique Cultural Educational Institutions Law, which enshrined the autonomy of *Yeshivot Ketanot*[33] and allowed their funding, without being subject to the Ministry of Education's curriculum, and, in fact, without Core Subjects being taught there at all.[34] An additional petition was filed, demanding that the law be invalidated, arguing that the State may not exempt itself from its obligation towards the students to provide them with a basic education. Unfortunately for the petitioners, this petition was rejected by the Supreme Court in 2014, as Judge Yitzchak Amit noted: "On the sensitive and volatile issue of education in the ultra-Orthodox sector, it is not the duty of the Court to remove the chestnuts from the fire."[35]

Launch of Programs to Integrate Haredim into the Israeli Society

Parallel to the battle to enforce the Core Subjects requirement in the Haredi educational system, policymakers began helping Haredi education graduates who wished to bridge their educational gaps and to integrate into the labor market.[36] In 2004, Project *Tevet* (lit. Momentum in Employment) was established in collaboration with the Joint Distribution Committee (JDC) and the Ministry of Industry, Trade and Labor, making the Haredi society one of its target groups. In 2007, the first *Shachar* (lit. Integration of Haredim) track was started in the army.[37] In 2009, a comprehensive study was conducted on the subject of Haredi employment by the National Economic Council,[38] and its conclusions led to the setting of unique employment targets for the Haredi society for the first time.[39] In 2012 and 2017, the Council for Higher Education's (CHE) Planning and Budgeting Committee (PBC) published the first and second five-year plan for the education of Haredim, respectively. In addition to the many funds that the State invests in these programs, Haredim also receive assistance from various philanthropic foundations, most prominent of which are the JDC, the *Kemach Foundation*, and the *Toronto Foundation*, which are supported by private donors around the world.

Over the years, the extent of the educational gap-closing tracks intended for Haredim has expanded. As of 2017 there were special tracks for Haredim in nineteen colleges and universities, which, beyond being adjusted to the Haredi lifestyle, also include modified admission requirements, funding, additional academic assistance, and curricula adjustment. The Haredi students also receive scholarships from the State and various philanthropic foundations.[40] The new five-year plan that was approved by the PBC in 2017 includes a budget of NIS 1.2 billion for this purpose for the next 6 years.[41] In addition to this assistance, the Ministry of Education operates, through an outside franchisee, free *Bagrut*-completing courses for Haredim.[42]

Army integration tracks are divided in two. The various *Shachar* tracks are mainly intended for married men and include partial educational gap-closing and professional training prior to the start of service, which allows them to serve in roles that prepare them for the labor market. The *Netzach Yehuda* tracks include service in gender-segregated battalions and companies, mostly in combat roles for only two years (instead of close to three years like the rest of Israeli men). In the remainder of the time, the soldier has the option to attend a preparatory program or an employment training track, while still benefiting from the army's support, with the understanding that these men lack the skills, expertise, and education that are relevant to the labor market. Additionally, Haredim benefit from adjusted classification, which allows them to integrate in preferred tracks and commanding roles, despite their low-profile classification as a result of their educational gaps.[43]

In terms of employment, the State operates various assistance programs. Over the years, eleven employment guidance centers were established throughout Israel, operated by the JDC, various municipalities, and the Ministry of Labor and Welfare,[44] which provide information and assistance for integration of Haredim into the labor market. The assistance includes, among others, classification and evaluation services, operation of free professional courses, vouchers for almost full funding of additional courses, scholarships for practical engineers, grants to employers to encourage them to hire Haredim, and support of Haredi entrepreneurs.[45]

Results of the Haredi-Integration Programs

The many efforts that have been invested in programs for Haredim achieved many of their goals, but the results show that there is still a long way to go. The dropout rate of Haredim from the pre-academic preparatory programs stands at 47% among men and 45% among women.[46] Additionally, 48% of Haredi men and 29% of Haredi women drop out during undergraduate studies, compared to 25% and 18% among other Jews, respectively.[47] Another characteristic that is unique to Haredim is the study fields and institutions they choose to attend. Thus, for example, in 2014 about 65% of Haredi men pursued degrees in law or business administration, for which there is low demand in the market, mostly in special gender-segregated programs for Haredim belonging to private colleges whose academic level is low, as reflected by their low bar exam passage rate.[48]

In terms of employment, the situation is also far from satisfactory. While Haredi women surpassed their set employment target, Haredi men are lagging far behind. Since 2015, the increase in the rate of employed Haredim has plateaued, and it even decreased somewhat.[49] Additionally, the employment quality of Haredim who work is quite low, their job extent and hourly wage are lower than that of the rest of the Jewish population, and the income of Haredi men is lower by about 43% than that of the other Jewish men as a result.[50] About 56% of Haredim are engaged in professions that belong to community and public systems, which include the fields of education, health, welfare, and junior clerical positions in the public and municipal administration, most of them with quite low income. In contrast, only about two percent of Haredim are employed in the computer field (mostly women) and only about half a percent in development positions (which is lower by about 80% than the rate in the general population).[51]

Despite the extensive allocation of resources by the State and philanthropic bodies, these data indicate the depth of the educational gaps of the graduates of the Haredi educational system, their difficulty in bridging them and integrating into the Israeli labor market, This position was explicitly expressed in an internal document by the CHE, which linked the high dropout rates of the Haredi educational system graduates from the tracks it opened to the educational gaps they struggle to overcome.[52]

OTD People

Those Who Leave the Haredi Society in Israel and Their Characteristics

Alongside the Haredi society, which has been on the receiving end of a considerable amount of attention in recent decades from researchers and policymakers, an additional population that has not received the same attention—OTD people—has been growing slowly. *Yotzim BeShe'ela* (lit. "Those who leave with a question") is currently the prevalent term in Israel to describe people who grew up in the Haredi society and have left it.[53] The term was coined as a mirror image to the expression "Returnees to the Faith" which describes a person's transition from a secular to a religious lifestyle (the word for "return" also meaning both "answer" and "repentance"). However, this term has its disadvantages, as there are those who leave the Haredi society and remain observant, and do not consider themselves *Yotzim BeShe'ela*, while some also refer to anyone who grew up in a religious family and became secular as a *Yotze BeShe'ela*. Some avoid using the term altogether because of its diverse connotations (both positive and negative), but today it is the most prevalent idiom to refer to the group. The term that has been widely accepted in English—OTD (Off The Derech)—is also controversial for similar reasons. This article deals with those who studied in Haredi educational institutions but today do not consider themselves Haredi, and subsequently the term "OTD individual/person/people/community" will be used in accordance with this definition. The rationale for the definition will become clear later in this article, as the discrimination that this group faces will be described.

The reported reasons for leaving the Haredi sect include the following: discomfort with, doubts about, and/or loss of faith in God or in religion; feeling of suffocation, desire to be independent, and difficulty to achieve self-fulfillment within the Haredi society; criticism of the Haredi society, which mostly leads to choosing an Orthodox or Traditional lifestyle; experiencing trauma and abuse (mostly sexual) within the Haredi world, which leads to the undermining of a youth's worldview. Sometimes these reasons are mixed, and cases where the leaving process starts because of one reason, but as time passes, a different reason becomes the top consideration, are commonplace.[54]

The lifestyle that Haredim have developed in recent decades, where boys study in religious schools from early childhood until their thirties, allowed it to create an undisturbed socialization process. This socialization process includes an earlier marriage age, an increase in the number of children, and increased educational gaps between the Haredi and Israeli societies. Additionally, it is also responsible for the high price that a Haredi person who chooses to go OTD, especially after one's teenage years, has to pay.[55] As a result, the process of going OTD starts mostly between the ages of 17 and 22,[56] a period during which a Haredi youth enjoys relative independence, because he or she is adult enough to be able to make decisions but still not married (the average marriage age in the Haredi society is 18 to 22 depending on the gender and sect).[57] A minority in the OTD community start the process at an earlier age, and another minority (which has been growing in recent years) choose to go OTD after marriage and children, a decision that often leads to divorce. The rarest cases are those where both spouses choose to go OTD together.

A parallel group to the OTD community is that of the youth who drop out of the Haredi educational institutions. These "dropout youths" continue to define themselves as Haredi, even though they do not continue in the acceptable path for their peers in the Haredi society.[58] In the past, the transition from the dropout youth group to the OTD community was quite rare, but in recent years the phenomenon of youths who belonged to the dropout youth group and go OTD after several years has grown, either because they saw the first group as a stopover or because they changed their worldview over the years. Today, the line between the two groups has been completely blurred. Another group that contributes to the blurred lines between Haredim and the OTD community and serves sometimes as another stop in the transition process is that of the "New Haredim," a term that describes those who consider themselves as belonging to the Haredi society according to their definition, but rebel against some of its conventions and choose to acquire an academic education, join the army, and integrate into the labor market.[59]

The Extent of the OTD Community

It is difficult to accurately assess the extent of the OTD community due to the lack of quantitative research on the phenomenon. According to Ministry of Education data, about 20% of boys and about 9% of girls who attend Haredi educational institutions and start the 7th grade, drop out before the end of the 12th grade,[60] but most of them belong to the aforementioned dropout youth group and it is possible that they will not go OTD. In recent years, the various methods to quantify the OTD community provide estimates in the range of between 7 and 10 percent of a Haredi youth cohort, which is about 1,000 to 1,500 youths who go OTD every year. The first study that was conducted on the phenomenon took place in 2014 by Out for Change, and was based on the CBS's annual Social Survey data. These results were later confirmed by the

CBS itself. In the study, OTD individuals were identified as those who defined the household in which they grew up when they were fifteen years old as Haredi, but at the time of the study did not consider themselves Haredi.[61] The study showed that among those born between 1972 and 1991 to Haredi families, about 12,300 people (7.8%) went OTD by 2012.[62] An additional analysis that Out for Change conducted indicates that the percentage has grown over the years and has currently reached about 10% among the youths. Currently, the Association is working on an expanded study, which will combine administrative data and surveys of the CBS and thus provide more reliable and detailed data on the size of the OTD community in recent years.

In 2017, the Agora Policy Institute, headed by Dr. Neri Horowitz, conducted a qualitative study for Out for Change, which included sociologically identifying and characterizing information about the OTD community. This study underscored the need to have a blueprint to help the OTD community to be used by government agencies and philanthropic foundations. The study is based on interviews with about one hundred OTD people and dozens of operatives in the field who work with the OTD community and Haredi dropout youth. The OTD people described the extent of the OTD phenomenon among family members, neighbors, and students in the institutions they had attended.[63] It appears from the interviews that the percentage of those who go OTD in the hard-core Haredi group is about 3 to 5%. Among the groups that have assimilated into the Haredi society—such as immigrants from Western countries; Returnees to the Faith; and the more open groups in the Haredi society, such as *Poalei Agudat Yisrael* (PAI) and part of the Lubavitch Hassidic sect—about 25% go OTD. Among the groups that have not assimilated into the Haredi society—mainly Neo-Breslov communities and Returnees to the Faith who do not live in Haredi-majority neighborhoods—about 10% go OTD. According to this estimate method, about 1,000 youths fully leave the Haredi society every year and several hundred more remain living in its margins.[64]

These estimates are reinforced by additional sources, In the 2016 and 2017 army recruitment years, about 2,850 and 3,070 yeshiva graduates (accordingly), enlisted in the army, of which 600 integrated into non-Haredi tracks.[65] According to unofficial estimates by people involved with these service projects, most of whom are enlisted in the general tracks are not Haredi today, and the same is true for about 10 percent of those who enlist in the Haredi tracks, but chose those service tracks because of the associated benefits therein.[66] According to data of Hillel—The Right to Choose, an organization that helps OTD individuals, it appears that over one thousand people go OTD every year. The number of people who contact Hillel has grown from less than 50 per year about a decade ago to about 250 in 2017,[67] and according to representatives of Hillel, less than one quarter of all OTD people join it.[68]

These studies did not look at the gender distribution in the OTD community, but from the impression of operatives in the field, it appears that today about 60 to 70% of them are men, while in the past their percentage was even higher. One possible explanation for the overrepresentation of men is their marriage age, which is often later by a year or two than that of women. Another reason may be the environment in the boarding schools, where most of the boys learn during adolescence and early adulthood, that allows them a greater degree of freedom than that of the girls, who mostly remain at home during their high school years, up to their marriage. As mentioned above, the Haredi cohorts are increasingly growing at a fast rate, so even if the percentage of those who go OTD will remain constant, their number will continue to grow, and within 5 to 10 years, about 2,000 youths are expected to leave the Haredi society every year.

Challenges and Trends of Going OTD

Graduates of the Haredi educational system face significant obstacles once they leave their community of origin because of gaps in their educational background. Most OTD people begin their path to the Israeli society where, in addition to the need to cope with the lack of basic education, they do not receive economic support from their family and they cannot continue to live in their parents' home. Sometimes, they even need to cope with their family's decision to completely sever the relationship with them, at least in the first few years after going OTD. This rift from the community in which they grew up and were educated in and the cultural gaps between it and the Israeli society adds another component to the difficulty of OTD individuals acclimating to Israeli society, and as a result, simple tasks, such as finding a job, become substantially more challenging. Alongside these difficulties, some OTD people are forced to deal with the emotional turmoil that results from losing their religious faith and from their separation from the community in which they were raised.[69]

As mentioned above, despite the great difficulties that the process of leaving entails, the extent of going OTD is increasingly growing over the years. Until 20 to 30 years ago, going OTD was a rare phenomenon; most OTD people were required to deal with absolute ostracism from their family, without a supportive community infrastructure, and as a result of lack of awareness, the secular society hardly helped them either. About 25 years ago, Hillel was established, and that marked the beginning of the secular effort to assist OTD people. At the beginning, the organization focused on absorbing the OTD people into Kibbutzim and volunteers' homes. Over time, the organization expanded and settled and today is working on building a community for OTD people and assisting with various services to over 1,000 people per year. The services include an emergency shelter, transitional housing, and social centers where OTD people who have joined the organization benefit from tutoring lessons, scholarships, assistance with finding employment, psychological counseling, and social events.

As the extent of the OTD phenomenon has grown, the difficulties facing the OTD community have partially decreased. Today, some of the young OTD people receive assistance from veteran OTD individuals, and the Haredi society also learned to contain them to some extent. Those who join Hillel get an opportunity to explore their capabilities and live their life to the fullest, according to the lifestyle they choose, in a supportive environment of friends and acquaintances who are in a similar situation as they are. OTD members who join Hillel receive the help of social workers, mentors, and volunteers. Alongside the growth in the number of the OTD people, the variety of types of OTD people has recently expanded and today the OTD community has branched out into subgroups with different characteristics.

Discrimination against the OTD Community and the Battle against It

Discrimination against the OTD Community

One of the first conditions that the aforementioned gap-closing assistance programs for Haredim have to meet is the adjustment to the Haredi lifestyle, which includes separation from non-Haredim and between men and women. As a result, OTD people are excluded from those programs, even though they suffer from identical knowledge gaps to that of Haredim, and in some cases their socioeconomic situation is even worse due to the separation from the family and lack of community support. This creates an absurd situation where a Haredi person who wishes to bridge the educational gaps he or she accumulated and earn an undergraduate degree receives a great deal of assistance from the State while their classmates in the same school who went OTD are excluded from these programs and have to pay for their studies at their own expense just because they chose to leave the Haredi society.

Had policymakers allowed OTD people to benefit from services similar to those of Haredim, in tracks intended for OTD people, or in a mixed framework with the general Israeli population, their decision to exclude OTD people from programs intended for Haredim would have been understandable. In fact, however, until 2013, the State has refused to give OTD individuals any assistance, and they had to face the challenges of bridging the educational gaps without receiving any support from the State, and, unfortunately, many OTD people "fell through the cracks." In some cases, the discrimination was deeply seated in the procedures, such as those that are used for programs in the employment field; according to those, "Haredi is an observant Jew who is unique in his stringent adherence to religious practices in his education and that of his children, the characteristics of the community to which he belongs, and his lifestyle, which distinguish him from the other observant Jews."[70] In other cases, such as procedures used by the PBC, the procedures included OTD people as well: "The student attended a Haredi institution from 9th to 12th grade" (where the identity of the institution as Haredi differs from boys to girls), but, in reality, only programs that are intended for Haredim were launched. In the case of the army, procedures for eligibility for the programs were not defined, only admission conditions thereto, which included a requirement to observe a Haredi lifestyle. It appears that in many cases this discrimination was not a result of a conscious decision, but of the limited extent of the OTD phenomenon in previous decades and the fact that the programs to assist Haredim were anyway required to provide separate programs.

The State's Responsibility

The dilemma regarding the limits of the State's involvement in the education of children who belong to non-liberal minority groups is not unique to Israel and is an ongoing debate in many countries that have multicultural populations. Society in general has an interest in educating its children, but beyond the clash between the parents' and the state's interests, it is important to remember that the interests of the children and of their parents are not necessarily identical.[71] The right to education is the most recognized socioeconomic right around the world; it is protected in the constitutions of 140 countries, as well as in a great number of international declarations. Israel recognizes it as a basic right as part of Basic Law: Human Dignity and Liberty, and it is also an article in the Convention on the Rights of the Child, which includes that right.[72] A central component of this right is receiving an education that is aimed in developing the personality, skills, and abilities of each student. Against that, there is the parents' right to teach their children as they see fit, as part of their right to autonomy and culture, but this right does not allow them to do as they please.[73]

One of the common means to balance the rights of the minority against that of the minority within the minority is the principle of the "Right of Exit"—the ability of individuals to leave the group affiliation to which they belong at any moment they see fit.[74] According to this principle, the state's responsibility toward someone who was born into a minority group is to ensure the existence of a reasonable possibility to get out of it; and as long as the possibility exists, individuals' remaining in the group reflects their choice to live in accordance with what is accepted within it, therefore the State should refrain from additional interference. As detailed above, the State allowed and funded the existence of educational institutions that do not provide basic education, and even fought to protect the Haredi institutions right to withhold a basic education to their enrolled students. The difficulty of OTD individuals to survive economically on their own is a direct result of the lack of a basic education that is required to live in dignity in the modern labor market, and thus the State of Israel does not provide the right of exit from the Haredi society.[75] This right is further impaired due to the exclusion of OTD individuals from the educational gap-closing programs that were launched for Haredim, which could have reduced the difficulty of leaving the Haredi society. Moreover, because the main (and sometimes only) justification that is presented to operate these programs are the education gaps with which Haredi education graduates face, it is unclear how one can justify the conditioning of the eligibility to receive the assistance by the current lifestyle of an applicant who wishes to earn a decent living and acquire a profession.

Beyond the moral and legal considerations, this discrimination is also contrary to the State's direct economic interest. Although OTD individuals already chose to leave the Haredi society, without assistance in closing the gaps, there is a high risk that they will not succeed in achieving an income level that will allow them to live in dignity and become productive citizens. Additionally, the difficulty in integrating into Israeli society may deter additional youths who wish to go OTD, but are fearful of the personal, social, and economic price they will have to pay, and as a result continue to live a lifestyle that is not in accordance with their faith. Clearly, this situation hurts both the would-be OTD people and the State, which has an economic interest in closing educational gaps for all of their citizens, regardless of religious belief. In fact, it is reasonable to assume that the amount of funds that is necessary to assist the OTD community is even lower than those needed to assist Haredim because, in contrast to Haredim, OTD people are interested in integrating into the Israeli society and do not require the establishment of separate infrastructure. Furthermore, providing education to the OTD community stops the cycle of neediness, because the OTD people's children will attain an education in the State educational institutions, in contrast to Haredim who may prevent basic education for their children just like their parents did, and require the State to continue to invest substantial amounts in closing the gaps for future generations as well.

The Founding of the Out for Change Association and Filing the Core Subjects Lawsuit

In 2013, the Out for Change Association was founded by OTD individuals for OTD individuals. The Association works to secure their rights through activism to change policy, provide development of programs, and raise public awareness of the OTD phenomenon. In its activity, the Association puts an emphasis on direct assistance of the State and public bodies to OTD individuals in order to give them the tools that will allow them to live up to their abilities and turn them into productive and economically-independent citizens. The activity is focused in the areas of closing educational gaps, military service, employment, and family (assistance in custody hearings in the Rabbinate Courts and in the civil courts in cases where one of the spouses is OTD). This includes legal and political battles to equalize the rights of the OTD community to that of Haredim, raising awareness of the public in general, and the policymakers in particular, to the OTD phenomenon and to the OTD community's needs, conducting and requesting research studies, development of programs to bridge the gaps, cooperation with government bodies and private entities to operate the programs, and making information of their rights accessible to the OTD community. One of the important characteristics of the organization's activity is changing the terminology of the discourse regarding the OTD community from one of welfare to one of rights. Out for Change believes the OTD community deserves State assistance as a basic right and should not be considered charity.

As part of its activities, the Association initiated and led a tort claim lawsuit that was filed near the end of 2015 on behalf of fifty-two OTD men and women, in which the government offices were sued for breaching their duties to provide the petitioners with basic education during their school years and for their refusal to assist them today in closing their obvious educational gaps. In response to the suit, the State Attorney asked to dismiss some of the petitioners, arguing that the statute of limitations had passed, and brought a third-party claim against the petitioners' parents and their educational institutions. These two moves are considered unusual on the part of the State, and during the first hearing the judge even expressed his discomfort with the strategy that the State Attorney used. Nonetheless, the State Attorney chose to pile up procedural hurdles on the petitioners and delay the hearing on the merits of the claims. Some of the petitioners withdrew their petitions due to pressure from their parents, who found themselves defendants in this lawsuit, while others were dismissed after the judge accepted the statute of limitations argument in August 2017. During 2018, an appeal of the latter decision was filed with the Supreme Court and it will be argued in 2020.[76] This lawsuit forces the court and the defendant government offices to address the two main discriminations from which the OTD community suffers: First, their discrimination as graduates of the Haredi educational system as compared to graduates of the Israeli educational system, in that they do not get to acquire a basic education that will allow them to live in dignity. Second, their discrimination as people who do not currently live a Haredi lifestyle as compared to the Haredim who receive assistance and support to bridge the gaps, a support that could have reduced the damage that was caused from the first discrimination.

The purpose of filing the lawsuit was not to receive monetary compensation for that small group of petitioners, but rather to raise awareness of the discrimination against the OTD community, confronting the State with the ramifications of its policies on the lives of tens of thousands of people, and creating leverage to stop this ongoing "double" discrimination. The lawsuit received great publicity in Israel and around the world, and it raised awareness of the battle for the rights of the OTD community.

The Association's Achievements

Since its founding, the Association has worked tirelessly to end the discrimination against the OTD community. During its years of operation, the Association has succeeded in bringing about a gradual change in the way policymakers treat the OTD community, and today we can point to many achievements in this regard.[77] The most significant change has occurred in the field of education where no official discrimination remains, although the realization of these rights is still deficient as a result of a lack of awareness on the part of the OTD community and the different institutes.[78] In 2016, an assistance program for graduates of the Haredi educational system was launched for the first time at the Hebrew University of Jerusalem and its Preparatory Program, which includes, tutoring lessons, eligibility for admission under special conditions, and extension of exam time. To date, similar programs have opened in five other academic institutions. In addition, the PBC has instructed the Kemach Foundation to stop conditioning the receipt of scholarships on maintaining a Haredi lifestyle and many OTD students have begun to benefit from these scholarships. The IDF passed a series of procedures which include: adjusted classification for all graduates of Haredi education; easement in being recognized as Lone Soldiers; and in 2018 even decided that OTD people are eligible to complete studies during the service, similar to those serving in the tracks for Haredim, although, again, this decision still lacks in implementation.[79] We also see a change in the field of employment, and after years of the policymakers' refusal to acknowledge the needs of the OTD, the Ministry of Labor, Welfare and Social Services has begun to revoke its discriminatory practices against the OTD. During the year 2018 the requirement to maintain a Haredi lifestyle was dropped from their criteria for eligibility to receive scholarships for courses in practical engineering and vouchers for vocational training. Today, the Ministry of Labor is working on developing additional vocational programs for the OTD, although the extent of the assistance to which they are entitled is still significantly lower in comparison to Haredim.

In early 2017, the Association made a strategic decision to expand its activities into the individual domain, thanks to a generous grant from the Charles and Lynn Schusterman Family Foundation. Since making this decision, the Association operates under two departments, the first—Policy and Development—includes the Association's aforementioned activities; and the second—Individual—includes counseling, vocational and academic guidance, rights-exercising services and legal assistance in family law for those who went OTD after they married.[80] The Individual Department also operates assistance programs for OTD people which include, among others, courses in basic English, mathematics, computer usage, introductory computer science, tutoring lessons, and workshops providing soft skills in the employment field. Additionally, the Individual Department has created an infrastructure for communal and social activity, including workshops and courses in the various fields of art and social events. The activities are concentrated in *HaSalon*[81]—Community Centers for the OTD which opened in Jerusalem and Tel Aviv, supported by a web-site with extensive information such as a handbook for the OTD, a virtual community center and information on the activities of the Association. Since 2019, the Individual Department's activity is financed by a joint project with the National Insurance Institute, the Ministry of Welfare, and a number of philanthropic foundations.

In Lieu of a Conclusion

In contrast to the common structure in dramatic plays, this article does not end with a climax. The battle for the rights of the OTD community did not and will not have a final scene in which the State's opposition collapses at once. The change is composed of many small steps accumulating together. One program joins another program, one OTD person joins another OTD person, one policymaker joins another policymaker, and, from year to year, the OTD phenomenon becomes a slightly more possible undertaking. Government offices that fought the Association in the past are treating it today as a partner in its activities. Media outlets that in the past showed no interest in covering the battle are now independently writing stories on this topic. Bridging the gaps that in the past were perceived among the OTD community as possible for only the privileged few, is becoming the appropriate and necessary norm.

This process is developing simultaneously with the change that the OTD community and its image are undergoing. In a story that aired at mid-2017 on Channel 10, Avishai Ben Chaim, Channel 10's Correspondent for Haredi Affairs, defined the OTD community as the "Official refresher of the Jewish-Israeli identity."[82] The question, "What can the OTD community do for the State?" has joined the question, "What does the State need to do for the OTD community?" and it appears that the answer is: "A great deal," and not just because of its increase in numbers. Representation of OTD people in the arts and industry is growing and deepening, the characteristics of the new lives of the OTD community are becoming increasingly diverse and interest in the OTD community is growing.

It is early to assess the ramifications that the OTD phenomenon has on the Israeli society and I doubt that I am the correct person to do so, but I would venture to say that there is room for conjecture. In the economic arena, I am confident that the OTD phenomenon will be found to be one of the main reasons that will prevent the abovementioned forecasted bankruptcy of the State. However, the contribution of the OTD community to the State goes beyond its members becoming productive citizens. It appears that in recent years OTD people have become a kind of inter-cultural bridge to and from the Haredi society, speaking both sides' languages, brokering between them, and criticizing them. On the one hand, the OTD community gradually exposes the Haredi society (especially the "New Haredim") to the possibilities that the Israeli society has to offer. On the other hand, the OTD community also has an effect on the Israeli culture, as its members are thoroughly familiar with the Jewish and Haredi cultures and traditions, and are interested in adjusting these mores into the twenty-first century.

While the economic effect of the OTD community remains limited to the borders of the State of Israel, it is important to remember that the cultural impact may extend far beyond that. In an era where great parts of world Jewry are dealing with a renewed definition of the place of the Jewish identity in a global world, OTD individuals, who are challenging the conventions on which they grew up, may (and already do) offer a fresh perspective on how to view Judaism and various ways to preserve it as a culture, nationality, or religion. Although it may sound overambitious, I dare to estimate that similar to the Enlightenment and Zionist Movements that preceded it, the OTD phenomenon is the next great herald of the Jewish nation.

Notes

1. Ultra-Orthodox Jews, who are known for their strict adherence to traditional Jewish law and rejection of modern culture, to be discussed in further detail below.

2. Writing this article would not have been possible without the assistance of Aharon Rose, Assaf Malchi, Yehuda Shohat, Dr. Lee Cahaner, Prof. Emeritus Menachem Friedman, and other people who have supported, commented on, and helped editing it, and I am forever grateful to them. Special thanks goes to Professor Emeritus Ron Hoz, Dr. Idit Kanfi, and Ruth Meller who recognized the article's potential even in its crude form, and to the editors, Professor Jessica Lang and Professor Ezra Cappell, who polished its final version. Last but not least, my dear mother who walked me through writing and translating the article, contributed to it throughout, and is also responsible for most of the good things in my life.

3. The changes that the Haredi ideology has undergone over the years and the migration from and to the Haredi society makes it difficult to define its characteristics. This article will focus on the Haredi society in Israel in recent decades.

4. Menachem Friedman, *The Haredi (Ultra-Orthodox) Society: Sources Trends and Processes* (Jerusalem: The Jerusalem Institute for Israel Studies, 1991), 9. For further details, see Benjamin Brown, *The Haredim: A Guide to Their Beliefs and Sectors* (Holon: Am Oved Publishers, 2017).

5. Kimi Kaplan, "The Study of Haredi Society in Israel: Characteristics, Achievements and Challenges" in *Israeli Haredim: Integration without Assimilation?* ed. Kimi Kaplan and Emmanuel Sivan (Tel-Aviv: Hakibbutz Hameuchad and Van Leer Jerusalem Institute, 2003), 224. For further details, see Haim Zicherman, *Black Blue-White: A Journey into the Charedi Society in Israel* (Tel Aviv: Miskal Publications, 2014).

6. Bezalel Cohen, *Economic Hardship and Gainful Employment in Haredi Society in Israel: An Insider's Perspective*, trans. Tamar Bash (Jerusalem: The Floersheimer Institute, 2006), 38–39.

7. Central Bureau of Statistics (Israel), *Measurement and Estimates of the Population of Ultra-orthodox Jews*, Israela Fridman, et al.

8. Gilad Malach, Maya Choshen, and Lee Cahaner, *Statistical Report on Ultra-Orthodox Society in Israel* (Jerusalem: The Center for Religion, Nation and State, 2016), 20.

9. Neri Horowitz, *Haredi Society 2016: An Overview* (Jerusalem: The Haredi Institute for Public Affairs, 2016), 23. Nachum Blass and Haim Bleikh, *Demographics in the Education System: Pupil Composition and Transfers Between Education Streams* (Jerusalem: Taub Center for Social Policy Studies, 2016), 17.

10. Cohen, *Economic Hardship and Gainful Employment in Haredi Society*, 34.

11. Jacob Lupu, *New Directions in Haredi Society Vocational Training and Academic Studies* (Jerusalem: The Floersheimer Institute, 2005), 7–61. Cohen, *Economic Hardship and Gainful Employment in Haredi Society*, 47.

12. The Knesset, Center for Research and Information, *Core Curriculum Studies in the Haredi Education System*, Eti Weissblei, 4, 19.

13. Lotem Perry-Hazan, *The Ultra-Orthodox Education in Israel: Law, Culture, and Politics* (Jerusalem: The Hebrew University of Jerusalem & Nevo, 2013), 156–158.

14. Institutions that are exempt from meeting the general requirements and instead receive special conditions which exempt them from following the provisions of the Compulsory Education Law. Malach & others, *Statistical Report on Ultra-Orthodox Society in Israel*, 61. Reuven Gal, Yehuda Morgenstern and Yael Elimelech, *Excellence in Mathematics in the Ultra-Orthodox Community* (Haifa: Samuel Neaman Institute, 2017), 13.

15. Weissblei, *Core Curriculum Studies in the Haredi Education System*, 13.

16. Perry-Hazan, *The Ultra-Orthodox Education in Israel*, 149–155.

17. Michal Chernovitzky and Dvora Feldman, *The Backyard of Education in Israel. The Haredi Educational System: Situation Report and Immediate Recommendations* (Israel: The Berl Katznelson Foundation, 2018), 30–31.

18. Having a *Bagrut* Certificate is a prerequisite to get into university and to get many jobs. Gal & others, *Excellence in Mathematics in the Ultra-Orthodox Community*, 18–19.

19. This testing method was chosen by the Haredi schools in order to prevent the girls from going to university and ensuring they will remain in the Haredi education system. Lupu, *New Directions in Haredi Society*, 98.

20. Malach & others, *Statistical Report on Ultra-Orthodox Society in Israel*, 82–86. As one can learn from the comparisons that appear in this report, the customary division in demographic studies in Israel is into three groups: 1. Jews that are not Haredi and others (Christians and other religions), 2. Arabs, 3. Haredim. This choice is a result of the unique characteristics of the Arab and Haredi populations. Accordingly, in most instances throughout the article, the data of the Haredi society will be compared to the other Jews and not to the average in Israel.

21. Bank of Israel, "Periodical Fiscal Review and Analysis of Research," 19–20.

22. Ministry of Finance, "Weekly Fiscal Review: December 17, 2017," 9.

23. Malach & others, *Statistical Report on Ultra-Orthodox Society in Israel*, 141

24. Central Bureau of Statistics (Israel), "Household Income and Expenditure: Data from the Household Expenditure Survey, 2016, General Summaries," table 13.

25. Lupu, *New Directions in Haredi Society*, 7–61. Cohen, *Economic Hardship and Gainful Employment in Haredi Society*, 33–44.

26. Ministry of Industry, Trade and Labor, Department of Research and Economics, *Haredi Employment Development Centers (MafteAch): Socio-Demographic Characteristics of the Applicants and the Programs in the Centers, Report No. 1,* Chagit Sofer-Fruman, 21. Eitan Regev, "Education and Employment in the Haredi Sector" in *State of the Nation Report, 2013,* ed. Dan Ben-David (Jerusalem: Taub Center for Social Policy Studies in Israel, 2013). Yohai Hakak, *Vocational Training for ultra-orthodox men* (Jerusalem: The Floersheimer Institute, 2004), 97–99.

27. Regev, *Education and Employment in the Haredi Sector,* 120–121.

28. Central Bureau of Statistics (Israel), "Press Release: Forecast of the population of Israel up to 2065."

29. Ministry of Finance, *Demographic Changes and Their Implications for Fiscal Aggregates in the Years 2014–2059,* Assaf Geva.

30. Gilad Malach, *Public Policy Strategy Pertaining to Israel's Haredi Population* (PhD diss., The Hebrew University of Jerusalem, 2013), 151. For a thorough review see: Kimi Kaplan, "The Study of Jewish Religious Society in Israel: Achievements, Missed Opportunities and Challenges," Magamot Vol. 52-2 (2017), 207–250.

31. Most remarkable is Eli Berman and Ruth Klinov, "Human Capital Investment and Nonparticipation: Evidence from a Sample with Infinite Horizons," *Discussion Paper No. 97.05* (Jerusalem: The Maurice Falk Institute for Economic Research in Israel, 1997). For a thorough review see Malach, *Public Policy Strategy,* 40.

32. The full paragraph is: "Education: Full autonomy of every stream in education will be guaranteed (incidentally, this rule applies in the Zionist Association and "Knesset Israel" at present); the Government will take no steps that adversely affect the religious awareness and religious conscience of any part of Israel. The state, of course, will determine the minimum obligatory studies—Hebrew language, history, science and the like—and will supervise the fulfillment of this minimum, but will accord full freedom to each stream to conduct education according to its conscience and will avoid any adverse effect on religious conscience." Translation of the full letter can be found at: Itamar Rabinovich and Jehuda Reinharz ed. *Israel in the Middle East: Documents and Readings on Society, Politics, and Foreign Relations, Pre-1948 to the Present* (Waltham, MA: Brandeis Univ. Press, 2008), 59.

33. Educational institutions for boys of high school age, sometimes in dormitories, where only religious studies are taught.

34. Weissblei, *Core Curriculum Studies in the Haredi Education System,* 7–10.

35. Tal Frost, "A Core for What? Ruling Commentary Following the Rubinstein Ruling: The Right to Leave and Education for Critical Thinking in the Framework of Core Studies in the Ultra-Orthodox Sector in Israel," The Bar-Ilan law Studies, Vol. 30 (2016), 564–566.

36. For a thorough review of the process see Lupu, *New Directions in Haredi Society*, 62–89, and Malach, *Public Policy Strategy*, parts 4–6.

37. Ministry of Industry, Trade and Labor, Department of Research and Economics, *Haredi Men in Technological Military Service: Integration of Graduates of 'Shahar' Programs in the Labor Market, Evaluation Research Report*, Assaf Malachi, 9–12.

38. The National Economic Council in the Prime Minister's Office, *The Ultra-Orthodox Sector in Israel: Empowerment and Integration into Employment*, Hagai Levin.

39. The National Economic Council in the Prime Minister's Office, "Committee for Examination of Employment Policy in Israel: Final Report," 13.

40. Council of Higher Education (Israel), *The Five-Year Plan of the CHE-PBC for the Ultra-Orthodox Population for the Years 2012–2016*, Gilad Malach, Lee Kahner and Eitan Regev.

41. Council of Higher Education (Israel). "The Multi-Year Plan 2017–2022, Press Conference." The Knesset, Center for Research and Information, *Government Assistance Programs for People from Ultra-Orthodox Backgrounds in the Fields of Higher Education, Employment and Military Service*, Itai Fiedelman, 5–13.

42. Government Procurement Administration, "Tender for Running a Preparatory Program for Matriculation Exams for Students in the Ultra-Orthodox Sector."

43. The Knesset, Center for Research and Information, *Army Service of the Haredi and for Those Who Left the Haredi Community*, Oriana Almasi, 10–14.

44. In the past, employment matters belonged to the Ministry of Economics.

45. Fiedelman, *Government Assistance Programs for People from Ultra-Orthodox Backgrounds*, 13–20.

46. This is not compared to the average among non-Haredim, because most of them do not need a preparatory program and are admitted to universities based on the *Bagrut* Certificate they received in high school.

47. Eitan Regev, "The Challenges of Haredi Integration into Academic Studies" in *State of the Nation Report, 2016*, ed. Avi Weiss (Jerusalem: Taub Center for Social Policy Studies in Israel, 2016).

48. Ilia Zatcovetsky and Reuven Gal, *Between (MACHA"R) Tomorrow and Today: Academic System for Haredim at a Cross-Road* (Haifa: Samuel Neaman Institute, 2015).

49. Ministry of Finance, "Weekly Fiscal Review: September 24, 2017."

50. Ministry of Finance, "Weekly Fiscal Review: December 17, 2017," 7.

51. Horowitz, *Haredi Society 2016*, 61.

52. Document No. 9444 that was sent to the CHE members ahead of the CHE meeting that took place on 05/23/2017, Art. 100. Not published.

53. In the past, the term *Chozrim BeShe'ela* meaning "Returnees with a question" was more common.

54. Neri Horowitz, *Haredi Disaffiliation: Risk, Potential and Social Policy* (Jerusalem: Out for Change, 2018), 11–16. The qualitative academic research on the subject of leaving the Haredi society is quite limited. The studies are based on a small number of interviews, most of which were conducted 10–20 years ago, before the increase in the extent of the OTD phenomenon to be described below. As such, the information that appears in the article is mainly based on the research of Dr. Neri Horowitz that was conducted during the years 2016–2017, and its findings are integrated with, and expand on, the preceding studies, most notably: Sarit Barzilai, *To Break a Hundred Gates: A Journey to the World of Those Who Go Out to the Question* (Tel Aviv: Miskal Publications, 2004). Orna Shani, *Haredim Migrating to Israeliness: The Discourse of the Ultra-Orthodox Men about the Defection from the Haredi Community and the Process of Their Integration into Israeli Society* (MA thesis, ben gurion university of the negev, 2005). Galia Weinberg-Cornik, *Between "Appearance" and Authenticity: Experiences, Meanings and Implications among "Going Out with a Question"* (PhD diss. Haifa University, 2012). Shlomi Doron, *Shuttling Between Two Worlds: Coming to and Defecting from Ultra-Orthodox Judaism in Israeli Society* (Tel Aviv: Hakibbutz Hameuchad Publications, 2013).

55. Menachem Friedman, "About Miracles": The Flourishing of the "Torah World" of Yeshivot and Kollelim in Israel" in *Handbook of Israel: Major Debates*, ed. Eliezer Ben-Rafael, Julius H. Schoeps, Yitzhak Sternberg and Olaf Glockner (Berlin/Boston: Walter de Gruyter GmbH, 2016), 241.

56. Horowitz, *Haredi Disaffiliation*, 16.

57. Central Bureau of Statistics (Israel), *Ultra-Orthodox Jews Geographic Distribution and Demographic, Social and Economic Characteristics of the Ultra-Orthodox Jewish Population in Israel 1996–2001*. Norma Gurovich and Eilat Cohen-Kastro, 37.

58. Zicherman, *Black Blue-White*, 121–127.

59. Ibid., 99–114.

60. Malach & others, *Statistical Report on Ultra-Orthodox Society in Israel*, 63.

61. This data collection method is limited by the percentage of survey respondents and a reliance on self-identification as a measure of the level of the family's orthodoxy level.

62. Fiedelman, *Government Assistance Programs for People from Ultra-Orthodox Backgrounds*, 4.

63. The limitations of this method are the inability to determine the degree it represents the sampled population and the possibility of underestimation due to "quiet" cases of going OTD; that is, OTD people who made the transition in a way that was not publicized within their extended environment.

64. Horowitz, *Haredi Disaffiliation*, 37–38.

65. Almasi, *Army Service of the Haredi and for Those Who Left the Haredi Community*, 14.

66. There is a limited phenomenon of Lubavitch Hassidim who enlist in a general service track, but this cannot explain the extent of the data. See also Asaf Malchi, *A Bridge to Employment: The Benefits of Military Service for Ultra-Orthodox Men* (Jerusalem, The Center for Religion, Nation and State, 2017), 43–52 and Almasi, *Army Service of the Haredi and for Those Who Left the Haredi Community*, 2.

67. Although it is possible that part of the growth can be explained by the increased awareness of the organization and the people who join it later on.

68. According to data that were received from Hillel. The data relating to the period from a decade ago is only an estimate because then the tracking was only partial.

69. Horowitz, *Haredi Disaffiliation*, 44–52.

70. It is interesting to note that the source of the criterion is the 4346/92 *Ma'ale vs. The Education and Culture Minister* decision by the High Court, which states: "We find that 'Haredim' **in terms of support in public institutions that perform cultural activities for 'Haredim'** refers to observant Jews . . ." (emphasis added).

71. Tammy Harel Ben Sharar, "Educational Autonomy, Core Curricula and Public Funding of Education—The 2008 Culturally-Unique Schools Act," *Law & Government (Mishpat Umimshal)* 12 (2009), 14–17.

72. Perry-Hazan, *The Ultra-Orthodox Education in Israel*, 257–260, 277–282.

73. Ibid., 304–307.

74. Frost, "A Core for What, 567–581.

75. Yael Simon, "'The Right to Leave' from a Non-Liberal Minority and the Model of 'Participatory Space': The French Education System and Preliminary Discussion in Israel," *Law & Government*, Vol. 12 (2009).

76. As of May 2019.

77. A detailed list of the achievements can be found in the Out for Change web-site.

78. The Knesset, Center for Research and Information, *Government Assistance for Individuals with Haredi Backgrounds in the Field of Higher Education*, Ido Avgar. For comparison, see Fiedelman, *Government Assistance Programs for People from Ultra-Orthodox Backgrounds*, 20–21 and Moshe Shenfeld, "Former Ultra-Orthodox Jews: From Falling Between the Cracks to a Genuine Opportunity." *Adult Education in Israel* 15 (2017), 23–37, which presents the snapshot in the education area as of 2014–2015.

79. Almasi, *Army Service of the Haredi and for Those Who Left the Haredi Community*.

80. The need for assistance in the field of Family Law touches on another challenge facing those contending with divorce proceedings and custody battles as a result of going OTD. For more details on the unique challenges this group faces see Horowitz, *Haredi Disaffiliation*, 18–20, 51–52.

81. This literally translates to: "The Living Room"

82. Avishay Ben Haim, "Light and Jerusalem: The Young People Who Leave Religion But Do Not Give Up on the Spirituality of Jerusalem," Channel 10. Updated 18/5/2017.

References

Bank of Israel. "Periodical Fiscal Review and Analysis of Research." http://www.boi.org.il/he/NewsAndPublications/PressReleases/Documents/%D7%94%D7%A1%D7%A7%D7%99%D7%A8%D7%94%20%D7%94%D7%A4%D7%99%D7%A1%D7%A7%D7%9C%D7%99%D7%AA%20%D7%94%D7%AA%D7%A7%D7%95%D7%A4%D7%AA%D7%99%D7%AA%20%D7%95%D7%9C%D7%A7%D7%98%20%D7%A0%D7%99%D7%AA%D7%95%D7%97%D7%99%D7%9D%20%D7%9E%D7%97%D7%A7%D7%A8%D7%99%D7%99%D7%9D.pdf.

Barzilai Sarit. To Break a Hundred Gates: A Journey to the World of Those Who Go Out to the Question. Tel Aviv, Miskal Publications, 2004.

Ben Haim, Avishay. "Light and Jerusalem: The Young People Who Leave Religion But Do Not Give Up on the Spirituality of Jerusalem." Channel 10. Updated 18/5/2017. http://10tv.nana10.co.il/Article/?ArticleID=1247021.

Berman Eli and Ruth Klinov. "Human Capital Investment and Nonparticipation: Evidence from a Sample with Infinite Horizons (Or: Jewish Father Stops Going to Work)," Discussion Paper No. 97.05. Jerusalem: The Maurice Falk Institute for Economic Research in Israel, 1997.

Blass Nachum and Haim Bleikh. Demographics in the Education System: Pupil Composition and Transfers Between Education Streams. Jerusalem: Taub Center for Social Policy Studies, 2016. http://taubcenter.org.il/wp-content/files_mf/transfersineducationeng.pdf.

Brown Benjamin. The Haredim: A Guide to Their Beliefs and Sectors. Holon: Am Oved Publishers, 2017 [Hebrew].

Central Bureau of Statistics (Israel). "Household Income and Expenditure: Data from the Household Expenditure Survey, 2016, General Summaries." https://www.cbs.gov.il/he/publications/doclib/2019/1719/h_print.pdf.

———. Measurement and Estimates of the Population of Ultra-Orthodox Jews. Israela Fridman, et al. [Hebrew]. https://www.cbs.gov.il/he/publications/DocLib/tec/tec25/tec25.pdf.

———. "Press Release: Forecast of the Population of Israel up to 2065." https://www.cbs.gov.il/he/mediarelease/DocLib/2017/138/01_17_138b.pdf.

———. Ultra-Orthodox Jews Geographic Distribution and Demographic, Social and Economic Characteristics of the Ultra-Orthodox Jewish Population in Israel

1996–2001. Norma Gurovich and Eilat Cohen-Kastro [Hebrew]. https://www.cbs.gov.il/he/publications/DocLib/pw/pw5/pw5.pdf.

Chernovitzky Michal, and Dvora Feldman. *The Backyard of Education in Israel. The Haredi Educational System: Situation Report and Immediate Recommendations.* Israel. The Berl Katznelson Foundation, 2018. http://www.berl.org.il/wp-content/uploads/2018/02/%D7%93%D7%95%D7%97-%D7%9E%D7%A2%D7%A8%D7%9B%D7%AA-%D7%94%D7%97%D7%99%D7%A0%D7%95%D7%9A-%D7%94%D7%97%D7%A8%D7%93%D7%99%D7%AA.pdf.

Cohen Bezalel. *Economic Hardship and Gainful Employment in Haredi Society in Israel: An Insider's Perspective.* Translated by Tamar Bash. Jerusalem: The Floersheimer Institute, 2006. http://fips.huji.ac.il/sites/default/files/floersheimer/files/cohen_economic_hardship_in_haredi_society_english.pdf.

Council of Higher Education (Israel). *The Five-Year Plan of the CHE-PBC for the ultra-Orthodox population for the years 2012–2016.* Gilad Malach, Lee Kahner and Eitan Regev. http://che.org.il/wp-content/uploads/2016/04/%D7%9E%D7%97%D7%A7%D7%A8-%D7%97%D7%A8%D7%93%D7%99%D7%9D.pdf.

———. "The Multi-Year Plan 2017–2022, Press Conference." http://che.org.il/wp-content/uploads/2016/09/%D7%AA%D7%9B%D7%A0%D7%99%D7%AA-%D7%94%D7%97%D7%95%D7%9E%D7%A9-%D7%AA%D7%A9%D7%A2%D7%96-%D7%AA%D7%A9%D7%A4%D7%91.pdf.

Doron Shlomi. *Shuttling Between Two Worlds: Coming to and Defecting from Ultra Orthodox Judaism in Israeli Society.* Tel Aviv: Hakibbutz Hameuchad Publications, 2013.

Friedman Menachem. "About Miracles": The Flourishing of the "Torah World" of Yeshivot and Kollelim in Israel" in *Handbook of Israel: Major Debates,* edited by Eliezer Ben-Rafael, Julius H. Schoeps, Yitzhak Sternberg, and Olaf Glockner. Berlin/Boston: Walter de Gruyter GmbH, 2016.

———. *The Haredi (Ultra-Orthodox) Society: Sources Trends and Processes.* Jerusalem: The Jerusalem Institute for Israel Studies, 1991 [Hebrew]. http://jerusaleminstitute.org.il/.upload/haredcom.pdf. English introduction can be found here http://en.jerusaleminstitute.org.il/.upload/haredcom.pdf.

Frost Tal. "A Core for What? Ruling Commentary Following the Rubinstein Ruling: The Right to Leave and Education for Critical Thinking in the Framework of Core Studies in the Ultra-Orthodox Sector in Israel." The Bar-Ilan law Studies, Vol. 30 (2016).

Gal Reuven, Yehuda Morgenstern and Yael Elimelech. *Excellence in Mathematics in the Ultra-Orthodox Community.* Haifa: Samuel Neaman Institute, 2017 [Hebrew]. https://www.neaman.org.il/EN/Files/6-479_20170720114027.373.pdf.

Government Procurement Administration. "Tender for Running a Preparatory Program for Matriculation Exams for Students in the Ultra-Orthodox Sector." https://www.mr.gov.il/officestenders/Pages/officetender.aspx?pID=562356.

Hakak Yohai. *Vocational Training for Ultra-Orthodox Men.* Jerusalem: The Floersheimer Institute, 2004 [Hebrew]. http://fips.huji.ac.il/sites/default/files/floersheimer/files/hakak_vocational_training_for_ultra_orthodox_men.pdf.

Harel Ben Sharar Tammy. "Educational Autonomy, Core Curricula and Public Funding of Education—The 2008 Culturally-Unique Schools Act." *Law & Government (Mishpat Umimshal)* 12 (2009) [Hebrew]. http://weblaw.haifa.ac.il/he/Journals/lawGov/Volume121/08-Harel.pdf.

Horowitz Neri. *Haredi Disaffiliation: Risk, Potential and Social Policy.* Jerusalem: Out for Change, 2018 [Hebrew]. https://www.leshinuy.org/wp-content/uploads/2018/12/%D7%99%D7%A6%D7%99%D7%90%D7%94-%D7%91%D7%A9%D7%90%D7%9C%D7%94-%D7%A1%D7%99%D7%9B%D7%95%D7%9F-%D7%A1%D7%99%D7%9B%D7%95%D7%99-%D7%95%D7%9E%D7%93%D7%99%D7%A0%D7%99%D7%95%D7%AA-%D7%97%D7%91%D7%A8%D7%AA%D7%99%D7%AA.pdf.

———. *Haredi Society 2016: An Overview.* Jerusalem: The Haredi Institute for Public Affairs, 2016. [Hebrew]. http://machon.org.il/wp-content/uploads/2016/03/%D7%94%D7%9E%D7%9B%D7%95%D7%9F-%D7%94%D7%97%D7%A8%D7%93%D7%99_%D7%AA%D7%9E%D7%95%D7%A0%D7%AA-%D7%9E%D7%A6%D7%91-%D7%94%D7%97%D7%9-1%D7%A8%D7%94-%D7%94%D7%97%D7%A8%D7%93%D7%99%D7%AA-2016-1.pdf.

Kaplan Kimi. "The Study of Haredi Society in Israel: Characteristics, Achievements and Challenges" in *Israeli Haredim: Integration without Assimilation?,* edited by Kimi Kaplan and Emmanuel Sivan. Tel-Aviv: Hakibbutz Hameuchad and Van Leer Jerusalem Institute, 2003 [Hebrew].

———. "The Study of Jewish Religious Society in Israel: Achievements, Missed Opportunities and Challenges," Magamot Vol. 52-2 (2017).

Lupu Jacob. *New Directions in Haredi Society Vocational Training and Academic Studies.* Jerusalem: The Floersheimer Institute, 2005. http://fips.huji.ac.il/sites/default/files/floersheimer/files/lupo_new_directions_3.pdf.

Malach, Gilad. *Public Policy Strategy Pertaining to Israel's Haredi Population.* PhD diss. The Hebrew University of Jerusalem, 2013 [Hebrew].

Malach Gilad, Maya Choshen, and Lee Cahaner. *Statistical Report on Ultra-Orthodox Society in Israel.* Jerusalem: The Center for Religion, Nation and State, 2016 [Hebrew]. https://www.idi.org.il/media/7882/haredi_shnaton.pdf. English abstract can be found here https://en.idi.org.il/media/4240/shnaton-e_8-9-16_web.pdf.

Malchi Asaf. *A Bridge to Employment: The Benefits of Military Service for Ultra-Orthodox Men.* Jerusalem: The Center for Religion, Nation and State,

2017 [Hebrew]. https://www.idi.org.il/media/10246/a-bridge-to-employment-the-benefits-of-military-service-for-ultra-orthodox-men.pdf. English abstract can be found here https://en.idi.org.il/media/9394/the-benefits-of-military-service-to-the-ultra-orthodox-sector-in-israel-en.pdf.

Ministry of Finance. *Demographic Changes and Their Implications for Fiscal Aggregates in the Years 2014–2059*. Assaf Geva. http://www.mof.gov.il/ChiefEcon/EconomyAndResearch/ArticlesSet/Article_20150518.pdf.

———. "Weekly Fiscal Review: September 24, 2017." http://mof.gov.il/chiefecon/economyandresearch/doclib/skiracalcalit_24092017.pdf.

———. "Weekly Fiscal Review: December 17, 2017." http://mof.gov.il/chiefecon/economyandresearch/doclib/skiraclacalit_17122017.pdf.

Ministry of Industry, Trade and Labor, Department of Research and Economics. *Haredi Employment Development Centers (Mafteach): Socio-Demographic Characteristics of the Applicants and the Programs in the Centers, Report No. 1.* Chagit Sofer-Fruman. http://employment.jdc.org.il/sites/default/files/reseaarches/%D7%9E%D7%A4%D7%AA%D7%97%20%D7%9E%D7%90%D7%A4%D7%99%D7%99%D7%A0%D7%99%D7%9D%20%D7%A1%D7%95%D7%A6%D7%99%D7%95%20%D7%93%D7%9E%D7%95%D7%92%D7%A8%D7%A4%D7%99%D7%99%D7%9D%20%D7%95%D7%AA%D7%A2%D7%A1%D7%95%D7%A7%D7%AA%D7%99%D7%99%D7%9D%20%D7%A9%D7%9C%20%D7%94%D7%A4%D7%95%D7%A0%D7%99%D7%9D.pdf.

———. *Haredi Men in Technological Military Service: Integration of Graduates of 'Shahar' Programs in the Labor Market, Evaluation Research Report*. Assaf Malachi. http://economy.gov.il/Research/Documents/X12244.pdf.

Out for Change. Associations' web-site. https://www.leshinuy.org/.

Perry-Hazan Lotem. *The Ultra-Orthodox Education in Israel: Law, Culture, and Politics*. Jerusalem: The Hebrew University of Jerusalem & Nevo, 2013 [Hebrew]. https://hinuchon.files.wordpress.com/2015/03/d794d797d799d7a0d795d79a-d794d797d7a8d793d799-d791d799d7a9d7a8d790d79c-d791d799d79f-d79ed7a9d7a4d798-d7aad7a8d791d795d7aa-d795d7a4d795.pdf.

Rabinovich Itamar, and Jehuda Reinharz, eds. *Israel in the Middle East: Documents and Readings on Society, Politics, and Foreign Relations, Pre-1948 to the Present*. Waltham, MA: Brandeis Univ. Press, 2008.

Regev Eitan. "Education and Employment in the Haredi Sector" in *State of the Nation Report, 2013* edited by Dan Ben-David. Jerusalem: Taub Center for Social Policy Studies in Israel, 2013. http://taubcenter.org.il/wp-content/files_mf/stateofnation_013eng8.pdf.

———. "The Challenges of Haredi Integration into Academic Studies" in *State of the Nation Report, 2016*, edited by Avi Weiss. Jerusalem: Taub Center for Social Policy Studies in Israel, 2016. http://taubcenter.org.il/wp-content/files_mf/stateofthenation2016.pdf.

Shani Orna. *Haredim Migrating to Israeliness: The Discourse of the Ultra-Orthodox Men about the Defection from the Haredi Community and the Process of Their Integration into Israeli Society.* MA thesis, Ben Gurion University of the Negev, 2005 [Hebrew].

Shenfeld Moshe. "Former Ultra-Orthodox Jews: From Falling Between the Cracks to a Genuine Opportunity." *Adult Education in Israel* 15 (2017).

Simon Yael. "'The Right to Leave' from a Non-Liberal Minority and the Model of 'Participatory Space': The French Education System and Preliminary Discussion in Israel." Law & Government, Vol. 12 (2009). http://weblaw. haifa.ac.il/he/Journals/lawGov/Volume121/07-Simon.pdf.

The Knesset, Center for Research and Information. *Army Service of the Haredi and for Those Who Left the Haredi Society.* Oriana Almasi. https://fs.knesset.gov. il/globaldocs/MMM/9c8c51fc-ce26-e811-80da-00155d0ad651/2_9c8c51fc-ce26-e811-80da-00155d0ad651_11_10796.pdf.

———. *Core Curriculum Studies in the Haredi Education System.* Eti Weissblei. https://fs.knesset.gov.il/globaldocs/MMM/ef546b58-e9f7-e411-80c8-00155d010977/2_ef546b58-e9f7-e411-80c8-00155d010977_11_10138.pdf.

———. *Government Assistance for Individuals with Haredi Backgrounds in the Field of Higher Education.* Ido Avgar. https://fs.knesset.gov.il/globaldocs/MMM/ d41dc3b8-f7c6-e811-80e7-00155d0aeea3/2_d41dc3b8-f7c6-e811-80e7-001 55d0aeea3_11_10815.pdf.

———. *Government Assistance Programs for People from Ultra-Orthodox Backgrounds in the Fields of Higher Education, Employment and Military Service.* Itai Fiedelman. https://fs.knesset.gov.il/globaldocs/MMM/4b506b58-e9f7-e411-80c8-00155d010977/2_4b506b58-e9f7-e411-80c8-00155d010977_11_7756.pdf.

The National Economic Council in the Prime Minister's Office. "Committee for Examination of Employment Policy in Israel: Final Report." http://www. boi.org.il/deptdata/papers/paper19h.pdf.

———. *The Ultra-Orthodox Sector in Israel: Empowerment and Integration into Employment.* Hagai Levin. http://en.keren-kemach.org/wp-content/uploads/ 2016/09/The-Haredi-Sector-in-Israel-%E2%80%93-Empowerment-Through-Employment-Integration.pdf.

Weinberg-Cornik Galia. *Between "Appearance" and Authenticity: Experiences, Meanings and Implications among "Going Out With a Question."* PhD diss. Haifa University, 2012.

Zatcovetsky Ilia and Reuven Gal. *Between (MACHA"R) Tomorrow and Today: Academic System for Haredim at a Cross-Road.* Haifa: Samuel Neaman Institute, 2015 [Hebrew]. https://www.neaman.org.il/EN/Files/6-434.pdf.

Zicherman Haim. *Black Blue-White: A Journey into the Charedi Society in Israel.* Tel Aviv: Miskal Publications, 2014 [Hebrew].

In Terms of OTD

Shira Schwartz

Setting the Path in OTD Terms

"Off the Derech"—the term itself has been talked and argued about by identifiers, anti-identifiers and researchers alike. To be OTD is primarily to be "off," as in, *she's a little off, that's a real turn-off,* or *off with his head!* For some people, the characterization is a compliment—*I really want to be off, if what I am off of is you.* For others, it evokes the feelings of delegitimization and the mechanics of power that defined them as deviant in the first place. Indeed, like many identity-based slurs, the term was authored by its opponents: members of the *frum* community, as a label for those who have "left," that is, who have ceased "being" *frum.* Its use today by OTDees themselves can be seen as a redemption of the slur, a way of taking ownership over and connecting through it, as a means of solidarity and visibility.

These two verbs that I highlighted above, "leaving" and "being," are central to the framing of OTD, and often accompany and accessorize it interchangeably. "*Is* she still *frum?*" can otherwise be expressed as, "Did she *go* off the derech?" Changing one's religious status is not simply a matter of changing beliefs or practices, but a kind of exit or departure that alters one's place in the world—their ontological status. To *be* frum is to be *part of* a *frum* community, so that when you no longer *are frum,* you have left that community, abandoned it, like a person, but also, like a place. But even more precisely, being "off the derech" means detaching yourself from a direction, a way of moving in the world, which has previously set the parameters for your existence. Leaving therefore does not only mean leaving people or even a place, but also the structure and mobility of that world itself. The path *is* the place. And it is everywhere, not only in Brooklyn. It is a way of creating continuity of being wherever you go. This is why leaving the path is so catastrophic. You lose ground everywhere.

Existing in this state of "offness" is disorienting and it comes with the suffering of losing our grip on the world. Often OTDees are so busy brushing off the negative, at times dangerous ramifications of this defining state of "offness," that we do not get the chance to pause and take stock of the losses we have accrued along the way, to reckon with what it means to go through this kind of detachment and to live forever in a spectral state of loss in relation to who and where we once were. Leah Vincent highlights some of this suffering in her recent *video*. "They said these things would destroy me and to some extent they did," she says, describing the trauma, violence, and alienation she experienced in the immediate aftermath of leaving.[1] The "they" that Vincent refers to here is her community and her family, who conditioned her life "on the derech" through the fear of what would happen to her if she went off of it. Her "they" is a relatable one. In a broader sense, "they" are all of the people who undermine an OTDee's right to self-definition by warning them of the "offness" they will experience once they get to the other side. *The secular world will destroy you*, they say. The notion that "they" could be right, is perhaps an OTDee's most frightening and difficult admission.

The destruction they had in mind was a spiritual one but it is also a material one. After all, if Orthodox Jews have learned anything from both their long and recent histories of anti-Semitism, it is that Jews are not safe in the non-Jewish world. This leads to a palpable fear that our way of life is the only one that will sustain us, not only religiously, but physically. Vincent's reframing of this cautionary warning applies to other kinds of destruction: social, emotional, and bodily, and opens up the layers of what an OTDee *actually* loses. Her courageous confession confirms the demise that the struggle to go off the path threatens. The fear of its truth is a sentiment shared by many of us. And yet, its confirmation has a lot more to do with the structure of the path than with its moral superiority, the way that losing one's community, social value, resources, sensibilities, even family—in short, their world—is a funda-

mentally dangerous and damaging experience. This essay is an attempt
to understand that struggle, the struggle to unmake and remake a world.

　　We leave because our worlds are no longer habitable. This is an
absolute stance that often leads to rejecting an entire way of life as wrong,
and the fervent embracing of whatever new one we choose is right; to
exit one world in order to become part of another one: a better one, a
safer one, a truer one. Where else would we get the courage to relinquish
everything familiar for the unknown? But the very absoluteness of the
binary "we/they" is a *frum* construction, one that pits individuals against
the societal norm in totalizing ways. This division forces a kind of wager
of all or nothing. In some ways, being OTD is an extremely Orthodox
move. It comes out of a conviction of absoluteness—there are rights
and wrongs, truths and falsehoods, insiders and outsiders, and nothing in
between. We follow our inherited sensibilities for purity away from their
origin—from their "path," and toward uncharted possibilities. This act is
more than one of exiting and entering; for these paths do not exist *for*
us, separately *from* us. The transition is not as easy as closing one door
and opening another. What results, is an active process of deconstructing
and building that demands and initiates a fundamental transformation
of self. This work is perhaps the hardest work a person can take on: the
act of re-making "world,"[2] and a form of auto-reproduction along with it.
What does it mean to create *without* and *against* family and community?
These acts of creation are typically attributed to parents, society, or divine
beings. Losing all of these as reproductive forces and guides, OTDees
must make themselves into their own and only source of creation.

　　A close and serious look at the phenomenology of this world-making
and auto-reproduction, of becoming OTD, and its cosmological and spatial
practices, can shed light on what holds both the *frum* and secular worlds
together, and on the practices of world-making at large. In this essay, I
will look at how worlds make us and how we make them, and why the
abandonment of one can break you. I will approach this analysis at first
through the terms of OTDees themselves, exploring in detail the linguistic construct of this identity category in relation to both its authors
and those entitled by it, looking at how these terms lay the foundation
for our understanding of this state of being. I will look both at what it
means to be "off"—to be held in a perpetually negative and relational
state, and at the invocation of the term "derech," path, as a descriptor
for it—a term that is at once spatial and bodily, one which highlights

our very mobility in the world. Framing these terms as openings into the orientations of being OTD, I explore them as descriptors that attempt to capture the bodily and spatial conditions that constitute OTD existence.

My attempt will work to examine both the layers and limits of OTD as an identity, particularly within the context of an identity politics that often operates outside it: the politics of difference and representation. An OTDee's concept of identity is conditioned through the ethic of sameness bred by the Orthodox community, and by the OTDee's own attempt to distance themselves from this community and their representation of it. Crucially, OTDees are oriented away from community, not toward it. But while their socialization has painted the world in large, absolute categories of negation: Jewish or non-Jewish, *frum* or *frei*, the secular world turns out to be more complex than this simplistic binary would have it. Entering this world demands yet another form of negation adjusting to complexity and abandoning prior models of identification, which the OTDee is more than willing to do. What then can be said of what OTD identity *is*? How do OTDees define themselves in their new, multicultural world of difference without the basic tools of representation required to enter? Leaving their primary identity category behind, they define themselves by what they are not, not by what they are, a crucial ingredient in contemporary identity politics. What therefore *is* identity for an OTDee?

Exploring the absence of identity for an OTDee pushes us to explore the limitations of representational identity politics. Paying attention to the ways that an OTDee loses identity can help us understand not only the social circumstances, but the underlying cosmological and ontological statuses that put people in positions to represent. Being OTD is an orientation away from one world and toward another, which pushes the analysis of OTD beyond identity and into ontology, the exploration of being part of the world, and cosmology, the exploration of how worlds come into being. The utter outsiderness that characterizes the OTDee experience calls into question the overall usefulness of looking at OTD merely as an identity category. The OTD positionality outlines not only an aspect of self, but the boundaries of multiple worlds within which OTDees dwell, and the entanglement of self with world. My methodology therefore explores OTD first and I approach the analysis of OTD this way in order to highlight the limits of meaning and identity that OTDees confront, and to gesture toward their world-breaking experience. This experience is one that defies coherence and signification in the above terms, and yet, it is by using these terms that we can arrive at the marker and outline of the negativity of OTD identity and existence, an identity that is always already and actively under erasure. I will therefore move to look at OTD not only as an identity but as an ontological orientation and cosmological origin and ending, exploring the different conditions of world and wordlessness that characterize OTD existence. I will do so by embracing a phenomenological lens, one that explicitly tracks these states of world-making, deepening this perspective to also account for the world-losing that characterizes an OTDee's origin. In line with this tradition's philosophical analysis of the conditions of experience, including those of the philosopher, my essay will develop its position in like terms, at times through what might also be called the auto-ethnographic, to learn what we can about being OTD from the source of its unfolding.

While philosophers have written through themselves as origin points of knowledge time and time again, the subjectivity of this move often goes unrecognized until a minor subject engages in a similar practice, making visible both their difference and the norms of the dominant subject-author himself. The naturalization of the majority and his world as the source of philosophical inquiry, written about previously and eruditely in their respective terms by scholars such as Sara Ahmed,[3] Elizabeth Grosz,[4] and Gayle Salamon,[5] has a foundational impact on framing knowledge itself as of the majority, at times delineating this outright and at other times, taking it for granted. My own practice attempts to use these same tools to make visible a subject position that is so very invisible, in the most material of senses, because of how urgently and completely the OTDee tries to pass unnoticed as different in the secular world. Writing through my own subject position allows me to interrogate the assumptions and structures that underpin existence in normative and norming worlds, like the ones that OTDees are trying to both leave and become part of, to make visible their normalization tactics and the challenges they present to those who try to exit or enter them. I do not assert that this essay will be exhaustive nor definitive of the entirety of OTD existence. I also do not intend for it to stand in for every individual OTDee. What I hope to do is to sketch a starting frame of analysis for a group of people who so often escape legibility and who so urgently demand an analytic of their own. I structure this starting point intentionally through difference, with the desire to account for it among OTDees, even if those differences are not inscribed here. I hope that my sketch resonates and allows more of us to zone in on resonances that are distinctly OTD, and I welcome further analytics that push us to consider the depth and diversity of OTD realities.

Orienting OTD:
Offness, Pathness and the Mechanics of Walking

It is by understanding how we become oriented in moments of disorientation that we might learn what it means to be oriented in the first place.

—Ahmed 2006, 6

To begin exploring the terms of OTD, we must first understand its basic components of "offness" and "pathness." To be *off* the derech is to exist in a perpetual relation to having been on it. The two states depend on one another negatively: to be off, one first has to have been on. Indeed, a friend once questioned how religious someone has to *have been* in order to claim the identity, "OTD." This is a tough question to answer, because some Orthodox communities are more porous than others, and because while the term has been instituted by those communities, it is also one that individuals identify with in order to connote undoing their affiliation with these communities. The OTD turn is a swerve off of a very specific, paved, and rigid path, that is collectively recognized by those on it as *"the* path." Registering your mobility away from this path defines your scope and direction in relation to it. *Where am I going? To the place that is far away from here.* It is fundamentally a negative stance, a definition of self through a motion that moves *away from.* And yet, OTDees often want to *move beyond* this opposition, to define themselves not in relation to, but separately from the Orthodox world. The particulars of the move *away from* set up a complex motion that is at once negative but also desires to be positive and free from the bounds of this relation.

This brings us to our second term, "derech" path. For it is not just a sense of negation that characterizes the OTD experience, but of being off of something structured, tangible, bound, directed, and a move into some*where* open and unknown. The experience of veering away from this kind of setness brings about the need to create a completely new orientation, a new way of being in the world. The breaking with "path" is often not an isolated, minor break, but one that erupts across one's entire world and shatters it, because the world itself is held together at every block by common foundations. The spatialization of the term "derech" gives us insight into the prior sense of "pathness" that an OTDee sets aside, abandons, and even escapes in swerving off. Because as it turns out, having such a rigid path prevents you from walking anywhere else, so that this path *becomes* your world. When you veer off of it, it is not just the path that you abandon but your entire sense of world. Walking the path necessitates an activation of your body to move. Stepping off of it triggers a breakdown not only in your world, but in you—in your very body and its way of navigating and making space.

"Orientations, then, are about the intimacy of bodies and their dwelling places," says Sara Ahmed in her phenomenological approach to queerness.[6] Ahmed frames the attachment between a body and its dwelling space as intimate. An OTDee undoes their most intimate, foundational attachments, of body and of place, in making a choice that is indeed queer, going after a set of spatial and bodily relations that veer from, problematize, and oppose social norms. It is the "offness" of the OTDee that reveals the "pathness" of the frum world to begin with. Their every move away from this world is characterized by the feeling of each of their bonds to it, both minuscule and significant, revealing their imposing and collective force through the moving, sensing body of the OTDee, as their world becomes undone.

> When we are oriented, we might not even notice that we are oriented: we might not even think "to think" about this point. When we experience disorientation, we might notice orientation as something we do not have . . . How do we begin to know or to feel where we are, or even where we are going, by lining ourselves up with the features of the grounds we inhabit, the sky that surrounds us, or the imaginary lines that cut through maps? How do we know which way to turn to reach our destination?[7]

As Ahmed notes, thinking itself is a property of disorientation, a response to negative space. The OTD move triggers that thinking, that noticing, for OTDees themselves, but notably also for their frum signifiers. The path of being *frum* becomes exposed in every step that an OTDee takes away from it. But as the term suggests, it does nothing to indicate where an OTDee is, only where they are not. What then of the OTD path? Can we think of OTD motion itself in terms of pathness? OTD is primarily an orientation, veering from the path and a certain direction

of moving in the world. The notion of "pathness" highlights two central elements that OTD identity breaks with, and in doing so, exposes
two central elements that *frum* identity is built on: body and space. It
is therefore common for frum people to refer to an OTDee's breaking
with tradition and belief as "leaving." For some OTDees, especially in
ultra-Orthodox communities, the leaving is tangible: they must leave
a physical, geographical place, a neighborhood and home where their
family and community reside and in which they are no longer welcome.
For others though, "leaving" signals a rupture with a set of practices,
relationships, and convictions. Still though, the socio-spatial centering
of Orthodox life in general, through communal dwelling that is often
enclaved or condensed around religious and social space that is exclusive
and segregated, and a set of social-spatial practices that allow a frum Jew
to exist as such wherever they go, makes it so that in untying oneself
from these, one also unties oneself from a way of inhabiting and moving
through space—their spatial sensibilities that have until now defined their
existence. The "leaving" is so poignant because it follows you everywhere,
into your very capacity to find and build "world." Because, as it turns
out, the structuring of that place was so effective that it structured *you*,
so that wherever you were, you were always tethered back to it—so that
you always stood as an outsider in the secular world. This impacted your
very ability to locate yourself outside of this *frum* world, to make a place
anywhere else. Not only did it structure you, but it was structured *through
you*, demanding your own body in order to carry it around and in order
to establish its features.

It is no surprise therefore that the new lives that OTDees attempt
to form are often referred to as their "journeys." The journey, the voyage
to the unknown and far away, connotes a process of open destination, so
that any bumps you may hit along the way are all tied together in the
ultimate goals of wandering and discovery. I would argue that journey is
not only used in its most trite sense here, the way that it is commonly
conjured up in any reference to stories of hardship or challenge in today's
popular culture. It is also very literal. OTDees do not know *where* they
are going, because their entire sense of place has been structured through
frum spatial practice. Michel de Certeau introduces the concept of spatial
practice, ways of making space through its navigation, in his analysis of
the pedestrian street-act of walking in a city. "Their story begins on the
ground level, with footsteps," he argues.[8] And for de Certeau, it is not

merely the built environment that makes space, but the myriad collection of individual footsteps that activate and shape it, fundamentally.

> Their intertwined paths give their shape to spaces. They weave places together. In that respect, pedestrian movements form one of these 'real systems whose existence in fact makes up the city.' They are not localized; it is rather they that spatialize.[9]

De Certeau points out that space itself is not given, and the spatializing capacity of footsteps and the foot-stepper. The OTDee is by their own terms a walker, even perhaps a runner, but most definitely, a foot-stepper. (It is no surprise that the primary organization that supports and advocates for OTDees is called Footsteps.) Crucially, OTDees stop walking in one direction and start stepping in another. But they do not simply walk into an already created space. It is their movements that make that space. Their oppositional motion changes their sense and orientation of place; it also changes space itself. "The starting point for orientation is the point from which the world unfolds: the 'here' of the body and the 'where' of its dwelling," says Ahmed.[10] Orientation is not only dependent on space but on *body*. Walking demonstrates this acutely because it requires the body to *move*. De Certeau's insight demonstrates how motion shapes and intervenes in space *through* the body.

The location of navigational points of "here" and "there," otherwise known as deixis, has been an important origin point for a number of philosophical studies of space. Emmanuel Kant engages this construct when he sets out his epistemological notion of inner and outer sense and therefore, inner and outer worlds.[11] Heidegger does so with his phenomenological reinterpretation of *dasein* as the self in relation to world,[12] Maurice Merleau-Ponty with his phenomenological analysis of perception through the motoricity of the body,[13] and de Certeau in his exploration of mobility through the act of walking.[14] After all, while all spatial awareness requires a basic sense of "here" and "there," this is even more overtly the case for walking, the very act of moving between the two.

Space begins with our sensing of these basic orientations. An OTDee undergoes a fundamental switch in the ordering of "here" and "there." As an Orthodox Jew, "here" was the Orthodox world, and "there" was everywhere else. There was a basic, undifferentiated otherness that everything beyond the *frum* world shared. But in leaving, these markers switch. Suddenly, an OTDee walks toward a new, open "here" that is always a move away from the Orthodox "there." The OTD move is a fundamental reversal of spatial orientation and a rupture in spatial perception—which is how world is held together for humans. But they also undergo a tremendous breakdown in the sense of "here" and "me," that is, their very sense of spatial and *self*-origin, and the intimate relationship between their body and the environment that holds it in place. That means that their sense of "the point from which the world unfolds" is disrupted, their cosmological and ontological sense of what the world is, how it functions, and their place in it.

Sensing Space Off the Derech

The OTD path is punctured and strung through space and the body. These penetrations are so devastating that they create an uneasy feeling that you cannot quite put your finger on, but if you could sum it up it would be something like this: I am never quite sure I exist. What I mean by that is that the properties and principles of this new world are so at odds with my own sensibilities that I do not possess a grasp on it and I am deeply uncertain if I am operating within it. Both, because when I reach to grasp in my normal, intuitive and proven ways, the world slips away, because in those moments, it seems to me that where it does exist is so far removed from where I am that I have no idea how to reach it. The distance is ontological: it is a difference between worlds, not simply world-views.[15] It is similar to the panic and dysphoria of the protagonist in *Night Thoughts of a Classical Physicist*, who experiences his world coming apart at the seams with the advent of Quantum Mechanics and cannot seem to function within this new physical reality.[16] What place does he have in this new world? Can he even exist in its structure? The OTD experience is not structured simply by the culture or social relations that an OTDee must part with, but by an entire ontology, a sense of what the world *is*, and a cosmology, a sense of its origin and how it operates. I often give the example to friends, in stammering to articulate my existence through shared language that we do not possess, that it is as if you were to jump out of the window and you did not come crashing down, because the very laws of gravity, the physical laws of the universe itself, are different. The laws of cause and effect, whose examination has been the start of so many of the greatest philosophical treatises, have been radically transformed. And while sometimes our journeys open up with elation as we learn that when doing prohibited act X, we do not get struck down by lightning. often, to our chagrin, we learn the opposite just as well: that when walking on firm ground, it falls out from under us.

The deactivation or unworlding of an OTDee has two parts: it means that you do not know how to move in the world anymore, but it also means that you lose the efficacy of the ways in which you moved before. The skills, values, sensibilities, and networks that you previously held cease to matter or to cohere with this new mode of being. They do not help in your continuous effort to exist, and they also lose all of their effectiveness. More fundamentally, your most basic sense of what holds you together and attaches you to the world, ruptures. Nothing is ready-at-hand for the OTDee, not even themselves. This is how you come to learn a fundamental cosmological principle of world-making that few seem to recognize: there is no "the" world; there are only "worlds." The dual-damage of swerving off often means that you cannot begin to take stock of what you have lost until you have managed to create a new reality for yourself that coheres and that holds you in it, a way of grasping the world again, a refuge in which you can exist. New bodies and new worlds must be made. You have experienced what happens when you let go of one and the barely-existing of reaching for another. And you realize, worlds get made through attachments, through our abilities to etch and stitch ourselves into them while creating them. That is, they start with our own bodily movements.

Maurice Merleau-Ponty argues that ruptures in the ability to grasp are fundamentally spatial interruptions when he explores a host of neural and visual injuries and the impact they have on the body's perception of both self and space. OTDees too must re-network their neurological faculties of spatial perception around their new environments. For a while, it becomes hard to grasp the world and to feel that the world grasps you back because ". . . for the normal person every movement has a background, and that the movement and its background are 'moments of a single whole,'" argues Merleau-Ponty.[17] But OTDees lack the integral background that typically sets points in a continuous order and makes them stick. They may be able to point to where things are abstractly, a kind of basic indexing, but they do not reach the level of intimate, bodily grasping: "But even if the instructions have for him an *intellectual signification*, they do not have a motor signification, they do not speak to him as a motor subject," as a subject that can *move*.[18] Those intimate bonds of body and world have not yet been re-paved: you walk on hard ground and expect it to drop out from underneath you at every moment. Conversely, you have to tell yourself that if you try to jump out of the window, you will come crashing down.

For Merleau-Ponty, as for many others, the two categories of space and time are the entirety of existence, including primarily, our own. "I am not in space and time, nor do I think space and time; rather I am of space and time . . . The scope of this hold measures the scope of my existence,"[19] so that when our perception of space changes, it is *we* who change too. Our very existence is made up of spatiality, so it is impossible to change one without changing the other. Conversely, a mere change of environment will not help us to get reoriented, to feel part of or attached to that world. The contours of the world are fundamentally bound to the contours of self so that this recreation of world can only happen through a simultaneous recreation of self. What gets undone in leaving the path is one's entire grasp on a world and on a self, and the contours of both. It is not a mere matter of learning how to index new things, to be able to recognize and point to a set of new secular objects and cues, but it requires an entirely new mode of grasping and, in doing so, the creation of an entirely new form of space and self. "There is not first perceptions followed by a movement, the perception and the movement form a system that is modified as a whole."[20] Movement and perception come together, so that the more we are able to move, the more we are able to perceive. It is a fundamentally bodily, spatial, material as well as a neurological act. An OTDee's loss of self and space are deeply entangled. As Merleau-Ponty tells us, we actively produce space through our modes of perception, which are our moving bodies. This production is not independent from its producer: we produce ourselves as we produce it. For OTDees, it is this task, of making a world, which is tantamount to the re-making of ourselves.

The Multiple Worlds of OTDees

"In an effort to shift their focus away from epistemology, the study of knowing, and its focus on human representation, social scientists and humanists alike have recently turned toward ontology, the study of being, and the framework of "world." They often trace the correlation of epistemology and the focus on human representation to Emmanuel Kant and his *Critique of Pure Reason*. Kant's epistemological reality is described by Bruno Latour in the following way:

> Under the name of a 'Copernican Revolution' Kant invented this science-fiction nightmare: the outside world now turns around the mind-in-a-vat, which dictates most of that world's laws, laws it has extracted from itself without help from anyone else. A crippled despot now ruled the world of reality.[21]

While Latour's description is somewhat dramatic, he highlights the kind of division that Kant creates between the nonhuman and the human, what anthropologists typically call, nature and culture. His approach also explores how, in doing so, Kant also creates an internal division within the human, that of the Cartesian divide between mind and body, making the former the determinate of the latter. Latour is invested in undoing both of these divisions and the epistemological hierarchy that Western science has created between the human and the nonhuman, culture and nature, respectively. Latour questions this binary and its hierarchy and in his work, aims to show the entanglement of humans and nonhumans and the networks they create. Latour's analysis is part of the larger interrogation within the social sciences of the strict division of nature and culture. While scientists have studied nature, social scientists and humanists alike have studied culture—the human production of meaning. Countering the saturated focus on representation and meaning across multiple fields, many of these scholars want to move beyond culture and into a more complex notion of what "is." These analyses look to move beyond questions of knowing and toward questions of being, or the very entanglement of the two.

The recent complication of this division has motivated a burgeoning interest in matters of ontology and the making of worlds or what "is" rather than on epistemological representations. This framework has brought about analytics that are no longer interested in the subjectivity of interpretation, signification, or meaning-making, which have the effect of convincing us that there is only one world that can simply be viewed differently, but in multiple worlds and the ontological differences that cohere *between* them. Offering a new way of accounting for difference, this framework has given rise to the concept not of multiple perspectives but of multiple worlds, an approach that has been championed by scholars such as Marisol de la Cadena,[22] Eduardo Viveiros de Castro,[23] and Annemarie Mol.[24] The difference between what Mol calls perspectivalism and the concept of multiple ontologies is not a difference in interpretation but in the thing itself, something that Henaré, Holbraad, and Wastell simplify as multiple worldviews vs. multiple worlds. Mol clarifies this further in relation to her object of study, disease, "In a world of meaning, nobody is in touch with the reality of diseases, everybody 'merely' interprets them . . . The disease *recedes* behind the interpretations . . . This multiplies observers—but leaves the object observed alone. All alone. Untouched."[25] For her, this kind of perspectivalism multiplies observers and interpretations, but in the admission of that multiplicity, we also admit that none of us is actually in touch with the thing itself. That is because to really be in touch with the thing requires moving beyond interpreting it, and into *it*—Kant's famously unknowable thing-in-itself. For Mol, the answer to resolving the gaps of perspectivalism and the gap between the thing as we perceive it and the thing in itself, is a change in framing and in method, away from viewing the world through the lens of meaning and toward an analysis of practice: of how humans *do* disease. She argues that the practices we perform to access, diagnose, handle and treat disease are actually ways of producing it. When we foreground "doing" rather than "meaning" as a way of knowing, we get more in touch with the thing itself through our manipulation of it. When this happens, Mol argues, reality multiplies.

> If practices are foregrounded there is no longer a single passive object in the middle, waiting to be seen from the point of view of seemingly endless series of perspectives. Instead, objects come into being—and disappear—with the practices in which they are manipulated. And since the object of manipulation tends to differ from one practice to another, reality multiplies.[26]

Analyzing practice can get us as close as we can to the "disease itself" and to our role in manipulating and making it, rather than merely pointing at, or referencing it. That is, it can get us closer to how we grasp the thing and the enactment of the thing that ensues from that attachment.

Mol calls this empirical philosophy.[27] Her revelation is that no knowledge happens without working itself through the ontological world. We know things by handling them, and both we and the things are enacted in this process.[28]

Marisol de la Cadena has proposed a similar notion in her use of Isabelle Stengers's term, "cosmopolitics." In her study of indigenous people in Peru, she looks at the differences between how indigenous people and outsiders enact politics, not by treating their oppositions as mere differences in perspective, but in ontology—in world. She asks what it would mean to take these differences seriously and to recognize their incongruence, that where outsiders might live in an ontology in which a mountain is a passive feature of environment meant for human enjoyment, indigenous people occupy a reality in which these mountains are active beings, or what she terms, earth beings. The incommensurability of these worlds means that when approaching people from outside any of our worlds, we may not possess the capacity to actually see them because they are not a mere matter of perspective, but being. Cosmopolitics takes account of these ontological and cosmological differences, differences in world and how the world operates.[29]

I want to propose that we need something similar to cosmopolitics and certainly a notion of multiple ontologies, in order to understand the movements that OTDees make and the conflicted state of their existence. One of the biggest motivations for and outcomes of the philosophy of multiple ontologies is the question of what we mean when we agree to disagree, that is, when we believe in a world of multiple perspectives. In a world of epistemology, there is no "there" there. We recognize that each person can have a different opinion and perspective on the world, but we ultimately do not believe that we are in touch with the world itself. This highlights an important difference between perspective and practice, and the limitations of the former. This is a difference that Mol highlights best when she talks about disease.

"This is the plot of my philosophical tale: that *ontology* is not given in the order of things, but that, instead, *ontologies* are brought into being, sustained, or allowed to wither away in common, day-to-day sociomaterial practices," she argues.[30] OTDees understand this, that belief is not simply a perspective but a *practice*, and a way of building a world. They understand that when they stop believing they stop possessing a world, and that losing faith is life-threatening because it unhinges the state of being in which they exist, because they stop *making* that existence real in their everyday sociomaterial and spatial lives. We do not agree to disagree, hardly ever. We disagree and choose an absolutely different path. In doing so, we create a rift between the world we once inhabited and practiced, and the one we are moving toward and creating. We also create rifts in ourselves, as the move to practice *ourselves* multiplies in ways that are fundamentally incommensurable. Bringing together phenomenology with analyses of practice gets us closer to how world-making and world-breaking occurs and the ways that bodies and space are brought in and out of being.

And while Mol argues that multiple objects "tend to hang together somehow,"[31] I remain fundamentally ambivalent about whether this sense of togetherness holds true for the multiple worlds of OTDees. I feel their break and weight in my body every time I move between them. I sense my proprioception changing, the sense of my body in space, both social and physical, and I sometimes get disoriented along the way. The change runs through my body—it is my body, my body multiple. There is a kind of transness and dysphoria to being OTD that, like the transness and dysphoria of gender, does not come in a one-size-fits-all form and which makes it difficult to identify the parts of you, both past and present, which in fact are you. When you do return to the frum world, you find yourself confronting the ghost or phantom of you, the "you" that you could not live as. Is this really a return at all? The journey through the gap gets easier the more you do it, because you learn its grooves, potholes, and dead ends. But you still feel it, and it still changes you, and the difference feels asymptotic: the closer you get to zoning in on it, the more you feel its absoluteness. The question is where you really live, which version of you is more authentic, which is *really* you—while at times its answer seems to achieve more and more certainty, its ultimate unsolveability surprises you. Because there are parts of ourselves, indeed entire versions of who we are, that we leave behind, that we cannot carry with us. The same goes for what we can bring back if we choose to revisit. When we "leave," we make a wager: where do I have a better chance of surviving? The question itself undoes the possibility of a full answer—because who do I even mean when I say "I" in this refracted context? If we really had all of the information necessary to solve that question, the sheer impossibility of the task and the depth of the losses we would accrue, I do not know if we would do it. It is important that we think it is doable. Otherwise, we would never make the move. And where would we be if we had not? *Who* would we be?

The Identity Politics of OTD:
Sameness, Difference, Negation

So far, we have approached the mechanics of making the self spatially, phenomenologically, ontologically, and cosmologically. But I would like to return to our initial framework for self-making: identity, in order to explore how these two frameworks approach the same concept, and what we might gain from exploring the OTDee self within both. What does it mean to occupy a negative identity, a negative orientation? When I say negative, I do not mean to conjure its colloquial use as un-jovial or non-enthusiastic, but rather its structural use, as something that is defined by its opposition, by an absence and by what it is not. As Hegel demonstrates, negative definitions are dialectical: they depend on one another.[32] Many social supremacist iterations of identity operate through negation as well, in areas such as race, gender, sexuality, class, and ability, so that to be one is not to be the other. The negative terms are united in relation; they depend on one another. Their existence is bound together with the relation and, therefore, with the opposition. The dependent relationship of negatives and originals has a lot to tell us about the relationship between these two oppositional groups of *frum* and OTD, and how these identities form one another in codependent ways. It also begs important questions about what it means to be defined through absence, to have your primary identity category refer to something you *once* were but no longer are. Who are you, when you are most strongly defined by what you are not? You try to build a new body, a new world, and a new identity for yourself, one based on "you" rather than on "them." You think you are trying to integrate, to become enlightened, to wake up and to *pass*. You hope that if you do those things, you will be transformed into the truer version of yourself, one that fits in with and makes sense to the rest of the enlightened world.

Your whole life has been structured by this "us" and "them," only you were always part of the "us." You knew of one primary source of difference that mattered: *goyishness*. And you knew one primary source of sameness that defined everything you were: *frumness*. Jews who did not fit this category filled a hybrid space: sometimes you related to them like they were *goyim* (Non-Jews) and sometimes you saw them as potential *frum* converts or "returnees"—because the source of all being was *frumkeit*. When you learned to think about difference it was always in relation to sameness: you were not taught to think, *how can I cultivate my difference?* It was always, *how can I overcome more and more subtle differences to make myself more and more similar to everyone else around me?* Sameness became your primary way of cultivating and thinking about identity. This is so much so that the notion of "identity" itself seems strange, because it has so little depth: because it is so one dimensional. On the other hand, this way of relating self to other highlights the basic mechanics of identification themselves: identifying *with*, possessing a commonality that is the same in both you and someone other than you. It is fundamentally about sameness. After all, negation and identification are two sides of the same coin.

But as it turns out, the *goyish*, secular world is a lot more replete with difference than we were ever taught it was. Not all non-Jews are the same, and people take their differences seriously. Explaining who you are in a world that is complicated by difference, rather than simplified by negation, is challenging. First, you have to learn that this is what is happening. It takes a lot of miss-readings and encounters with difference in order to recognize that how you approach society is *different* from what everyone else seems to be doing; that you do not construct your sense of self or world in the same way. You always knew this in your bones but you always thought of it as a phantom limb that would eventually go away once you finally grew a new body. Only that is not how bodies work, you learn.

Recognizing this radical difference in the way I and others were processing the social world was a turning point for me in how I related to being OTD. I realized that this thing that I was doing, trying to relate to everyone through sameness rather than through difference, was fundamental to my way of moving through the world; that there was no way to undo it without undoing myself, and that it was also a part of my cultural sensibilities. Recognizing this break *between* self and world yet again, brought me in touch with a break *in* self, and also in this new world into which I thought I was trying to seamlessly enter. These gaps and fissures put me in direct encounter with the multiplicity of my worlds, and the selves that were torn between them in parts and bits that seemed impossible to hold together in one place. In a secular world structured through the politics of representation, what does it mean to de-identify with your primary identity category, so much so that you cannot represent it? And in a larger landscape of political identity which works to cultivate a politics of difference through these individual representations, what does it mean to possess a cultural specificity that works against this? And finally, what does it mean to need to translate yourself into these terms in order to become visible, but upon doing so, to realize that you have now completed your own erasure? The task seems impossible.

While friends and colleagues argued over the nuances of terms like "identity" and "culture," I did not have tools for understanding these political frames. My culture and communal identity were not things I was working to preserve—they were things I was actively trying to get rid of, and to get out of me. But the failed attempts to completely do so taught me more about the limitations these terms have for describing and handling the set of circumstances that I found myself in, and my experience in this world. After all, one can change a culture. I had certainly done so. I now had a new set of terms, practices, and social norms that were very much a part of me. But despite the robust analytics that exist for exploring hybrid identities and double consciousness, what I was struggling with was far more severe than a sense of identity: it was my sense of the world, and my existence within it. Suddenly, community was the highest moral standard. In order for you to even show up recognizable in a space, you had to demonstrate your own affiliations with and support for communities and a recognition of their ultimate sacredness. While this approach brought a sense of solidarity, empowerment, visibility, and survival for many members of minority communities around me, and with good reason, the demand was deeply disorienting to an OTDee who knew the dangers of community all too well. It was like on the outside, nobody recognized just how threatening being that closely entangled with one another could also be. While other people were struggling to become visible *through* community, I was trying to become visible without it. Our mismatched sensibilities made it so that I had to either agree to these terms of representation once again in order to pass, or risk the possibility that there was no "there" on the other side. Nobody wants to nor knows how to tell a room of non-Jews just how much community has taken from them. Nobody wants to reveal just how "other" they actually are. That revelation feels life-threatening for the OTD passing-project. And nobody, just nobody, wants to have to show their body bags at the door, to expose just how difficult it is to get to the other side, and how many of us do not make it.

How to exist then as an OTDee who seems to have *no place*? At first I tried to translate the space, to see if its practices, sensibilities, and orientations could be transplanted into another world. In that attempt, I learned that it was not just my space that I was trying to carry over, but my self—the self that could only come into being through a very particular ecology, and the self I was determined to resurrect through its recreation. Really, it was myself that I was not sure could survive the foundational break with place. Who was I outside of this extended environment? I had grown into being through the sinews of the *frum* world. Its flesh was my flesh, its motion was my motion. Place was like a body that I was not sure I could exist without. But when mine grew sick, I had to find a way to perform a superhuman transplant of inconceivable proportions: to build a new body. Not all identity categories share this ability, to transition outside of them. And yet, our inability to ever completely cut loose, brings OTD mobility back into conversation with a host of identity categories that resist undoing. The ontological difference of being OTD teaches us that this is far more than an identity category, but a relationship to the world, and a practice of world-making. Perhaps this is unique to OTD. But perhaps, in re-looking at what it holds in common with other attempts to veer away from one's ontological foundations, we might explore how identity politics that are solely based on representation offer us limited perspective on our differences. An OTD ontology of multiple worlds, and attention to the cosmological processes that bring those worlds into and out of being, might show us "a path" toward understanding what holds us together and what breaks us apart, from ourselves and from one another.

An OTD Analytic:
Future Multiplicities and Directions for Work

I propose that we move beyond a strictly cultural, representational, linguistic, and identity-based analytic for understanding the transient being of the OTDee, and with that, the strict division between the frum and frei worlds in analyzing OTD existence. Instead, I suggest we follow Annmarie Mol's call to study how bodies that are multiple do, and I would add, also do not, hang together. The OTD move is fundamentally a spatial and bodily practice. It is the attempt to leave the very world that defines you and to survive outside it, with the added caveat of returning from time to time and in doing so, undoing some of that definitive division. The attempt itself is one of both suicide and world-making in its quintessential form, as it picks up on all of the tacit, minute and un-analyzable elements that make up existence. We feel the losses of each of these, and their absence fills our lives with a presence that can feel unsurmountable. When we try to "move on," there is just so much not only that we need to learn, but that we need to be able to *do* and *build* in order to make it. This is why it is so very hard to leave; it is also why, "they" are right: it *is* dangerous *out there*. Attending to the multiplicity of OTD reality opens up the possibility of studying its remarkable achievement, of breaking, building, and holding together the multiple realities, gaps, and fissures of OTD existence.

For Michel de Certeau, "pathness" is semiotic, and pedestrians who follow walking-paths do so by reading space, sometimes following it and sometimes re-routing themselves through it. De Certeau's insight into the relationship between reading and moving highlights the agency of the individual who operates within a larger spatial system. But the reading is not simply a matter of interpretation: we move through contact with ground, and as we move, we mark it. This is an act of inscription that is at once ontological and semiotic. Our bodies make their "impressions," to borrow a term from Sara Ahmed.[33] Our imprints and etchings change the materiality of space and of us. Movement really highlights the way that path-making is at once a kind of etching that gives way to and necessitates reading, and how it is also a change in the world itself, through practice. The OTD journey, as it is often called, requires a lot of new knowledges. It is common to view this need for both research and activist work alike, through the lens of literacies: there are myriad kinds of learning that an OTDee needs to do, knowledge that they need to become literate in, in order to transition into and function in the secular world. These can range from strict, academic literacies like learning how to speak English, to use a computer, or how to study science. They also include institutional literacies, like how to apply for college, interview for a job, access resources, develop cultural literacies, like learning the varieties of secular music or accessing a museum, as well as social and bodily literacies like how to act at a party, how to flirt, how to dress your body in shorts, shave your beard for the first time, or date. The "knowing" of these things has a learning curve. It takes a while for an OTDee to learn all that they must in order to succeed in the outside world. But what I want to suggest is that this learning curve is not simply information-based. Learning in these cases is actually a way of *making*, "The motor experience of our body is not a particular case of knowledge; rather, it offers us a manner of reaching the world and the object."[34] The learning process as we call it does not consist simply of acquiring new information, but of reaching for and grasping a new world and way of being. It requires practicing new selves and new worlds into existence. That is precisely why it is so, so hard. The OTD journey is not just epistemological, but cosmological, a way or re-ordering and re-making your sense of world and self.

This new self is in many ways, absolutely opposed to the old one, in its goals, practices, and orientations. The old self, like a phantom limb, flutters in and out of existence: it is there but it is not there. It is bound up with a prior body, and also, a prior space. Its mode of grasping is no longer effective in this new reality. Like Donna Haraway's cyborg, an OTDee is composed of parts that are ontologically different, and that do not ultimately cohere.[35] An OTDee's struggle therefore is often aimed at achieving this impossible coherence, either by trying to figure out a way to make them all work together, or by amputating their Orthodox body parts. And yet, those parts are stubborn. Not only do they show up as phantoms, disrupting the OTDee's ability to move, they also sometimes resist cutting. The more we build bodies that function in different ways, we create splits inside ourselves resulting in multiple versions of ourselves, multiple bodies. It is a trauma, the whole ordeal, and surviving and even thriving depends on our ability to become more than one and less than many, so that all versions of ourselves can hang together. The ultimate achievability of this feat is still under exploration in our collective journeys.

The story of Sodom and Gomorrah provides an important example of a biblical OTD narrative, not for its moral equivalence but for its structural and spatial parallel. The story is after all about what happens when you actively part with a way of life and refuse the social norm. In this story, Abraham's nephew, Lot, is being exited from a place that God's messengers are about to destroy because of its corrupt ways, "Get up and exit this place because God is destroying it," they are urged.[36] But going is not so easy. Lot delays; his sons-in-law delay; until the People of God must urge him again to take his remaining family and leave. There is a lot of doubt and hesitation that plagues anyone confronting the choice to leave their security and stability—their world behind. It is the ultimate journey. Indeed it took messengers of God to remove Lot and his remaining family from the city.

But the angels convince Lot, and Lot manages to convince his remaining family. The angels warn Lot to flee to the hills and to never look back, "And when he took them out, and he said 'save yourself, do not look behind you and do not pause anywhere in the area, flee to the hills so that you are not erased.'"[37] But even this is too much for Lot, for he knows he will not survive in the unknown, unstable hills. He beseeches the People of God to allow him to take refuge in a nearby city: because when leaving one world, one needs to at least be able to touch down in another. Lot and his family convince the People of God to create a refuge for them and to spare this city. And just as we think that all of the delaying is done, the person who is only known to us as "Lot's Wife," cannot stand to walk away without pausing, and gazes back at her origin in flames.

There is so much hesitation in leaving the path. Sometimes, something yanks us out against our will. But once we have made that first move, like Lot and his family, we cannot afford to turn around and wax sentimental about what we are losing. If we did, we would surely, like Lot's Wife, become frozen in place, *immobile*. Because who could withstand that suicidal view? We mourn Lot's Wife, and all of those like her that we have lost, who did not make it to the arduous but life-saving hills on the other side. Nobody wants to have to go through this. This is something we do not get to say enough, because we are so busy defending the choice. We leave because we have to. We leave because our world is no longer habitable, and the only way to survive is to get out. Learning the various factors that make a person feel that they must leave in order to survive will teach us a lot about the hazards that take shape within the frum world, which make it unlivable for some. Exploring what could be changed about Orthodox worlds to make them more survivable is a justice project worth taking up by Orthodox Jews, OTDees, scholars and activists alike. Paying attention to how OTDees unbuild and rebuild themselves and their worlds is an act of empathy, witnessing and world-making.

Notes

1. Leah Vincent, "Leah Vincent Sheds Light On Her Ultra-Orthodox (Judaism) Upbringing," *Real Women Real Stories*, Youtube, October 12, 2016, video, 6:41. https://www.youtube.com/watch?v=P_3aPsTKQv8.

2. My use of world is both colloquial and philosophical. On the one hand, OTDees leave their religious, familial, and communal worlds. This leaving however ruptures an OTDee's sensibilities and capacities for making and sustaining their existence. It has the collective effect of rendering the world itself not-at-hand, in the Heideggerian sense of not available for use. My analysis borrows from the phenomenological terminology of "world" and "being in world" in order to understand how an OTDee's transition between religious and secular life is also a transition between spaces. And because these spaces are totalizing in the ways that they construct existence, complete with their own cosmologies, practices, and social structures, moving between them can lead to a state of "worldlessness"—losing all of the things that create a world for someone and their sense of being in it. Exploring that motion can tell us a lot about how "world," in both the colloquial and philosophical senses, is created and also unmade.

3. Sara Ahmed, *Queer Phenomenology: Orientations, Objects, Others* (Durham, NC: Duke University Press, 2006).

4. Elizabeth Grosz, *Volatile Bodies: Toward a Corporeal Feminism* (Bloomington: Indiana University Press, 1994).

5. Gayle Salamon, *Assuming a Body: Transgender and Rhetorics of Materiality* (New York: Columbia University Press, 2010).

6. Ahmed, *Queer Phenomenology*, 8.

7. Ibid. 6.

8. Michel de Certeau, *The Practice of Everyday Life*, trans. Steven Rendall (Berkeley: University of California Press, 1984), 97.

9. Ibid.

10. Ahmed, *Queer Phenomenology*, 8.

11. Emmanuel Kant, *Critique of Pure Reason*, trans. Kemp Smith (London: Palgrave Macmillan, 2007), 167–68.

12. Martin Heidegger, *Being and Time*, trans. Joan Stambaugh (Albany: State University of New York Press, 1996).

13. Maurice Merleau-Ponty, *The Phenomenology of Perception*, trans. Donald Landes (New York: Routledge, 2012).

14. de Certeau, *Practice of Everyday Life*.

15. Amiria Henaré, Martin Holbraad, Sari Wastell, "Thinking Through Things" in *Thinking Through Things: Theorising Artefacts Ethnographically*, ed. Amiria Henaré, Martin Holbraad, Sari Wastell (New York: Routledge, 2007), 10.

16. Russell McCormmach, *Night Thoughts of a Classical Physicist* (Cambridge, MA: Harvard University Press, 1991).

17. Merleau-Ponty, *The Phenomenology*, 113.

18. Ibid.

19. Ibid., 141.

20. Ibid., 113.

21. Bruno Latour, *Pandora's Hope: Essay's On the Realities of Science Studies* (Cambridge, MA: Harvard University Press, 1999), 6.

22. Marisol de la Cadena, *Earth Beings: Ecologies of Practice Across Andean Worlds* (Durham, NC: Duke University Press, 2015). Also see, Elizabeth Povinelli *Economies of Abandonment: Social Belonging and Endurance in Late Liberalism* (Durham, NC: Duke University Press, 2011).

23. Eduardo Viveiros de Castro, "Exchanging Perspectives The Transformation of Objects into Subjects in Amerindian Ontologies," in *Common Knowledge*, v.10(3) (2004): 463–84.

24. Annemarie Mol, *The Body Multiple: Ontology in Medical Practice* (Durham, NC: Duke University Press, 2003). Also see, Karen Barad, *Meeting the Universe Halfway and the Entanglement of Matter and Meaning* (Durham, NC: Duke University Press, 2007).

25. Mol, *The Body Multiple*, 11–12.

26. Ibid., 5.

27. Ibid., 1.

28. Mol's approach is praxis oriented rather than phenomenological per se. In general, the ontological turn in anthropology and science and technology studies often takes more of a practice-based approach. Bringing both ontological approaches of phenomenology and practice together can offer us more insight into OTD being, how it is experienced and how it is made. The sensation and perception of being in the world is completely enmeshed with one's abilities to do things that enact the world and make use of it, which is precisely what a praxis-analysis offers us.

29. de la Cadena, *Earth Beings*, 280.

30. Mol, *The Body Multiple*, 6.

31. Ibid., 5.

32. G. W. F. Hegel, *Phenomenology of Spirit*, trans. A.V. Miller (Oxford: Oxford University Press, 1977), 10, 76.

33. Sara Ahmed, *The Cultural Politics of Emotion* (Edinburgh: Edinburgh University Press, 2004), 8.

34. Merleau-Ponty, *The Phenomenology of Perception*, 141.

35. Donna Haraway, *Simians, Cyborgs, and Women: The Reinvention of Nature* (New York: Routledge, 1991), 181.

36. Genesis, 19:14.

37. Ibid., 19:17.

Bibliography

Ahmed, Sara. *The Cultural Politics of Emotion*. Edinburgh: Edinburgh University Press, 2004.

———. *Queer Phenomenology*. Durham, NC: Duke University Press, 2006.

Barad, Karen. *Meeting the Universe Halfway: Quantum Physics and the Entanglement of Matter and Meaning*. Durham, NC: Duke University Press, 2007.

de Certeau, Michel. *The Practice of Everyday Life*. Translated by Steven Randall. Berkeley: University of California Press, 1984.

de la Cadena, Marisol. *Earth Beings: Ecologies of Practice Across Andean Worlds*. Durham, NC: Duke University Press, 2015.

Grosz, Elizabeth. *Volatile Bodies: Toward a Corporeal Feminism*. Bloomington: Indiana University Press, 1994.

Haraway, Donna. *Simians, Cyborgs, and Women: The Reinvention of Nature*. New York: Routledge, 1991.

Hegel, G. W. F. *Phenomenology of Spirit*. Translated by A.V. Miller. Oxford: Oxford University Press, 1977.

Heidegger, Martin. *Being and Time*. Translated by Joan Stambaugh. Albany: State University of New York Press, 1996.

Henaré, Amiria, Martin Holbraad, and Sari Wastell. *Thinking Through Things: Theorising Artefacts Ethnographically*. New York: Routledge, 2007.

Kant, Emmanuel. *Critique of Pure Reason*. Translated by Norman Kemp Smith. London: Palgrave Macmillan, 2007.

Latour, Bruno. *Pandora's Hope: Essays on the Reality of Science Studies*. Cambridge, MA: Harvard University Press, 1999.

McCormmach, Russell. *Night Thoughts of a Classical Physicist*. Cambridge, MA: Harvard University Press, 1991.

Merleau-Ponty, Maurice. *The Phenomenology of Perception*. Translated by Donald Landes. New York: Routledge, 2012.

Mol, Annemarie. *The Body Multiple: Ontology in Medical Practice*. Durham, NC: Duke University Press, 2008.

Povinelli, Elizabeth. *Economies of Abandonment: Social Belonging and Endurance in Late Liberalism*. Durham, NC: Duke University Press, 2011.

Salamon, Gayle. *Transgender and Rhetorics of Materiality*. New York: Columbia University Press, 2010.

Viveiros de Castro, Eduardo. "Exchanging Perspectives The Transformation of Objects into Subjects in Amerindian Ontologies." *Common Knowledge*, v.10(3) (2004): 463–84. Durham, NC: Duke University Press.

Notes from the Field

Footsteps' Evolution and Approach to Supporting Individuals Leaving the Ultra-Orthodox Community

RACHEL BERGER, TSIVIA FINMAN, LANI SANTO

Footsteps' Founding, History, & Evolution

Every year, thousands of ultra-Orthodox Jewish men and women across the globe attempt to explore the world beyond their insular communities. These individuals struggle to redefine their lives despite punitive reactions from family and friends, insufficient or nonexistent secular education, entrenched gender roles, and, in some cases, a limited command of English. Those who choose to leave their communities of origin are extraordinarily self-determined and motivated, and yet many face devastating loss, intense isolation, tremendous gaps in their knowledge of secular society, and cultural disorientation.

As the leading organization in North America providing comprehensive services to this population, Footsteps offers a range of services, including social and emotional support, educational and career guidance, financial assistance and scholarships, workshops and social activities, access to legal representation for divorce and custody battles, and other life-saving resources. Through its programs, Footsteps fosters social and professional networks, celebrates individual and collective accomplishments, and promotes the issues and concerns of its members. Footsteps provides a safe and non-judgmental space where individuals can grapple with big questions, find like-mindedness, and gain the confidence and skills to lead a life of their choosing.

Footsteps was founded in 2003 by a formerly ultra-Orthodox woman from the Chabad/Lubavitch community, Malkie Schwartz, who envisioned a world in which all who choose to leave insular religious communities have the resources they need to flourish and to lead self-determined, richly integrated lives within mainstream society. Assisted by secular relatives, Malkie wanted to provide a framework of support to others she met who were on a similar path, but who did not have access to similar resources and struggled with homelessness, lack of vocational and life-skills, loss of family and community support, and a lack of knowledge about the secular world at large.

From a one-person start-up that met in coffee shops and college classrooms, Footsteps has since professionalized, moving into a space of its own in 2008, hiring an experienced nonprofit manager, Lani Santo, as Executive Director in 2010 to take the reins from its visionary founder, and building a board to serve as ambassadors and guide the organization's strategic direction. In the years between 2010 and 2019, the organization's annual budget grew from under a half a million dollars to over three million. Footsteps has a program space in lower Manhattan, and an additional satellite office in Rockland County to serve those emerging from communities in upstate New York, including Monsey and remote upstate hamlets such as Kiryas Joel and New Square. Additionally, while the vast majority of ultra-Orthodox Jews in America reside in the greater New York metropolitan area, Footsteps has expanded its distance programming to those seeking support from across the country and abroad. Footsteps also provides organizational support and guidance to leaders of grassroots efforts and other not-for-profits that serve the concerns of this population both locally and beyond our geographic service area.

With 15 years serving this community, Footsteps has issue expertise and a wealth of knowledge about insular ultra-Orthodox communities and has served as a thought leader, contributing to the public's understanding of these insular communities and of the issues that arise for individuals leaving them. Academics, journalists and authors, lay professionals, and members of the public have turned to the organization to gain a better understanding of a highly insular and complex ecosphere. The organization has acted as cultural translator for the courts, the press, and lay professionals across a spectrum of fields that directly serve our members.

In 2015, Footsteps helped design a landmark study undertaken by Nishma Research to better understand individuals who had left Orthodox communities. For the first time, there was an attempt to identify and quantify an emergent segment of the Jewish community, which would bolster years of anecdotal experience about those who leave. In addition to exploring reasons for leaving, which are varied not only across this population, but may be multifaceted for each individual, the survey also identified a community in and of itself. That is to say, even if those who have left do not participate in activities with others who have left, they may share points in common. The survey was completed by 885 individuals; it successfully identifies unique characteristics specific to this population, and explores reasons for leaving relationships with origin communities and families, Jewish identity, and ongoing needs, among others.[1] We explore some of the survey findings throughout this article.

Footsteps' Founding Vision, Mission, and Core Values

As our community evolves, our Vision and Mission Statements guide our work. These not only define what the organization is, and what it seeks to achieve, but also define what it is not. Our work is grounded in the underlying premise that healthy, happy, empowered individuals strengthen families and communities, whether these are birth families and origin communities or any new ones that are sought out post-initial transition, including the newly emerging formerly ultra-Orthodox community itself. Understanding what Footsteps is *not* trying to achieve is as important as what we are working toward, since perceptions persist that our organization's agenda seeks to discourage religious observance and/or disconnection to origin families and communities. This has never been the intent of organizational leadership, as it limits the possibilities of our members achieving what they may ultimately define as the best lives for themselves. Moreover, the range and intensity of repercussions for embarking on this transition may be enormous and is most profoundly a decision that only an individual can make for themselves. Leaving is far from easy, and life in the secular world may present a different set of hardships, especially for those who do not have the skills or knowledge to navigate it. Our vision is as follows:

Footsteps envisions a world in which all who choose to leave insular religious communities are able to live self-determined lives, have the resources to flourish and thrive within them, and are fully supported in achieving the educational and cultural acclimation necessary for a richly integrated life within mainstream society.

Footsteps' founding vision creates space for a diverse community where the Self is honored, regardless of observance, and the belief that individuals have the capacity to define and pursue what is in their best interest, without judgement, is promoted. As this chapter further discusses below, it is not our intent to replicate the entirety of what is lost, but to provide critical interventions to facilitate personal growth trajectories. Additionally, while we have gained issue expertise to focus on a specific population emerging from Jewish communities, Footsteps' vision also locates our work in a larger context where ultra-insular forms of religion that disconnect their adherents from the mainstream are on the rise. We occasionally hear from individuals from Christian, Muslim, and other restrictive faith backgrounds who feel similarly disconnected from society and are isolated within their respective religious sect.[2]

Our Mission Statement was updated in 2016 to reflect our values, clarify our current target population, and refine our organizational purpose: "*Footsteps supports and affirms individuals and families who have left, or are contemplating leaving, insular ultra-Orthodox Jewish communities in their quest to lead self-determined lives.*"

Footsteps' Vision and Mission are grounded in the organization's Core Values. These articulate the culture that Footsteps strives to create, within our membership, internally, as a staff and board, and externally, through our interactions with the public and our supporters. We seek to uphold the following ideals:

- *Respect*—we honor personal choice, respecting diverse lifestyles and maintaining individuals' safety and privacy as they build self-determined lives. We listen and learn from others, valuing different opinions, beliefs, working styles, expertise, and approaches.

- *Inclusive Community*—we build and model a diverse, accepting community that supports self-expression and allows people to lead lives that are true to themselves without imposing personal beliefs and practices on others.

- *Integrity*—we promote authenticity and transparency, owning our responsibility and considering the impact our actions have on others.

- *Self-Determination*—we affirm individuals' rights to determine the course of their own lives. We create opportunities for our members and staff to engage with and contribute to the organization in exciting and meaningful ways. We take responsibility as a force for positive change in the communities and arenas in which we work.

- *Continuous Improvement*—we value reflection and constant learning. We take stock on a regular basis, celebrating accomplishments, identifying assets, and exploring areas for improvement so that we can live and work with a sense of meaning and purpose.

A Note on Terminology

The acronym "OTD" is reclaimed from the slur within Orthodox communities that describes individuals who have strayed "Off The *Derech*," translating the Hebrew word *derech*, "path," as "the path of Orthodox Judaism." Many individuals use this reclaimed slur to self-identify, and it is widely used, although not universally so; others describe themselves as XO (ex-Orthodox), popularized in the 1990s in online blogs and message forums, and other slurs such as the Yiddish word "*frei*," meaning literally, "free" or "*apikores*," literally "apostate," have also been reclaimed, but are less widely used. Other terms such as post-Orthodox, culturally Jewish, and formerly Orthodox are used to self-identify, but a significant number of individuals resent labels entirely. For the sake of brevity, we choose to utilize the term OTD with hesitance, given that we, alongside many of our members, feel conflicted about the term.

Demographics

So, who are Footsteps members? Fifteen years ago, a typical Footsteps member was a single, young man from a Chasidic background, seeking a basic education and a chance to socialize with others like himself. He most likely would have self-described as atheist, and would have likely been living in ultra-Orthodox Brooklyn and have told very few people about his true beliefs.[3] Today, thanks to the addition of more support and community-building programs, Footsteps' membership is more diverse than ever. Forty percent of the organization's membership identifies as women or as gender non-conforming. Approximately 30 percent of Footsteps members are parents, and this figure will grow, as we currently are expanding our family supports. Previously, the vast majority of our members were from Brooklyn. Today, 30 percent of our members live in Rockland and Orange Counties, where Footsteps maintains a satellite location. Approximately 20 percent of Footsteps members identify as LGBTQ. About 20 percent of our members identify as traditionally Jewish in one way or another. Our membership is diverse in terms of community of origin, with individuals transitioning from every Chassidic denomination, including and not limited to Satmar, Belz, Bobov, Ger, and Chabad/Lubavitch, as well as Yeshivish and Litvish or a combination of the above. These demographic shifts have impacted the organization's services. Each population requires catered support, and as the membership body grows, members challenge the organization to craft additional responses to their needs. At the outset, Footsteps' primary target population was young men and women who were focused on getting a high school equivalency degree and into college. Today, Footsteps offers so much more.

Footsteps' Program Model

What began in 2003 as a roving support group is today a dual-purpose social service agency and community-building organization, with nearly 20 staff, a budget of $3 million in fiscal year 2019, and numerous partnerships. To achieve its goals, Footsteps has developed robust services and programming that can be broken into three core concepts, (1) Community Engagement, (2) Support Services, and (3) Partnerships and Collaborations.

Community Engagement

Community is the force that drives individuals—both those who recently transitioned and those who left years ago—to Footsteps. Both within and beyond the Footsteps membership, those who left report that their top interest is to meet people like themselves who understand where they came from.[4] To address this need (as well as many others), Footsteps offers social and community events, peer-led support groups and workshops, peer mentoring, and opportunities for seasoned members to give back. These offerings connect members internally to each other as well as externally to allies. Most large community events are open to non-members, since we know that the concept of membership does not appeal to all. Major events such as Thanksgiving Dinner and our Camp Footsteps weekend each currently attract over 200 individuals, and increasingly are attended by families with children. More than 800 individuals take part in community-building programming every year, both locally in New York City and beyond.

Support Services

Many individuals who come for community stay for services. These services ensure that our members have critical resources in education, career readiness, legal supports, mental health and wellness, and crisis supports. Footsteps uses a membership model for those who wish to access our supports. These include:

1. The signing of a membership agreement that requires each new member to maintain the confidentiality of their peers, and to co-create a safe and respectful community aligned with Footsteps' mission and values;

2. A symbolic one-time membership fee of twenty-five dollars that is waived if it poses financial hardship;

3. An in-person initial interview with a social-worker to assess the elements of our programs and services that would be the most useful.

Over the years, we have examined the efficacy of this membership model, and whether it creates a barrier to entry to those who might otherwise participate in our programs; ultimately, we have found that it represents a symbolic moment of action for the vast majority of our members who live in a "pre-transition" stage for *many years* before this defining moment. It reflects an important first step toward a chosen life. It also has been an effective deterrent to those who are truly not prepared to leave. The act of joining or affiliating with an organization, is triggering to some—to paraphrase Groucho Marx, we are sensitive that there are some potential members that will not join "any club that would have me as a member"—but these mentioned benefits, we have found, outweigh this consideration.

At the core of our support service programs is the peer support model articulated above, coupled with one-to-one offerings by social workers and other professional staff, not to mention a highly skilled volunteer network that provides tutoring, mentorship, coaching, and occasionally internships or job offers. Our Support Services include a scholarship fund that has awarded over $1 million to date, two micro-grant programs, short-term crisis supports, financial counseling, and referrals to the Hebrew Free Loan Society, just to name a few. As the organization has grown, we most recently expanded our Family Justice program to provide more tailored supports to parents. Our supporters recognize that investment in our members' at this critical juncture is vastly impactful and can make the difference between self-sufficiency and dependency. Our Support Services assist more than 300 members a year through a combination of one-to-one and group work. An additional 125 members annually access our Economic Empowerment programs.

Partnership and Collaboration

A single organization with finite resources cannot, and we believe should not, attempt to be everything to those walking through its doors, nor should it attempt to "reinvent the wheel." Collaboration with other organizations and service providers lies at the core of Footsteps' program model. In the areas of career readiness, job placement, and legal services, Footsteps has developed formalized, funded partnerships with specializing agencies. We have countless other partners in the education, workforce development, and mental health fields, where we have developed the cultural competency of their teams and created pipelines for our members. In this way, those in our membership who may find navigating resources in the secular world overwhelming, instead are provided wraparound care, with follow up from Footsteps staff and partner organizations who are truly culturally competent and can anticipate their specific needs.

Exploring the Model

As an organization, Footsteps has evolved along with its members. We see a five-year intense transition phase for most of our members, characterized by an inner realization, an initial transformation, and its aftermath on an individual's family, friendships, income, and housing. Afterwards, there is a climb toward stability, setting and attaining individualized goals, and potentially, a process of reconciliation and integration of current and former identities. Of course, no two journeys are the same, and our program model is designed to provide space for those at any point in the journey. As the organization continues to support those at the onset of a transition, the community also supports members who have fully done so. A significant portion of members successfully reach sufficient degrees of self-actualization and cease attendance at Footsteps programs once they gain a foothold in a life of their choosing. Yet, a growing portion of those perceive the Footsteps community itself as an intrinsic social network, and many stay—or join at later stages of their own journey—to support those newly leaving, or to find resources they may need once again. As we celebrate our 15th-year anniversary, our identity as a community and organization has shifted to reflect this diversity.

Our theory of change is that our members will be best served by offering a balance of concrete supports and services, nurturing and strengthening the emerging community of formerly religious individuals, and connecting them to broader Jewish and secular communities. Footsteps serves as a central hub and often as a second family for this burgeoning community, and as a bridge from ultra-Orthodoxy to the wider Jewish community and to secular society at large. In this way, and as complex as it is to do so, we recognize that regardless of our members' distinct and varied personal affiliations, we are supporting a distinct and growing segment of the Jewish community. We explore this reality in depth later in this article.

The core elements of our model can be captured as follows: **Essential Services → Community Building → Activism and Movement Building**, where each subsequent activity builds off of the success of what preceded it.

Central Tensions at Footsteps

At its essence, Footsteps creates a supportive environment where individuals choose to journey from a black-and-white world to one filled with shades of gray, that is, from a homogenous world with a mapped out trajectory to a diverse world filled with possibility and nuance. There are two central tensions inherent to the transition Footsteps members undergo and that inform the organization's strategy, tone, and decisions: the tension between *the secular and the Jewish* and the tension between *moving forward and staying connected to the past*. Perhaps not coincidentally, these are two central tensions that mainstream Jewish communities have grappled with since the flourishing of the American Jewish community in the twentieth century.

Tension between Secular and Jewish Identities

Footsteps' membership is united by the fact that everyone is seeking to break away from a deeply religious past. Leaving the fold is fraught with tension and paradox, at least at the onset. This is why Footsteps cultivates a non-sectarian space that does not assume religious belief, affiliation, or practice. To best serve our members, Footsteps' first priority is to offer a neutral space so that members who no longer identify or are grappling with Judaism have a space to explore their options. For Footsteps, cultivating an "inclusive community" means that the organization has to make space for individuals who define themselves in all sorts of ways, from atheist and culturally Jewish, to formerly ultra-Orthodox and spiritual, to formerly Jewish, to Jewish and practicing, and beyond. Many of our members will explore many of these possible affiliations before identifying one that feels healthy and authentic.

In initial meetings with Footsteps staff, more than 20 percent of members report having experienced abuse of one form or another.[5] This further complicates their relationship with their Jewish identity, and is a fundamental concern of Footsteps. Ultra-Orthodoxy is not only highly insular, it is an all-encompassing way of life. Every moment of someone's day, every desire, and every need is in service to living "the right way." Dress codes, dietary restrictions, religious language, *Shabbos* and holiday rituals, and places where traumatic experiences may have occurred like synagogues, *mikvahs* (ritual baths), and *yeshivas* can all be sources of pain for our members and can trigger visceral and/or a physical reaction and/or a sense of a loss of agency. Instances of abuse may have taken place within religious spaces and/or by religious leaders or teachers, the very institutions and individuals entrusted with the care of community members.

Many have shared with us that they experienced religious practices and rituals as forms of control over their individual needs and desires. Some directly associate places, practices, and rituals with the abuse they experienced while living an ultra-Orthodox life. And still others have shared that the experience of leaving ultra-Orthodoxy was so painful that any association with religious practice arouses deeply uncomfortable or painful feelings. Our members may experience what is increasingly being understood as Religious Trauma Syndrome, which can include both the effects of prolonged exposure to the source of trauma within harmful religious communities and/or the psychological impact of severing one's ties to one's identity or origin community.[6] We have found that symbols of faith or demonstrations of religious ritual can be off-putting, alienating, or even bring about symptoms of PTSD or Complex-PTSD. In this way, some maintain that every member of Footsteps has experienced some degree of religious trauma.[7]

As a result, during the initial stages of the journey, defined by strong feelings of pain, loss, sadness, and anger, Footsteps members often require a clean break to achieve healthy outcomes. Individuals may stop engaging in any ritual and/or identify as atheist. They may simply want out. Our Religious Practices Policy recognizes these realities and limits religious ritual at member gatherings. Those who practice must do so privately. Footsteps will accommodate religious dietary restrictions to those that observe, but unlike other Jewish pluralistic communities, the most observant practitioners within our groups do not define what is practiced or observed in communal spaces. Our central value is choice, and we aim to create a space in which all choices are treated with respect. At Footsteps, pluralism is a commitment to the diversity of religious practice, including no religious practice.

An example of our values in action is displayed at our annual summer weekend program, "Camp Footsteps." Religious practices like a Friday night *Kabbalat Shabbos* prayer service are held in private settings alongside other programming, so that those who do not wish to participate do not feel sidelined for their choices. Jewish cultural experiences, such as a *tisch or kumsitz* (Jewish singing) are welcome, if members lead these activities themselves, just as traditional American campfire songs are welcome. In 2017, Camp Footsteps was held at Camp Kutz, a Reform summer camp in Orange County, New York. Camp Kutz is a kosher-style camp that does not have an Orthodox *hechsher* (seal of approval), which is thus acceptable to most of our members. Footsteps reached out individually to the two dozen or so individuals who had requested kosher, *hechshered* accommodations for themselves or their children. These conversations with staff created a space for members to talk about their personal (and often evolving) religious practice, or those of their family members.

Footsteps' efforts to create space for all people, no matter their often evolving religious practices, takes purposeful intentionality, requiring time, patience, and flexibility. The fact that Footsteps makes this investment is immensely important to members, who feel reassured, validated, and supported in their choices. Footsteps' desire to meet members where they are and to respect their needs is fundamental to the organization's reputation as safe and respectful.

In practice, it can be difficult to maintain a balance of member needs. Our partnership model, however, means we can create pathways for interested members who seek to reclaim elements of their Jewish identity. By offering pathways through partnerships, we can offer a breadth of support to our members, specialize in what we do best, and work with external organizations and ally communities that can introduce Footsteps members to new networks and experiences.

Increasingly, members have asked for support entering various parts of the wider Jewish community. A new formalized Footsteps/Moishe House partnership provides leadership development and community networking to those in their twenties and thirties who are interested in connecting to a post-college Jewish community. Footsteps partnered with Moishe House in 2017 to create the first residence led by Footsteps members, which caters to formerly ultra-Orthodox millennials and connects them to broader peer networks. The Moishe House program model provides subsidized housing and a program budget to residents, who cultivate Jewish community for their peers. The fit was mutually beneficial as both organizations seek to empower young people who wish to cultivate ownership over their Jewish identity, and in this way we can support the Jewish communal experience some of our members ask for, without compromising the comfort of other members who do not wish to engage at all.

There are many additional examples: A selection of our members has enjoyed presenting and participating in Limmud, a Jewish learning community. Romemu, a renewal synagogue on Manhattan's Upper West Side, infuses its services and programming with Chassidic melody, philosophy, and storytelling, and has made itself particularly welcoming to formerly Orthodox individuals. And in the last few years Footsteps has prepared a list of synagogues that have reached out to Footsteps to welcome our members with free or discounted tickets during the High Holidays.

As our membership has matured and evolved, many participants have independently sought pathways to alternative Jewish spaces, and in the future we anticipate facilitating additional connections to Jewish communal spaces to meet member demand. Individuals at the onset of their transition may have little or no knowledge of Jewish experience beyond the community and practice in which they were raised. Non-Orthodox ritual, services, and communal spaces might not feel like authentic expressions of Jewish identity. However, as we have observed over the years and as confirmed through the Nishma survey, people in the later stages of the transition, or post-transition, often reclaim their relationship to Judaism and Jewish identity and practice on their own terms.[8] In fact, the notion of being "culturally Jewish," which is often derided in ultra-Orthodox communities, is how many of our members ultimately see themselves—though for this population, reclamation of Jewish culture, combined with high literacy of Jewish life, ritual, language, etc., means this is a different type of cultural Judaism.

So, while our members may not see themselves as affiliated, their ultimate degree of affiliation is similar to many other young American culturally identified Jews (although members' Jewish identity invariably will reflect elements of ultra-Orthodox or Chasidic culture). For example, the Nishma study showed that over 50 percent of Footsteps members regularly/sometimes participate in *Shabbos* meals, 44 percent regularly/sometimes listen to Jewish music, 34 percent regularly/sometimes light *Shabbos* candles, and 24 percent regularly/sometimes engage in Jewish study/spiritual inquiry.[9]

People who leave ultra-Orthodoxy are also making their mark on the broader Jewish community. Those who leave bring a wealth of Jewish knowledge which often makes them assets in non-Orthodox Jewish spaces. There are significant numbers of Footsteps members who teach in non-Orthodox Sunday and Hebrew Schools, lead prayer services, or chant weekly Torah. For those men who were ordained in their former Orthodox lives, some may even become chaplains or officiate life-cycle events. They may be driven to these jobs out of financial necessity, or perhaps nostalgia for elements of these spaces; they may wholeheartedly subscribe to the tenets and values of these other Jewish spaces or they may not. Either way, because of their knowledge and skills, they help to educate the wider community, and demonstrate a unique voice of change and cultural understanding, one that moves well beyond early transition points of need and loss.

Tension between Moving Forward and Staying Connected to the Past

There is no way to erase the past; even if an individual self-actualizes within a secular context, each individual's personal history emerging from an insular ultra-Orthodox community will be a reality for the rest of their life. Consequently, a central part of the journey is learning to balance the tension between one's chosen and hard-fought identity and the community, family, and cultural milieu from which one emerges. Footsteps' philosophy maintains that where appropriate, integration of the various parts of Self is healthy and is a key element that contributes to self-actualization.

Family and community ties complicate the notion of a clean break with the past. The Nishma research indicated something that we have observed over the years: for many, family relationships do improve over time, although these range by community and by family member (e.g., those emerging from Satmar communities experience less reconciliation than those emerging from Chabad/Lubavitch, and similarly, less reconciliation overall with their fathers than mothers).[10] Those who are raising ultra-Orthodox children due to custody arrangements are often mandated by the courts to live within the bounds of community norms in order to maintain access to their children. Others, who have little secular education or vocational training, are often employed within the Orthodox community for a number of years before their transition to a desired secular life is complete.

Still others require as much psychological distance from origin communities and families as possible, and for lengthy periods of time.

It is quite challenging to maintain proximity for those who are shunned by their families and communities. It is equally painful for those who face continued abuse or re-traumatization if they maintain contact. Thus maintaining a proximity and relationship to family while leaving is not always possible.

Prior to Footsteps, leaving an ultra-Orthodox lifestyle often meant leaving family members behind. Shulem Deen documents in his memoir, *All Who Go Do Not Return*, that though he and his ex-wife initially had an agreement for shared custody, this quickly changed once the larger ultra-Orthodox community became involved.[11] The community began to shame his children for having a "different" kind of father—one who wore jeans. Their relationship began to suffer. His ex-wife took him to family court, claiming that since he had Internet at his home, he was a bad influence. The judge reduced his arrangement from regular weekend overnights to a few hours a week to monthly supervised visits. His children grew anxious in his presence, as his son Hershy said: "Mommy says you want to turn us into goyim."[12]

As shown in the Netflix documentary *One of Us*, in which one Footsteps member fights for custody of her seven children, Shulem is certainly not the only formerly ultra-Orthodox individual to experience alienation from a spouse and children. However, increasingly, men and women within the Footsteps community are successfully navigating the very real and complex challenges, compromises, and emotions to sustain the relationships that they care about deeply. Eli Mandel and his wife, Rikki, have both written publicly about the efforts they make to sustain their relationship—she is ultra-Orthodox and he is no longer.[13] He writes that after he left ultra-Orthodoxy, "many friends and acquaintances . . . told us they feel that our marriage could no longer work, and took strong positions against our marriage. But Rikki and I felt differently, and we persevered. Setting out on this new life was almost like getting married all over again; we had to relearn to respect each other and each other's choices."

For some members, the end (or the beginning) of an unhappy marriage is the catalyst for a religious shift. If this is the case, and they are parents, there is an increasing understanding among Footsteps members that maintaining a relationship with their children can and should be their right and responsibility. With the support of Footsteps' Family Justice Program and other legal efforts, they are beginning to win court battles so that they are legally entitled to custody and visitation.[14] An enormous challenge lies ahead in this area and Footsteps is working on both strengthening the service offerings to members and a legal reform strategy.

What's Next: Moving towards Advocacy

Before Footsteps was founded, leaving ultra-Orthodoxy was a solitary journey. "I left in the middle of the night with only $50 to my name," says Deena, who embarked on her journey before 2003. Today, many people, even those deeply ensconced in the ultra-Orthodox world, know about Footsteps or can find it online as they begin to take their initial forays toward leaving. While the journey will always be difficult, today people have access to approximately 1,700 members, a peer network estimated at over 5,000, and specialized resources designed for and by this community. Beyond Footsteps, the North American landscape has changed, especially in New York. Two additional resources stand out: Freidom (formerly OTD Meetup), a social group run by and for formerly ultra-Orthodox individuals, provides weekly social and cultural activities, and Formerly Fundamentalist caters to individuals from a variety of fundamentalist backgrounds.

There are also burgeoning meetups and emerging organizations across the United States and the world. A partial listing includes: Hillel: Open Gates (which predates Footsteps in its founding) and Out for Change, both located in Israel; Mavar and Gesher UK in England; Forward in Montreal; Pathways in Melbourne; and other peer-led initiatives in Los Angeles, Baltimore, and Florida. Footsteps runs a quarterly conference call for individuals across the world to connect with one another and the organization. People can also connect online through dozens of Facebook groups, WhatsApp groups, and other online forums.

As the community of formerly ultra-Orthodox has grown, individuals' attitudes toward their own identities have shifted. As Deena said, "I left and I tried to forget who I had been. I didn't think about my old life for twenty-five years, until my kids were grown up and out of the house." Today, the term OTD is used, by many, with pride. And a campaign called "It Gets Besser" encourages people to share their accomplishments and joys. Many Footsteps members report feeling transformed by sharing their stories with a supportive audience.

Externally, awareness of this experience has fueled a tremendous support network of donors and volunteers. The larger Jewish community has also become interested in learning more about, and supporting Footsteps and its members. Synagogues host our members and Jewish communal organizations that once declined to fund Footsteps now support the organization.

Recent population surveys, including the 2013 Pew Study on American Jews and the 2011 UJA-sponsored Jewish Community of New York study, highlighted the growth of the ultra-Orthodox population, both absolutely and as a percentage of the larger Jewish community.[15,16] Growing awareness of the size and strength of the ultra-Orthodox community has also spurred awareness about those who leave, changing attitudes, challenging misconceptions, and leading toward greater interest and willingness to embrace this emerging community.

Until recently, Footsteps focused entirely on service provision and community building. People who wished to advocate for change around issues affecting the formerly ultra-Orthodox did so on their own. Examples include Naftuli Moster's Yaffed, which seeks to improve secular education within Chasidic yeshivas, and Fraidy Reiss's Unchained At Last, which seeks to end child marriage and forced marriage in the United States, whether in Jewish communities or not.

As Footsteps has grown and awareness around the issues that deeply affect our members has increased, particularly after the release of *One of Us*, the organization has begun to explore ways to build a movement and advocate for systemic change. In 2018, Footsteps began developing a plan for legal reform in secular courts, which time and time again discriminate against parents leaving the ultra-Orthodox community in custody battles. Footsteps also recently hired its first Director of Field and Movement Building, with the vision of supporting reform efforts and mobilizing the public around issues of concern to those leaving ultra-Orthodoxy.

Increasingly, Footsteps members are showing up as advocates for themselves and their community. Footsteps members, and the OTD community at large, are creating spaces that cater to their needs, and are shaping the narrative around their stories. Footsteps plays a crucial role behind the scene in developing and supporting the next generation of leadership. A new microcosm of thriving OTDers is also burgeoning. In ultra-Orthodox Brooklyn neighborhoods, including Kensington, Ditmas Park, and Crown Heights, OTD communities are springing up. This merging of old and new identities to create a new branch of the Jewish tree was unimaginable ten years ago.

We see the future of the organization, and the emergence of a movement, as only sustainable if it is run primarily by those who have personally experienced leaving ultra-Orthodoxy.[17] Footsteps has invested in leadership from within—from adding members to the board of directors, to increasing the number of staff who grew up ultra-Orthodox, to creating a Member Advisory Committee to ensure that members and the organization have a two-way feedback loop. Footsteps also invests in the community by offering micro-grant funding, collaborating with organizations with aligned missions, and creating pathways to other leadership opportunities, be they on college campuses, with community foundations, or with other organizations where community members find resonance.

Looking ahead, we see a bright future. This movement out of ultra-Orthodoxy brings a new voice into the Jewish world—a voice of choice and change. There are thousands of individuals who are building off of their experiences growing up in and leaving the ultra-Orthodox world to create social change, raise awareness, and reform societal injustices. We are here to support and affirm all of the brave individuals who choose to embark on this journey into a new world. We are here to amplify the voice of this movement and propel it forward as it grows stronger and larger.

Notes

1. Mark L. Trencher, "Starting a Conversation: A Pioneering Survey of Those Who Have Left the Orthodox Community," *Nishma Research*, June 19, 2016, http://nishmaresearch.com/assets/pdf/Report_Survey_of_Those_Who_Left_Orthodoxy_Nishma_Research_June_2016.pdf.

2. Individuals that reach out to Footsteps from other fundamentalist communities (such as ex-Mormon, Jehovah's Witness, ex-Muslim, etc.) are connected to resources and supports; ultimately, the organization's issue expertise has evolved to serve those emerging from Jewish communities, and therefore, we offer limited services to those from other faith backgrounds. Additional joint programming in partnership with organizations that serve those from other faith backgrounds bolsters our work.

3. For the first few years of Footsteps' existence, 80% of membership was male identified. In 2018, there is more parity in our membership with about 60% identifying as male. Footsteps' investment in critical supports, including our family justice work, has lowered the barriers for women and gender non-

conforming individuals who wish to leave. Our Support Services programming is utilized about equally by men and women.

4. See Trencher, "Starting a Conversation," 11.

5. This figure reflects the percentage of abuse reported at the initial interview with Footsteps' staff. We believe the rates are much higher.

6. "Understanding Religious Trauma Syndrome: Trauma from Leaving Religion," British Association for Behavioural and Cognitive Psychotherapies, http://www.babcp.com/Review/RTS-Trauma-from-Leaving-Religion.aspx.

7. Batya Ungar-Sargon, "Why Do So Many Jews Who Leave the Ultra-Orthodox Community Commit Suicide?" *Gothamist*, August 12, 2015, http://gothamist.com/2015/08/12/ultra_orthodox_jewish_struggle.php.

8. Trencher, "Starting a Conversation," 8.

9. Ibid., 10.

10. Ibid., 58.

11. Shulem Deen, *All Who Go Do Not Return* (Minneapolis: Graywolf Press, 2015), 276.

12. Ibid., 279.

13. Eli Mandel, "Seder with My Orthodox Wife and Kids," *Times of Israel* (Jerusalem, Israel), March 11, 2015.

14. Sharon Otterman, "When Living Your Truth Can Mean Losing Your Children," *New York Times* (New York, NY), May 25, 2018.

15. "A Portrait of Jewish Americans: Findings from a Pew Research Center Survey of U.S. Jews," Pew Research Center, October 1, 2013, http://www.pewforum.org/files/2013/10/jewish-american-full-report-for-web.pdf.

16. "Jewish Community Study of New York: 2011 Special Report on Poverty," UJA-Federation of New York, June 2013, https://www.ujafedny.org/assets/785329.

17. We simultaneously feel that it is important to have outside issue experts and allies at the staff and board levels, so that we are drawing from diverse professional settings as well as ensuring that the broader Jewish and secular communities are invested as allies and supporters.

Bibliography

"A Portrait of Jewish Americans: Findings from a Pew Research Center Survey of U.S. Jews." Pew Research Center. October 1, 2013. http://www.pewforum.org/files/2013/10/jewish-american-full-report-for-web.pdf.

Batya Ungar-Sargon. "Why Do So Many Jews Who Leave The Ultra-Orthodox Community Commit Suicide?" *Gothamist*. August 12, 2015. http://gothamist.com/2015/08/12/ultra_orthodox_jewish_struggle.php.

Deen, Shulem. *All Who Go Do Not Return*. Minneapolis: Graywolf Press, 2015.

"Jewish Community Study of New York: 2011 Special Report on Poverty." UJA-Federation of New York. June 2013. https://www.ujafedny.org/assets/785329.

Mandel, Eli. "Seder with My Orthodox Wife and Kids." *Times of Israel* (Jerusalem, Israel). March 11, 2015.

Otterman, Sharon. "When Living Your Truth Can Mean Losing Your Children." *New York Times* (New York, NY), May 25, 2018.

Trencher, Mark L. "Starting a Conversation: A Pioneering Survey of Those Who Have Left the Orthodox Community." Nishma Research. June 19, 2016. http://nishmaresearch.com/assets/pdf/Report_Survey_of_Those_Who_Left_Orthodoxy_Nishma_Research_June_2016.pdf.

Winell, Dr. Marlene. "Understanding Religious Trauma Syndrome: Trauma from Leaving Religion." British Association for Behavioural and Cognitive Psychotherapies. http://www.babcp.com/Review/RTS-Trauma-from-Leaving-Religion.aspx.

Educational Attainments among Disaffiliates from Ultra-Orthodoxy

MIRIAM R. MOSTER

Introduction

Classical sociologists projected that education and modernization would have a secularizing effect, leading to a decline in religion.[1] Research throughout the first two thirds of the twentieth century seemed to corroborate their projection, as survey data indicated a positive correlation between educational attainment and secularity or apostasy.[2] Some, however, explained the positive correlation between secularity and educational attainment by pointing to a self-selection process whereby individuals who identify as secular are more likely to go on to enroll in college or pursue an academic career.[3] Regardless, beginning in the seventies as more individuals began pursuing a college education, researchers began observing that there was no longer a clear positive relationship between secularity and educational attainment, leading some contemporary sociologists to reject the thesis of the secularizing effect of education in favor of social theories.[4]

More recent research has been mixed, in part due to a reframing of what constitutes secularity and religiosity. Recent studies distinguishing between various forms of religion (new movements vs. traditional) and aspects of religious practice and belief have found that while some forms and features of religion correlate negatively with educational attainment, others—such as congregational affiliation—correlate positively.[5] Given the nuance introduced with some of the new literature, the explanatory power of education as secularizing no longer seems clear cut.

While many researchers have theorized about the relationship between education and secularity since it appeared to take a turn in the seventies, few have focused on apostates from fundamentalist groups and none to my knowledge have explored the relationship between education and secularity among recent disaffiliates from Orthodox Judaism (herein also referred to as exiters or OTD, an acronym for "Off the Derech," or off the path).[6] The OTD phenomenon can be particularly illuminating as disaffiliates from fundamentalist groups are not like the secular individuals of no religion of other studies. Moreover, as Hasidic disaffiliates in particular come from communities which tend to shun secular education, a case study of disaffiliates from Hasidism with attention paid to the chronology of their attainment of education can shed light on the relationship between education and secularity.

Admittedly, secularity is not an easy term to define. According to Casanova, if secularization is to be defined as the marginalization of religion and the "relocation of persons, things, functions, meanings, and so forth, from their traditional location in the religious sphere to the secular spheres," then the deprivatization of religion that began in the eighties would be antithetical to secularization.[7] Heilman found this to be the case with Orthodox Judaism as the ultra-Orthodox, rather than becoming marginalized and privatized in the modern world, have morphed into a "public American Orthodoxy."[8] The distinction between religiosity and secularity in the modern world is murky, and insofar as Chasidim exert control in public spheres, Chasidism may be said to have a secular character. In other ways, too, Chasidism (and contemporary ultra-Orthodoxy in general) is very much a product of modern times. And just as Chasidim might not be purely a-secular, disaffiliates may not be purely secular, as many disaffiliates continue to identify Jewishly in practice or belief, even if not in the same ways they had when they practiced as Chasidim—raising the question of whether their Jewishness once disaffiliated qualifies as a religious identity or as a secular one. Others have grappled with similar questions in studies of Jewish identity in general, debating under what circumstances Jewishness constitutes a strictly religious identity as opposed to a secular ethnic or cultural identity.[9] Parsing Jewish religious and secular identity seems to remain a somewhat open question. For the purposes of the present study, however, secularity is defined strictly in terms of an individual's self-identification as religiously disaffiliated.[10]

Exiters in Context

Exiters from Orthodoxy range from the formerly modern Orthodox to the formerly ultra-Orthodox. Ultra-Orthodoxy includes the Litvish and Chasidic communities, both of which encompass a range of constituents that vary in their adherence to particular modes of dress and stringencies. One of the more conspicuous differences between the various denominations of ultra-Orthodox Judaism is in their approach toward secular education. Whereas some ultra-Orthodox schools embrace secular learning within a dual curriculum that also devotes time to religious studies, others eschew secular studies.

More specifically, most male Chasidim living in New York receive a negligible secular education.[11] Their primary education typically consists of one and a half hours of basic English and math, four days per week, in some cases taught by a Chasidic adult male who is himself unfamiliar with the subject matter he is meant to teach.[12] After the age of thirteen (when boys turn Bar Mitzvah), they typically receive no secular education at all, and instead spend their days studying religious texts.[13] Their studies often begin early in the morning and last well into the evening, and a school day of fourteen hours is not uncommon.[14] This practice all but guarantees that adolescent Chasidic males are not only denied a basic secular education in the school setting, but that they also do not have the leisure to read or otherwise educate themselves independently. As a result, many adult male Chasidim are functionally illiterate, most are unlikely to ever attend college, and the Chasidic community is consequently plagued by high rates of poverty.[15]

Low educational attainment among male Chasidic exiters might therefore be expected given their deficient primary and secondary education. On the other hand, the Haskalah movement of the late eighteenth through the late nineteenth centuries gave rise to the enlightened disaffiliate, setting a precedent for higher educational attainment among all Orthodox disaffiliates today, including Chasidic disaffiliates.[16] And recent data on Jewish educational attainment reinforces this post-enlightenment tendency. A Pew report noted that "highly educated Jews tend to be less religious than Jews with fewer years of schooling."[17] The report goes on to clarify that this is true both when religiousness is measured as a matter of Orthodoxy as well as when the sample is limited to non-Orthodox Jews: non-Orthodox Jews are more highly educated than Orthodox Jews; and among non-Orthodox Jews, "Jews with college degrees are less likely to say religion is very important to them or that they believe in God with absolute certainty compared with Jews with lower levels of educational attainment."[18] Glaeser and Sacerdote similarly found that "Jews are by far the most educated and by far the least likely to attend services. Within Judaism, the two more educated groups (reform and conservative) have lower attendance levels than the less educated orthodox Jews."[19] Furthermore, twentieth-century Jewish educational attainments overall have been especially pronounced, giving reason to believe that patterns related to educational attainment among disaffiliates from Judaism may be more pronounced as well.[20]

That being the case, Jewish disaffiliates should be expected to have high rates of BA attainment overall. Male Chasidic exiters, in contrast, will likely have lower rates of BA attainment than Jews overall due to their inadequate secular education, but higher rates of BA attainment than their religious counterparts. (Male educational attainment in particular has been found to correlate more strongly with secularity than female educational attainment.[21]) It also stands to reason that male Chasidic disaffiliates' rates of BA attainment will positively correlate with the duration for which they have identified as OTD, as this permits them the requisite time to make up for their deficient education and to pursue a BA.

Contemporary Disaffiliates' Educational Attainments

Survey data published in the summer of 2016 by Nishma on those who left the Orthodox community finally makes an evaluation of their educational attainments possible and the data indeed diverges drastically from trends noted in other studies.[22] A limitation of Nishma's data is that it was conducted as an opt-in panel and lacks a sampling frame. Nonetheless, it is the best available data at present. According to Nishma's report, 61 percent of all respondents (including those who formerly affiliated with denominations other than Chasidism) had obtained at least a BA, a rate that is similar to the 58 percent of Jewish Americans with BAs, and to the 60 percent of non-Orthodox Jewish New Yorkers with BAs.[23] Among male disaffiliates from Chasidism, in contrast, only 26.3 percent had obtained BAs—a rate that is less than half of that of Jewish Americans, and one that is also lower than the 32.3 percent of American males who, as of the 2015 census, had obtained at least a BA.[24]

Although rates of BA attainment are lower among male OTD Chasidim than they are among the US male population, other disaffiliates, and American Jews, disaffiliated Chasidim at least five years out of the community would nonetheless be considered highly educated in comparison to religious Chasidim. Additionally, the numbers are skewed by the crippling effects of a deficient primary and secondary education.

Exemplifying this, rates of educational attainment among formerly Chasidic individuals within their first four years of leaving Chasidism are similar to those of their religious counterparts: according to UJA's *Jewish Community Study of New York*, 63 percent of male Chasidim had a high school diploma or less, 21 percent had some college credits or an associate's degree, and 16 percent had a bachelor's degree or more (see figure 1).[25] Similarly, in the present study, among those >1 to 4+ years out of the community, 61 percent have a high school diploma or less, 21 percent have some college credits or an associate's degree, and 17 percent have obtained a BA (see figure 1 and table 1). Their low

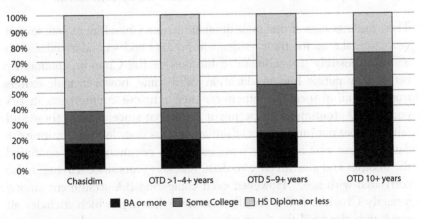

Source: Data on Chassidim come from Cohen, Miller, and Ukeles, Jewish Community Study, 218; data on OTD derived from Mark Trencher, "Starting a Conversation: A Pioneering Survey of Those Who Have Left the Orthodox Community" (Nishma Research, 2016).

Figure 1. Educational attainments among male Chasidim and Chasidic disaffiliates.

Table 1. Educational Attainments Among Male Chasidic Disaffiliates

Time since leaving	Total	H.S. or less	Some College	BA or more
OTD (all years)	156	76 (49%)	39 (25%)	41 (26%)
>1–4+ years OTD	75	46 (61%)	16 (21%)	13 (17%)
5–9+ years OTD	46	21 (46%)	15 (33%)	10 (22%)
10+ years OTD	35	9 (26%)	8 (23%)	18 (51%)

Source: Derived from Mark Trencher, "Starting a Conversation: A Pioneering Survey of Those Who Have Left the Orthodox Community" (Nishma Research, 2016).

educational attainments in the first few years after leaving the community are likely a consequence of the inadequate education they received within the Chasidic community. However, among Chasidic males out of the community 5 to 9+ years, educational attainments begin to shift: more than half either are pursuing or have completed a college degree and fewer than half have only a high school diploma or less (see table 1). By ten years or more OTD, more than 50 percent have obtained a BA, a rate that begins to approach that of non-Orthodox Jews and is significantly higher than the rate of BA attainment in the US population.

Explaining Disaffiliates' Academic Attainments

These findings suggest that male disaffiliates from Chasidism require several years to make up for their inadequate primary and secondary education and also possibly to acclimate to life outside the Chasidic community before they pursue higher education. With time, however, male exiters from Chasidism seem to outperform their religious counterparts in BA pursuit and attainment. Some might argue that since data on those still religious does not (and cannot) distinguish years since leaving, limiting the data to those who are many years out of the community may confound the findings and give an edge to disaffiliates, as years since leaving is also correlated with age.[26] However, even comparing BA attainment among formerly Chasidic males for all years since leaving (which includes all ages) with the total for those who remain religious (which again spans all ages), exiters still have higher rates of BA attainment.

Moreover, since rates of educational attainment for formerly Chasidic males who had left Chaisidism in the last 1 to 4+ years are most similar to rates of academic attainment for those within the community, the secularizing effect of education cannot have been a catalyst for exiting. For had it been, those who leave would have at least begun pursuing higher education prior to leaving, in which case their rates of BA attainment (or BA pursuit) would dwarf those of the currently Chasidic, and rates of those with a high school diploma or less would be far lower. Rather, the change in educational attainment based on time since leaving indicates that (1) secularization/disaffiliation likely preceded their access to education, and (2) some other/mediating factor(s) must explain both their disaffiliation and their higher rates of educational attainment.

Literature on the relationship between secularity and educational attainment does not adequately account for rates of BA attainment among former Chasidim—or among disaffiliates from other denominations of Orthodox Judaism. Secularization theory would not pertain, for while disaffiliates' college years may further influence their levels of belief, observance and disaffection—and this can provide fertile ground for a future study—many ex-Chasidim are nonetheless self-identifying as disaffiliated prior to enrolling in college.

The findings of the present study also stand in contrast to Massengill and MacGregor's finding that among Americans born after 1960, not only do those of no religion (religious "nones") underperform compared to the religiously affiliated, but even disaffiliates, whom they identify as those who were raised religious and identified as religious by age sixteen but disaffiliated later, end up performing similarly to religious affiliates in educational attainment.[27] They note that the social networks fostered by religious affiliation may explain adherents' educational attainments, in contrast to the lower attainments of "nones" who lack those networks.[28] This explanation would not account fully for the educational attainments of the formerly ultra-Orthodox. Among Chasidim, for instance, intra-religious social connections might aid adherents and disaffiliates who choose to pursue certain lines of work, but they would certainly not aid an individual seeking an education, as secular education is shunned and information regarding education is difficult to come by in the Chasidic community. Moreover, Massengill and MacGregor point to religious social networks to explain commensurate educational attainments between religious affiliates and disaffiliates; not to explain discrepant attainments as is the case here.

On the other hand, the new networks individuals tap into after leaving their religious community may, but even then only partially, better account for their academic attainments. And as noted earlier, disaffiliates do attain BAs at rates similar to those documented for non-Orthodox Jews. In explaining Jewish achievement, Burstein appeals to social capital, a combination of human capital and particularity, arguing that the social and support networks (human capital) geared toward education (Jewish particularity) established by the Jewish community, foster, and consequently explain, Jewish achievement.[29]

The OTD community does benefit from Jewish social and support networks geared toward education. Footsteps is a key organization that enables one of the most undereducated groups in the country to achieve high rates of BA attainment by providing support in the form of GED prep and college scholarships, among other things. Other informal forms of support come through Facebook groups such as "OTD University" where individuals offer college guidance to fellow disaffiliates. Disaffiliates can also access various forms of support through other Jewish scholarship funds and resources in the broader Jewish community. Nonetheless, the explanatory power of social capital goes only so far as Footsteps was a decade or so old as of Nishma's survey, and it is therefore not clear that the resources they provide would have helped the most likely to be educated of the disaffiliates—those ten or more years out of the community. OTD Facebook communities are also a more recent phenomenon.

Massengill and MacGregor also argue that the stable and grounding environment of a religious upbringing confers protection against deviance in adolescence, which may explain disaffiliates' educational attainments later in life.[30] There is insufficient data on deviance among disaffiliates from Chasidism, but a perusal of the literature available raises questions about this supposition.

Some within the ultra-Orthodox community have attributed disaffiliation to an unstable upbringing, claiming that OTD individuals are often the products of broken homes or victims of childhood abuse.[31] Deviant youth (whether merely deviating from religious stringencies or displaying harmful behaviors) are labeled at-risk and OTD interchangeably, which may indicate that deviance in adolescence is not uncommon among disaffiliates who then go on to have high rates of BA attainment.[32] However, this might simply be a semantic error—an incorrect conflation of at-risk adolescents with OTD adults.[33]

Some maintain that many at-risk youth ultimately return to the faith.[34] On the other hand, others have found that labeling an individual as disaffiliated, even if that individual would not have considered him- or herself a disaffiliate to begin with, can serve as a catalyst for that individual's disaffiliation.[35] That may well be the case with at-risk Orthodox adolescents. Labeled OTD by others, they perhaps begin to embrace this given name and identify as disaffiliated even if that was not their initial intention. However, as the two populations have received little academic attention, it is hard to know for certain. In any case, lack of data along with anecdotal evidence of unstable home environments and deviance among some OTD individuals in their youth, render the theory that disaffiliates from ultra-Orthodoxy have high rates of academic attainment due to the stable, religious environment of their adolescence both unverifiable and questionable.

Another theory that does not adequately account for the educational attainments of Chasidic disaffiliates attributes the changing relationship between secularity and educational attainment after the 1970s to the normalization of college education among religious adherents.[36] Schwadel suggests that the influx of religious students into colleges diminished the social pressure toward secularization.[37] By this reasoning, the secularizing influence when it existed was not from education and the new knowledge and learning that contradicted religious belief, but rather from the social pressure inherent in an environment where the majority of people were secular.

Though the predicament of ex-Chasidim does not contradict this theory, neither does it lend support to it, since Chasidic disaffiliates likely disaffiliated prior to attending college, in which case the lack of a secularizing influence in the college setting becomes irrelevant. But social pressure can be invoked to make a different case. Within the Chasidic community, social pressure pushes individuals strongly to remain religious and to refrain from attending college in the first place. Though social pressure cannot easily explain their disaffiliation, it may explain their inclination toward academic pursuits after disaffiliating: surrounded by so many college-educated fellow-disaffiliates, OTD individuals may be responding to social pressure in their new, secular environment among their OTD peers when they pursue a college education. Prior to the influx of religious students into colleges, peer pressure in academic settings encouraged secularization. Here, social pressure among secular and disaffiliated peers would be encouraging education.

Schwadel also argues that as the highly educated are more likely to be early adopters and innovators, the highly educated were the early adopters of secularity.[38] He notes further that secularity might have begun among the upper class (who were more likely to be highly educated) as a status differentiator but then diffused to the rest of society.[39] By these accounts, when secularity was still rare and novel in the general population, it was the domain of the highly educated, but as secularity became more common, it trickled down to the less educated leading to the current circumstances where a growing number of individuals who never attended college identify as secular while a growing number of college students now identify as religious. However, this can hardly be true among Chasidim who are barely educated to begin with—and in fact, education is the second of two things disaffiliates are adopting, the first being secularization—which only begs the question: if early adopters are the highly educated, what explains the early adoption of education?

Among additional characteristics of early adopters, Rogers identifies the possession of a "favorable attitude toward education."[40] Perhaps, then, exiters' favorable attitude toward education motivates their disaffiliation. Or, put another way, coming from a community where secular education is shunned, self-selected individuals find themselves compelled to leave Chasidism in order to pursue higher education; hence the higher rate of BA attainment among disaffiliates. In her study of Amish disaffiliates, Sullivan similarly found that "there was a trend of leaving the Amish church explicitly for the opportunity of more education for some of the participants."[41] Relatedly, in their study of various Protestant denominations, Smith and Sikkink argue that since fundamentalist identity is "dependent on a religious enclave," individuals' actions (such as the pursuit of higher education) that take them beyond the enclave threaten their retention within the group.[42]

While the attribute of favoring education may pertain, this attitude as sole motivator is somewhat questionable on the grounds that, for the rare Chasid who is interested in a college education, niche institutions do exist, such as Machon L'Parnassa, which caters to ultra-Orthodox individuals seeking a college education in a culturally sensitive context.[43] Leaving in order to pursue a college education would also not explain higher rates of BA attainment among disaffiliates overall, including those among the formerly modern Orthodox who could easily have pursued BA degrees at secular and even elite institutions while remaining religious. Among the modern Orthodox, according to UJA data, 55 percent of males had obtained a BA compared to 86.6 percent of modern Orthodox men surveyed by Nishma who went OTD.[44] Nevertheless, what remains a compelling argument is that some OTD individuals may constitute a self-selected group possessing a number of the attributes found among innovators and early adopters (Rogers lists thirty-two in total). These traits and propensities may then help explain both individuals' disaffiliation and their subsequent academic achievement. But here again, we are limited to conjecture due to paucity of data.

Patai has pointed to a "heritage of education," specifically the heritage of Talmud study, to explain Jewish achievement, and some might contend that that same heritage can explain exiters' rates of BA attainment.[45] Others have similarly pointed to a Jewish legacy of education and literacy to explain contemporary Jewish achievement.[46] Chasidim participate in this heritage, for while Chasidim shun secular education, they do not in any way shun all education. Continuing in the heritage of education of their forebears, Orthodox boys are said to be trilingual in ancient Hebrew, Aramaic, and either Yiddish or English depending on the denomination; and Talmud study can be intellectually rigorous. By this reasoning, OTD individuals may be responding to the premium placed on education in their community of origin as they pursue higher education once they leave the fold.

However, while it might be tempting to attribute BA attainment among disaffiliates to a religious legacy of learning, that cannot be the whole answer. For if this culture of learning were to explain disaffiliates' educational attainments, disaffiliates in other time periods would have been highly educated as well, for that same reason. And yet, in Ancient Rome as well as during the Middle Ages, disaffiliates from Rabbinic Judaism tended to be less educated and less likely to be literate than their religious counterparts among whom learnedness was prized.[47] Furthermore, secular Jews today boast disproportionate academic achievement, despite not partaking in the cultural heritage of traditional religious learning. Glazer found similarly that Jewish-American immigrants displaying high academic attainment were unlikely to have been religiously affiliated, and had not partaken in what he termed the "great tradition" of Torah and Talmud study of traditional Rabbinic Judaism.[48]

A better explanation for exiters' achievements might be found in what Lee and Zhou have dubbed "stereotype promise," which they define as "the social psychological process through which exceptional academic outcomes become a self-fulfilling prophecy."[49] Along these lines, as disaffiliates assimilate into secular society, they join a culture with positive stereotypes about Jewish achievement. A legacy of high-achieving disaffiliates from the Haskala period would further reinforce this percep-tion, and the highly educated secular Jews and veteran OTD individuals that disaffiliates go on to encounter would lend additional credence to this narrative, bolstering disaffiliates' confidence in their ability to suc-ceed academically.

Conclusion

All in all, educational attainments of Orthodox disaffiliates, and specifi-cally those of Chasidic disaffiliates, are probably best explained by the confluence of factors noted above. As innovators forging new identities for themselves in a secular world, some may be interested in education to begin with or may be self-selected in other ways that are conducive to academic pursuits. Social capital in the form of Jewish organizations, scholarship funds, and a growing OTD community for guidance, provides disaffiliates with the resources to embark on an academic journey. Social pressure toward, or social expectation of, academic pursuit would be fostered by the new community they join of fellow-OTD individuals as well as by secular Jews who already boast disproportionate academic achievements. Witnessing their peers' success may inspire individuals in the OTD com-munity who had not necessarily had their sights on academic endeavors at the outset of their journey away from ultra-Orthodoxy to enroll in col-lege. This community of high achieving peers may embolden even former Chasidim to pursue higher education despite lacking the foundations for such study. And stereotype promise becomes a self-fulfilling prophecy as many formerly OTD individuals go on to attain BA degrees.

Acknowledgments

Many thanks to Dr. Michael Staub, Dr. Steven Cohen, Dr. Zalman Newfield and to my husband, Naftuli Moster, for their comments on this chapter.

Notes

1. See Alan Aldridge, Religion in the Contemporary World (Massachu-setts: Polity Press, 2013), chapter 2. Aldridge offers a comprehensive overview of secularization theory in the works of Durkheim, Marx and Weber.

2. James Henry Leuba, *The Belief in God and Immortality: A Psychological, Anthropological and Statistical Study* (Chicago, IL: Open Court, 1921), 286; Joseph Zelan, "Religious Apostasy, Higher Education and Occupational Choice," *Sociology of Education* 41, no. 4 (1968): 378; Arthur C. Wickenden, "The Effect of the College Experience Upon Students' Concepts of God," *The Journal of Religion* 12, no. 2 (1932): 265–66; Rodney Stark, "On the Incompatibility of Religion and Science: A Survey of American Graduate Students," *Journal for the Scientific Study of Religion* 3, no. 1 (1963): 14.

3. Robert Wuthnow, "Science and the Sacred," in *The Sacred in a Secular Age*, ed. Phillip E. Hammond (Oakland, CA: University of California Press, 1985), 191; Fred Thalheimer, "Continuity and Change in Religiosity: A Study of Academicians," *Pacific Sociological Review* 8, no. 2 (1965): 108. Interestingly, Thalheimer references a study published by Marvin Nathan in 1932 that found that Jewish disaffiliates were more likely to disaffiliate prior to attending college.

4. See, for instance, Rebekah P. Massengill and Carol Ann MacGregor, "Religious Nonaffiliation and Schooling: The Educational Trajectories of Three Types of Religious 'Nones,'" in *Religion, Work, and Inequality: Research in the Sociology of Work*, ed. Lisa A. Keister, John Mccarthy, and Roger Finke (Emerald Group Publishing, 2012), 183–203; Philip Schwadel, "Explaining Cross-National Variation in the Effect of Higher Education on Religiosity," *Journal for the Scientific Study of Religion* 54, no. 2 (2015): 401–18; Jeremy E. Uecker, Mark D. Regnerus, and Margaret L. Vaaler, "Losing My Religion: The Social Sources of Religious Decline in Early Adulthood," *Social Forces* 85, no. 4 (2007): 1667–692.

5. See, for instance, James R. Lewis, Michael P. Oman-Reagan, and Sean Currie, "The Religion of the Educated Classes Revisited: New Religions, the Nonreligious, and Educational Levels," *Journal for the Scientific Study of Religion* 55, no. 1 (2016): 102; Michael J. McFarland, Bradley R. E. Wright and David L Weakliem, "Educational Attainment and Religiosity: Exploring Variations by Religious Traditions," *Sociology of Religion* 72, no. 2 (2011): 166–88; Darren E. Sherkat, "Religion and Higher Education: The Good, the Bad, and the Ugly," *SSRC Web Forum* (2007); Schwadel, "Explaining Cross-National Variation in the Effect of Higher Education on Religiosity," 401–18; Jonathan P. Hill, "Faith and Understanding: Specifying the Impact of Higher Education on Religious Belief," *Journal for the Scientific Study of Religion* 50, no. 3 (2011): 533–51.

6. On the relationship between apostasy from fundamentalist religion and educational outcomes, see Christian Smith and David Sikkink, "Social Predictors of Retention in and Switching from the Religious Faith of Family of Origin: Another Look Using Religious Tradition Self-Identification," *Review of Religious Research* 45, no. 2 (2003): 198, 202; Jessica Sullivan, "A Recipe for Success in the 'English World': An Investigation of the Ex-Amish in Mainstream Society" PhD diss., Western Michigan University, (2018) https://scholarworks.wmich.edu/dissertations/3358, 108. Sullivan's dissertation on Amish disaffiliates touched briefly on disaffiliates' educational attainments, finding that 60 percent of the

25 ex-Amish sampled had gone on to pursue a GED or college education—an education that would have been closed off to them within the Amish community.

7. Jose Casanova, *Public Religions in the Modern World* (Chicago: University of Chicago Press, 1994), 13.

8. Samuel C. Heilman, *Sliding to the Right: The Contest for the Future of American Jewish Orthodoxy* (Berkeley: University of California Press, 2006), 299.

9. See Charles Kadushin, "Asking About Religion," in *Socio-Demography of American Jewry* (2011) https://www.brandeis.edu/ssri/conferences/demographyconf/plenary1.html, 8; Harriet Hartman and Moshe Hartman. "Jewish Identity and the Secular Achievements of American Jewish Men and Women," *Journal for the Scientific Study of Religion* 50, no. 1 (March 2011): 151; Debra Kaufman, "The circularity of secularity: The sacred and the secular in some contemporary post-Holocaust identity narratives," *Contemporary Jewry* 30, no. 1 (2010): 119–139.

10. I have defined secular here simply as identifying as OTD. However, individuals within this population hold a range of beliefs and vary in their levels of observance. Even the duration for which one has identified as OTD can be ambiguous, as two respondents identifying as having been OTD for the same number of years may be defining their "leaving" differently. Cragun and Hammer note that ambiguity is a shortcoming in a lot of the literature on secularity, as a given term (i.e. disaffiliate, secular, or exiter) takes on different meanings in different studies. See Ryan T. Cragun and Joseph H. Hammer, " 'One Person's Apostate is Another Person's Convert': What Terminology Tells Us About Pro-Religious Hegemony in the Sociology of Religion," *Humanity & Society* 35, no. 1–2 (2011): 149–75.

11. Yoel Finkelman, "Ultra-Orthodox/Haredi Education," in *International Handbook of Jewish Education*, ed. Helena Miller, Lisa D. Grant, and Alex Pomson (New York: Springer, 2011), 1065; Samuel C. Heilman, *Sliding to the Right: The Contest for the Future of American Jewish Orthodoxy* (Berkeley: University of California Press, 2006): 86. Although Nishma's survey distinguished Chabad from other Chasidic sects, in the present study I have included Chabad respondents among the Chasidim as Chabad is, after all, a Chasidic sect, and, despite other differences between the sects, many Chabad male students in New York receive an inferior secular education as is the case in other Chasidic sects.

12. Alisa Partlan, *Non-Equivalent: The State of Education in New York City's Hasidic Yeshivas*, ed. Naftuli Moster (New York: Yaffed, 2017), 4.

13. Ibid., 31.

14. Ibid., 31, 38.

15. Ibid., 5; Steven M. Cohen, Ron Miller, and Jacob B. Ukeles, *Jewish community study of New York: 2011: Comprehensive Report* (New York: UJA-Federation, 2012), 220.

16. Raphael Patai, *The Jewish Mind* (New York: C. Scribner's Sons, 1977), 281–83; Joseph Jacobs, "The Comparative Distribution of Jewish Ability," *Journal of the Anthropological Institute of Great Britain and Ireland* 15, no. 365 (1886): 358.

17. *In America, Does More Education Equal Less Religion?* (Washington, DC: Pew Research Center, 2017), 12.

18. Ibid.

19. Edward L. Glaeser and Bruce L. Sacerdote, "Education and Religion," *Journal of Human Capital* 2, no. 2 (2008): 7.

20. Paul Burstein, "Jewish Educational and Economic Success in the United States: A Search for Explanations," *Sociological Perspectives* 50, no. 2 (2007): 209–10; Patai, *The Jewish Mind*, 339; Richard Nisbett, *Intelligence and How to Get it* (New York: W. W. Norton, 2009), 171–72.

21. Robert Wuthnow, *The Restructuring of American Religion* (Princeton, NJ: Princeton University Press, 1988), 225–26; Seth W. Norton and Annette Tomal, "Religion and Female Educational Attainment," *Journal of Money, Credit and Banking* 41, no. 5 (2009): 980; Leuba, *The Belief in God and Immortality*, 283. Baker and Whitehead find that the gender gap disappears among highly educated liberals. They argue that perceived gender gaps are not due to innate gender differences but to other factors. A key factor in the present study is the highly gendered culture disaffiliates have left. See Joseph Baker and Andrew L. Whitehead, "Gendering (Non)Religion: Politics, Education, and Gender Gaps in Secularity in the United States," *Social Forces* 94, no. 4 (2015): 1636.

22. Nishma is a private research firm specializing in sociological and marketing research for the Jewish community. The study, produced by Mark Trencher, was guided by Steven M. Cohen (who directed UJA's Jewish Community Study of New York); Mark I. Rosen, Director of Field Experience Programs in Brandeis's Hornstein Program; and Zalman Newfield (PhD, NYU), among others. Of the 885 respondents for Nishma's "Starting a Conversation," 313 were former Chasidim, and of those, 158 were male. Four individuals out of the 885 respondents did not identify gender, former religious affiliation, or the number of years they have been OTD. Those individuals have been excluded from the present study. Thirty individuals who identified as formerly Chasidic provided neither their gender nor their highest level of education. Of those, two did not identify the length of time for which they had identified as OTD; the rest remain roughly in proportion to the identifiers of educational attainment and gender in terms of the duration for which they have identified as disaffiliated. The present study is admittedly limited by respondents' omissions as well as by the sample size, but this is inevitable since the population of disaffiliates is so much smaller than that of religious affiliates, and disaffiliates are more difficult to reach. Whereas Orthodox individuals are concentrated in particular neighborhoods, exiters span the globe and often relocate for work or college, living apart from other disaffiliates and their former communities. Relative to the population size of OTD individuals, the sample, while small, may nonetheless be revealing.

23. Mark Trencher, *Starting a Conversation: A Pioneering Survey of Those Who Have Left the Orthodox Community* (Nishma, 2016), 95; *A Portrait of Jewish Americans*, 42, 43; Cohen, Miller, and Ukeles, *Jewish Community Study*, 218.

24. Camille L. Ryan and Kurt Bauman, "Educational Attainment in the United States: 2015," *U.S. Census Bureau*, 2.

25. Cohen, Miller, and Ukeles, *Jewish Community Study*, 218.

26. In contrast to educational attainment in the U.S. population, which is negatively correlated with age, educational attainment among Chasidim and exiters is positively correlated with age, likely due to a decline in the secular education provided in Chasidic yeshivas in recent years.

27. Massengill and MacGregor, "Religious Nonaffiliation and Schooling," 197.

28. Massengill and MacGregor, "Religious Nonaffiliation and Schooling," 198. This may also help account for high rates of Jewish American BA attainment. Not all secular Jews are like the secular "nones" of other studies. While "secular" in comparison to the Orthodox, I would argue that in some respects reform and conservative Jews may nonetheless be comparable in their religious affiliation and participation to mainstream Christians or even the more religious and more highly educated mainline Protestants and Catholics.

29. Paul Burstein, "Jewish Educational and Economic Success in the United States: A Search for Explanations," *Sociological Perspectives* 50, no. 2 (2007): 215.

30. Massengill and MacGregor, "Religious Nonaffiliation and Schooling," 188, 198–99.

31. Shimon Russell, "Hefker Velt Revisited," *Mishpacha*, February 1, 2017, http://www.mishpacha.com/Browse/Article/7192/Hefker-Velt-Revisited; Lawrence Kelemen, "Why are So Many Kids Today 'Off the Derech'?" *Jewish Action* 73, no. 4 (2013): 27.

32. Yonason Martin, "'Off the Derech' vs. At Risk," *Hakshiva*, Dec. 6, 2016, https://hakshiva.org/off-derech-vs-risk/; Lazer Brody, "Off-the-Derech Youth," *Lazer Beams* (blog), Feb. 26, 2018, http://lazerbrody.typepad.com/lazer_beams/2018/02/the-most-painful-problem-in-the-jewish-world-today-is-the-off-the-derech-off-the-path-at-risk-youth-who-grew-up-in-religio.html; "Going Off the Derech," *Yeshiva World*, April 18 2012, https://www.theyeshivaworld.com/coffeeroom/topic/going-off-the-derech. Brody defines Off the Derech youth as "off the path, at risk." In a thread entitled "Going off the Derech" in which a mother solicits advice regarding her OTD adolescent son, respondents use the terms "at-risk" and "off the derech" interchangeably.

33. Yonason Martin, "'Off the Derech' vs. At Risk," *Hakshiva*, Dec. 6, 2016, https://hakshiva.org/off-derech-vs-risk/.

34. Hella Winston, *Unchosen: The hidden lives of Hasidic rebels* (Boston, MA: Beacon Press, 2005), 55.

35. Merlin B. Brinkerhoff and Kathryn L. Burke, "Disaffiliation: Some Notes on 'Falling from the Faith,'" *Sociological Analysis* 41, no. 1 (1980): 44–45.

36. Philip Schwadel, "Birth Cohort Changes in the Association Between College Education and Religious Non-Affiliation," *Social Forces* 93, no. 2 (2014): 722.

37. Ibid., 722.

38. Schwadel, "Birth Cohort Changes in the Association Between College Education and Religious Non-Affiliation," 723.

39. Schwadel, "Explaining Cross-National Variation in the Effect of Higher Education on Religiosity," 415.

40. Everett M. Rogers, *Diffusion of Innovations*, 3rd ed. (New York: Macmillan, 1983), 258.

41. Sullivan, "A Recipe for Success in the English World," 108.

42. Smith and Sikkink, "Social Predictors of Retention in and Switching from the Religious Faith of Family of Origin," 202.

43. Heilman, *Sliding to the Right*, chapter 5.

44. Cohen, Miller, and Ukeles, *Jewish Community Study*, 218.

45. Patai, *The Jewish Mind*, 524.

46. Nathan Glazer, "The American Jew and the Attainment of Middle Class Rank," in *The Jews: Social Patterns of an American Group*, ed. Marshall Sklare (New York: Collier-Macmillan, 1958), 143.

47. Nisbett, *Intelligence and How to Get it*, 174–75; Paola Tartakoff, *Between Christian and Jew: Conversion and Inquisition in the Crown of Aragon, 1250–1391* (Philadelphia, PA: University of Pennsylvania Press, 2012), 69, 72, 74–75; Paola Tartakoff, "Testing Boundaries: Jewish Conversion and Cultural Fluidity in Medieval Europe, c. 1200–1391," *Speculum* 90, no. 3 (2015): 731–32.

48. Nathan Glazer, "Culture and Achievement," in *Culture Matters: How Values Shape Human Progress*, ed. Lawrence E. Harrington and Samuel P. Huntington (New York: Basic Books, 2000), 56.

49. Jennifer Lee and Min Zhou, *The Asian American Achievement Paradox* (New York: Russell Sage Foundation, 2015), 125.

References

A Portrait of Jewish Americans. Washington, D.C.: Pew Research Center, 2013. http://www.pewforum.org/2013/10/01/jewish-american-beliefs-attitudes-culture-survey/.

Aldridge, Alan. *Religion in the Contemporary World*. Massachusetts: Polity Press, 2013.

Baker, Joseph O., and Andrew L. Whitehead. "Gendering (Non) Religion: Politics, Education, and Gender Gaps in Secularity in the United States." *Social Forces* 94, no. 4 (2015): 1623–645. https://doi.org/10.1093/sf/sov119.

Brinkerhoff, Merlin B., and Kathryn L. Burke. "Disaffiliation: Some Notes on 'Falling from the Faith.'" *Sociological Analysis* 41, no. 1 (1980): 41–54. https://www.jstor.org/stable/3709857.

Burstein, Paul. "Jewish Educational and Economic Success in the United States: A Search for Explanations." *Sociological Perspectives* 50, no. 2 (2007): 209–28. https://doi.org/10.1525/sop.2007.50.2.209.

Casanova, José. *Public Religions in the Modern World.* Chicago: University of Chicago Press, 1994.

Cohen, Steven M., Ron Miller, and Jacob B. Ukeles. *Jewish community study of New York: 2011: Comprehensive Report.* New York: UJA-Federation, 2012. http://www.jewishdatabank.org/studies/details.cfm?StudyID=597.

Cragun, Ryan T., and Joseph H. Hammer. "'One Person's Apostate is Another Person's Convert': What Terminology Tells Us about Pro-Religious Hegemony in the Sociology of Religion." *Humanity & Society* 35, no. 1–2 (2011): 149–75. https://doi.org/10.1177/016059761103500107.

Finkelman, Yoel. "Ultra-Orthodox/Haredi Education." In *International Handbook of Jewish Education*, edited by Helena Miller, Lisa D. Grant, and Alex Pomson, 1063–086. New York: Springer, 2011.

Glaeser, Edward L., and Bruce I. Sacerdote. "Education and Religion." *Journal of Human Capital* 2, no. 2 (2008): 188–215. https://doi.org/10.1086/590413.

Glazer, Nathan. "Culture and Achievement." In *Culture Matters: How Values Shape Human Progress*, edited by Lawrence E. Harrington and Samuel P. Huntington, 49–63. New York: Basic Books, 2000.

———. "The American Jew and the Attainment of Middle Class Rank." In *The Jews: Social Patterns of an American Group*, edited by Marshall Sklare, 138–46. New York: Collier-Macmillan, 1958.

"Going Off the Derech." *Yeshiva World.* April 18 2012. https://www.theyeshivaworld.com/coffeeroom/topic/going-off-the-derech.

Hartman, Harriet, and Moshe Hartman. "Jewish Identity and the Secular Achievements of American Jewish Men and Women." *Journal for the Scientific Study of Religion* 50, no. 1 (March 2011): 133–53. https://doi.org/10.1111/j.1468-5906.2010.01556.x.

Heilman, Samuel C. *Sliding to the Right: The Contest for the Future of American Jewish Orthodoxy.* Berkeley: University of California Press, 2006.

Hill, Jonathan P. "Faith and Understanding: Specifying the Impact of Higher Education on Religious Belief." *Journal for the Scientific Study of Religion* 50, no. 3 (2011): 533–51. https://doi.org/10.1111/j.1468-5906.2011.01587.x.

In America, Does More Education Equal Less Religion? Washington, DC: Pew Research Center, 2017. http://www.pewforum.org/2017/04/26/in-america-does-more-education-equal-less-religion/#.

Kadushin, Charles. "Asking About Religion." *Socio-Demography of American Jewry* (2011) https://www.brandeis.edu/ssri/conferences/demographyconf/plenary1.html.

Kelemen, Lawrence. "Why are so Many Kids Today 'Off the Derech'?" *Jewish Action* 73, no. 4 (2013): 27–28.

Lee, Jennifer, and Min Zhou. *The Asian American Achievement Paradox.* New York: Russell Sage Foundation, 2015.

Leuba, James Henry. *The Belief in God and Immortality: A Psychological, Anthropological and Statistical Study.* Illinois: Open Court, 1921.

Lewis, James R., Sean E. Currie, and Michael P. Oman-Reagan. "The Religion of the Educated Classes Revisited: New Religions, the Nonreligious, and Educational Levels." *Journal for the Scientific Study of Religion* 55, no. 1 (2016): 91–104. https://doi.org/10.1111/jssr.12246.

Martin, Yonason. "'Off the Derech' vs. At Risk." *Hakshiva.* Dec. 6, 2016. https://hakshiva.org/off-derech-vs-risk/.

Massengill, Rebekah P., and Carol Ann MacGregor. "Religious Nonaffiliation and Schooling: The Educational Trajectories of Three Types of Religious 'Nones.'" In *Religion, Work, and Inequality: Research in the Sociology of Work,* edited by Lisa A. Keister, John Mccarthy, and Roger Finke, 183–203. Binkley, UK: Emerald Group Publishing, 2012.

McFarland, Michael J., Bradley RE Wright, and David L. Weakliem. "Educational Attainment and Religiosity: Exploring Variations by Religious Tradition." *Sociology of Religion* 72, no. 2 (2010): 166–88. https://doi.org/10.1093/socrel/srq065.

Nisbett, Richard. *Intelligence and How to Get it.* New York: W. W. Norton, 2009.

Norton, Seth W., and Annette Tomal. "Religion and Female Educational Attainment." *Journal of Money, Credit and Banking* 41, no. 5 (2009): 961–86. https://doi.org/10.1111/j.1538-4616.2009.00240.x.

Partlan, Alisa. *Non-Equivalent: The State of Education in New York City's Hasidic Yeshivas.* Edited by Naftuli Moster. New York: Yaffed, 2017.

Patai, Raphael. *The Jewish Mind.* New York: C. Scribner's Sons, 1977.

Rogers, Everett M. *Diffusion of Innovations.* 3rd ed. New York: Macmillan, 1983.

Russell, Shimon. "Hefker Velt Revisited." *Mishpacha.* February 1, 2017. http://www.mishpacha.com/Browse/Article/7192/Hefker-Velt-Revisited.

Ryan, Camille L., and Kurt Bauman. "Educational Attainment in the United States: 2015." *US Census Bureau* (2016). https://www.census.gov/library/publications/2016/demo/p20-578.html.

Schwadel, Philip. "Birth Cohort Changes in the Association between College Education and Religious Non-Affiliation." *Social Forces* 93, no. 2 (2014): 719–46. https://doi.org/10.1093/sf/sou080.

———. "Explaining Cross-National Variation in the Effect of Higher Education on Religiosity." *Journal for the Scientific Study of Religion* 54, no. 2 (2015): 402–18. https://doi.org/10.1111/jssr.12187.

Sherkat, Darren E. "Religion and Higher Education: The Good, the Bad, and the Ugly." In *SSRC Web Forum*. 2007.

Smith, Christian, and David Sikkink. "Social Predictors of Retention in and Switching from the Religious Faith of Family of Origin: Another Look Using Religious Tradition Self-Identification." *Review of Religious Research* 45, no. 2 (2003): 188–206. https://doi.org/10.2307/3512582.

Stark, Rodney. "On the Incompatibility of Religion and Science: A Survey of American Graduate Students." *Journal for the Scientific Study of Religion* 3, no. 1 (1963): 3–20. https://doi.org/10.2307/1385002.

Sullivan, Jessica R. "A Recipe for Success in the 'English World': An Investigation of the Ex-Amish in Mainstream Society." Western Michigan University (2018). PhD diss. 3358.

Tartakoff, Paola. "Testing Boundaries: Jewish Conversion and Cultural Fluidity in Medieval Europe, c. 1200–1391." *Speculum* 90, no. 3 (2015): 728–62. https://doi.org/10.1017/S0038713415001402.

———. *Between Christian and Jew: Conversion and Inquisition in the Crown of Aragon, 1250–1391*. Pennsylvania: University of Pennsylvania Press, 2012.

Thalheimer, Fred. "Continuity and Change in Religiosity: A Study of Academicians." *Pacific Sociological Review* 8, no. 2 (1965): 101–08. https://doi.org/10.2307/1388476.

Trencher, Mark. "Starting a Conversation: A Pioneering Survey of Those Who Have Left the Orthodox Community." *Nishma Research*, 2016. http://nishmaresearch.com/social-research.html.

Uecker, Jeremy E., Mark D. Regnerus, and Margaret L. Vaaler. "Losing My Religion: The Social Sources of Religious Decline in Early Adulthood." *Social Forces* 85, no. 4 (2007): 1667–692. https://doi.org/10.1353/sof.2007.0083.

Wickenden, Arthur C. "The Effect of the College Experience Upon Students' Concepts of God." *The Journal of Religion* 12, no. 2 (1932): 242–67. https://doi.org/10.1086/481162.

Winston, Hella. *Unchosen: The Hidden Lives of Hasidic Rebels*. Boston, MA: Beacon Press, 2005.

Wuthnow, Robert. "Science and the Sacred." In *The Sacred in a Secular Age*, edited by Phillip E. Hammond, 187–203. Oakland, CA: University of California Press, 1985.

———. *The Restructuring of American Religion*. Princeton, NJ: Princeton University Press, 1988.

Zelan, Joseph. "Religious Apostasy, Higher Education and Occupational Choice." *Sociology of Education* 41, no. 4 (1968): 370–79. https://www.jstor.org/stable/2112158.

Representation, Recognition and Institutionalization of a New Community

Reflection on the Mediatization of Former Ultra-Orthodox Jews

Jessica Roda

Culture is not passed through the genes but is created by people
and perpetuated in social interaction[1]

Introduction

While I sit quietly writing this article, the critiques continue to pour
in on the Netflix documentary *One of Us*. This documentary looks
at the difficulties faced by those who leave the ultra-Orthodox Jewish
world (a community known as OTD—*Off the Derech/Off the Path*). The
consequences of this media spotlight have been fortuitous, but the images
that the renowned documentary filmmakers Heidi Ewing and Rachel
Grady (*Jesus Camp*, 2006) have chosen to show will certainly have an
impact on the general public. In this respect, these images have already
had an influence on the interpretation of the ethnography that I do on
the contemporary lives of the ultra-Orthodox Jewish community in New
York and Montreal. Torn between the problems[2] related to leaving the
ultra-Orthodox world and the emotion expressed by the individuals that
I have had the privilege to meet, I have a lot of difficulties distancing

myself from the harrowing testimonies on the screen. As such, it is my anthropological experience, caught between the emotion of these personal experiences, as expressed in the images, and the need to account for the way in which this community's daily life is structured, that has led me to offer my reflections on the role and impact that the mediatisation of OTDs in that mass media has had, starting with the documentary *One of Us*. This coverage in the mass media, as well as in social media, appears to me to be a central element in the process of defining and recognising this growing community. In this respect, I have often focused my thoughts on two points: how would this community come to exist if it were not for social media and how this community has been institutionalised through the media's lens? In fact, one of the unique aspects of this exodus process from the ultra-Orthodox Jewish world is the collective organization of the community, which is facilitated through social media, thus allowing a translocal community to be created, one which essentially functions, at first, through the virtual world rather than through direct physical contact.[3]

In this article, I will first set out the basic consequences that arise from the mediatisation of a controversial social phenomenon in the mass media. Then I shall plunge into the heart of the documentary *One of Us*. I will reflect on the message that the three protagonists have chosen to express. This will allow me to analyze what the documentary provoked as well as its position in the field of cinematic productions on the ultra-Orthodox Jewish world, be they fictional or documentary.

Mass Media as a Medium for Shaping Knowledge and Potential Compassionate Feeling

It is generally known and accepted that the media are a powerful communication tool. This power comes from their use of multiple mediums, especially images, which are highly charged emotionally and have no other equivalent. Furthermore, since the mid-2000s, the role of the mass media in people's daily lives has grown tremendously, especially in the last decade thanks to expanded access to high-speed Internet, the ubiquity of mobile phones, the extraordinary advances in web search abilities as well as newer forms of communication, such as the emergence of blogs, YouTube and other social media. More recently, there has been the emergence of broadcast mass media, such as Netflix, Amazon video, and iTunes video.[4] Today, the media are omnipresent in our daily lives and serve as a basic and common reference point. A simple example is evident when a public personality becomes the target of sexual or criminal accusations and these accusations are mediatized through the mass media. This generally leads to social and professional marginalization, ahead of any due process, if there is any due process. In this perspective, for some people, social media are seen as symbolic substitutes for the judicial system. In the case of an accusation/investigation where the accused has been found "not guilty" by the legal system, there are still consequences due to the ongoing mediatization of the issue, often leading to the social exclusion of the person in question. Recently, we have been witness to such cases. Consider the drop in popularity for the French presidential candidate François Fillion over a scandal about fictitious jobs, the downfall of Jian Gomeshi after being accused of sexual assault for which he was eventually found "not guilty," or the viral aspect of public accusations of sexual aggression with the #metoo on social media following the Weinstein affair. These are significant examples of the power the media have to formally establish an image and a message of which the concerned community eventually become aware.[5] The mass media[6] thus largely contribute to framing an audience's knowledge and comprehension of a given topic. This digital revolution, in which access to information is facilitated, has deeply transformed the usual power dynamics. For example, Foucault's work as well as that of researchers in the Actor Network Theory (ANT),[7] who have worked on the media, have contributed to a better understanding of power: "[power is] being reproduced everywhere in a huge network of linkages, apparatuses, and habits within everyday life."[8] It is in this perspective that we can no longer deny the influence of the mass media on cultural and social changes. Power no longer lies solely in the hands of institutions, leaving the individual thus powerless. Ulf Hannerz[9] explains that this influence goes well beyond the cultural content available by the mediatization of the phenomenon or the event.[10] In this perspective, I argue that the mediatization of OTD life, because of its intrinsic connection with the ultra-Orthodox Jewish community, acts as an agent of change on both communities (ultra-Orthodox Jews, both current and former) as well as on outsiders. More interestingly, this mediatization in the mass media appears as a means to reinforce the recognition process, as "being normal," that the people having doubts or leaving the community experience.[11]

Showing abuse, violence and suffering on the screen often makes the front page of newspapers since sensationalism and extravagance are seen as more appealing to the general public. This strategy to attract the largest number of viewers/readers and to bring specific attention to a cause is nothing new. In this respect, Mitchel Stephens and Albert Gabriele[12] tell us that, through the transmission of information using sensationalist means or unique/exceptional story, the public gains in education and the cause gathers greater attention. Nevertheless, the consequences of showing one story on the screen to talk about a broader phenomenon can end up working against the stated goals. In 1999, Susan Moeller highlighted the negative aspects of the international news media coverage of famine, war, and death. She noticed compassion fatigue: "If images of starving babies worked in the past to capture attention for a complex crisis of war, refugees, and famine, then starving babies will headline the next difficult crisis."[13] We can reflect on the consequences of following such a media strategy focused on human suffering, where sensational language and images abound.

Beyond this acknowledgment, the mediatization of human suffering and victims remains the predominant element when appealing to spectators to take an interest in that specific phenomenon, to develop feelings of compassion or, even more recently, scathing reactions in regard to this mediatization. In all these cases, the attention from the media and the general public risks being significant. On this particular topic, it is not surprising that OTDs are portrayed on screen through a lens of suffering, exclusion and abuse; phenomena that are experienced by many individuals, but are not exclusive. A few years back, we saw films such as The Chosen (Jeremy Kagan 1981) A Price Above Rubies (Boaz Yakin 1998), Kadosh (Amos Gitai, 1999), and Mendy: A Question of Faith (Adam Vardy 2003) show on screen these personal tensions between Hassidic religious life and modern life, but not until very recently it was fiction in which the actors were often from outside the community. Ultra-Orthodox communities, most notably the Hassidic community, like many other isolated communities situated on the margins of society and considered exotic compared to the norm, have always fascinated us and shall continue to do so. It seems that over the past two decades media and film coverage of these communities has increased. It is interesting to note that this development has occurred simultaneously with public personalities considered marginal from the ultra-Orthodox Jewish world who publically engage with the outside world while maintaining their ties with the religious world in a different way (Rachel Freir, Mindy Pollak in Canada, Lipa Schmeltzer) with individuals emancipated from their community. Just from this fact, we can understand the complexity of the ultra-Orthodox world and the multiple realities that define it.

Beyond these hybrid realities, a media and cinema genre has developed, one in which former ultra-Orthodox Jews participate. The community composed of those who have left has in fact forged a place on the Internet, going so far as to develop a collective culture that is its own, combining linguistic and cultural heritage with ultra-Orthodox, often Hassidic, ritual while renouncing institutions and religious beliefs. Indeed, those who have left have been portrayed in various essays as well as in radio and video reports. The recent mediatization of these experiences·has shown that the general public has misunderstood aspects of ultra-Orthodox culture, notably Hassidic, continuing the curiosity that many citizens have while spotlighting the taboos and difficulties that the community faces (sexuality, gender segregation, relationships with the non-religious word, non-religious education). In this media presence, the Netflix documentary *One of Us* seems to be a significantly influential piece due to the many reactions that it has provoked in the mass media, specialized media, civil society, as well as in the Orthodox, ultra-Orthodox and Liberal Jewish communities.

One Social Reality as a Collective Representation or the Centrality of Suffering

On Sunday, September 10, I arrived in Toronto for a *Meet-Up* of OTDs,[14] organized by Gene Steinberg. Gene travelled from New York specifically for the world premiere of the Netflix documentary *One of Us* at the Toronto Film Festival with other members of the OTD *Meet-Up*. The members of the OTD community anxiously awaited this documentary. In 2008, the Montreal documentary filmmaker Eric Scott was one of the very first to show on screen the issues and complexities related to the exodus from the ultra-Orthodox Jewish world via the documentary *Leaving the Fold*. However, with this new documentary, thanks to its visibility and its subtitling in four languages (French, Spanish, Italian and German), the directors will probably establish, perhaps even institutionalize, a world-wide image of the OTD community as well as their counterpart, the ultra-Orthodox community. If so, what image have these directors chosen to give? Which reality have they decided to mediatize? But more importantly, what message will they convey about this particular religious culture in order to peak the curiosity of as many viewers as possible?

The trailer for the film presents the individual transitions of the film's three protagonists, whom we continuously encounter throughout the film, as well as their secrets and their torment, accompanied by a musical crescendo culminating in police sirens. The trailer leaves us with the impression that the documentary is somewhat sensationalist. After all, it has already been proven that showing suffering, exclusion and marginalization on the big screen makes a film more successful since it provokes strong emotions, favors compassion and incites the viewer to support the cause.

Heidi Ewing and Rachel Grady had wanted to experience the ultra-Orthodox world for several years, specifically the Hasidic world, but they had few leads as to how this could be done. As New Yorkers, both of them share common space with the ultra-Orthodox Jewish communities and they had a great curiosity for these very insular groups. Thanks to Footsteps,[15] a New York-based organization that offers programs and resources for those wanting to become independent of their community, the producers gained access through the spectrum of people who had left the community. The originality and, dare I say, the strength of this film, is that the directors were able to follow three individuals over several years, even in their intimacy. This long-term project has, in particular, allowed Etty's and Ari's transition from a "religious body" to a "secular body" to be documented. The third protagonist is the American actor Luzer Twersky, who appeared in the Maxime Giroux film *Felix & Meira* (2014) and the Pearl Gluck short film *Where is Joel Baum* (2012). His transition occurred several years earlier. Through his humor, which appears regularly in the documentary, and his specific detachment in relation to his past, he incarnates balance and allows the viewer to take a few steps back from the drama we see in Etty's and Ari's lives. There is even a scene in which we see Luzer participate in a supper called "Shabbos meal for ex-Chasidic Jews,"[16] being particularly emotional when savoring *hallah* (Shabbat bread), reciting chants, and exchanging a few words in Yiddish. While transcending religious codes on the separation of the genders, on the use of musical instruments, or even on technology (the producers are filming at this moment—it may or may not be a real Shabbat (Friday) evening—but in the documentary it appears as such), we clearly understand the cultural, symbolic, and implicit emotional weight underlying this Friday evening amongst OTDs in which Luzer Twersky is participating. There are also several moments where we see Ari questioning his decision and more broadly doubting. He is talking with several people from the community. Often he is very well received, while at other moments he is excluded. On several occasions, we have to ask ourselves if everyone who appears on the screen, especially those interacting with Ari, has consented to being filmed. Nevertheless, these few nuanced moments, with respect to how the community reacts to *apikoyres* (heretic) life paths, appear only very discretely so that the viewer keeps them in his/her mind. The story's narrative around suffering and the abuse, which appear only implicitly in the film, is definitely what the viewer is likely to retain.

Being familiar with those who have left the Hassidic community, I was deeply moved by this documentary. Taken aback by the sadness and anger in Etty's and Ari's lives, I was nevertheless left disoriented by the significant on-screen adaptation of both the drama and the suffering. Although Luzer Twersky's narrative offers some lightness or neutrality on these exoduses and there are few nuanced passages with Ari, Luzer or people from the community, the film's aesthetics, through its photography and sound track focusing on Etty's struggle to get a divorce and the ensuing custody battle, reinforce the film's dramatic narrative. I then pondered the key role in the narrative that the directors gave to suffering. Make no mistake about it, an exodus experience without tragedy, with family acceptance, as I have at times been able to observe, would not have been as appealing on the big screen. However, there is nevertheless a real paradox: on one side, there are those who have left the community and who are working hard to transform their image, that of having belonged to a community depicted as unbalanced and abused; and on the other side, there is a constant media focus on their suffering. As such, does a film adaptation of Etty's and Ari's transitions, freeing themselves from their ultra-Orthodox Jewish lives in which they endured both physical and sexual abuse, not give legitimacy to those who specifically say that these exoduses basically occur because of traumatism and an unstable family environment? What are the consequences of focusing the debate on the suffering aspect of the experience to the detriment of another when social reality has many aspects? As the anthropologist Saida Hodzic[17] recently explained in her work *The Twilight of Cutting*, in which she deals almost exclusively with the debate surrounding female genital cutting in Ghana and more broadly in Africa, in addressing the issues of human rights, what happens when we focus the debate on one reality over another?

These two documentary filmmakers chose to shed light on experiences which are unknown to the general public so as to give significance to these individual transformations within a religious context. This was done by choosing to focus on experiences of abuse, violence, and rejection. They achieved this in a brilliant way, paying homage to the three protagonists and the great Footstep counselor, Chani Getter, who appears as the main source of emotional support for Etty. But here again, the religious world does not necessarily present a good first impression, opposing reason and liberalization. It is interesting to note here that according to Hjarvard[18] the relationship between mediatization and secularization is strongest at the societal level since mediatization is part of the differentiation process by which religious institutions and beliefs have become set apart and marginalized in society.[19] In this perspective, we can assume that the documentary's narrative is pursuing a broader narrative in the media that consists of marginalizing religious institutions and reinforcing the secularization of society to support a specific voice. This could explain the predominant role of the media and the importance of the mediatization of the experience of exiting religion for the consolidation of the OTD community.

This reflection on the centrality of suffering is not to deny or diminish the suffering experienced by those who left. This is a reality. It accompanies a reflection on why the producers decided to adopt this angle knowing that there are other dimensions to consider in the transition process. Reality is much more complex and the individual feeling of ambivalence[20] seems to be particularly dominant, something hardly captured by the media. Beyond this, sociologists of religion have shown that even the most secluded religious group are influenced by the social changes in their broader environment, at a different level, within a different timeline and through different mechanisms, but they are nevertheless still influenced. In this perspective, we can hope that the changes that have happened in the broader society about the degree of acceptance of abuse will continue to influence the treatment of such issues by more secluded societies.

More broadly, this particular scandalous portrayal of a religious world, something that also appears in their previous production *Jesus Camp* (2006), leads us to question how individuals with opposing worldviews can live together and, more specifically, the position that religion has in the secular mass media. As such, someone can reflect on the concept of living-together and multiculturalism in our so called "secular" society. Do we not speak of accepting otherness within the limits of a similarity with the majority, which is to say not overly different, not too visible, not too audible, and publicly not too religious? Can we think of such a citizen project as being above and beyond political exploitation, such as a real social project, unless this living-together is only considered within the framework of an extraction of another's identity which does not correspond to the social norms of the society in question? Such questions are particularly relevant to understanding the tension between religion and secularism in the mainstream media. Indeed, today the approach to religion and to secularisation forms the basis of the thesis of a mediatization of religion. As such, *One of Us*, by mediatizing the religious, must be thought of as the continuation of a difficult dialogue between religion and secularism.

As such, I am reminded of an episode of the TV show *Banc Public* on Télé Québec. Journalists wanted to make a documentary on the Hassidic community in Montreal and to include the stories of those who have left the Montreal community and received support from the organization Forward.[21] Before accepting the invitation, I spoke quite extensively with the journalists to be sure that it would be a nuanced documentary, avoiding sensationalism about the Hassidic community. After more than an hour-long interview in which I explained the numerous nuances around an exodus experience, the ways in which the community was multilayered, while addressing the issue of cultural relativism in our societies, I was anxious to see the final result. The evening of the premiere, we got together with several members of Forward. There were many reactions, but I was particularly troubled by the result, which was contrary to what I was told it would be, especially that it ran contrary to what I suggested. The journalists and producers decided to orient the narrative around the suffering and drama of the exodus. It was far from being nuanced. It simply added to the mass media's difficult discourse on non-Christian religious communities, especially the Muslim and Hassidic communities, all the more significant given the debts on reasonable accommodations,[22] the Charter of Values[23] and the more recently adopted Bill 62,[24] an Act to foster adherence to State religious neutrality and, in particular, to provide a framework for requests for accommodations on religious grounds in certain bodies. In this debate, what is not always noticed is that such a mediatization can have positive results for the OTD community. After the Télé Québec documentary *Quitter la communauté juive orthodoxe*[25] aired, Forward received much support. Several people contacted the organization to volunteer for different activities or just to offer financial support for the group. In this respect, I saw the positive aspect of such mediatization, but I remained frustrated by the caricatural and exceptional images that were used to discredit such a result. The mediatization of the lives of OTDs and especially their difficult transition appears as a dominant tool to give a voice to this community, allowing it to exist and be implicitly supported by a part of public opinion, including potential donors. On this note, our focus shifts toward how the documentary was received by different viewing publics, its media coverage and, more generally, what it is creating socially.

The After Release:
"Whether you say something good or say something bad, just say something"

Studies in media, religion and culture concur that mediatization is not a process with a unified outcome or consequences.[26] Rather its outcomes are unpredictable, diverse, and complex.[27] One can wonder how people make sense of a documentary, available on a global movie platform such as Netflix, in which individuals are seen suffering because of their religious communities.

The documentary, *One of Us*, has garnered a lot of media coverage. An avalanche of articles, Facebook posts, and videos broadcast on various platforms (YouTube, Netflix or Instagram) has highlighted a wide range of points of views on the subject. The documentary did indeed make a lot of noise. This was to be expected given the journalistic nature of the production (infiltrating a community), the notoriety of its directors and the social influence of Netflix. There have been interviews with the producers and numerous articles in the general news media (*New York Times*,[28] Charlie Rose,[29] Build Series,[30] Vox.com,[31] *Village Voice*,[32] *The Wrap*[33]) in the Jewish press (Forward, Tabletmag, *Times of Israel*,[34] Haaretz, Jerusalem

Post, the podcast The Yiddish Voice[35]) and even in the specialized press dealing with cinema (*Filmmaker* magazine, *Variety* magazine, *Indiewire*, *Alliance of Women Film Journalists*, *Film Courage*, Filmwax radio). For me, the most interesting reactions were those from social media, especially the discussions within the religious Jewish communities. Among them, I can identify three categories: denial of the protagonists' stories; compassion associated with critique (absence of nuances and the focus on suffering); and compassion with a desire to enter into a dialogue and to change mentalities. It is interesting to see that the documentary has been seen by many people within the community. The ultra-Orthodox *underground* scene, both masculine and feminine, using the Internet and connected to social media, is alive and well established.

Yakov Horowitz, an activist in the education field, from inter-community dialogue to the defence of victims of physical and sexual abuse within the ultra-Orthodox communities, quickly expressed his opinions on the documentary. In his comments entitled "Yakov Horowitz on the documentary *One of Us*—Part 2, "Do You Care If I Am Happy?" watched by over 1,300 people on Facebook and more than 600 on YouTube, Rabbi Horowitz expresses himself as follows:

"I think this film really should generate honest discussions in our community about what our relationship should be, what it is that we should be doing, to support, and help people who are making the choice of leaving the community, to leave religion and sometimes leave the community. I think this is very healthy, this is a healthy discussion, we were not taught into school, this is not what many of us are a accustom[ed] to doing, and it is important to hear things from their perspective. Very often we see, specially guys, [. . .] dress a certain way, they exude a certain energy, we may find it offensive, it is not about you, they are not doing it because of you, it is not easy for them to leave their family and their community, but just to be supportive. I asked to Luzer Twersky what his message for everybody would be and he said, he is very very happy that people are talking about this, he is be[ing] contact[ed] by many people including [that] he was invited to a forum with some Hasidische people who are still in the community. The problem of the community to discuss this, he was very happy that it is generating this level of conversation. I want to mention another point, don't always assume that the person leaving is bitter and angry, some are and some for good reasons. [. . .] Every situation is different; and to some degree it is really not different from each of us when we come to a different setting or a new setting. [. . .] I think it is an important conversation, it is a conversation we should have with our friends, our children. [. . .] When something comes up that is in the news, and around, it is a wonderful opportunity to have discussions about it, so let us continue the dialogue, I am going to post [an]other fragment of the film. I definitely do want to talk about some of the hard issues, perhaps the most challenging one is dealing with these custody cases. What to do, it is very complicated, when a spouse abandoned religion, visitation, custody, back and forth between this different worlds. It is very difficult, and and I really believe we have to talk about it."[36]

Horowitz's comments clearly show that the documentary has generated a discussion on various difficult subjects. As for the invitations that Luzer Twersky has received from the ultra-Orthodox community, there was one notable one on October 24th when he and Ari Hershkowitz went to Monsey to discuss their experiences with Hassidic author Chany G. Rosengarten. The discussion lasted just over an hour and was broadcast on Instagram Live and Facebook Live, and since has been available on YouTube.[37]

Let's look at one of the earliest exchanges, when Chany Rosengarten talked of Ari's feelings while watching the documentary. Then Luzer Twersky responds via https://www.chanyrosengarten.com/

CHANY: I am feeling nervous about this because . . . this is a very important documentary; it is very relevant to my viewers of orthodox community. I feel that it is important because it talks about important topics. It is very painful; I think many people can relate to it. People are going into a lot of pain. At the same time, coming from [the] Hasidish community and being part of Hasidish community, the story, the three anecdotes are kind of views in support of a message. And the message is for or about leaving the community, the support that people need, and the importance of the community.

The three painful stories are in support of the message, with almost seems like a commercial for footsteps. [. . .] I hear the pain being use[d] as a way [of] labelling the community by his pain, people are feeling offended.

LUZER: The agenda of the film is to tell a story. [. . .] I am assuming that they wanted to tell a story about three people. They are not telling the story of the community, then people ask why they don't present the positive side of the community. There is [a positive side] in there, some of it, because otherwise it would not be difficult to leave. You give up a lot of good things, and it is also evidence that I go back to do this things, that there is a beauty in there. There is a loss! Not only the loss that you see that Etti has or that I had, my family, but there is also a spiritual loss, an emotional loss of community. It is not necessarily criticizing anything specific, it is telling a story of what happens when people leave, and being held back, you are making it more difficult for them. So it is less a put down or an attack on the community, [. . .] That is not the process of the movie, but it is what it does because it makes you question how can we do this better.

This exchange informs us, on one side, of the multiple reactions and feelings to the suffering shown on the screen and, on the other side, the numerous semantic possibilities to which the cinematic production subscribes. It would appear to be a catalyst of the state of the ultra-Orthodox world's society. It shines light on the tensions, disagreements, taboos, and, more generally, connects various actors from this religious world (those leaving the community, the marginalized, the double-lifers, traditionalists). In fact, it has provoked exchanges, dialogues, both voluntary and involuntary, complicit and contentious. Thus, beyond the critiques the documentary has received since its release, notably on its lack of nuance due to the focus on three stories of suffering and the marginalization of the religious, it should be credited with providing spaces for dialogue as well as private and public debate within the community.

As for the position of One of Us within the documentary film genre, it follows a logic of addressing topical subjects from the perspective of an individual's story, selected for its exceptional aspect. The long-term consequences remain unpredictable, but it is certain that this

documentary fits into the recognition approach and the institutionalization of a community that has been emancipated from the private sphere,
from the margins and from shame. This community has now been seen
and heard. It is proud of its accomplishments.

Notes

1. William Shaffir, Robert Brym and Morton Weinfeld (eds.), *The Jews in Canada* (Toronto: Oxford University Press, 1993), 122.

2. This consists of going beyond general assumptions, namely understanding the underlying reasons for a social phenomenon seen as problematic. In this specific situation, it is understanding the underlying problem behind this exodus and more generally doing an ethnography of how this community is constructed.

3. This phenomenon of entering and leaving the religious world is not new (see Assaf David, " 'My Tiny, Ugly World': The Confession of Rabbi Yitzhak Nahum Twersky of Shpikov," *Contemporary Jewry* 26, no. 1 [2006]: 1–34). Religious history is filled with sufficient personal experiences. However, what is unique in this situation is the organization within this emerging community.

4. Couldry Nick and Andreas Hepp, "Conceptualizing Mediatization: Contexts, Traditions, Arguments," *Communication Theory* 23 (2013): 192.

5. The public outcry over the Weinstein affair is due to an openness to such criticism and especially for this specific kind of issue. Major revolutions and social transformations occur within a contextual framework: a series of events ending in a major transformation or, in other words, a point of no return.

6. Here I follow Raymond Williams as quoted by Jeffrey Shandler in *Jews, God and Videotape. Religion and Media in America* (New York: New York University Press, 2009), 9, who uses the term media in its complexity, knowing that it includes various communication technologies (print, audio, visual, digital and so forth) as well as the "specialized capitalist sense" in which a particular institution or service (such as a newspaper publisher, radio station, recording label or video production company) serves as a "medium for something else."

7. The Actor Network Theory has been developed by Michel Callon, Bruno Latour, Madeleine Akrich and other scholars from the Centre de sociologie de l'innovation de Mines ParisTech (Centre for Sociological Innovation at Mines ParisTech).

8. Couldry and Hepp, "Conceptualizing Mediatization: Contexts, Traditions, Arguments," 194.

9. Hannerz Ulf (ed.), *Medier och kulturer* (Stickholm: Carlssons, 1990).

10. Ibid.

11. Fader Ayala, "ultra-Orthodox Jewish interiority, the Internet, and the crisis of faith," *HAU: Journal of Ethnographic Theory* 7, no. 1 (2017): 185–206.

12. Stephens Mitchel, *A History of News*, 3rd ed. (Oxford: Oxford University Press, 2006). Albert Gabriele, *Sensationalism and the Genealogy of Modernity: a Global Nineteenth Century Perspective* (New York: Palgrave Macmillan, 2016).

13. Moeller Susan, *Compassion Fatigue: How the Media Sell Disease, Famine, War and Death* (New York: Routledge, 1999).

14. https://www.meetup.com/otdmeetup/, accessed November 7, 2017.

15. https://www.footstepsorg.org/, accessed November 7, 2017.

16. Cf. https://www.youtube.com/watch?v=DohaTVDTJRw, accessed November 7, 2017.

17. Hodzic Saida, *The Twilight of Cutting. African Activism and Life after NGOs* (Chicago: Chicago University Press, 2017).

18. Hjarvard Stig, "The Mediatisation of Religion: Theorising Religion, Media and Social Change," *Culture and Religion* 12, no. 2 (2011): 130–33.

19. I would like to nuance this by mentioning that religious institutions adjust to the media logic, they also might use it and take advantage of it according to their needs (Lövheim Mia, "Mediatisation of religion: A critical appraisal," *Culture and Religion* 12, no. 2 (2011): 157. In this perspective, we can think of the ways the secular world, and notably people leaving the community, is portrayed by the Ultra Orthodox media where the absence of nuances is also particularly relevant.

20. The concept of ambivalence within the ultra-Orthodox world has been developed in Finkelman Yoel, "The Ambivalent Haredi Jew," *Israel Studies* 19, no. 2 (2014): 264–93.

21. http://forwardorg.org/, accessed November 7, 2017.

22. In 2007, the Québec Premier Jean Charest announced the establishment of the Consultation Commission on Accommodation Practices Related to Cultural Differences in response to public discontent concerning reasonable accommodation (cf. Report, https://www.mce.gouv.qc.ca/publications/CCPARDC/rapport-final-integral-en.pdf), accessed November 7, 2017.

23. Cf. Dagenais Maxime, "Québec Values Charter," *The Canadian Encyclopedia*, accessed November 7, 2017, http://www.thecanadianencyclopedia.ca/en/article/the-charter-of-quebec-values/

24. Cf. http://www.assnat.qc.ca/en/travaux-parlementaires/projets-loi/projet-loi-62-41-1.html, accessed November 7, 2017.

25. Cf. Broadcast *Banc Public* « *Quitter la communauté juive ortho-doxe* », 2016, http://bancpublic.telequebec.tv/emissions/emission-27/29119/quitter-la-communaute-juive-ultra-orthodoxe

26. Lövheim, "Mediatisation of Religion: A Critical Appraisal," 161.

27. See Stolow Jeremy, "Religion and/as Media," *Theory, Culture and Society* 22, no. 4 (2005): 119–45. Meyer Birgit, ed., *Aesthetic Formations. Media, Religion, and the Senses* (New York: Palgrave Macmillian, 2009). Morgan David, "Mediation or Mediatisation: The History of Media in the Study of Religion," *Culture and Religion* 12, no. 2 (2011): 137–52.

28. https://www.nytimes.com/2017/10/19/movies/one-of-us-review.html, accessed November 7, 2017.

29. https://charlierose.com/videos/31081, accessed November 7, 2017.

30. https://www.youtube.com/watch?v=jPJCwvttdYg, accessed November 7, 2017.

31. https://www.vox.com/culture/2017/10/19/16496048/one-of-us-review-hasidic-grady-ewing-netflix, accessed November 7, 2017.

32. https://www.villagevoice.com/2017/10/17/hasidic-jews-struggle-to-break-from-the-sect-in-netflixs-one-of-us/, accessed November 7, 2017.

33. https://www.thewrap.com/one-of-us-review-netflix-heidi-ewing-rachel-grady/, accessed November 7, 2017.

34. http://jewishweek.timesofisrael.com/new-netflix-documentary-one-of-us-adds-to-growing-ex-orthodox-genre/, accessed November 7, 2017.

35. https://overcast.fm/+DeFiqnj0k, accessed November 7, 2017.

36. https://www.youtube.com/watch?v=I9jky60oqPY, accessed November 7, 2017.

37. https://www.youtube.com/watch?v=s7LV7E6Uh_o, accessed November 5, 2017. As of November 3, there were over 700 views on YouTube and over 5000 on Facebook.

Bibliography

Assaf, David. "'My Tiny, Ugly World': The Confession of Rabbi Yitzhak Nahum Twersky of Shpikov." *Contemporary Jewry* 26, no. 1 (2006): 1–34.

Couldry, Nick, and Andreas Hepp. "Conceptualizing Mediatization: Contexts, Traditions, Arguments." *Communication Theory* 23 (2013): 191–202.

Fader, Ayala. "Ultra-Orthodox Jewish Interiority, the Internet, and the Crisis of Faith." *HAU: Journal of Ethnographic Theory* 7, no. 1 (2017): 185–206.

Finkelman, Yoel. "The Ambivalent Haredi Jew." *Israel Studies* 19, no. 2 (2014): 264–93.

Fornäe, Johan. "Culturalizing Mediatization." In *Mediatized Worlds. Culture and Society in a Media Age*, edited by Hepp Andreas and Friedrich Krotz, 38–53. Basingstoke: Palgrave Macmillan, 2014.

Gabriele, Albert. *Sensationalism and the Genealogy of Modernity: A Global Nineteenth Century Perspective*. New York: Palgrave Macmillan, 2016.

Hepp, Andreas, Stig Hjarvard, and Knut Lundby. "Mediatization: Theorizing the Interplay Between Media, Culture and Society." *Media, Culture & Society* 37, no. 2 (2015): 314–24.

Hodzic, Saida. *The Twilight of Cutting. African Activism and Life after NGOs*. Chicago: Chicago University Press, 2017.

Hjarvard, Stig. "The Mediatisation of Religion: Theorising Religion, Media and Social Change." *Culture and Religion* 12, no. 2 (2011): 119–35.

Lövheim, Mia. "Mediatisation of Religion: A Critical Appraisal." *Culture and Religion* 12, no. 2 (2011): 153–66.

Meyer, Birgit (ed.). *Aesthetic Formations. Media, Religion, and the Senses.* New York: Palgrave Macmillian, 2009.

Morgan, David. "Mediation or Mediatisation: The History of Media in the Study of Religion." *Culture and Religion* 12, no. 2 (2011): 137–52.

Moeller, Susan. *Compassion Fatigue: How the Media Sell Disease, Famine, War and Death.* New York: Routledge, 1999.

Shaffir, William, Robert Brym, and Weinfeld Morton, eds. *The Jews In Canada.* Toronto: Oxford University Press, 1993.

Shandler, Jeffrey. *Jews, God and Videotape. Religion and Media in America.* New York: New York University Press, 2009.

Stephens, Mitchel. *A History of News*, 3rd ed. Oxford: Oxford University Press, 2006.

Stolow, Jeremy. "Religion and/as media." *Theory, Culture and Society* 22, no. 4 (2005): 119–45.

Williams, Raymond. *Keywords: A Vocabulary of Culture and Society.* New York: Oxford University Press, 1983, 2014, 203.

Filmography

The Chosen (1981, Jeremy Kagan United States)
A Stranger among us (1992, Sidney Lumet)
A Price Above Rubies (1998, Boaz Yakin, United States)
Kadosh (1999, Amos Gitai, United States)
Mendy: A Question of Faith (Adam Vardy 2003, United States)
Ushpizin (2006, Giddi Dar, Israel)
Holy Rollers (2010, Antonio Macia and Kevin Asch, United States)
Where is Joel Baum (2012, Pearl Gluck, United States)
Fill the Void (2012, Rama Burshtein, Israel)
Fading Gigolo (2013, John Turturro, United States)
Félix et Meira (2014, Maxime Giroux, Canada)
Menashe/Brooklyn Yiddish (2017, United States)

Documentary

Bonjour ! Shalom ! (1991, Garry Beitel, Canada)
A Life A part (1997, Oren Rudavsky, Menachem Daum)
Trembling Before G-d (2001, Sandi Simcha DuBowski, United States)

Divan (2006, Pearl Gluck, United States)
Leaving the Fold (2008, Eric Scott, Canada)
Shekinah. The Intimate Life of Hasidic Women (2013, Abby Jack Neidik, Canada)
Only for God: Inside Hasidism (2013, National Geographic)
Sacred Sperm (2015, Ori Gruder, Israel)
Kosher Love (2017, Evan Beloff, Canada)

The Social Practices and Linguistic Spaces of Shababniks in Brooklyn

Gabi Abramac

The Translocality of Fieldwork: Nechama's Bakery in Mea She'arim

On a Thursday night in August 2017, I was at Nechama's Bakery in Mea She'arim in Jerusalem, choosing pastries and trying to pick out the person I was supposed to meet. Thursday was the night, I was told, when *apikorsim*, Hasidic wayward youngsters or those who just hang out near the yeshiva showing no interest in studying, come to hang out at Nechama's, located up the block from the Mir Yeshiva. Nechama's smelled of freshly baked pretzels, fluffy cheese pastries, challas, rugelach, and other baked goods. Their kaisereich rolls looked like beautiful little works of art, and I very discreetly took out my silenced smart phone to take a picture, which might capture the cuteness of these little pastries. As I was putting my phone back into the bag, I met the gaze of a teenage girl who had spotted the phone. Nothing out of ordinary goes unnoticed in Mea She'arim, which is known for its rigorous standards.

An article published in *Haaretz* in 2012 referred to Jerusalem's Haredi neighborhoods as "an intimidating and mysterious labyrinth," which can appear hostile to most secular visitors.[1] A friend of mine once described Mea She'arim as "a very special neighborhood . . . once one gets past all the dirt and the treacherous traffic everywhere, it's love." Mea She'arim is indeed an overcrowded, curious place where one can see

335

women in Yerushalami burkas and find the last kosher Viennese bakery or a graffitied Palestinian flag created by Neturei Karta.

On my visit to Mea She'arim, I was accompanied by a Jerusalemite friend, a fellow linguist. He wore a t-shirt and a knitted kippah. I was dressed in as orthodox a manner as possible. In the course of my five years of fieldwork among Hasidim I have picked up on even the most subtle of nuances and learned to adapt my clothing across the Haredi spectrum. My friend kept saying that I would be better off walking around Mea She'arim on my own. The fact that I, who fit in so well and looked so religious, was chatting with a guy who looked conservative, at best, could only undermine the impression I was trying to create, he claimed. As I had arrived much earlier than my scheduled appointment at Nechama's, Ivri and I checked out the stores on Rechov Malchei Israel and Rechov Meah Shearim. I bought a skirt and some head bands, which would come in handy for my further research in *frum* communities, we leafed through books at Manny's and the Feldheim bookstore, and then headed back to the bakery to meet Shmulik—an Israeli Shababnik whom my American Shababniks had suggested I should meet.

Yet Shmulik never showed up. He apologized, explaining that he had got stuck at a wedding. It was another failed meeting, an occurrence with which an ethnographer who works with hidden heretics is all too often confronted. Ivri and I sat down in front of a store, ate our cheese pastries, did some people watching—a mesmerizing activity in bustling Meah Shea'rim at dusk—then bought some dips and Yerushalmi kugel and eventually went home.

There is a little game I play in my head whenever I find myself in odd situations and unusual places: I try to go back over the events that brought me there. I remember hopping down the terraced cemetery in Tzfat one cold and pitch-black night in January 2014, trying to read the inscriptions on the tombstones with the flashlight on my phone, and thinking to myself, "How on Earth did I wind up here?" Similarly, that Thursday night, as I was walking back to my rented house in the Old City of Jerusalem, I was thinking of the odd stream of events that had taken me from Brooklyn to Mea Shea'rim in search of Shababniks.

My sociolinguistic research on Hasidic communities in New York started in the summer of 2012 with the initial goal of analyzing the use of Yiddish in different Hasidic communities and investigating language contact, language ideologies, and variables that influence language choices.

In the course of my research, inevitably, I also came across people who left their *frum* communities, and I became curious about the linguistic biographies of former New York Hasidim. I wanted to know more about their language shifts and linguistic attitudes: about the processes of English acquisition, whether they abandoned Yiddish as they acquired English, how they felt about secular Yiddish literature and the community of secular Yiddish speakers, how important Yiddish was to their new identity, how they felt about passing Yiddish on to future generations, and so on.

And then, in November 2016, I discovered a totally different group of former Hasidim: young men—whom I refer to as Shababniks—who left the Haredi fold in Israel and relocated to Brooklyn between 2011 and 2015. I wanted to learn more about their social patterns, languages, values, and identity, and to ascertain the points of overlap and divergence between them and American *Off the Derech* (OTD). I have examined the intersection of their identities by focusing on four main categories: their in-group kinship ties, their post-migration professional lives, their leisure activities, and their linguistic repertoire. I have further cross-referenced these findings with the data gathered during my previous study of New York OTD.

The Superdiversity and Complexity of the (Formerly) *Frum Velt*

On various sociocultural levels Hasidic society is quite diverse. One of my informants once said that the word *frum* almost looked like an abbreviation for the term *from frum to modern*, pointing to the measure of fluidity and internal diversity within the community. The communities of formerly *frum* Jews likewise display a diversity of their own. However, what all former Haredim have in common is that they creatively restructure their social practices and adapt to new and overlapping (linguistic) spaces. They negotiate their identities against the backdrop of both the Haredi community and the world at large. In the U.S., for non-English speakers, this also includes multilingual processes by which those who leave the fold construct social landscapes and build conceptual common ground.

I employ the theoretical concept of superdiversity to analyze the sociopolitical, economic, and linguistic changes, which Hasidim and ex-Hasidim face in the globalized, neoliberal, and digital postmodern age.

Superdiversity is a concept introduced by Steven Vertovec. It is designed to denote a degree and kind of complexity that surpasses anything previously experienced in any given society.[2] Superdiversity encompasses new patterns of inequality and prejudice, new models of segregation, space, and contact, new forms of cosmopolitanism and creolization, of secondary migration patterns and community organization. The concept is well suited to describe and analyze the heterogeneity of Hasidic and formerly Hasidic societies. It draws attention to the "diversification of diversity" and seeks to find a "new way of talking about diversity" from a perspective that surpasses notions of multiculturalism or multilingualism.[3] According to Arnaut and Spotti, "in sociolinguistics, 'diversity' is firmly lodged in a long tradition of variationist studies that endeavor to correlate variously distributed (sets of) linguistic features with stratifications of different sorts."[4] While I also take other related concepts concerned with mobility, migration, and socio-spatial interconnectedness, such as "translocality,"[5] "liquid modernity,"[6] and "global complexity"[7] into account, I have found the framework of superdiversity to be uniquely suited to an analysis of Hasidic society that combines sociolinguistic, anthropological, and religious perspectives.

Methodology

My research is based on ethnographic fieldwork, extensive qualitative interviews, and digital ethnography. In my interviews I used the form of biographical narratives, which I supplemented with semi-structured interviews. I find that life stories and a biographical approach are particularly helpful when exploring the intersection of identity, migration, religion, and language acquisition. Life stories tell us how the speakers make sense of the world around them and rationalize their behavior and roles.[8] On this basis, shared stories connect the individual and communal dimensions and constitute and reflect reality.[9] Autobiographical narratives provide us with an understanding of how individuals make sense of their experiences and how these constitute elements and instruments of identity construction.[10] Narrative is an organizing concept in our lives because humans shape and make sense of narrated experiences and beliefs by telling stories.[11]

My fieldwork observations draw on my participation in numerous social events, which included Shabbat dinners, Pesach Seders, leisure time activities (barbecues, time at the beach, nature trips) and Psytrance parties, which play an enormously important role in many Shababniks' lives. While the process of gaining access both to their online communication on platforms like WhatsApp, Facebook, and Instagram and to their collective offline activities went fairly smoothly, scheduling individual interviews proved to be a rather more challenging task. During the week, the Shababniks had very busy schedules, and in their free time they preferred to hang out with their "Shababnik family." Setting time aside for an interview was not their priority. Consequently, while my access in terms of participant observation was virtually limitless, gathering their biographical narratives turned out to be a laborious task indeed.

As a supplement to ethnographic fieldwork, digital ethnography[12] provided further insights into the sociolinguistic changes Shababniks undergo and enriched my understanding of how they construct the meanings of their new community and negotiate plural identities.

Encountering Shababniks

In November 2016, on a Friday night, I was speaking to a former Pupa Hasid, in a Starbucks off the N train at Kings Highway in Brooklyn, whom I had already interviewed several times. As a former English teacher at a Hasidic school, he was a fount of knowledge regarding attitudes toward English and its acquisition by Hasidic boys. As the meeting dragged on, my informant invited me to join him for a Friday night dinner at the house of his Israeli friends in Crown Heights. We went to a decrepit building in Maple Street and climbed up to the apartment on the top floor. The place looked rather shabby and some of the furniture seemed to be falling apart, but the apartment was bustling with life. There were more than 20 young people there and the smell of good food permeated the place. The *Shabbos tish* comprised three tables, differing in height and size. The seating consisted of sofas, chairs, stools, armchairs, and just about anything on which one could conceivably sit. Our host, Yoni,[13] served a typical heymish meal: wine for the Kiddush, challah, dips, salad, fish, gefilte fish, soup, chicken soup with lokshen, kugel and farfel, and compote. This *tish* differed from innumerable others of its kind only in that there was also weed, which was passed around with dessert. Everyone spoke Hebrew and the whole event looked like an expat get together. When people started addressing me in Hebrew I told them that my Hebrew was very basic, adding that I spoke Yiddish, which I knew was of little interest to most Israelis. Yet, to my surprise many of them switched to Yiddish. It transpired that most of them spoke Yiddish and that they came from Hasidic families in Israel.

I left the gathering intrigued and wanting to know more about these people. Who exactly were they? Were they related to each other? How long had they been in America? How did they get there? How did they leave the Haredi world in Israel? How did their Israeli Haredi Yiddish compare to New York Hasidic Yiddish? To what extent did they speak Yiddish in their daily lives? What did they do for a living? Were they in touch with the American OTD scene? A few weeks later, I returned to that same apartment to conduct my first interview with Yoni, who had been our host that evening.

Shababnik: The Term

In Israel, the common term for people who have left the Haredi fold is *yotzim leshe'elah* ("those who have left to question"). Converts or those returning to halakhic Judaism are generally referred to as *hozrim bitshuva* ("repentant returnees [to the way of the Torah]"). My interviewees, however, did not identify as *yotzim leshe'elah*—they never had any philosophical questions. They were simply the misfits and troublemakers known in Israel as *Shababnikim*.[14] I had never heard the term before. As Yoni explained, *frum* communities in Israel used a variety of terms to describe them: "*Shababnikim* are the religious, doing balagan, doing trouble . . . *Shababnikim* . . . and yes . . . that's the names they call it. So we used to be *Shababnikim* . . . I think every family, every religious, every Hasidut calls it different. Whatever, these are the names that people make."

Although I could not be sure whether all my respondents would identify with the term, I started to use it in my extended discussions with the former Hasid who had introduced me to the group. Given that it was based on Yoni's explanation and its usage in the Israeli religious context, this choice seemed justified. There were times when respondents would laugh at the word, but they went along with it all the same. I also frequently came across the term Shababniks (instead of the Hebrew form *Shababnikim*).

In ethnographic fieldwork, "gatekeeper" is the term that denotes a community member who can facilitate access into a field and establish contacts for a researcher. I think that a more appropriate term for my gatekeeper Eli would be *shadchan*. He was my key informant, acting in some ways like a research assistant. Eli was a former Hasid who had become fluent in Hebrew while studying at a yeshiva in Israel, and who spent a lot of time with Shababniks. He was able to answer many questions, help me with the analysis of certain concepts, point me in various interesting directions, schedule interviews, and get me invited to many in-group gatherings. His fluency in Hebrew, which I lack, helped me interpret certain events and occurrences, which my respondents narrated. As the Shababniks' Yiddish skills tend to be restricted to simple everyday usage, they were unable to express complex thoughts or narrate their life story in Yiddish. Yiddish was the language of their home and their early childhood. It was not even the language of the street. There were times when they could not find an adequate term in Yiddish or English, and Eli was crucial in interpreting the concepts they were trying to articulate.

In Israel, the term *Shababniks* (*Shababnikim*) denotes Yeshiva dropouts, typically from Bnei Brak, Jerusalem or Ashdod, who are usually involved in some sort of criminal activity: petty theft, robbery, credit card scams or other financial crimes, or the sale of soft drugs. The term comes from the Arabic word *shabab*, which means young man or naughty boy. Some sources claim that the term is in fact an acronym derived from the biblical phrase "Semach bahur b'yaldutecha"—"O youth, enjoy yourself while you are young!" (Ecclestiastes 11: 9).[15] Yet my Shababniks identified no more with this explanation than they did with the term *yotzim leshe'elah*.

Ordinarily, Shababniks are *batlanim*, they hang out in groups, smoke cannabis all day long and openly show their contempt for the norms of the community. They are frequently portrayed and discussed online. In a post in the JTF Discussion Forum, for example, Shababniks were described as

> a new and growing phenomenon of a breed of severely wayward fearless young lapsed-Haredi criminals who wear black kippot and even lay tefillin, but who have viciously turned on their own kehillos, mugging and robbing them ruthlessly and nastily, at the same time praying to Hashem to help them in their crimes! Shababniks have no respect for the rabbis, rebbes or police.[16]

Elsewhere, individual Shababniks have been described as "a yeshiva drop-out,"[17] "a kid who hangs out on the streets and doesn't learn,"[18] a "no goodnik-shababnik" or "a person from a haredi family who thinks secular but for cultural reasons dresses with a Kippa and like a Hareidi [sic]."[19]

The *Forward's* long-standing (anonymous) columnist in all language-related matters, Philologos, explained that a Shababnik was a young man on the fringes of the Haredi community who still holds his religious beliefs but lives in a state of limbo: he is neither studying in a yeshiva nor can he apply for a legal job since he would be subject to military conscription if it became known officially that he has terminated his religious studies.[20] In 1999, the term Shababnik was also mentioned in a policy proposal by Tahar Ilan, which was submitted with the Tal Commission's report on the draft deferment for yeshiva students. Ilan noted that one of the commission's tasks had been to "create courses and frameworks that would enable "yeshiva dropouts and young haredi men who hang out in the streets (known as 'shababniks') to serve in the army."[21]

Being a Misfit and the Trajectory of Leaving

Most of the Shababniks I interviewed described themselves as having been troublemakers from a very early age: "I was always a troublemaker," "I was always a bad boy," "All my life I used to make problems." The problems tend to begin with a lack of interest in the yeshiva curriculum followed by increasing conflicts with the rules and growing disdain for the norms of the community, which they showed more and more openly. At a young age, the most common form of transgression tends to be the acquisition of a radio or cell phone or accessing the forbidden press. Most of the Shababniks describe these activities as innocent attempts to gain greater access to information, "to get the news," but also as a rebellion against the hermetic norms suffocating them. Increasingly strong-willed and not afraid to confront the authorities in the yeshiva, when caught with cell phones or radios they would demand that the yeshiva return the confis-cated objects, knowing full well that this would lead to their expulsion.

Most of them began to skip school when they were twelve or thirteen and then spent their days wandering the streets of the Haredi neighborhoods. One respondent described how he used to spend his days at the *Kotel* in Jerusalem and just talked to anyone who showed an interest. At this point, they were rarely interested in establishing contact with the non-Haredi world. They thought that secular Israelis were "very *nebech*" ("pitiable") and viewed them with "*rachmones* (compassion), a great deal of *rachmones*." In accordance with the communal narrative, they also believed that anyone outside of the community lived a hard life without fulfillment, and that everybody who left ended up being depressed.

In some cases their parents, in an attempt to bring them back into the fold, would seek the help of therapists. Having failed to find an adequate school for them, the parents would typically send them to "kiruv" yeshivas, a sort of a correctional facility where in fact the bonds between the transgressors were only strengthened. On their account, this was the point at which they started doing nothing all day long and discovered marijuana and the Internet. In their narratives of this state of limbo, marijuana features with increasing prominence. Neither did they want to return to the Haredi fold nor did they know where else they might want to be. In this situation weed offered a welcome escape. This stage involved no contact with the non-Haredi world or the opposite sex, just directionless time spent together doing nothing. At this point, the relationships with their families were tense and antagonistic. Many of them reported that their mothers had cried a lot. Some of the families tried to arrange *shidduchim* for them, desperately hoping that the marital bond would lock them into the system.

Some Shababniks view service in the Israeli Defense Forces as a means of transitioning from the Haredi community to mainstream society. Some within the Haredi community have suggested that sending a Shababnik to the IDF might be a sort of *pikuach nefesh* (saving their life) but most warn against allowing Shababniks to fall into the hands of the IDF. The relationship of the Shababniks and their (former) community to the IDF is a complex issue worthy of further exploration. The Israeli government is obviously aware of the fact that yeshiva dropouts are evading military service. In his aforementioned policy proposal on draft deferment for yeshiva students, Ilan suggested the authorities should insist that the leading rabbis issue "an explicit instruction, or at least a sincere call" urging Shababniks to join what is now the haredi *Netzah Yehuda* battalion.[22] As the proposal acknowledged, conscription of the Shababniks would lead to the induction of large numbers of young men who had been shunned by their families. As Ilan explained, in some cases "induction may improve the relationship between the soldier and his family because he has returned to a framework, and a distinctly religious

framework at that. Sometimes," however, "induction exacerbates the rift."
The IDF would need to take into account that Shababniks might well
not be able to return to their families when on furlough. The establishment of a system of adoptive families from the religious sector and an
organization of the kind that the Friends of Nahal Haredi have since
become should be considered.[23]

According to my Shababnik respondents, an estimated 30 percent
of their fellow Shababniks went to the army, either voluntarily or because
they were drafted. One respondent recounted how he thought about
joining the IDF but had not been eligible for military service because
he had been in prison for dealing hashish. One Shababnik suggested
that one could always evade the army: "there's a lot of tricks you can
do, like I did, I brought a paper from a psychiatrist that said that I'm
unfit because of a mental issue . . ." Those who do join the IDF are
often confronted with a heavy backlash from their (former) community.
Pashkevilim, posters displayed publicly in Haredi neighborhoods, are used
to shame them. On them, a Haredi soldier may find himself described
as a "common Shababnik, bitter, and unsatisfied," as a "frivolous youth"
attracted to the idea of "trading in souls," as a "a young punk" in search
of meaning in "the military missionary system," as a "hedonist on a
spiritual decline" or as someone whose "hatred of the Torah scholars is
driving him insane."[24]

A major change occurred in the lives of my respondents when they
discovered that *heymish* bakeries in New York were looking for workers
during the matzah baking season. Initially, the Shababniks would go
back to Israel after the matzah season. Yet eventually they stayed. In
America, they gradually changed their appearance, gave up their religious
observance and morphed into the group I encountered: modern young
Israeli expats with a *frum* background. This subculture has established
specific in-group relationships and a common attitude that affects all
aspects of its members' lives.

America: The Reinvention of the Self
and Creation of a New Shababnik Community

Relocation to New York has facilitated new changes in the lives of the
Shababniks and reinforced transformations already under way. The new
environment offered them the leeway and opportunities to reshape their

social and professional life. Their initial experience of Hasidic New York was one of stigmatization. As one of them explained: "I was a seventeen-year-old coming to America by himself, they knew I'm not a *yeshiva bucher*, you know, they knew I'm not a *yeshiva bucher*, they knew I'm a Shababnik right away. . . ." Soon they came in contact with American OTDs and other Jews on the fringes of the Hasidic communities. It was in this shared social space that they began to communicate with women (other than their female relatives) for the first time. They described this as a scary experience. Previously, the Shababniks had lived in an entirely homosocial world. When I asked one of my informants whether they had had any girlfriends in Israel, he gave me a puzzled look and answered: "No, no girlfriends. Nothing. We did nothing. We were only smoking weed. Weed was our girlfriend." In America, the Shababniks gradually began to modify their appearance, eventually discarding all outward signs of their former affiliation with Haredi culture and blending into mainstream society. As a general rule, they tended to dissociate themselves from the American OTD community they met quite early on. Apparently there is too much potential for cultural dissent between these two groups.

The social cohesion among Shababniks is very strong. They often speak about their circle of friends as "family." Their kinship ties function as a substitute family with very strong and nurturing connections. Some of the Shababniks maintain that their "new" families are actually more tight-knit, understanding, loving, and caring than their biological families were. They attribute this to the fact that, above and beyond their religious education, siblings in Hasidic families tend not to have a lot in common. The social cohesion of this substitute family is reinforced by the shared cultural background and the similar personal trajectories of its members. The performance of kinship displays an array of modified Jewish traditions and rites that both accommodate the traditions of their past and strongly express their new identities. They take a great deal of pride in caring for other members and in preparing hot meals for each other. They attribute this mutual attachment to the experience of being alone in a new country and thus compelled to rely upon each other.

Over time, the Shababniks have generally reestablished fairly good relationships with their biological families. Usually this means that they are able to maintain respectful and diplomatic relations and visit them a few times a year. My assumption, which the interviews confirmed, was that these relationships benefited from the geographical distance. Had the Shababniks stayed in Israel, their families would be constantly confronted with their secular life style. One of them told me that he had cut his *peyes* off only on arrival in America because he did not want to cause his parents additional pain.

In economic terms, Shababniks rely heavily on the American Hasidic network and mainly work in Hasidic-owned businesses. In stark contrast to their idle days in Israel, they now display the tenacious drive to succeed and strong work ethic typical of many immigrants. "Making it work," making money, and constantly making plans for new money-making schemes are prominent themes in this group. As several respondents explained, they do not work in Hasidic businesses because they yearn to be close to the community, but because it is the best way to earn money: "I work in a construction company and my boss is ex-Hasidic too. That's the best way to make the money. Not because we want to be Hasidic people." Some of the Shababniks do not think that their motivation to succeed is driven solely by their immigrant mentality and attribute it simply to the fact that they are growing up and maturing. Others insist that their changed attitude has everything to do with the fact that they came to America.

The Shababniks' Linguistic Repertoire

The participants of my study came from the following Hasidic sects: Premishlan, Skver, Gur, Vizhnitz, Rachmastrivka, Boyan, Skver, and Chabad. One participant was a former Yerushalami Haredi. All of them grew up in Yiddish-speaking homes. Even though some of them were raised in sects such as Gur, where Yiddish is barely spoken, usually they had one Yiddish-speaking American parent or there was some other specific reason why Yiddish was spoken at home.

At a very young age they shifted to using Modern Hebrew with their friends, in the street, and with their siblings. Yiddish was mainly used for communication with parents or elderly community members. Hebrew remains their language of in-group communication. Yiddish is used as a secret language when they do not want to be understood by "outsiders"; for instance, when communicating with Yiddish-speaking American Hasidim or speaking to their parents in Israel on the phone. In all other domains of life they use English to communicate with wider society, i.e., with non-Hebrew and non-Yiddish speakers.

Due to their poor writing skills, which reflect the education patterns of Israeli yeshivot, where Yiddish is an oral language of instruction and debate but not a written language, the Shababniks never write in Yiddish. They recognize that American Hasidim are versed in using Yiddish as a written language but claim that, in Israel, only older people share this skill. Likewise, they tend to have picked up their English from their surroundings and not by means of systematic study. This linguistic repertoire is clearly reflected in their WhatsApp communication: while Shababniks text in Hebrew, they generally leave voice notes in Yiddish or English.

In this context, the analysis of narrative content, context, and form takes into account narrative production on the macro- and micro-level. The macro-level analysis focuses on the historic, political, economic, and cultural context, while the micro-level analysis examines issues of language choice, setting, interlocutors, narrative functions and so on.[25] Shababniks' narratives also reveal language ideologies at the macro level and the attempts of their communities to maintain Yiddish.

> Yoni: My first language was Hebrew. At cheyder we spoke Hebrew and at my house we spoke Yiddish. So it was like both, you know? Usually in Hasidut Gur they are not speaking Yiddish. These days yeah, they are not speaking Yiddish, but at my house we spoke Yiddish because my mom came from America, like from different Hasidus, my mom came from Skver, so she spoke Yiddish . . . They always used to tell us "Yoni, talk Yiddish," they used to tell us always to talk Yiddish.

All the respondents felt positively about Yiddish, describing it as a "special" language, rich in distinctive words and expressions. One respondent described it as a pan-Jewish and translocal language. He recalled how one of his co-workers could not understand that a worker from Israel and a worker from America spoke the same language. He added that he had a friend in Israel who wanted to move to America but could not find a job in New York because he spoke neither English nor Yiddish. Clearly, then, their ability to speak Yiddish plays an important role in allowing them to gain employment in New York and thus leave the Israeli Haredi fold to join the Brooklyn Shababniks.

In terms of their attitudes toward, and experiences with, "secular" Yiddish the narratives of the Shababniks and the American OTDs I interviewed differ entirely. Many American OTDs have been in touch with non-Haredi Yiddish speakers in New York and have attended Yiddish-language events; some have written for the secular Yiddish press or told me that they enjoyed reading books written by famous Yiddish authors. Presumably, because Yiddish is so clearly associated with a limited range of specific forms of communication for them, none of the Brooklyn Shababniks showed any interest in the vibrant Yiddish culture scene in New York.

Leisure Time, the Psytrance Tribe, and Psytrance "Spirituality"

Many of the Shababniks spend the bulk of their leisure time hanging out together as a group. In addition to Friday night dinners, their weekends are spent "chilling out" together, spending time outdoors, and attending Psytrance parties. All their social events are marked by a blasting Psytrance beat in the background. In many cases Shababniks tend to have huge TV screens at home on which they play videos of Psy parties or Psytrance psychedelic visuals.[26] Psytrance parties and membership in the Psytrance tribe play a salient and important role in Shababniks' narratives about their current lifestyle.

The Shababniks I interviewed had already become part of the Psytrance subculture in Israel, which happens to be one of the hottest places for Psytrance. Psytrance was brought to Israel by young Israeli backpackers who traveled to India after they were discharged from the IDF and came across psychedelics and Goa trance music. Upon their return to Israel, they recreated what they had experienced, transforming Goa trance into the psychedelic trance genre. In the 1990s, Psytrance parties were held on Israeli beaches, in the desert, and in woods.[27] The parties, held on Shabbat and Jewish religious holidays, became imbued with a specific form of "spirituality." The intensity of the parties was heightened by psychedelics, lending them a "quasi-religious atmosphere."[28]

For Shababniks, PEDMC (Psytrance electronic dance music culture) is about much more than simply a musical event; it provides a sort of a substitute spirituality and a sense of belonging as part of the Psytrance "tribe." While little research has so far been undertaken on the significance of Psytrance for former Haredi youngsters, some has focused on the significance of Psytrance in Israel more generally.[29] Some of its findings can also be applied specifically to former Haredi youngsters who attend Psytrance parties. What Schmidt has to say about the crisis and demythologization of Zionism among Israeli youth, for example, can likewise be applied to the crisis and demythologization of Haredi values among former Haredi youngsters. Reynolds has observed that youngsters are turning "to rave culture for the meaning and sense of belonging they once derived from religion,"[30] and this is certainly something Shababniks also speak about: "Yankl: You know, in Psytrance: first of all it's drugs, but this is not the only reason. Second, it's . . . Psytrance is peace and love. There's a lot of meaning in Psydance, it's not only the music."

Israeli Psytrance organizers in New York often run theme-based parties, such as Purim parties, Psylloween (Psytrance Halloween), and Hanukka-themed Psy parties. As PEDMC meets a *heymish* background, the Palm Shtrimpin Festival, for instance, advertises a Psytrance "Connection Gathering," promising "An Intimate Shabbos Experience & Heimish Music Festival."[31] All the ads for Psytrance events feature various positive key words and concepts. This particular "Heimish festival" listed love, dancing, art, music, healing, vibes, spirituality, sustainability, culture, transformation, and science. All of these supposedly bring the participants together for a "higher purpose." Other concepts propagated on digital platforms promoting PEDMC events include "acceptance of light" and "mindfulness."

Although some of my younger American OTD respondents also said that they attend Psytrance parties, I would argue that the Shababniks' strong enthusiasm for PEDMC is very much rooted in their Israeliness.[32] In his discussion of Psytrance in Israel, St. John suggests that the popularity of Psytrance in Israel is in many ways a response to the everyday pressures and crises in the region. He sees PEDMC as a refuge from social obligations, loyalty to the state, and "the burden of sacrificial mythologies." The self-identification of Israeli Psytrancers should be seen as a response to the "absence of the freedoms enjoyed by youth elsewhere around the world."[33] These conclusions also apply directly to the Shababniks. To be sure, they live in a society within a society, which is seemingly disconnected from the problems of Israeli society at large, yet young Haredim are in fact confronted with a similar set of challenges to those other young Israelis face: security issues, financial uncertainty, a rigorous schedule, the expectation that they succeed in their studies, show themselves to be loyal to their community, and re-enact specific narratives of martyrdom and superiority.

For Shababniks who participate in the Psytrance culture, this also entails an element of doing what is cool outside of the shtetl and of consuming the forbidden fruit. One Shababnik recalled his first encounter with Psytrance culture for me in detail. His group of yeshiva dropouts had subsequently decided to throw their own Psytrance party. He described his initiation into Psytrance as a life-changing experience, which helped him clarify his life goals:

> Avi: When I was 21 or 22 maybe, someone brought me to a party, a dance party in the nature . . . like a Psytrance party, and this was my first time I saw the parties—what's going on and I was shocked. I remember my first time when I went to a party and I felt very uncomfortable there because I was still with the peyes and everyone was all like crazy, with all the hair and everything, but I saw what was going on. I saw the vibes at the party, and everyone on drugs and I was very shocked and then we did the same party but only us. The guys from yeshive. We took like 30–40 guys and we did our own party and this was my first time when I took MDMA. It opened up my mind and I started . . . I don't know exactly how to explain the process and I don't even know exactly what it did, but I know that from that point I started changing my behavior, I started like thinking what I wanna be, what I wanna do, and what exactly I, I mean till then I didn't know what exactly I wanna do, like what kind of life I wanna have.

Relevant data show that the Psytrance culture—in the form of recruitment for PEDMC parties, the exchange of emotions of anticipation before parties, logistical planning in the case of an out-of-city festival, and the exchange of experiences after parties involving a substantial amount of visuals and digital footage—also plays a major role in the Shababniks' online activities. Brooklyn Shababniks will often post pictures from PEDMC events on social media with captions expressing love for their "Psytrance family" and using slogans such as "Only together we are really one!" In line with the suggestion that Israeli Psytrancers "mix and match both real and imagined identities and social roles to the extent that what emerges is a modified replica of their source culture,"[34] I would argue that the membership of Shababniks in the Psytrance tribe constitutes a substitute form of communal belonging.

Liquidity of the Self and the Diversification of Diversity

Before rebuilding their new identity as young, life-loving Israeli migrants, the Shababniks' trajectory was marked by the stigma of transgression and disobedience and feelings of worthlessness. "Stigma," as Frideres explains,

> is the identification of a trait or attribute of an individual that is used to differentiate individuals into different categories, groups or other boundaried social entities and has a negative value. Each stigma represents a social identity in a particular context. Hence you may be "stigmatized" in one context but not in another.[35]

The stigmatization experienced by Shababniks in Israel and their placement in *kiruv* yeshivas prior to their immigration to the United States strengthened the bond between them and created a strong sense of social solidarity within their subculture and in their dealings with the superculture. As these young men rebuild their lives on a new continent, this stigma is finally gone. Shababniks focus their energy on making their present comfortable and enjoyable, and on dreaming up big plans for their future. Their discourse abounds with new money-making schemes, enterprises they want to start, and places where they might travel or settle. While some of their goals may not be entirely realistic and feasible, the optimism they show and the creativity of their ideas stand in marked contrast to their previously aimless life.

I was particularly astonished to discover that most Shababniks still identify as believers. One of my informants even continues to believe that Hasidic rebbes can perform miracles. He recalled how the late Lubavitcher Rebbe miraculously helped his mother conceive after six barren years of marriage. I discussed this at length with my ethnographic *shadchan*. As he explained,

They don't believe that most of the restrictions that Haredim keep, the most Halacha, is actually from God. So they really believe in God, but it's not like they believe in God and they are totally contradictory because they believe in all the laws and they just don't wanna do it. They are kinda a little bit more sophisticated and they also believe that all these laws, and these Jewish halachos and minhagim is not really what God wants you to do.

Shababniks even see this belief as an "Israeli Haredi thing." Several respondents in fact claimed that most of those who leave the fold are still believers: "Almost everyone" among the former Haredim in Israel, one of my respondents told me, "believes in God. Almost everyone. 99%." The Shababniks are in fact divided into one more and one less religious group. Even so, they all say that one day they would want to build a Jewish home that relies on traditional values. The particular group I surveyed tends to look down upon organizations that help Haredim transition to the secular world and consider those who use their services as weak and not very resourceful.

There are a number of key differences that distinguish the transition of Shababniks from that of American OTD individuals. First, the Shababniks left as a group. The group I have been working with was in fact established by a merger of two earlier groups. They went through their entire transition together and the extensive mutual support within the group minimized the potential need for external help. Unlike many male American OTD individuals who had to learn English as a co-territorial language, the Shababniks were fluent in the language of their Israeli surroundings. Shababniks were also less isolated than American OTD individuals because they did not feel alien in Israel. In their own words, they were among other Jews, which made them feel more self-confident and not really as newcomers to the wider society. None of the Shababniks had been married, so they were able to leave without having to take wives or children into consideration. Given that they are now far removed from their biological families, relations with them are, as already mentioned, less tense. Finally, the community they have built for themselves is very strong and supportive and characterized by tight-knit caring relationships akin to those common in the Hasidic world.

Even within the wider Psytrance tribe important distinctions are maintained. Some of the younger American OTDs attend Psytrance parties but they do not mix with Shababniks. Conversely, Shababniks keep their distance from Israeli trancers. As Avi explained,

> I also have friends that came from the secular world, and the connection is different. It's much different. I mean, you can see it still. We are two groups. In one group all of us Psytrance family, and there's one group of ex-Hasidim and one group of secular Israelis.

Shababniks sometimes us Psytrance jargon in their daily lives, referring to "expanded consciousness" or the "practicing of mindfulness," thus incorporating these foreign philosophies into their new identity, perhaps as a substitute for the religious certainties they have abandoned. Schmidt has suggested that the stupendous rise of the Psytrance scene in Israel can be seen as "part of their [the Israeli devotees of Psytrance] ardent search for a viable supplement to a cultural ethos with which they no longer overtly identify."[36] For Shababniks, Psytrance facilitates a radical dissociation from the structures of Haredi life.

In various respects, then, Shababniks display liquid and plural identities that enable them to be Yiddish-speaking employees in Hasidic-owned businesses in Brooklyn in the morning, Shabbos meal hosts in the evening, and Israeli migrant Psytrancers in America the next day. As a result of their multiple identities they inhabit both spaces shared with OTD individuals and spaces that are distinctly their own.

Conclusion

This chapter presents a study of the collective identity of a group of young Israeli men who have broken away from the highly structured Haredi society in Israel. In Brooklyn, Shababniks have created an alternative substitute community for themselves with its own values, beliefs, and forms of behavior. Mine is the first study of the collective trajectory of Shababniks in a transcontinental context. In exploring their models of collective and individual change, I have employed the concept of trans-locality, which Greiner and Sakdapolrak introduced to describe forms of simultaneity and identity formation that transcend boundaries.[37] The concept facilitates the simultaneous treatment of localities and mobilities within a holistic context. The translocal perspective allows these processes to be researched in a less linear and more open-ended way that captures the diverse and contradictory effects of interconnectedness between places, institutions, and actors. The trajectory of the Shababniks and their narratives reveal the diversity of genres, styles, and registers that constitute "super-diverse repertoires."[38] At the macro level of narrative analysis, the translocal approach facilitates a form of assessment of changes within Hasidic communities and the fluidity and discontinuity characteristic of the Shababniks, which integrates notions of "movements and flows on the one hand with notions of fixity, groundedness and situatedness in particular settings on the other."[39]

The world of former Israeli Haredim is multidimensional and diverse and I have obviously engaged only with one very specific group. In terms of further research, I hope this chapter will draw attention to the ex-*frum* Psytrance scene, an incredibly interesting and multilayered topic, which has not yet been explored in the scholarly literature. Other emerging topics in these narratives are the relationship between Shababniks and the IDF and the issue of Shababniks who serve prison time for criminal offenses. How are they later reintegrated into society and how does their identity change in confinement? Does prison "reform" them or distance them even further from their faith and their communities of origin? How has Haredi society responded to Shababnik IDF veterans, given its decades-old fierce opposition to (compulsory) service in the IDF?

The trajectories of American OTD individuals and Shababniks, both those who stay in Israel and those who emigrate, certainly merits further comparative attention. What can we learn about the commonalities and peculiarities of the processes unfolding in (ex-)*frum* communities translocally? In terms of their community structure, culture, and context, how much do Hasidic communities in New York, Israel, Antwerp, or London have in common and to what extent do they differ? What can these groups learn from each other? These are all important questions and I hope we will see more comparative studies taking a multi-site approach to various Haredi contexts. It is precisely the translocal perspective that brought me to Mea She'arim on that hot Thursday night in August 2017. I had been interacting with Shababniks who narrated their previous lives to me and I wanted to meet Shababniks who were going through the stages of change that already lay in the past for my primary respondents. In a way, my search for Shababniks in Mea She'arim was like time travel, taking me back to the roots, locations, and patterns of the lives of the young men I had been studying. In the sweet air of

Nechama's, I was looking for their past selves in an attempt to put the puzzle of their experiences together and complete the Gestalt.

Notes

1. Yuval Ben-Ami, "Eating Pious Pastries in Mea She'arim," *Haaretz*, December 10, 2012, https://www.haaretz.com/jewish/food/eating-pious-pastries-in-mea-she-arim.premium-1.483847?=&ts=_1505046493849.

2. Steven Vertovec, "Super-diversity and its Implications," *Ethnic and Racial Studies* 29, no. 6 (2007): 1024–054.

3. Simon Fanshawe and Dhananjayan Sriskandarajah, *"You Can't Put Me In A Box": Super-diversity and the End of Identity Politics in Britain* (London: Institute for Public Policy Research, 2010), 33; Jenny Phillimore, "Approaches to Health in the Age of Super-diversity: Accessing the NHS in Britain's Most Diverse City," *Critical Social Policy* 31, no. 1 (2011): 5–29; Jan Blommaert and Ben Rampton, "Language and Superdiversity: A Position Paper," *Diversities* 13, no. 2 (2011): 1–21; Sinfree Makoni and Alastair Pennycook, "Disinventing and Reconstructing Languages," in *Disinventing and Reconstructing Languages*, ed. Sinfree Makoni and Alastair Pennycook (Clevedon, UK: Multilingual Matters, 2007), 29.

4. Karel Arnaut and Massimiliano Spotti "Superdiversity Discourse," in *International Encyclopedia of Language and Social Interaction*, ed. Karen Tracy, Cornelia Ilie, and Todd Sandel (Malden, MA: Wiley/Blackwell, 2015), p. 3 (electronic version).

5. Clemens Greiner and Patrick Sakdapolrak, "Translocality: Concepts, Applications and Emerging Research Perspectives," *Geography Compass* 7, no. 5 (2012): 373–84.

6. Zygmunt Bauman, *Liquid Modernity* (Cambridge: Polity, 2000).

7. John Urry, *Global Complexity* (Cambridge: Polity, 2003).

8. Jerome S. Bruner, *Acts of Meaning* (Cambridge, MA: Harvard University Press, 1990); Charlotte Linde, *Life Stories. The Creation of Coherence* (New York: Oxford University Press, 1993).

9. Doris Schüpbach, *Shared Languages, Shared Identities, Shared Stories* (Frankfurt am Main: Peter Lang, 2008), 279.

10. Rina Benmayor and Andor Skotnes, "Some Reflections on Migration and Identity," *Migration and Identity. International Yearbook of Oral History and Life Stories* 3 (1994): 1–18.

11. Bruner, *Acts of Meaning*; Elinor Ochs, "Narrative," in *Discourse Studies: A Multidisciplinary Introduction* vol. 1: *Discourse as Structure and Process*, ed. Teun A. van Dijk (London: Sage, 1997), 185–207; Catherine Kohler Riessman, *Narrative Analysis* (Newbury Park, CA: Sage, 1993).

12. Natalie M. Underberg and Elayne Zorn, *Digital Ethnography: Anthropology, Narrative, and New Media* (Austin: University of Texas Press, 2013); Pia Varis, "Digital Ethnography," in *The Routledge Handbook of Language and Digital Communication*, ed. Alexandra Georgakopoulou (London: Taylor & Francis, 2016), 56–68.

13. To protect their privacy, I have assigned aliases to all of the participants in the study. I conducted all the interviews in Brooklyn, between November 2016 and July 2017. The interviews were conducted in English—in most cases in a rather idiosyncratic English that tended to involve a fair amount of code switching between English, Yiddish, and Hebrew.

14. In this discussion, when I am not referring specifically to Shababniks, I use a range of terms interchangeably to refer to people who have left Haredi communities such as formerly *frum*, former Haredim, ex-Hasidim, people who leave the Haredi fold, or OTD. Some authors also refer to defectors (Lynn Davidman, *Becoming Un-Orthodox: Stories of Ex-Hasidic Jews* (New York: Oxford University Press, 2015), lapsed Haredi, formerly religious or *datlashim* (Florence Heymann, "La *kippa* dans la poche. Sortir du sionisme religieux en Israël," *Ethnologie française* 43 [2013/4]: 651–59). I have also heard pejorative terms such as "Hasidic bums."

15. Samuel C. Heilman, *Defenders of the Faith: Inside Ultra-Orthodox Jewry* (New York: Schocken, 1992), 162.

16. wonga66, "The 'Shababnik': The New Breed of Haredi Punk/Gangster," post in JTF Discussion Forum, January 17, 2010, http://jtf.org/forum/index.php?topic=41973.0.

17. Neta Sela, "West Side Story, Meah Shearim Style," *YNet News*, April 9, 2008, https://www.ynetnews.com/articles/0,7340,L-3529543,00.html.

18. FailedMessiah, "Money Can't Buy Love—But It Can Buy Rabbis, Kol Koreh's and Protesters," *FailedMessiah* (blog), April 9, 2008, http://failedmessiah.typepad.com/failed_messiahcom/2008/04/money-cant-buy.html.

19. Scott, San Diego, CA, "Lashon haRa against the groom?"and shadoil, Jerusalem, "Waste," responses to Sela, "West Side Story," April 9, 2008, https://www.ynetnews.com/articles/0,7340,L-3529543,00.html.

20. Philologos, "What Do the Kenya Mall Terrorists and Naughty Jewish Children Have in Common," *Forward*, October 6, 2013, http://forward.com/culture/184859/what-do-the-kenya-mall-terrorists-and-naughty-jewi/.

21. Shahar Ilan, *Draft Deferment for Yeshiva Students: A Policy Proposal* (Jerusalem: The Floersheimer Institute for Policy Studies, 1999), https://fips.huji.ac.il/sites/default/files/floersheimer/files/ilan_draft_deferment_for_yeshiva_students_english.pdf, 10.

22. Ilan, 18.

23. Ilan, 19.

24. Roi Yanovsky and Tali Farkash, "Three Arrested on Suspicion of Inciting against Haredi Soldiers," *Ynet News*, January 13, 2016, https://www.ynetnews.com/articles/0,7340,L-4752374,00.html.

25. Aneta Pavlenko, "Autobiographic Narratives as Data in Applied Linguistics," *Applied Linguistics* 28, no. 2 (2007): 174.

26. Psytrance or psychedelic trance is a form of electronic dance music (EDM). It is a subgenre of trance music that remains close to trance's original roots, i.e., it focuses on a repetitive sound with hypnotic and spacy melodies. Psytrance is characterized by its pounding rhythm, which is layered with complex melodic lines and high energy riffs. It includes a number of genres, among them Goa trance, Progressive Psychedelic, Full on, Dynamic Psy, and Darkpsy.

27. Katie Bain, "Psytrance and Israel," *Red Bull Music Academy Daily*, September 19, 2016, http://daily.redbullmusicacademy.com/2016/09/psytrance-israel-feature.

28. Joshua I. Schmidt, "(En)Countering the Beat: Paradox in Israeli Psytrance," in *The Local Scenes and Global Culture of Psytrance*, ed. Graham St. John (New York: Routledge, 2010), 134.

29. Graham St. John, *The Local Scenes and Global Culture of Psytrance* (New York, London: Routledge, 2010); Schmidt, "(En)Countering the Beat."

30. Simon Reynolds, *Generation Ecstasy: Into the World of Techno and Rave Cultures* (Boston: Little Brown, 1998), 288, quoted in Schmidt, "(En)Countering the Beat," 228.

31. Palm Shtrimpin Festival, "PSF Presents: Connection Gathering 2017," May 18, 2017, https://www.facebook.com.events/1678762735753680/?active_tab=about.

32. It is worth noting that Shababniks, if they travel abroad, also tend to opt for the same "exotic" destinations in South America or Asia that are popular with young Israelis taking a gap year between their service in the IDF and entry into the labor market.

33. Graham St. John, "Freak Media: Vibe Tribes, Sampledelic Outlaws and Israeli Psytrance," in *Continuum: Journal of Media & Cultural Studies* 26, no. 3 (2012): 442–43.

34. St. John, *Local Scenes*, 143.

35. James S. Frideres, "Immigrants, Integration and the Intersection of Identities," working paper for Canadian Heritage, 2002, http://canada.metropolis.net/events/diversity/immigration.pdf, 9.

36. Schmidt, "(En)Countering the Beat," 144.

37. Greiner and Sakdapolrak, "Translocality."

38. Jan Blommaert and Albert Maria Backus, "Superdiverse Repertoires and the Individual," in *Multilingualism and Multimodality. Current Challenges for*

Educational Studies, ed. Ingrid de Saint-Georges and Jean-Jacques Weber (Rotterdam: Sense Publishers, 2013), 11–32.

39. Greiner and Sakdapolrak, "Translocality," 375.

References

Arnaut, Karel, and Massimiliano Spotti. "Superdiversity Discourse." In *International Encyclopedia of Language and Social Interaction*, edited by Karen Tracy, Cornelia Ilie and Todd Sandel, 1–7. Malden, MA: Wiley/Blackwell, 2015, online edition.

Bain, Katie. "Psytrance and Israel." *Red Bull Music Academy Daily*, September 19, 2016. http://daily.redbullmusicacademy.com/2016/09/psytrance-israel-feature.

Bauman, Zygmunt. *Liquid Modernity*. Cambridge: Polity Press, 2000.

Ben-Ami, Yuval. "Eating Pious Pastries in Mea She'arim." *Haaretz*, Dec. 10, 2012. https://www.haaretz.com/jewish/food/eating-pious-pastries-in-mea-she-arim. premium-1.483847?=&ts=_1505046493849.

Benmayor, Rina, and Andor Skotnes. "Some Reflections on Migration and Identity." *Migration and Identity. International Yearbook of Oral History and Life Stories* 3 (1994): 1–18.

Blommaert, Jan, and Albert Maria Backus. 2013. "Superdiverse Repertoires and the Individual." In *Multilingualism and Multimodality*, edited by Ingrid de Saint-Georges and Jean-Jacques Weber, 11–32. Rotterdam: Sense Publishers, 2013.

Blommaert, Jan, and Ben Rampton. 2011. "Language and Superdiversity: A Position Paper." *Diversities* 13, no. 2 (2011): 1–21.

Bruner, Jerome S. *Acts of Meaning*. Cambridge, MA: Harvard University Press, 1990.

Davidman, Lynn. *Becoming Un-Orthodox: Stories of Ex-Hasidic Jews*. New York: Oxford University Press, 2015.

FailedMessiah. "Money Can't Buy Love—But It *Can* Buy Rabbis, Kol Koreh's and Protesters." *FailedMessiah* (blog), April 9, 2008. http://failedmessiah. typepad.com/failed_messiahcom/2008/04/money-cant-buy.html.

Fanshawe, Simon, and Dhananjayan Sriskandarajah. *"You Can't Put Me In A Box": Super-diversity and the End of Identity Politics in Britain*. London: Institute for Public Policy Research, 2010.

Frideres, James S. "Immigrants, Integration and the Intersection of Identities." Working paper for Canadian Heritage, 2002. http://canada.metropolis.net/ events/diversity/immigration.pdf, 9.

Greiner, Clemens, and Patrick Sakdapolrak. "Translocality: Concepts, Applications and Emerging Research Perspectives." *Geography Compass* 7, no. 5 (2013): 373–84.

Heilman, Samuel C. *Defenders of the Faith: Inside Ultra-Orthodox Jewry.* New York: Schocken, 1992.

Heymann, Florence. "La *kippa* dans la poche. Sortir du sionisme religieux en Israël." *Ethnologie française* 43 (2013/4): 651–59.

Ilan, Shahar. *Draft Deferment for Yeshiva Students: A Policy Proposal* (Jerusalem: The Floersheimer Institute for Policy Studies, 1999), https://fips.huji.ac.il/sites/default/files/floersheimer/files/ilan_draft_deferment_for_yeshiva_students_english.pdf,

Linde, Charlotte. *Life Stories. The Creation of Coherence.* New York: Oxford University Press, 1993.

Makoni, Sinfree, and Alastair Pennycook. "Disinventing and Reconstituting Languages." In *Disinventing and Reconstituting Languages*, edited by Sinfree Makoni and Alastair Pennycook, 1–41. Clevedon, UK: Multilingual Matters, 2007.

Ochs, Elinor. "Narrative." In *Discourse Studies: A Multidisciplinary Introduction* vol. 1: *Discourse as Structure and Process*, edited by Teun A. van Dijk, 185–207. London: Sage Publications, 1997.

Palm Shtrimpin Festival. "PSF Presents: Connection Gathering 2017." May 18, 2017. https://www.facebook.com/events/1678762735753680/?active_tab=about.

Pavlenko, Aneta. "Autobiographic Narratives as Data in Applied Linguistics." *Applied Linguistics* 28, no. 2 (2007): 163–88.

Phillimore, Jenny. "Approaches to Health in the Age of Super-diversity: Accessing the NHS in Britain's Most Diverse City." *Critical Social Policy* 31, no. 1 (2011): 5–29.

Philologos. "What Do the Kenya Mall Terrorists and Naughty Jewish Children Have in Common." *Forward*, October 6, 2013. http://forward.com/culture/184859/what-do-the-kenya-mall-terrorists-and-naughty-jewi/.

Riessman, Catherine Kohler. *Narrative Analysis.* Newbury Park, CA: Sage Publications, 1993.

St. John, Graham. *The Local Scenes and Global Culture of Psytrance.* New York: Routledge, 2010.

St. John, Graham. "Freak Media: Vibe Tribes, Sampledelic Outlaws and Israeli Psytrance." *Continuum: Journal of Media & Cultural Studies* 26 no. 3 (2012): 437–47.

Schmidt, Joshua I. "(En)Countering the Beat: Paradox in Israeli Psytrance." In *The Local Scenes and Global Culture of Psytrance*, edited by Graham St. John, 131–48. New York: Routledge, 2010.

Schüpbach, Doris. *Shared Languages, Shared Identities, Shared Stories.* Frankfurt am Main: Peter Lang, 2008.

Scott (San Diego, CA). "Lashon haRa against the groom?" *YNet News* (comment), April 9, 2008. https://www.ynetnews.com/articles/0,7340,L-3529543,00.html.

Sela, Neta. "West Side Story, Meah Shearim Style." *YNet News*, April 9, 2008. http://jtf.org/forum/index.php?topic=41973.0.

Shadoil (Jerusalem). "Waste." *YNet News* (comment), April 9, 2008. https://www.ynetnews.com/articles/0,7340,L-3529543,00.html.

Underberg, Natalie M., and Elayne Zorn. *Digital Ethnography: Anthropology, Narrative, and New Media.* Austin: University of Texas Press, 2013.

Urry, John. *Global Complexity.* Cambridge: Polity, 2003.

Varis, Pia. "Digital Ethnography." In *The Routledge Handbook of Language and Digital Communication*, edited by Alexandra Georgakopoulou, 56–68. London: Taylor & Francis, 2015.

Vertovec, Steven. "Super-diversity and its Implications." *Ethnic and Racial Studies* 29, no. 6 (2007): 1024–054.

wonga66. "The 'Shababnik': The New Breed of Haredi Punk/Gangster." JTF Discussion Forum, January 17, 2010. http://jtf.org/forum/index.php?topic=41973.0.

Yanovsky, Roi, and Tali Farkash. "Three arrested on suspicion of inciting against Haredi soldiers." *Ynet News*, January 13, 2016. https://www.ynetnews.com/articles/0,7340,L-4752374,00.html.

The OTD Struggle

Telling a More Compelling Story

Naftuli Moster

One of the greatest challenges inherent in leaving an ultra-Orthodox lifestyle is the transition from a copiously scripted life to one that is at once unscripted and in a sense doomed by a narrative of failure. Much research has been done in the fields of anthropology, sociology, and journalism on the Orthodox lifestyle and the script that adherents follow, and the disparaging narrative about those leaving the community has been studied as well. This paper will illuminate the role OTD literature plays as a coping mechanism that allows its authors to rewrite and thereby take control of their narratives and lives; as well as the role it plays for other OTD individuals by providing a new script for those looking to start a life outside of their native community.

The Ultra-Orthodox Script

The term *haredi* (ultra-Orthodox) is an umbrella for two main groups: the Yeshivish or Litvish, and the Hasidic. Both follow scripted lifestyles as prescribed by their leaders and their religious texts. The Yeshivish tend to follow a strict interpretation of the Torah and *halacha* (Jewish law), with less emphasis on *kabala* (texts and practices related to the soul and spirit), in contrast to the Hasidim who emphasize the spiritual and mystical aspect of Jewish practice.[1]

361

Within Hasidism, different sects are similar in the way they pray and live according to halacha (Jewish law) and Hasidic traditions and values, but they differ with regard to the spiritual leader they follow and minor practices and customs unique to each sect.[2] Despite their differences, all ultra-Orthodox individuals lead very scripted lives in terms of their daily routine, mode of dress, education, and lifecycle events. The scripts may vary slightly by sect, but they are fundamentally the same in their strict adherence to minhag (Jewish tradition) and halacha.

A child born into an ultra-Orthodox home is groomed from an early age, often as early as birth, to believe in God, to fear Him, to love Him, and to fulfill His commandments. Ultra-Orthodox children are surrounded by Jewish objects, images, languages, and texts from infancy and onward. These tools introduce them to the script they will follow for the rest of their lives. Even babies' toys often have religious significance and religious texts and messages inscribed on them, as a stroll into any toy store in an ultra-Orthodox neighborhood will reveal. Puzzles and card games are often related to Torah and Jewish holiday themes.

Ultra-Orthodox Jews not only follow the Torah and halacha to the strictest extent, but also set metaphorical "fences" by imposing additional restrictions to ensure that rules are not broken even unwittingly and that obligations are fulfilled properly.[3] Ultra-Orthodox toddlers are initially exposed to Jewish studies and literature only, starting with the Hebrew letters and an introduction to Jewish holidays, songs, role models, and the Hebrew calendar among other things, establishing the primacy of the ultra-Orthodox way of life. Children from a very young age are taught to recite blessings before and/or after many daily and mundane activities, including eating, using the bathroom, and hearing thunder or sighting lightning during a rainstorm. The ultra-Orthodox script dictates which foods they may and may not eat and when the permitted foods may be eaten. The script even dictates which shoe must be put on first when dressing, and in what order shoes with laces are to be tied; how to cut one's fingernails and toenails; with whom an individual may and may not converse; and more.[4]

Other aspects of the script are unique to one gender or the other. To give several examples: Perhaps the earliest aspects of the ultra-Orthodox script are the bris (ritualistic circumcision) a baby boy must undergo on his eighth day and the vacht nacht the night before the bris when flocks of children and adults sing and pray beside the newborn's crib.[5] As the infant grows into a toddler he is groomed to follow ultra-Orthodox dictates. At the age of three, at an *upsherin* ceremony, a boy's hair, which had not been cut or trimmed since birth, is shorn except the two sides for *peyos* (sidecurls); the toddler then puts on a *yarmulke* (skullcap) which he is required to wear at all times, and *tzitzis* (ritual fringes) which he wears during waking hours.[6] This trend of altering the dress-code and appearance increases in scale over time, as boys who become bar mitzvah put on a hat and a black or dark blue jacket over a white shirt to further complement the traditional garb worn by the members of their community. For Hasidic males, the garb typically changes again after a young man marries, when he begins to wear a *shtreimel* (round fur hat) on Shabbos, holidays, and special occasions.

Not only does their script tell them how to observe rituals and *mitzvot* (commandments), how to conduct themselves in various circumstances, and how to dress at different stages in life, the script even dictates what individuals should strive to become as adults. It dictates that boys strive to be rabbis and scholars; consequently, boys' education in yeshiva places a strong emphasis on Judaic studies, leaving almost no time for secular studies.[7] On average, most Hasidic yeshivas and many Litvish yeshivas teach boys only one and a half hours of English and math per day up until the age of thirteen. No other secular subjects are taught, and past the age of fourteen no secular subjects are taught at all.[8] Ultimately, by following this script, "The boy is expected to become a *talmid hacham*, a learned man, and an *ehrlicher Yid*, an honest Jew."[9]

Girls and women follow a somewhat different script. Their lives are not marked by the same rites of passage as those of boys, such as a *bris* at eight days, a haircut at three years, and a bar mitzvah at thirteen, but they too are fully immersed in the Jewish and ultra-Orthodox life and culture with little exposure to anything else.[10] (The Bat Mitzvah celebration, common in other Jewish communities, is understated among Hasidic and Litvish families; similarly, the Kiddush celebrating the birth of a Hasidic girl is typically a more modest celebration than that of the bris which marks the birth of a boy.)

Modesty in dress is a central concern for girls and women, as is housekeeping and caring for younger siblings so as to assist their mothers and to prepare them for their roles as mothers and wives.[11] After marriage, the laws of menstrual purity become more central to women's scripts. By following her script, "The girl is expected to be a *Yiddisher mama*, a Jewish mother, and a *Yiddisher tochter*, a Jewish daughter married to a *talmid hacham* and an *ehrlicher Yid*."[12]

The scripted lifestyle of the ultra-Orthodox also impacts the way adolescents choose to express their individuality. While in the secular world adolescents often exhibit rebellious or deviant behaviors, Kamen, in his study of Bobov Hasisim notes that in the ultra-Orthodox world often the opposite is the case.[13] There, adolescents at times "rebel" by becoming even more religious and connected to their teachers and spiritual leaders. This allows for a radicalized identity as an ultra-Orthodox or Hasidic Jew; other expressions of identity are rarely entertained or tolerated. In other words, adolescent exploration concludes with a strengthened commitment to their script in contrast to the deviance from it that is more typical in the secular world.[14]

The secular world would strike the Hasid as wholly unscripted. And the insularity of the ultra-Orthodox communities makes the secular world not only inaccessible but also inconceivable. Ultra-Orthodox and Hasidic communities, some of which are situated in the heart of New York City, rarely engage with the secular world around them. Most shops located within the community are run by Orthodox individuals who dress as all members in their community do, and who speak the same language—for Hasidim, mostly Yiddish.[15] Advertisements, radio broadcasts, newspapers, magazines, and news websites follow strict modesty laws and report mostly on Jewish news from an Orthodox angle.[16] Role models hailed in school by their religious teachers and written about in ultra-Orthodox newspapers and magazines are almost exclusively male rabbis, with the occasional recognition of (religious) first aid providers.

The nature of ultra-Orthodox education is further insulating. This is so by design according to Krakowski, who suggests that yeshivas attempt to provide an entirely different worldview to their students, countering the worldview held by average Americans.[17] Heilman believes yeshivas are designed in such a way as to provide for an enclavist culture, one that cuts off the outside world and seeks to protect their children from external influences.[18] Regardless of whether their intention is to counter the message of the secular world or to block it out entirely (or both at once), the consequences of this lack of education are often permanent, especially for ultra-Orthodox. While girls receive a more well-rounded education and Hasidic women are more likely than men to interact with the secular world, their worldview tends to be narrowed through other means, according to Fader, such as through the strong emphasis on modesty and the "hyperbolization," of their religious identity.[19] As a result of their insularity, the ultra-Orthodox script is the only script the average Hasid or other ultra-Orthodox individual knows.

Ultra-Orthodox Narratives

In addition to living scripted lives, ultra-Orthodox children also take part in a narrative about themselves in which they essentially define themselves through their religious and familial narrative history. For instance, children's namesakes often extend back to a rabbi, prophet, or biblical character. Other aspects of their narrative derive from the Torah, Talmud, and other sacred texts which affirm their status as a chosen people and assure them that their script is the key to living a virtuous and meaningful life.

The ultra-Orthodox world has also crafted a narrative about all who are different from them. The ultra-Orthodox way of life, which would seem restrictive, is portrayed as liberating, while the secular and seemingly freer life is portrayed as enshackling, empty, and meaningless; a life to be demonized and reviled.[20] These messages are conveyed in sermons by rabbis, lectures to schoolchildren, and posters in the neighborhood. The clear message is that the non-Orthodox are script-less and therefore aimless, foolish, and vulgar.

The narrative about those who were raised ultra-Orthodox but then left is even more bleak. In these communities it is common to berate those who have gone "off the *derech*" (OTD, off the ultra-Orthodox path), and to talk about them in the same manner as one would speak of gentiles and secular Jews—in derogatory ways. Moreover, the motives and mental well-being of those who are OTD are often called into question. There is no shortage of stories in the ultra-Orthodox press, school lectures, and publications depicting the OTD community as mentally ill, selfish, and unrestrained. To many, going OTD is viewed as both a spiritual and physical death sentence. Though not commonplace, it not unheard of for parents to sit shiva for a living but no longer religious child; and tales circulate within the community of OTD drug abuse and suicide.

A handful of recent articles clearly demonstrate this perception: Dov Fischer, in an opinion piece in Cross-Currents, depicts OTD individuals as baalei taava (people driven by desire) seeking physical pleasures and freedom from ultra-Orthodox rules.[21] In "Night Light" by Michal Marcus, a piece of short fiction published in the ultra-Orthodox magazine, Mishpacha, in October of 2016, the OTD antagonist is portrayed as a financially struggling pseudo-intellectual, selfish and incapable of holding her life together.[22] OTD individuals are often mistakenly identified as "at risk," a term more appropriate for those who resort to self-destructive behaviors—despite the fact that most OTD individuals are self-sufficient adults. Parents and siblings will often accuse the child going off the derech of selfishness and intentionally harming the family name—carrying great consequences to the rest of the family remaining religious, especially to the marriage prospects of related individuals.[23] Their decision to become not religious effectively taints the family name, making it less desirable for members of the community to become associated.

All in all, the narrative the ultra-Orthodox community tells of the OTD individual stands in stark contrast to the narrative they tell of themselves: whereas they are self-disciplined, those who are OTD are out of control; whereas they are pure, those who are OTD are promiscuous; whereas they are learned, those who are OTD are failures and dropouts—and when those who are OTD seem learned, they are studying meaningless and trivial things rather than pursuing truth; whereas they are self-respecting, those who are OTD lack dignity; whereas they are a community of kindness, those who are OTD are self-serving; whereas they will achieve the world to come, those who are OTD have life neither in this world nor in the next.

Leaving Ultra-Orthodoxy: Scriptless and Doomed

With that, the reader can now imagine what it is like for individuals from ultra-Orthodox communities to suddenly find themselves on the other side. The script by which they have lived their lives is rendered obsolete and the disparaging narrative about secular people now applies to them. Relationships with family members become strained, and in many cases OTD individuals are estranged and abandoned by family.[24]

As Shaffir states:

> In light of the Haredi lifestyle's total grip over the individual, the thought of exiting presents a virtually insurmountable challenge. Not only does the decision involve severing ties with family and friends—a feature commonly reported in the accounts of disaffiliation and defection—but, in this case, demands contact with a way of life which is utterly foreign.[25]

Individuals who leave the community face many practical challenges as well. According to Berger, after following a script for every aspect of their lives, it is challenging for "exiters . . . entering the new secular society for the first time . . . with neither preparation nor the necessary skills . . . to make decisions rather than follow prescribed routes."[26]

Davidman and Greil found that in contrast to people who become religious or switch denominations, who often feel like they have "found themselves" through the new narrative and script they adopt and the welcoming community embracing them, those who are OTD experience the opposite.[27] Shaffir noted that even ex-cult followers have an easier time since they are already familiar with the secular world they are rejoining.[28] Until recently, no group offered guidance and support or a script for the newly non-religious as they integrated into larger society.[29] In the past few years, however, several non-profits and social support groups have been formed in the U.S. and abroad to help OTD individuals on their journey out. Still, the support is far more limited than the support and guidance individuals receive within the religious community.

Additionally, as individuals leave with no alternative narrative, many assume the narrative that members of the ultra-Orthodox community tell of defectors: they see themselves as failures, worry they have lost their minds, and wonder if they are as depraved and selfish as the community painted them. A striking demonstration of this is the fact that many who leave refer to themselves as OTD. For lack of an alternative, the only language available to them by which to define their new identity is the disparaging terminology the ultra-Orthodox community used to define them. (This seems to be specific to the United States, as in Israel individuals who leave their religious community are referred to as "yotzim" [exiters].) This choice to accept a derogatory label is likely in part due to the lack of another, more appropriate label, and may be a reflection of their lacking a narrative for themselves.

Making matters worse, aspects of the narrative the ultra-Orthodox tell of OTD-ers are occasionally confirmed when OTD-ers are driven to drugs and suicide. The absence of a path or script and the anxiety that comes with it, along with the lack of a standard education, general (secular) knowledge, and applied skills among ultra-Orthodox individuals who leave, leads many to struggle financially, socially, and emotionally in the period immediately following their departure from their communities and families. Lack of education can have a particularly crippling effect. Unlike children attending non-ultra-Orthodox schools who receive an education in a variety of areas including English, math, science, history, geography, music, graphic design, sports, and even business, boys attending ultra-Orthodox and primarily Hasidic yeshivas typically receive only the scantest instruction in English and math, and little else.[30] The legacy of a poor education causes many of those who choose to leave their native communities to question their worth and to inadvertently accept the view of them held by those who remain in their communities. (Full disclosure: I run an organization that works to improve secular education in the Hasidic community.)

Leaving the ultra-Orthodox community typically comes after intense questioning and doubts.[31] Departure involves a complete breakdown of everything the individual once believed in and the way he or she saw him- or herself as well as the people surrounding him or her.[32] An existential crisis, described by Victor Frankl as "a sense of futility and emptiness, a feeling of meaninglessness," often comes with departure and continues to reaffirm the ultra-Orthodox community's narrative about the OTD community.[33] Essentially, the individual questions the script that has dictated his life, but does not have a script with which to replace it—which can cause severe anxiety, again reaffirming the narrative that OTD individuals are not psychologically or mentally well.

In addition to the challenges and trauma resulting from the loss of community and script, the process of leaving in and of itself is traumatic.[34] Whether due to being shunned by family, estranged from their community, or being treated as someone who has suffered a mental breakdown, the experience can leave individuals feeling alone and helpless.[35] This trauma continues to reaffirm that narrative of emotional and mental instability. One of Shaffir's interviewees sums up the pain associated with going OTD by saying, "A person can really go mad from such an experience. It's a terrible loneliness . . . You cut off everything that you had . . . And nobody cares about you . . . Nobody cares about you as a person."[36] Those who leave the community risk being abandoned by the people who profess to love them and feel rejected or unwelcome by the outside world that they attempt to join.[37]

Leaving the community may also result in divorce, the loss of custody of one's children, the loss of access to financial resources, and the loss of a place to live.[38] These struggles can lead, again, to anxiety and even depression—not because these individuals are mentally unwell, but rather because their circumstances are so dire that even the healthiest of individuals would struggle in such a position. Nonetheless, that anxiety or hopelessness continues to reaffirm the narrative the ultra-Orthodox tell about OTD individuals.

Winston, after doing extensive research on the ultra-Orthodox community with a focus on those leaving it, concludes:

> But ultimately, it was not this focus on the primacy of the group over the individual that was troubling to me, but rather the extent to which fear seemed to regulate behavior and maintain conformity in these communities, ultimately reproducing their way of life, one generation after the next.[39]

The fear instilled in them growing up continues to consume some of them even after they have gone OTD.[40] The fear ingrained within them when they were part of the community—fear of upsetting God, of upsetting the community and family, fear of divine retribution or social and communal retribution—often contributes to their anxiety upon leaving, which in turn plays into the narrative told about them and others like them within the community, which they, too, often cannot help but internalize.

Berger, Shaffir, Davidman, and Greil all describe a journey that is filled with anxiety and fear.[41] Without a script, little is known or certain about an individual's future once he or she chooses to leave. Guilt is a final contributing factor for OTD individuals who suffer the consequences of the disparaging narrative put forth by members of their community. In a community where family is both central and close knit and where family image is a top priority, OTD individuals are often consumed by guilt for betraying their families and blemishing the family name.[42] And going OTD is not without consequences to the individual's family—it will often affect the marriage prospects of the OTD individual's siblings. For some, the guilt alone is sufficient to keep them living within the community despite their lack of faith. For those who do go OTD, the guilt can cause them great anxiety; additionally, it affirms the narrative of the selfishness of those who go OTD: they care only for themselves and not about consequences to their family.

Re-writing the Narrative

With such a damning narrative and so many challenges, it is unsurprising that OTD suicide seems to occur at a more frequent rate than suicide within the general population. (I use "seem" because a formal study of these contrasting rates has yet to be conducted, but anecdotal evidence suggests this to be the case.) At the same time, there are many OTD success stories of individuals who try and succeed in rewriting their narrative. Recently, a proliferation of literature by OTD individuals attempts to set the record straight and document the stories of those who leave. The literature presents individuals who struggle with scriptlessness after leaving the community but then find their place in society and go on to achieve normalcy and success. Memoirs include Shulem Deen's *All Who Go Do Not Return*, Leah Lax's *Uncovered: How I Left Hasidic Life and Finally Came Home*; Leah Vincent's *Cut Me Loose: Sin and Salvation after My Ultra-Orthodox Girlhood*; Deborah Feldman's *Unorthodox: The Scandalous Rejection of My Hasidic Roots* and more. There have also been a number of OTD bloggers over the years.[43] Indeed, OTD literature has become a sub-genre of memoir. Long-form articles have made appearances in non-Orthodox Jewish publications as well as in mainstream media.[44]

Often, OTD authors choose to remain anonymous; but even behind their anonymity is an eagerness to share their journey and rewrite the narrative of those who go OTD. These articles and books paint an entirely different picture from the one narrated from within ultra-Orthodox communities. OTD memoirs contain hardship and heartbreak but also a journey of self-discovery and self-actualization.

Researchers have noted a unique desire by OTD-ers to tell their stories. Berger stresses the eagerness of OTD individuals to share their stories in their own words.[45] And Winston notes a similar phenomenon when she conducted her research, writing: "Indeed, as word of my research spread, some people actually sought me out for interviews."[46] Clearly there is a desire to share a narrative that is not being told and not being recognized. The presence of multiple autobiographies and memoirs by OTD individuals as well as the many articles published routinely on websites and blogs such as *The Jewish Daily Forward*, *Kveller*, and *Off the Derech*, suggest the need to tell a story that works against the dominant narrative being told by the community.

Narrative as Therapy

OTD personal writings that reclaim and redefine the experience of departure are productive in several ways: first, they may help provide something of a script for those contemplating leaving. In part, the difficulties of scriptlessness are alleviated by organizations such as Footsteps in the U.S. and Hillel in Israel that help individuals who choose to leave their religious communities enroll in an educational institution, find employment, and find their own paths. Yet many who go OTD do not join these organizations until well after their initial stages of leaving, believing, perhaps, the narrative told about these organizations within the ultra-Orthodox community. New literature may provide new disaffiliates more help with finding a script than any organization could on its own, and the literature itself often corrects the narrative about these organizations. The secular world is utterly foreign to those raised within the confines of an ultra-Orthodox community, but others have successfully transitioned and future OTD individuals will be able to borrow from these new publications and learn how to transition into a secular world themselves.

Additionally, this rewriting of the OTD story can take the form of narrative therapy. Narrative therapy emphasizes that the act of telling a story is subjective to the individual and so often resists a more dominant and more oppressive narrative. The narrative approach focuses on the individual who feels misunderstood because the oft-repeated storyline sees his or her actions as deviant and applies labels to him or her.[47] This is particularly common among the OTD population where, before and after leaving, these individuals internalize a narrative that secular people and those who leave the community to join them are troubled misfits. The OTD individual needs an outlet in which he or she can present an alternative narrative, one that fits better with his or her subjective experience.

Narrative writing has been shown to improve individuals' physical and emotional well-being. The emotional effect of writing is akin to the results achieved by therapy insofar as it enables individuals to organize and attain a semblance of control over past events as they make those events cohere in a meaningful way.[48] A meta-analysis conducted by Pasqual Frisina, Joan Borod, and Stephen Lepore revealed that narrative writing not only predicts greater health in healthy individuals, but it can ameliorate symptoms of anxiety and depression in individuals already suffering from poor mental health.[49] This would bode well for OTD individuals experiencing anxiety or depression in the early stages of leaving.

Narrative writing may offer these individuals an outlet to share their side of the story, one that is filled with strength, determination, and ambition, as opposed to the story of anger, trouble, and failure that is being told about them by members of their former community. It enables them to write a script for future defectors, and paint a picture that is more promising to combat the negative narrative repeated by the religious community. Narrative therapy, or even simply the act of writing independently, or sharing their story verbally in a non-clinical setting, may help individuals rewrite their history and ensure a more positive future for themselves and for others.

Notes

Many thanks to my wife Miriam Moster for her comments on this paper.

1. Samuel C. Heilman, *Defenders of the Faith: Inside Ultra-Orthodox Jewry* (Oakland, CA: University of California Press, 1992), 239; Samuel C. Heilman, "Who Are the Haredim?" in *Non-Equivalent: The State of Education in New York City's Hasidic Yeshivas*, ed. Naftuli Moster (New York: Yaffed, 2017), 12; Gershom Gerhard Scholem, *Major Trends in Jewish Mysticism* (New York: Random House Digital, Inc., 1961), 325.

2. William Shaffir, "Boundaries and Self-Presentation among the Hasidim: A Study in Identity Maintenance," in *New World Hasidim: Ethnographic Studies of Hasidic Jews in America*, ed. Janet S. Belcove-Shalin (Albany, NY: SUNY Press, 2012), 34.

3. Abot 1:1.

4. *Kitzur Sh. Ar.* 72:14, 3:4.

5. Dovid Zaklikowski, "The Night Preceding the Circumcision," *Chabad*, http://www.chabad.org/library/article_cdo/aid/145054/jewish/The-Night-Preceding-the-Circumcision.htm.

6. "The Basics of the Upsherin," *Chabad*, Chabad-Lubavitch Media Center, http://www.chabad.org/library/article_cdo/aid/710724/jewish/The-Basics-of-the-Upsherin.htm.

7. Heilman, *Sliding to the Right*, 86.

8. Alisa Partlan, *Non-Equivalent: The State of Education in New York City's Hasidic Yeshivas*, ed. Naftuli Moster (New York: Yaffed, 2017), 31.

9. Solomon Poll, *The Hasidic Community of Williamsburg: A Study in the Sociology of Religion* (New York: Schocken Books, 1969), 54.

10. Winston, *Unchosen*, xii.

11. Lynn Davidman and Arthur L. Greil, "Characters in Search of a Script: The Exit Narratives of Formerly Ultra-Orthodox Jews," *Journal for the Scientific Study of Religion* 46, no. 2 (2007): 206; Poll, *The Hasidic Community of Williamsburg*, 73.

12. Poll, *The Hasidic Community of Williamsburg*, 54.

13. Robert Mark Kamen, *Growing up Hasidic: Education and Socialization in the Bobover Hasidic Community* (New York: AMS Press, 1985), 83.

14. Ibid.

15. Heilman, *Sliding to the Right*, 116.

16. Ibid.

17. Heilman, *Sliding to the Right*, 249.

18. William Shaffir, "Disaffiliation: The Experiences of Haredi Jews," in *Leaving Religion and Religious Life*, ed. Mordekhai Bar-Lev and William Shaffir (Greenwich, CT: JAI Press, 1997), 208.

19. Moshe Krakowski, "Moderate Ultra-Orthodoxy: Complexity and Nuance in American Ultra-Orthodox Judaism," *Religion & Education* 39, no. 3 (2012): 262.

20. Heilman, *Sliding to the Right*, 86.

21. Fader, *Mitzvah Girls*, 14, 146.

22. Abot 6:2; Winston, *Unchosen*, 144; Davidman and Greil, "Characters in Search of a Script," 205–06; Roni Berger, "Leaving an Insular Community: The Case of Ultra Orthodox Jews," *Jewish Journal of Sociology* 56, no. 1/2 (2014): 76.

23. Dov Fischer, "Random Thoughts on Another Flawed Survey of Orthodox Jews," *Cross-Currents*, June 29, 2016, http://cross-currents.com/2016/06/29/random-thoughts-on-another-flawed-survey-of-orthodox-jews/.

24. Michal Marcus, "Night Light," *Mishpacha Magazine*, Oct. 13, 2016, http://www.mishpacha.com/Browse/Article/6568/Night-Light.

25. Winston, *Unchosen*, 37; David Lehmann and Batia Siebzehner, "Power, Boundaries and Institutions: Marriage in Ultra-Orthodox Judaism," *European Journal of Sociology/Archives Européennes de Sociologie* 50, no. 2 (2009): 288.

26. Berger, "Leaving an Insular Community," 85–86; Winston, *Unchosen*, 114; Annette Mahoney, "Religion and Conflict in Marital and Parent-Child Relationships," *Journal of Social Issues* 61, no. 4 (2005): 697.

27. Shaffir, "Disaffiliation: The Experiences of Haredi Jews," 209.

28. Berger, "Leaving an Insular Community," 89.

29. Davidman and Greil, "Characters in Search of a Script," 212–13.

30. Shaffir, "Disaffiliation: The Experiences of Haredi Jews," 216.

31. Shaffir, "Disaffiliation: The Experiences of Haredi Jews," 214.

32. Poll, *The Hasidic Community of Williamsburg*, 73; Heilman, *Sliding to the Right*, 86.

33. Berger, "Leaving an Insular Community," 84–85.

34. Berger, "Leaving an Insular Community," 85.

35. Viktor Emil Frankl, *The Feeling of Meaninglessness: A Challenge to Psychotherapy and Philosophy* (Milwaukee, WI: Marquette University Press, 2010), 41.

36. See, for instance, the trauma described by Shulem Deen, Leah Vincent, and Deborah Feldman in their memoirs.

37. Winston, *Unchosen*, 172; Berger, "Leaving an Insular Community," 77.

38. Shaffir, "Disaffiliation: The Experiences of Haredi Jews," 215.

39. Winston, *Unchosen*, 15; Davidman and Greil, "Characters in Search of a Script," 213.

40. Berger, "Leaving an Insular Community," 85–86.

41. Berger, "Leaving an Insular Community," 85, 87; Shaffir, "Disaffiliation: The Experiences of Haredi Jews," 216; Davidman and Greil, "Characters in Search of a Script," 206.

42. Shaffir, "Disaffiliation: The Experiences of Haredi Jews," 218.

43. Winston, *Unchosen*, 169.

44. Shaffir, "Disaffiliation: The Experiences of Haredi Jews," 219.

45. Berger, "Leaving an Insular Community," 85, 87; Shaffir, "Disaffiliation: The Experiences of Haredi Jews," 216; Davidman and Greil, "Characteeristics in Search of a Script," 206.

46. Winston, *Unchosen*, xxiii.

47. Alan Carr, "Michael White's Narrative Therapy," *Contemporary Family Therapy* 20, no. 4 (1998): 486.

48. Crystal L. Park and Carol Joyce Blumberg, "Disclosing Trauma Through Writing: Testing the Meaning-Making Hypothesis," *Cognitive Therapy and Research* 26, no. 5 (2002): 612–13.

49. Frisina, Pasquale G., Joan C. Borod, and Stephen J. Lepore. "A Meta-Analysis of the Effects of Written Emotional Disclosure on the Health Outcomes of Clinical Populations," *The Journal of Nervous and Mental Disease* 192, no. 9 (2004): 632.

References

Belcove-Shalin, Janet S., "Introduction: New World Hasidim." In *New World Hasidim: Ethnographic Studies of Hasidic Jews in America*, edited by Janet S. Belcove-Shalin, 1–30. New York: SUNY Press, 2012.

Berger, Joseph. *The pious ones: The World of Hasidim and Their Battles with America*. New York: Harper Collins, 2014.

Berger, Roni. "Leaving an Insular Community: The Case of Ultra Orthodox Jews." *Jewish Journal of Sociology* 56, no. 1/2 (2014): 75–98. https://doi.org/10.5750/jjsoc.v56i1/2.83.

Brodesser-Akner, Taffy. "The High Price of Leaving Ultra-Orthodox Life." *New York Times*. March 30, 2017. https://www.nytimes.com/2017/03/30/magazine/the-high-price-of-leaving-ultra-orthodox-life.html.

Carr, Alan. "Michael White's Narrative Therapy." *Contemporary Family Therapy* 20, no. 4 (1998): 485–503. https://doi.org/10.1023/A:1021680116584.

Davidman, Lynn, and Arthur L. Greil. "Characters in Search of a Script: The Exit Narratives of Formerly Ultra-Orthodox Jews." *Journal for the Scientific Study of Religion* 46, no. 2 (2007): 201–16. https://doi.org/10.1111/j.1468-5906.2007.00351.x.

Deen, Shulem. "Breaking Away: Former Hasidim Find Fulfillment in the Secular World." *Steinhardt Foundation*, Winter 2017, http://www.steinhardtfounda-tion.org/contact/winter_2017/winter_2017_deen.htm;

Erikson, Erik. "Eight Ages of Man." In *Klassiekers van de kinder-en jeugdpsychiatrie II*, edited by Fop Verheij, 258–75. Uitgeverij Van Gorcum, 2008.

Fader, Ayala. *Mitzvah Girls: Bringing up the Next Generation of Hasidic Jews in Brooklyn*. Princeton, NJ: Princeton University Press, 2009.

Fischer, Dov. "Random Thoughts on Another Flawed Survey of Orthodox Jews." *Cross-Currents*, June 29, 2016, http://cross-currents.com/2016/06/29/random-thoughts-on-another-flawed-survey-of-orthodox-jews/

Frankl, Viktor Emil. *The Feeling of Meaninglessness: A Challenge to Psychotherapy and Philosophy*. Milwaukee, WI: Marquette University Press, 2010.

Frisina, Pasquale G., Joan C. Borod, and Stephen J. Lepore. "A Meta-Analysis of the Effects of Written Emotional Disclosure on the Health Outcomes of Clinical Populations." *The Journal of Nervous and Mental Disease* 192, no. 9 (2004): 629–34. https://doi.org/10.1097%2F01.nmd.0000138317.30764.63.

Heilman, Samuel C. *Defenders of the Faith: Inside Ultra-Orthodox Jewry.* Berkeley: University of California Press, 1992.

Heilman, Samuel C. *Sliding to the Right: The Contest for the Future of American Jewish Orthodoxy.* Berkeley: University of California Press, 2006.

Heilman, Samuel C. "Who Are the Haredim?" In *Non-Equivalent: The State of Education in New York City's Hasidic Yeshivas,* edited by Naftuli Moster, 12–15. New York: Yaffed, 2017.

Heilman, Uriel. "An Unorthodox Journey." *Hadassah Magazine,* July 2017, http://www.hadassahmagazine.org/2017/07/17/an-unorthodox-journey/.

Kamen, Robert Mark. *Growing up Hasidic: Education and Socialization in the Bobover Hasidic Community.* New York: AMS Press, 1985.

Krakowski, Moshe. "Moderate Ultra-Orthodoxy: Complexity and Nuance in American Ultra-Orthodox Judaism." *Religion & Education* 39, no. 3 (2012): 257–83. https://doi.org/10.1080/15507394.2012.716343.

Lehmann, David, and Batia Siebzehner. "Power, Boundaries and Institutions: Marriage in Ultra-Orthodox Judaism." *European Journal of Sociology/Archives Européennes de Sociologie* 50, no. 2 (2009): 273–308. https://doi.org/10.1017/S0003975609990142.

Lovinger, Robert J. "Considering the Religious Dimension in Assessment and Treatment." In *Religion and the Clinical Practice of Psychology,* edited by E. P. Shafranske, 327–64. Washington, DC: American Psychological Association, 1996.

Mahoney, Annette. "Religion and Conflict in Marital and Parent-Child Relationships." *Journal of Social Issues* 61, no. 4 (2005): 689–706. https://doi.org/10.1111/j.1540-4560.2005.00427.x.

Marcus, Michal. "Night Light." *Mishpacha Magazine,* Oct. 13, 2016, http://www.mishpacha.com/Browse/Article/6568/Night-Light.

Park, Crystal L., and Carol Joyce Blumberg. "Disclosing Trauma through Writing: Testing the Meaning-Making Hypothesis." *Cognitive Therapy and Research* 26, no. 5 (2002): 597–616. https://doi.org/10.1023/A:1020353109229.

Partlan, Alisa. *Non-Equivalent: The State of Education in New York City's Hasidic Yeshivas,* edited by Naftuli Moster. New York: Yaffed, 2017.

Poll, Solomon. *The Hasidic Community of Williamsburg: A Study in the Sociology of Religion.* New York: Schocken Books, 1969.

Scholem, Gershom Gerhard. *Major Trends in Jewish Mysticism.* New York: Random House Digital, Inc., 1961.

Shaffir, William. "Boundaries and Self-Presentation among the Hasidim: A Study in Identity Maintenance." In *New World Hasidim: Ethnographic Studies of Hasidic Jews in America,* edited by Janet S. Belcove-Shalin, 31–68. Albany, NY: SUNY Press, 2012.

Shaffir, William. "Disaffiliation: The Experiences of Haredi Jews." In *Leaving Religion and Religious Life*, edited by Mordekhai Bar-Lev and William Shaffir, 205–28. Greenwich, CT: JAI Press, 1997.

"The Basics of the Upsherin." *Chabad*. Chabad-Lubavitch Media Center. http://www.chabad.org/library/article_cdo/aid/710724/jewish/The-Basics-of-the-Upsherin.htm.

Winston, Hella. *Unchosen: The Hidden Lives of Hasidic Rebels*. Boston, MA: Beacon Press, 2005.

Zaklikowski, Dovid. "The Night Preceding the Circumcision." *Chabad*. http://www.chabad.org/library/article_cdo/aid/145054/jewish/The-Night-Preceding-the-Circumcision.htm.

Off the Derech and into the Wild

Navigating Jewish American Identity

Ezra Cappell

> *But the path of the just is as the shining light, that shineth more and more unto the perfect day.* Rashi says: But the way of the righteous is like the light of dawn: which shines and illuminates from the first ray of dawn . . . until the day is perfect: Until midday, which is the brightest time of day.
>
> —Rashi's Commentary on *Proverbs* 4:18

> The greater part of what my neighbors call good I believe in my soul to be bad, and if I repent of anything, it is very likely to be my good behavior. What demon possessed me that I behaved so well?
>
> —Henry David Thoreau

> The pure righteous do not complain of the dark, but increase the light; they do not complain of evil, but increase justice; they do not complain of heresy, but increase faith; they do not complain of ignorance, but increase wisdom.
>
> —Rabbi Abraham Isaac Kook

I

So what can I tell you about Yonatan Ben? Yoni was small and scrawny; he was an asthmatic who would never be found without an inhaler in

379

the front pocket of his pants, but in yeshiva he would often lead morning prayers with a clear, pure voice. Along with the inhaler, Yoni kept an Ace comb in his pocket—it must have been a challenge to convince that mane of curly black hair to remain in place. Yoni had this endearing habit of scrunching up his nose in a failed effort to push his eyeglasses back up into their proper place. But every morning Yoni would wash *negel vasser*[1] with a plastic trough and two-handled cup that he kept under his bed just as our rebbe instructed. He would make the blessing to ritually cleanse his body, and get down on the floor of his bedroom, which was covered in an orange, shag carpet and complete as many push-ups as his weakened lungs and thin arms allowed.

Yoni loved to play stoop baseball and I was often his double-play partner in this elaborate game of skill, luck, and invention. Yoni would do his best Phil Rizzuto play-by-play as he imagined himself Willie Randolph scooping up a scorching grounder hit by Davey Lopes, step on an oil spot that was kind of shaped like second base and effortlessly throw across the street to first, brilliantly completing a double play thus preserving the Yankees' World-Series-clinching victory.

I'd often come to Yoni for Shabbos and when we'd get to his house on Friday afternoon, instead of immediately running to play ColecoVision (Yoni, who like me, had few of the expensive gadgets our wealthy classmates spoke of at recess in respectfully hushed tones, had somehow acquired this cutting-edge game, a system even more technologically advanced than Atari!) and before we'd run to the arcade on the boardwalk to play game after game of Ms. Pacman, we had cooking duties to perform. I would watch with incredulity as Yoni spent hours making the soup and frying the chicken for his family's Shabbos meals. Yoni would expertly prepare the *chulent* in a Crock Pot slow-cooker; he would add all the ingredients: first the beans, then perfectly cubed potatoes, expertly sliced carrots, and lastly a large cut of *flanken*[2] he had defrosted the night before. The next day on the holy Shabbos we would rise for morning prayers to the aroma of *chulent* filling the house. Only after the hours of Shabbos preparations were complete, would he put the leash on Snoopy, a tremendous mutt of a dog that Yoni smothered with hugs, and we would finally be free to run to the boardwalk, with Snoopy pulling us along to where Ms. Pacman, Asteroids, and the mighty Donkey Kong awaited.

Did I mention Yoni was the best student in our class? Perhaps the whole school. But why stop there? Yoni was my best friend and though he was often in and out of the hospital for debilitating asthma attacks that left him unable to breathe on his own for weeks at a time, between the hospital stays and the nebulizers, he willed himself into becoming one of the most gifted athletes I have ever seen grace a basketball court. He was a natural point guard with a sweet shot from about fifteen feet, Yoni's real talent was in spreading the ball around to each of his teammates, communicating with and encouraging the other players after a missed free-throw or lay-up. At the end of eighth grade when we graduated from our elementary school yeshiva in Long Beach, we each went off to different yeshiva high schools in the New York area: Yoni to Cedarhurst, while I went to Queens. Though we now played on crosstown rival teams, we still remained as close as ever and continued to spend many *Shabbosim*[3] together. I wasn't the least surprised when Yoni was named captain of his yeshiva high school basketball team and when we played a game against his school, I was proud to see Yoni standing at center court with a "C" ironed onto his uniform waiting to talk with the referees.

Yoni was a natural at whatever he put his mind to. Although Yoni's parents had divorced when he was very young, and though he rarely saw his father who lived in Mexico, and though his mother's second husband was not particularly kind to Yoni or well-suited to be a father, and though Yoni had lost a sister to a congenital heart defect, and though Yoni's twice-divorced mother suffered from numerous ailments that severely limited her mobility, leaving Yoni, the youngest member of the family to be "the man of the house," he never allowed these challenges to define him or even alter in the slightest his preternaturally upbeat, joyful demeanor. At his shul in Long Beach Yoni would leap from his bench to help any child who had lost his place in the prayer book. Unlike the rest of us yeshiva boys, fairly overflowing with anger and hostility at our troubled (if still mostly privileged) lives, I do not recall ever seeing Yoni commit a wantonly cruel act. Once, I even saw him squander an entire recess saving a fledgling pigeon in our schoolyard. Yoni carefully cut open a small milk carton to house the tiny, struggling creature. And when Yoni's enormous dog Snoopy (I think he was some sort of German shepard/Labrador retriever mutt), became too old to walk, I would hold the front door open as Yoni struggled to carry him out of the house and into the yard to, as Yoni said, "take care of his business." What can I say? I know it sounds invented, too impossibly good to be true, like I'm laying it all on way too thick. But I have to tell you: Yoni was simply a great kid.

So imagine how I felt at the conclusion of Yom Kippur 1987, not yet having broken the fast,[4] the phone was already ringing as I was about to walk in through the front door of my parents' house in Tannersville. On the line was my other best friend, Steve, from my Long Beach days. I remember the first thing Steve said to me was: "Are you sitting down?" I thought he was joking. People only said such ridiculous things like that on TV. But Steve repeated the request, saying he wouldn't continue if I didn't sit down. So I sat. I then heard Steve say: "I have some bad news. Yoni is dead."

II

The fire took place on the night of Yom Kippur. Right after they finished their pre-fast meal and before heading to shul, Yoni's mother would have placed her hands firmly upon her son's head and bestowed the traditional priestly blessing: "May God make you like Ephraim and Menashe. May God bless you and watch over you. May God shine His face toward you and show you favor. May God be favorably disposed toward you and grant you peace."

A few hours before the fire, Yoni had stood in shul at Bachurei Chemed, perhaps, as he often did, leading the prayers for the youth minyan, cantillating the Byzantine words of the many prayers, annulling all of his vows and the vows of his fellow congregants, devoutly praying that God inscribe him, his family, and friends in the book of life for one more year.

Shortly after learning of Yoni's death the entire congregation gathered together and as part of *musaf* they recited the *Unetaneh Tokef* prayer:

All mankind will pass before You like a flock of sheep. Like a shepherd pasturing his flock, making sheep pass under his staff, so shall You cause to pass, count, calculate, and consider the soul of all the living; and You shall apportion the destinies of all Your creatures and inscribe their verdict. On

Rosh Hashanah will be inscribed and on Yom Kippur will be sealed—how many will pass from the earth and how many will be created; who will live and who will die; who will die after a long life and who before his time; who by water and who by fire, who by sword and who by beast, who by famine and who by thirst, who by upheaval and who by plague, who by strangling and who by stoning. Who will rest and who will wander, who will live in harmony and who will be harried, who will enjoy tranquility and who will suffer, who will be impoverished and who will be enriched, who will be degraded and who will be exalted. But Repentance, Prayer, and Charity annul the severe Decree.[5]

The Long Beach firefighters found Yoni's body wedged behind his bedroom door; crouched in the corner by the doorframe directly beneath the plastic basketball hoop that had kept us entertained for so many years of play. He peacefully slept that evening as his room filled with smoke—Yoni must have woken into the worst asthma attack of his life. Disoriented, he would have crawled toward the door desperate to suck some clean air through the gap by the floor.

A few hours earlier, having completed her Sidney Sheldon novel, Yoni's mother was ready for sleep. Not wanting to violate the prohibition of "making or extinguishing a fire"[6] on the holiest day of the year, to darken the room for sleep, she threw a bath towel over her reading lamp.

And so on his last Shabbos, as everyone blissfully slept, resting for the most solemn and holy day of the Jewish year—a long, full day of repentance and prayers—instead of the usual smell of Yoni's pungent *chulent* stewing, his house, located just a few short yards from the Atlantic ocean, slowly filled with smoke. Before awaking to the flames, how many perfectly placed double-play balls did Yoni dream of, never to be turned?

III

The funeral was the next day. I was in Tannersville with my family for Yom Kippur in the Northern Catskill Mountains, and I almost didn't make it to the funeral. A freakish early fall snowstorm began just as I got the call from Steve (the record-setting blizzard would dump twenty-two inches of snow and wreak havoc across the entire Northeast), but as it turned out, it wasn't the storm that almost forced me to miss Yoni's funeral, it was my junior high school rebbe. My parents remained Upstate, closing the house for the year as Yom Kippur always signaled the end of the summer season in Tannersville; I had gotten a ride back to "the city" with family friends just before the storm made the mountain roads impassable.

Thankfully, my buddy Steve had arranged for our eighth-grade rebbe to pick me up after they finished morning prayers at his yeshiva nearby in Far Rockaway. The rabbi would take me, as well as Steve and a few other students from their school who had known Yoni, to the funeral in Hewlett. The funeral was set to begin at 11 a.m. and my former rebbe was supposed to pick me up by 10:15. I had never been to a funeral before and I stood outside our house on Cedarhurst Avenue waiting in the unusually cold early-fall weather, anxiously looking toward West Broadway and past the *shtiebel*[7] on the corner for the rabbi's station wagon. By 10:45 I was thinking: Should I take a taxi? How long would it take for a taxi to arrive? Maybe if I walked down the block to the train station I could find a taxi and I might convince the driver to quickly take me to Hewlett. Maybe if I told him my best friend just died, he'd understand. Only I didn't know the name of the funeral home. But how many funeral homes could there be in Hewlett? Yeah, that could be a problem. What about money? That could also be a problem. Surely the rabbi would come soon. He wouldn't want us to miss the funeral, would he? Just as I was about to go run to the train station, the rabbi pulled up to the curb. It was 11:25. As I stepped into the car I asked my former rebbe, "Why so late?" He replied: "It was *gevaldik*![8] After davening the whole school recited *k'pitel* after *k'pitel* of *Tehillim*[9] assuring Yonatan Ben's soul a smooth transition to *Olam Ha'bah*[10]!"

The funeral home was packed with hundreds of mourners. In addition to Yoni's entire school there were people from all over Long Island who had heard about the terrible tragedy and came to pay their respects. Everyone apparently came to the funeral, with the exception of the best friend of the deceased. We had to push ourselves into the room overflowing with people. The funeral was just concluding, but I could hear the unmistakable wail of Yoni's mother and I could see people (was that his older sister? was it Adam?) throwing themselves on the coffin as some of Yoni's friends struggled to carry the small coffin through the mob.

The next morning on the way to school, I remember all the kids on the van patting me on the back, trying to say something, trying to comfort me. A few hours later I was in *shiur* having *chavrusah*[11] with my Talmud study partner, when our rebbe called my name and, with a brusque hand-gesture, beckoned me to follow him into the hallway. The sing-song recitation of the ancient Aramaic still percussed in my ears as the classroom door closed behind me and I stood facing my rebbe in the hallway.

The rabbi began: "I've spoken to the rebbe of your friend, Yonatan Ben, *Zecher Tzaddik Livracha*.[12] I've been hearing all sorts of things about your friend, *nebuch*, who was *nifter*.[13] His rebbe told me he was a wonderful boy, a true *tzaddik*[14] in the making. His life was Torah . . . Well Torah and basketball. Correct?"

I nodded at this and added: "Yes rebbe, he was the best." If he was trying to make me feel better with this little speech, it certainly wasn't working too well yet.

"So, *mestumah*, had he lived, he might have been a true *gadol b'torah*[15] . . ." his voice trailed off, but I could see his eyes narrowing.

"So Cappell, can you tell me why *hakodesh boruch hu*,[16] who knows all and sees into the *neshamahs* (souls) of everyone, takes someone like Yonatan Ben away from us? Why? So young? So soon? Why would *hakodesh boruch hu* do such a thing?"

I didn't answer. For a moment I thought it was a rhetorical question. Apparently, by the way he was looking at me, I soon realized that my rebbe really expected an answer. He asked me again:

"Why Cappell? Why would *Hashem* do something like this?"

Looking down I noticed the nearly eighth-of-an-inch gap between the floor tiles in the hallway. What kind of shoddy job had they done when they "re-modeled" the school this past summer? I finally looked up and attempted an answer.

"Rebbe, I don't know. I wish I knew, but I don't."

Undeterred, my rebbe plowed ahead.

"Cappell (he always stressed the last syllable of my name, the annoying way he drew my name out made it sound like a shofar blow, almost like a willowy *tekiyah* of sorts: Ca-ppeeeelllll). You don't know? I'll tell you why *Hashem* does these things: because of Yonatan Ben's friends, that's why."

I just stared at the red beard moving up and down before me. The beard seemed to be getting closer to my face the longer the rabbi spoke.

"*Hashem* takes away such a person to send a message to his friends. Yonatan Ben was without sin, so why should he, *nebuch*, be taken so early?"

A long pause by my rebbe as he stared at me and I tried to stare through the floor.

"But what about you, Cappell? Did you *daven*[17] today with *kavaneh*,[18] or did you sleepwalk through the whole *davening*? When was the last time you reviewed our *sugya*?"[19]

The hallways seemed to be closing in, and I was surrounded by the red sea of my rebbe's beard; I was lost in a thicket of scraggly red hair.

"Cappell, there is still hope! The *gedolim*[20] teach us that it is never too late! As long as we are alive there is time to get back on the right *derech*, the *derech Hashem*, the path of the Torah. If you are still breathing, there is always time. We just *davened* two days ago on Yom Kippur in the *Unetaneh Tokef*: ". . . *but repentance, prayer and righteousness avert the severe decree . . .*"

"Severe decree," were the last words I heard—that, and my rebbe yelling from the top of the stairs: "Cappell, where are you going! Come back! We're not done yet!"

I didn't slow down to catch my breath until I was halfway down 108th Street and only a few short blocks from Queens Boulevard. I wasn't sure where I was headed, but my feet seemed to be taking me to a familiar place: Jacey's Billiards, where I proceeded to blow that day's pizza lunch money (and the next as well) for time on a table toward the back. I set up for Nine-ball. The year before, the old timers had patiently taught me how to power break so you could win a match on the opening shot. I shot game after game by myself. The few scattered regulars paid me no mind. After a while of listening to the break of the billiard balls, I managed to calm down; I felt my breathing begin to slow and the pounding in my head settled into a dull thud.

Yoni was dead. My rebbe thinks it's my fault for not *davening* hard enough, for not learning enough *Gemarah*. His words: "What path are you on, Cappell?" haunted me. I kept seeing that red beard. But what was the *derech Hashem*, the path of God that my rebbe spoke of? How would I ever find it? I was still far too angry and confused, raw and overwrought, to go back to school. What path was I traveling on? I sort of knew it wasn't really my fault Yoni had died. Didn't I? But what path did I want to be on? I had no clue.

I shot one more game before collecting the billiard balls. I paid Jacey, who nodded at me, and then I quickly found myself alone again on Queens Boulevard. Now what? What *derech* would I take? My grandparents lived a few blocks from here down Yellowstone and I thought about walking to their house, but then I figured they'd probably be out shopping for some sale items at King Kullen or visiting with friends. Instead, I began the slow walk back to school where I knew the rest of my day as a yeshiva student awaited. I knew one thing for certain: I would never play stoopball beside the boardwalk with Yoni again. I was sixteen years old.

IV

This question of just what *derech* I would pursue, was, for a while at least, quelled during a year of focused study at a seminary in Jerusalem, where I, along with thousands of other yeshiva high school graduates from around the United States, enrolled before starting my college education. During the last months of the 1980s after a long day of studying Talmud, I would often head into town toward Ben Yehuda Street to meet up at Apple Pizza with friends from various Jewish day schools. Once we made it into town, in addition to the pizza, we sometimes availed ourselves of the seemingly nonexistent minimum drinking age in Israel (after all, if you could be trusted to carry an Uzi submachine gun on public transportation, perhaps you could also be trusted to drink a beer or two, or so our theory went), and we would enjoy a quick Goldstar or Maccabee beer.

To not be *mivatel Torah*[21] along the way—wasting time that might otherwise be productively used studying the Torah—I would bring some *sefer* or holy text along with me. For these purposes, our large folio editions of the Babylonian Talmud would not work, for unlike *The New York Times*, which I would later learn to artfully fold neatly into columns while occupying approximately eighteen inches of space on a packed early-morning New York City subway car, our large folio-sized *Gemarahs* were way too large for perusing on an Israeli bus. Choosing texts entirely for their portability, I quickly discovered in our yeshiva library pocket editions of Jewish mystical classics. On these nightly bus trips into town, I made my way through all sorts of hagiographies of *chassidic* leaders, miracle men, the Baal Shem Tov, and Rabbi Dov Ber of Mezeritch; from there I moved on to Rabbi Yisroel Salanter and the *Mussar*[22] movement. At some point I even found a book containing several chapters and stories concerning my own familial *chassidic* lineage: Rabbis Yisrael Taub and Shaul Yedidya Elazar Taub, the Modzitzer Rebbes, whose Hebrew names I carried with me. The first Modzitzer was the leading song-maker of Eastern European Jewry, the author of a famous commentary on the Hebrew Bible, and my great-great-grandfather. There were many other volumes I eagerly read, but unfortunately I soon exhausted the meager supply of non-folio-sized books in our small yeshiva library.

With this introduction, I quickly gravitated toward the more weighty texts of Jewish Gnosticism and mystical knowledge. In an old, used English bookstore off Jaffa street, I found a beat-up copy of Gershom Scholem's *Major Trends in Jewish Mysticism*; studying that difficult text brought me full circle back to a book I had already been exposed to in yeshiva high school in Queens: *Mesillat Yesharim, the Path of the Just,* by Rabbi Moshe Chaim Luzzatto, otherwise known by his acronym, the Ramchal. *Mesillat Yesharim* is the Ramchal's most widely read text and, as I was daily reminded by my rebbes in yeshiva, its aim was to perfect the character and personality of all who read its contents. The general notion of most of my high school *rebbeim* was that I wasn't applying myself too diligently to the Ramchal's teachings: my character was still far from perfect.

The Ramchal's book is built upon a *Beraita* from the *Babylonian Talmud, Avodah Zarah 20b:*

> From here Rabbi Pineḥas ben Ya'ir would say: Torah study leads to care in the performance of mitzvot. Care in the performance of mitzvot leads to diligence in their observance. Diligence leads to cleanliness of the soul. Cleanliness of the soul leads to abstention from all evil. Abstention from evil leads to purity and the elimination of all base desires. Purity leads to piety. Piety leads to humility. Humility leads to fear of sin. Fear of sin leads to holiness. Holiness leads to the Divine Spirit. The Divine Spirit leads to the resurrection of the dead.[23]

In *Mesillat Yesharim,* the Ramchal systematically goes through each of these enumerated steps showing his readers how they may acquire these traits toward perfection, which constitutes "the path of the just."

One night, after having gone into town, I was taking my usual bus back to my yeshiva and all the while immersed in Luzzatto's text. Enthralled by the Ramchal's words (the Maccabee beer and the very late hour didn't help either) I completely missed my stop and emerged from the bus in the middle of Mea Shearim; it would be a long walk back to my yeshiva through this ultra-Orthodox community. Standing on the street in Mea Shearim, I gathered my thoughts to plan the most direct path back to my yeshiva. I looked around and it seemed as if every *chassid* that passed me on the street suspiciously eyed my un-peyosed cheeks and my non-chassidic garb. As I attempted to plot my *derech*, my path, the humor and irony of getting lost in a text called *The Path of the Just* causing me to stumble so far afield of my yeshiva, was not entirely lost on me, even at the green age of eighteen.

Many years have passed since that wayward bus trip through Jerusalem, and though I haven't thought of myself as a yeshiva student in decades (and though my character still needs perfecting), my old, well-traveled copy of *Mesillat Yesharim* is still with me, patiently perched on my living-room bookshelf. Its moment of utility recently arrived when I had occasion to compose a *d'var Torah* with my son, and I went in search of that small volume. I located the book—right between my old trusty *Jastrow's Dictionary* and a full monogrammed set of *Mishnah Berurah*. I picked up the dog-eared volume, caressed its cover, and much like Proust's "petites madeleines," the memory of an evening lost in Mea Shearim came flooding back. I laughed at the image of my younger self, so distraught at the prospect of being late for *davening*. How earnest and devout my faith was, how important all the rituals seemed—as if each commandment were a matter of life and death. Before even opening my *Messilat Yesharim* and reading its contents with my son, I recalled my desperation that evening in Mea Shearim, my need to find the right *derech*, the one path that would lead me back to my yeshiva.

V

This story of finding "one's path," or perhaps as the Ramchal intended it, the "correct" path, seems to be as important to me today as it was nearly thirty years ago, only for quite different reasons. Recently I have been immersing myself in many Jewish texts concerned with the "derech," but these texts are far different from the holy texts I was taught in yeshiva: I am referring to the wave of recent "OTD" or Off the Derech memoirs recently published. These books might collectively constitute a new subgenre of contemporary Jewish-American literature. Most of these memoirs have been published by formerly observant people chronicling their struggles at establishing productive, meaningful lives outside of their ultra-Orthodox birth communities. Early on in many of these narratives the protagonist will suffer some sort of spiritual shock or crisis of faith that leads the person through a series of small rebellions and transgressions against the Torah and its *taryag mitzvoth* (613 commandments). Usually these rebellions involve eating some form of non-kosher food, which in an ironic reversal of the Ramchal's path toward perfection, inevitably leads the protagonist to violate ever more prohibitions. From the perspective of their ultra-Orthodox birth communities, these memoirists ultimately find themselves "Off the Derech"—literally, "off the path,"—the one true path of Torah.

One of these recent OTD memoirs is Shalom Auslander's, *Foreskin's Lament*. At the approximate midpoint of Auslander's memoir he violates the laws of Shabbos for the first time by traveling to the Spring Valley Mall and eating non-kosher food. Afterwards Auslander is in a taxi heading back towards his observant family in Monsey, New York, and he is terrified that God will strike him down in retribution for his many sins:

> [W]e swerved back into our lane just moments before colliding head-on with a blue pick-up. I wondered how many Sabbaths my driver had violated, and why God hadn't killed him yet, and if he'd violate Sabbath again next weekend and if I would, too, when I suddenly remembered Rabbi Blowfield saying the Sages saying that not only is violating the Sabbath like violating all 613 commandments, but that observing the Sabbath is like observing all 613 commandments, and then it hit me: If I violated Sabbath this weekend but observed it next weekend, transgressional speaking, wouldn't I pretty much break even?[24]

Through this passage, with its mathematical formulations of commandments and transgressions, Auslander strongly suggests the need for a reckoning and revitalization within the Orthodox and ultra-Orthodox world. It is this rigid and unforgiving world of Orthodoxy that Auslander, like so many other contemporary OTD memoirists, feels the need to break away from and leave behind. Which brings us to an overwhelming question: how did we get here?

VI

To answer that previous question we'll need to go back nearly 2,000 years to ancient Babylonia:

> We learned in our Mishnah: And furthermore, Rabbi Eliezer said: One may even cut down trees to prepare charcoal for the purpose of circumcision on Shabbat. With regard to this issue, the Sages taught in a *baraita*: In the locale of Rabbi Eliezer, where they would follow his ruling, they would even cut down trees on Shabbat to prepare charcoal from it in order to fashion iron tools with which to circumcise a child on Shabbat. On a related note, the *baraita* relates: In the locale of Rabbi Yosei HaGelili they would eat poultry meat in milk, as Rabbi Yosei HaGelili held that the prohibition of meat in milk does not include poultry.
>
> The Gemara relates: Levi happened to come to the house of Yosef the hunter. They served him the head of a peacock [*tavsa*] in milk and he did not eat. When Levi came before Rabbi Yehuda HaNasi, the latter said to him: Why did you not excommunicate these people who eat poultry in milk, contrary to the decree of the Sages? Levi said to him: It was in the locale of Rabbi Yehuda ben Beteira, and I said: Perhaps he taught them that the *halakha* is in accordance with the opinion of Rabbi Yosei HaGelili, who permits the eating of poultry meat in milk. Given the possibility that their rabbi rules that it is permitted, I cannot come and prohibit it, and I certainly cannot excommunicate them for it.[25]

There is much in this Talmudic passage that would seem surprising, perhaps even heretical, to a student of contemporary Jewish Orthodoxy. At a time when many Orthodox American rabbis have been blacklisted[26] by the Israeli rabbinate on trumped up charges of heresy and "problem conversions," here is a Talmud passage that clearly regards halacha[27] as a living structure, one capable of embracing a multiplicity of perspectives and practices. Instead of excommunicating Jewish people for alternate viewpoints, this passage, indeed much of the ancient Babylonian Talmud, embraces difference, argument, and open debate. Witness Levi's viewpoint that engenders an overarching respect for alternate halachic interpretations and perspectives on kashrut and Shabbos.

The contemporary ultra-Orthodox perspective is quite different, bearing little resemblance to the apparent respectful restraint of the ancient rabbis. In 1997 Rabbi Avi Weiss published an essay titled, *Open Orthodoxy! A Modern Orthodox Rabbi's Creed*. In his essay, Rabbi Weiss declares a more "open and inclusive" form of Orthodoxy in America. His creed places an "emphasis on halacha as well as a broad concern for all Jews, intellectual openness, a spiritual dimension, and a more expansive role for women."[28] Yet ever since Weiss's essay was published the ultra[29]-Orthodox movement has been attacking and denigrating this far more progressive form of Jewish Orthodoxy.

As we can discern from the Talmudic passage above, Rabbi Weiss's open and inclusive form of Orthodox Judaism isn't so much a break from Jewish tradition, instead it signals a homecoming—a return to a Judaism that embraces multiple perspectives and validates a difference of beliefs and experiences. Open Orthodoxy seems more closely aligned with the Judaism glimpsed in the Mishnah or on the folio pages of the Babylonian Talmud than on the holy streets of Brooklyn or Monsey.

Orthodoxy has traveled a straightened path from Levi's statement in the Babylonian Talmud: "Given the possibility that their rabbi rules that it is permitted, I cannot come and prohibit it, and I certainly cannot excommunicate them for it," to this recent edict from the Council of Torah Sages: "Internet usage should by all means be avoided . . . children should not be given Internet access. For those who must have Internet access . . . it is assur [prohibited] to have Internet access without an effective filter."[30] To publicize their prohibition in 2012, the council rented out and filled the vast Citi Field in New York City,[31] to hold a community-wide rally against the perils of the Internet and the heresy it spreads. Oftentimes community members who do not adhere to every edict and stricture of their ultra-Orthodox rabbinate, are branded heretics and are ultimately excommunicated from the only home and community they have ever known. Once branded, these individuals immediately become pariahs and are ostracized even by their own families.

Many of the OTD narratives feature brave protagonists forced out of their communities, others have willingly left, but these memoirists are turning their experiences both as insiders and outsiders of the ultra-Orthodox community into the subject of their writing and research. Far from remaining passive victims of the injustices many of them have faced, OTD writers have found productive ways to combat the hatred and intolerance they were shown by their descent communities, and in so doing they forge their own "consent" communities of like-minded individuals. Many of these writers shine an unwelcome light on the unjust practices and customs of the cloistered communities of their birth.

So how did we get from a respectful understanding of alternate perspectives on halacha to the disdain for modernity that filled Citi Field in that rally against the Internet? We might get some answers to this question by examining a different passage from the Babylonian Talmud, Tractate *Sanhedrin* 99a, and look toward Maimonides,[32] whose interpretation of this passage might help us understand how Orthodoxy has embraced such an intolerant worldview.

> The Mishnah teaches that those who have no share in the World-to-Come include: And one who says: The Torah did not originate from Heaven. The Sages taught in a *baraita* that with regard to the verse: "Because he has despised the word of the Lord and has breached His commandment; that soul shall be excised; his iniquity shall be upon him" (Numbers 15:31), this is a reference to one who says: "The Torah did not originate from Heaven." Alternatively, one can explain: "Because he has despised the word of the Lord;" this is a reference to an *epikoros*, who treats the word of God with contempt. Alternatively, one can explain: "Because he has despised the word of the Lord;" this is a reference to one who interprets the Torah inappropriately. "And has breached His commandment;" this is a reference to one who breaches the covenant of flesh, who refuses to circumcise his foreskin. "Shall be excised [*hikkaret tikkaret*];" "*hikkaret*" refers to being excised in this world, and "*tikkaret*" refers to being excised from the World-to-Come. From here Rabbi Elazar HaModa'i says: With regard to one who desecrates consecrated items, e.g., intentionally rendering them impure; and one who treats the intermediate days of the Festivals with contempt; and

one who breaches the covenant of Abraham our forefather; and one who reveals aspects in the Torah that are not in accordance with *halakha*; and one who humiliates another in public, even if he has to his credit Torah study and good deeds, he has no share in the World-to-Come.[33]

This Talmudic passage discusses several broad categories for exclusion from the world to come, yet the key in understanding the ways that normative Orthodox religious practice has developed is in the methodology of how this passage (and thousands of other passages) have been interpreted. To understand how halacha developed over many centuries we will turn to Maimonides's interpretation of this section from the Talmud.

For the past eight centuries we have been using the Rambam as our main source for halacha. Let's take a look at the Rambam's *Hilchot Teshuvah*, one of the fourteen volumes of his classic work *Mishneh Torah*, in which Maimonides includes among the categories of those who have no portion in the world to come: "nonbelievers, heretics, those who deny Torah . . . those who cause the many to sin, and those who depart from the ways of the community." The Rambam continues:

One who secedes from the paths of the congregation, although he committed no transgressions, but remains separated from the congregation of Israel, observes no commandments together with them, does not include himself in their troubles, nor afflicts himself on their fast-days, but follows his own path as the rest of the people of the land, acting as if he was not one of them, he has no share in the World to Come. One who commits transgressions high-handedly like Jehoiakim, whether his acts were against minor or against major commandments, he has no share in the World to Come. Verily, he is one of whom it is said: "He reveals a face in the Torah not according to law," seeing that he hardened his forehead, exposed his face and is not ashamed to disobey the Torah.[34]

So the Rambam teaches that one who secedes from the paths of the community, and here is the kicker: even if he committed no sin, forfeits his share in the world to come. Even in my supposedly "modern" Orthodox yeshiva, I was taught by my *rebbeim*[35] that God is so wonderful and fair-minded that he will only punish a person for *committing* an evil deed and not just for *thinking* about an evil deed. Conversely, we were taught that this benevolent and all-knowing God will reward a person even for only having thoughts of good deeds, regardless of whether the person follows through and actually fulfills the *mitzvah*, the good deed.

Yet in this passage, Maimonides rules that separating oneself out from the community and "following your own path," even without committing any sin, is worthy of permanent banishment from the eternal paradise of the world to come. This ruling, made by Maimonides in Egypt over eight centuries ago, continues to profoundly shape the lives of many men and women in twenty-first century America and beyond. One of the more disturbing aspects of this ruling is its vague openendedness. What actually constitutes "following one's own path"? True, the Rambam lists four examples:

a) observes no commandments together with them,

b) does not include himself in their troubles,

c) nor afflicts himself on their fast-days,

d) but follows his own path as the rest of the people of the land, acting as if he was not one of them

Each of these categories is completely open to rabbinic interpretation. How can a rabbinic authority be sure that a person observes absolutely "no commandments with his community"? With 613 commandments in the Torah, has such a person truly not observed any of them with his community?

In the next two categories, what does the Rambam mean by "their troubles" and "their fast days"? Once again these are rather vague designations. How, for instance, does the Rambam define this community? Which brings us to the last category the Rambam mentions, which is perhaps the most nebulous of them all: "he follows his own path." This open-endedness wouldn't be so disturbing if it followed a general pattern in Maimonides's thinking and writing style. Yet throughout the many volumes of the *Mishneh Torah*, the opposite is true: the Rambam is almost always quite explicit about what constitutes a transgression and writes with great precision and clarity about what constitutes a prohibition.

For example, in the same section, while discussing who is considered an atheist, Rambam give his readers five distinct categories:

> There are five categories of atheists; (1) he who says that there is no God and no Omnipotence; (2) he who says that there is an Omnipotence but that there are two or more such; (3) he who says that there is One Lord; but that He is corporeal and has a form; (4) likewise one who says that He alone is not the First Cause and Creator of all; (5) likewise he who worships a star, or planet, or any other as a mediator between him and the Lord of the universe; every one of these five is an atheist.[36]

So given the precision of his writing elsewhere, why is the Rambam so vague and open-ended in this key category of people who are barred entry into the never-ending, paradisiacal community of *Olam Ha'bah*, the World to Come? More importantly, why should this ancient ruling matter to so many men and women born into ultra-Orthodox communities around the world? My own experience in yeshiva (as well as the experiences of several OTD memoirists) might help reveal the full effect of the Rambam's ancient ruling concerning "following one's own path."

But before we get to those experiences we should mention that not every Torah scholar agrees with the Rambam's ideas concerning who is considered an atheist. In his illuminating book *Must a Jew Believe Anything?*, Menachem Kellner quotes the RAAVID's (R. Abraham ben David of Posquieres) attack on the Rambam, quoting the Raavid as saying that many "greater and better" scholars disagreed with the Rambam.[37] Here is the Raavid's complete gloss on the Rambam's passage from the *Mishneh Torah*:

> Hasagot HaRaavad: **He who says that there is One Lord but that He is corporeal and has a form.** Why does he call such one an atheist? Many greater and better than he followed this opinion according to what they saw in phrases, and more particularly in the texts of the Agadot (legends of the Talmud) which misdirect opinions.[38]

Here, we can clearly see that not all the rabbinic authorities agreed with Maimonides's conception of who is a heretic. The Raavid, a non-

Aristotelian thinker, rejects the Rambam's categorization. Although the Rambam was not *the* final word on this concept—yet his is the *only* word we follow today. The Rambam's main effort in the *Mishneh Torah*, and in many of his other commentaries as well, was in codifying halacha, simplifying it into a system of belief. In doing so the Rambam strips out the many disagreements and divergent opinions that is the lifeblood of the Babylonian Talmud. In doing so, perhaps he was inadvertently setting the stage for where ultra-Orthodox Judaism situates itself today centuries later, where even the slightest deviation from what is considered the one and only *derech* is often met with a pitiless decree of banishment.

Maimonides ends his commentary on the Mishnah, "Helek, Sanhedrin, Chapter Ten," with a systematic codification of his famous creed:[39] the thirteen principles of faith. In yeshiva we were taught to recite these fundamental beliefs daily as part of our morning prayers. Yet concerning these rather dogmatic principles of faith, in his introductory remarks on Maimonides's interpretation of Sanhedrin Chapter X, Isadore Twersky says:

> The systematic formulation of a specific number of basic principles of belief provided the impetus for the creation of an extensive literature on dogma and triggered a long, sometimes acrimonious debate concerning the role of dogma in Judaism"[40]

When one considers Maimonides's words at the conclusion of the chapter, it is not difficult to understand why this debate became acrimonious (and why in yeshiva we were all forced to daily recite Maimonides's Thirteen Principles of Faith):

> When a man believes all of these fundamental principles and his faith is thus clarified, he is then part of that "Israel" whom we are to love, pity, and treat, as God commanded, with love and fellowship. Even if a Jew was to commit every possible sin, out of lust or mastery by his lower nature, he will be punished for his sins but will still have a share in the world to come. He is "one of the sinners in Israel." But if a man gives up any of these fundamental principles, he has removed himself from the Jewish community. He is an atheist, a heretic, an unbeliever who "cuts among the plantings." *We are commanded to hate him and to destroy him* (italics mine)"[41]

How different this Orthodox Judaism is from Rabbi Avi Weiss's conceptual framework for an Open Judaism and how diminished a worldview this seems compared to the lively give and take, debate and tolerance seen in that earlier passage from the Babylonian Talmud? One can draw a direct line from Maimonides's directive to "hate the heretic" and the cruel judgments of so many contemporary *batei din* (religious courts) that have excommunicated so many people deeming them "off the derech" and no longer a part of the community.

VII

> I wasn't the first one to be expelled from our village, though I'd never known any of the others. I'd only heard talk of them, hushed reminiscences of ancient episodes in the history of our half-century-old village, tales of various subversives who sought to destroy our fragile unity. The group of Belzers who tried to form their own prayer group, the young man rumored to have studied the books of the Breslovers, even the rebbe's own brother-in-law, accused of fomenting sedition against the rebbe.
>
> But I was the first to be expelled for heresy.[42]

So begins Shulem Deen's memoir, *All Who Go Do Not Return*, which chronicles his life after being excommunicated from his ultra-Orthodox community. As we saw in Maimonides's ruling, if one follows "one's own path as the rest of the people of the land," you will be labeled a heretic. For many of the OTD memoirists, a similar accounting takes place before they too are banished from the only community they have ever known. In Leah Vincent's memoir: *Cut Me Loose* (2014) we glimpse a similar interaction where her seemingly "petty transgressions"[43] are subsumed under the over-arching and all-encompassing vague category of "heresy"—of following one's own path. Among Vincent's crimes against the Torah are communicating with a boy by sending him an innocent letter, and purchasing a sweater deemed by her mother to not be *tznius*,[44] or modest. At first Vincent is only cut off financially, but once she has been branded a heretic, she is almost completely abandoned by her family—her father refuses to even speak to her. After her mother discovers she has purchased an immodest sweater and therefore in the eyes of her mother (and following the Rambam's ruling), she is attempting "to follow her own path as the rest of the people of the land," Vincent's mother calls to confront her daughter about the sweater: ". . . you keep on messing up and hurting people. Disappointing people."[45] Her mother tells Vincent she will "have to figure out how to get by on [her] own."[46]

In his recent memoir, *Why Not Say What Happened: A Sentimental Education*, Morris Dickstein recounts his "heresy," which was the innocent abridgment of the weekly portion of Torah reading, one of his responsibilities as a summer employee of an Orthodox hotel in the Catskills. Depending on the vagaries of the Jewish lunar calendar, occasionally a double portion of Torah reading will be required during the Sabbath prayers. On one such weekend, Dickstein, who was the official *baal koreh* or "Torah reader" for the summer congregation, only had time to prepare the first half of the double portion. Instead of showing some level of understanding or *rachmones*, the community is outraged at Dickstein's attempt to shorten the weekly portion to be read and thoroughly embarrasses him in public, which is a far worse sin than not fully preparing the Torah reading. The Talmud teaches that "one who humiliates another in public has no share in the World-to-Come."[47] This episode leads to Dickstein's growing awareness of the "punctilio of ritual, the unbending Orthodox need to dot every *i*."[48] This terrible scene becomes a watershed moment for the young Dickstein, who is basically banished from this unyielding Orthodox community. As time passes, the Orthodox community's focus on the minutia of halacha pushes Dickstein further and further away from the world of his youth and leads him firmly toward the intellectual world of secular culture and academia. Dickstein writes: "I grew fiercely alienated from such a sterile formalism unconnected to actual experience."[49] In discussing the barren landscape of his Talmudic classes, Dickstein notes: "We were directed solely to halacha, the legal side of the Talmud, while ignoring the aggadah, the tales, legends, and reports of everyday life that might have engaged us more, besides giving us some sense of the actual world, the lives of Jews in their Babylonian exile, where these arguments unfolded."[50]

In the eyes of Orthodox communal authorities each of these small transgressions, be it an immodest sweater, a change in the Torah reading, speaking to another community member about going to college, are all subsumed under the overarching Maimonidean heretical category of "following your own path." Leah Vincent perfectly encapsulates the predicament of these memoirists: "I felt like I was caught in a garish nightmare, my parents getting stricter and stricter, my petty transgressions ballooning into terrifying sins."[51]

There has been a vast array of research using the recently published Pew Research Center's Study of Jewish Americans, which shows that there has been a demographic explosion in Orthodox life and communities in America. Clearly Orthodox life is growing in North America at unprecedented levels. As Stephen Cohen sums up in a recent article: "In 40 years, far fewer Jews will identify as Conservative and Reform, and far more will identify as Orthodox."[52]

Yet there lurks in the shadows a disturbing counternarrative to all these positive data points; there is an often-ignored underside to this development in the wake of the Shoah as so many devastated Chassidic and ultra-Orthodox communities have repopulated themselves. While American freedoms and opportunities have provided the perfect breeding ground for these communities to flourish and grow, it has also led to a concurrent increase in the growing ranks of the disaffected and those who either choose to leave or are forced to leave their ultra-Orthodox enclave.

As Shulem Deen makes clear in his memoir, this leave-taking is sometimes a conscious choice by individuals who no longer feel they belong to a deeply religious community, whereas just as often the individuals are forced out by their communities for having subversive thoughts or for generally not conforming to the many strictures and customs of the community. In Shulem Deen's case he was forced out by a *beis din*.[53] Deen acknowledges that since he no longer adhered to the core beliefs and practices of his New Square community in Orange County, New York, home to the Skverer Chasidim, perhaps the *beis din* was right and it was time for him to leave: "But it was just as well. I no longer belonged here, in this village, in this community, among these people. It would not be easy, but this was bound to happen. It was time to go."[54]

At first Deen accepts his banishment from New Square since he knows he will still be with his family, even if they will all be living together in a nearby town and not in the community he has called home for his entire adult life. But this feeling of acquiescence at the decision of the *beis din* morphs into utter horror when those same community leaders make certain that Deen will be separated, not just from the larger Skverer community, but also from the people he cares most deeply about: his children. These Skverer leaders exert tremendous pressure within the community and within the family court system to make certain that Deen is systematically barred from spending time with his children. Deen's harrowing story, detailed in his memoir, is one of the many stories of OTD people who are labeled or adopt the label of *Off the Derech*—being off the path of their ultra-Orthodox communities.

In his introduction to *Mesillat Yesharim*, the Ramchal writes that the whole purpose of his book is to teach his readers to conform all of their "traits and . . . actions to what is just and ethical." He concludes his introduction with the following words:

> May God be with our aspirations and keep our feet from stumbling, and may there be fulfilled in us the supplication of the Psalmist, beloved of his God (Psalms 86:11), "Teach me, O God, Your ways; I shall walk in Your truth. Make one my heart to fear Your Name." Amen, so may be His will.[55]

There is certainly something unjust and unethical about the cruel treatment Shulem Deen (as well as the other OTD memoirists we have been discussing) receives from his ultra-Orthodox community. Yet for me that evening so many years ago when I perceived myself to be a member in good standing of a Torah community, the many communal strictures, prohibitions, and requirements all made perfect sense to me. Despite being lost in Mea Shearim, my path seemed neatly laid out before me. Sunrise was only a few hours away and soon morning prayers would begin. Knowing I could not be late to *shacharis*, I would seek the straightest path back to the *bais medrash* doors so that I might continue to "walk in God's truth." After all, the Ramchal does not give his readers options: his book is titled *Mesillat Yesharim*, the *path* of the just, not *Messilot Yesharim*, the *paths* of the just. There is only one correct path—every other path is a clear deviation from God's way.

So where does this leave me today? That day in Jerusalem so many years ago I did make it back to my Yeshiva in time for morning prayers. But what about now? What path, what *derech*, am I on today?

VIII

These days, as a professor of literature, I am more powerfully drawn to a writer like the Israeli poet Yehuda Amichai, than the Ramchal and his philosophy of the one, true path toward righteousness and God. Amichai's poetry is suffused with the complexity and complications of the modern Jewish experience; he offers his readers the gift and the burden of choice: to those open to modernity there are numerous paths to take—each with its own set of consequences and outcomes. His poem "Through Two Points Only a Straight Line Can Pass: Theorem in Geometry," expresses the straitened lives of a "one path" philosophy:

A planet once got married to a star,
and inside, voices talked of future war.
I only know what I was told in class:
through two points only one straight line can pass.

A stray dog chased us down an empty street.
I threw a stone; the dog would not retreat.
The king of Babel stooped to eating grass.
Through two points only one straight line can pass.

Your small sob is enough for many pains,
as locomotive power can pull long trains.
When will we step inside the looking-glass?
Through two points only one straight line can pass.

At times I stands apart, at times it rhymes
with you, at times we's singular, at times
plural, at times I don't know what. Alas,
through two points only one straight line can pass.

Our life of joy turns to a life of tears,
our life eternal to a life of years.
Our life of gold became a life of brass.
Through two points only one straight line can pass[56]

I see my own experience in yeshiva reflected in the many OTD memoirs I have been reading, Euclidean geometry pushed to its limits: straight lines and new squares inevitably lead to constrained, boxed-in lives. Isn't it time Orthodoxy moved from a simple geometric formulation of religious observance toward a topological approach to Jewish life? Just because Orthodox Judaism operates today from a medieval Maimonidean perspective, it does not necessarily have to continue on the same *derech*. If the late twentieth century advances in civil and women's rights movements have taught us anything, it is that the future does not have to be a carbon copy of the past. Perhaps eight centuries of hating heretics are enough. After all, as Amichai reminds us, there are many paths, and not just one, which we can each take to lead a vibrant and meaningful Jewish life in the contemporary world. And so to paraphrase one of Maimonides's thirteen attributes of faith: *Ani ma'amim beeumah shlemah*, I believe with a perfect faith in a more forgiving place, an Orthodox Jewish life where manifold worlds of understanding and practices, where different paths toward righteousness are not just tolerated but celebrated.

IX

At the end of each week, at *shalosh seudos*, the traditional third meal of the Sabbath, my family would gather round the dining room table and sing songs and tell stories about my grandfather's grandfather, Reb Yisroel, the first Modzitzer Rebbe. The Modzitzer's *niggunim* (musical compositions), are to this day sung in synagogues around the world. My grandfather told me about how, when he was a little boy in Poland, he would sit in *his* grandfather's lap while the great rebbe composed a new *niggun*,[57] a new tune to honor each Shabbos. At another family *shalosh sheudos*, my grandfather told me the following story:

> Rabbi Azriel David Fastag, was a Hasid of the Modzitzer Rebbe, and Reb Fastag, like many of the chassidim were composers of music. They would come from all over Poland to stay for Shabbos with the rebbe and they would share their *niggunim* with the second Modzitzer Rebbe, Rabbi Shaul Yedidya Elazar. Reb Fastag was in a ghetto that had been set up by the Nazis and now he was being transported by cattle car to the extermination camp of Treblinka. While in the cattle car and under the most difficult circumstances imaginable, much like the previous Modzitzer Rebbe in his darkest hour, he began to compose a

niggun. A tune. Reb Fastag was thinking about the Rambam's *Thirteen Principles of Faith*, particularly the twelfth principle: "*Ani Ma'amin b'Emuna Sheleima, b'vias HaMoshiach; v'af al pi she'yismamaya, im kol zeh, achakeh lo b'chol yom she'yavo,* I believe with perfect faith in the coming of the *Moshiach*; and even though he may tarry, nevertheless, I wait each day for his arrival." Reb Fastag's tune was set to this line. Geshuri writes about this story in his book about *chassidishe* music and he says that everyone in the cattle car starting to sing this *d'veykus niggun*, which gave them the strength to face the evil of the Nazis. Geshuri writes that Reb Fastag was only sad that his rebbe, the Modzitzer, would never learn of this tune. With the help of a Japanese official[58] the rebbe had already miraculously escaped to Shanghai, China, before coming to New York and then *Eretz Yisroel*. Reb Fastag cried out in the cattle car that he would give his place in *oylem habah* (the world to come) to anyone who would share his *niggun* with the Modzitzer Rebbe. Two Modzitzer chassidim who were with Reb Fastag in the cattle car decided to make an escape and leapt from the moving train. One of them died immediately from the fall, but the other chassid survived. This chassid did in fact bring this *niggun* to the rebbe, who said of Reb Fastag's tune: "With this *niggun* we went to the gas chambers, and with this *niggun* we will one day soon greet the Moshiach."[59]

After telling this story, Grandpa, whose first wife was murdered at Auschwitz and who had himself survived Nazi brutality at Breendonk and Mechelen concentration camps, led the family in singing Reb Fastag's slow, *d'veykus niggun*[60] to *Ani Ma'amin*. Each note of the song was a testament to his abiding faith.

I was recently reminded of this story and my grandfather's abiding faith, when, as part of a Holocaust educational travel class I annually taught at the University of Texas at El Paso, I took a group of my students to Poland and we spent several days at Auschwitz studying the history of this Nazi extermination camp. At Auschwitz we entered the bunker that had been used to house children, and we immediately heard music coming from deep inside the children's bunker: the sound was the unmistakeble, plaintive notes of Reb Fastag's Modzitz tune as recorded by Reb Ben Zion

Shenker. A scholar at Auschwitz confirmed the story my grandfather had told me years before about this *niggun*. In his telling of the story, our guide added that Reb Fastag's *niggun* had not only made its way back to the Modzitzer Rebbe, but that the tune had also spread throughout the Nazi concentration camp system. He told us that many victims of the Nazis sang this *niggun* as they were marched to the gas chambers.

X

My grandfather's life began with him sitting on his grandfather's lap, inspiring the Modzitzer Rebbe to compose his famous *niggunim*. Many decades later, when, after a series of strokes mostly robbed my grandfather of the power of speech, he was living out his last days at the Bialystoker Nursing Home on the Lower East Side of New York. From the window beside his bed my grandfather would gaze out across the street at the old *Forverts* building—a most fitting view for a Yiddish writer. Before Shabbos, I would bike down from my apartment in the East Village to visit with him. Sitting together we would sing the Modzitzer *niggunim* of his youth. Among the songs we would sing was Reb Fastag's *niggun* to Ani Ma'amin, Maimonides's 12th attribute of faith that my grandfather had taught me so many years earlier. My grandfather beside me, I would sing the words of Maimonides and focus with perfect *kavanah* on each of the great sage's words: "Ani Ma'amin b'Emuna Sheleima, b'vias HaMoshiach; v'af al pi she'yismamaya, im kol zeh, achakeh lo b'chol yom she'yavo." After several minutes of singing, the words would begin to fade away leaving only me, Grandpa, and this wordless Modzitzer tune.

Reb Fastag's *niggun* seemed to encompass all that I loved about Judaism and all that I had learned from my grandfather. It was a tune filled with understanding and mercy. It seems to be a tune of which I can never get enough. Even now, upon being woken in the middle of the night by one of my children who has had a nightmare, I will turn to that Modzitzer tune to calm my child's fears and restore a measure of peace.

Sometimes, while I am alone reading or out walking in the mountains behind my house in the desert, I will find that the piercing silence is punctuated by the swayed rhythm of my humming. When I am completely still and I remember to listen, the tune in my head and upon my lips sounds a lot like *ani ma'amin, ani ma'amin, ani ma'amin.*

Notes

1. *Negel vasser* is the Yiddish term for the ritual washing of one's hands upon awakening from sleep.

2. *Flanken* (short ribs) is a cut of meat used in many traditional Eastern European Jewish dishes.

3. The plural form of the Yiddish term for the Jewish Sabbath.

4. Yom Kippur is the holiest and most solemn day of the year and Jews are supposed to refrain from eating any food or drinking any water during the holiday.

5. *The Complete Artscroll Machzor—Yom Kippur* (Mesorah Publications, New York, 1986), 533.

6. Orthodox halachic authorities have banned the use of electricity on Shabbos (Yom Kippur has even more strictures and prohibitions than the Sabbath).

7. *Shtiebel* is a Yiddish word for "little house," and it is a small, informal gathering place for communal prayer.

8. *Gevaldik,* is a Yiddish word meaning "great" or "fantastic."

9. Chapters from the book of *Psalms*.

10. *Olam Ha'bah*—is the world to come.

11. A *chavrusah* session is a joint learning partnership or joint study session. This is a traditional way of Talmud study in *yeshivot* around the world.

12. *'Ztl*—is an acronym that stands for, "Zecher Tzaddik Livracha," which translates as "in blessed memory of a righteous person."

13. *Nifter* is a Yiddish/Hebrew word meaning "deceased."

14. A title given to righteous people.

15. *Gadol b'torah* is a great person in Torah learning.

16. The Holy Blessed One—a name for God.

17. Pray.

18. *Kavanah* literally means "intention." It refers to the focus and mindfulness necessary for Jewish rituals and prayers.

19. *Sugya* is the component of the Talmud comprising rabbinical analysis of and commentary on the Mishnah. In this context it also refers to the section of the Talmud currently being studied in class.

20. The word *Gedolim* is the plural form of the Hebrew word that means "big" or "great," and it refers to the most important and revered rabbis.

21. *Mivatel Torah* is literally "wasting the Torah," or wasting time that could be occupied with Torah study. This concept could be derived from numerous sources, including the Mishnah in Pirkei Avot 4:10, which reads as follows: "Rabbi Meir says: Minimize business and engage in Torah. Be humble of spirit before everyone. If you neglect the Torah, many reasons for neglecting it will be presented to you. And if you labor in Torah, [He (God)] has abundant reward to grant you."

22. The *Mussar* movement is a Jewish ethical and educational movement that stresses morality and discipline.

23. https://www.sefaria.org/Avodah_Zarah.20b

24. Shalom Auslander. *Foreskin's Lament* (New York Riverhead: 2007), 134–35.

25. The Babylonian Talmud, Tractate *Shabbat* 130a

26. As *The Jewish Telegraphic Agency* (JTA) recently reported: "Some 160 rabbis, including several prominent American Orthodox leaders, appear on a list of rabbis whom Israel's haredi Orthodox-dominated Chief Rabbinate does not trust to confirm the Jewish identities of immigrants." https://www.jta. org/2017/07/08/news-opinion/united-states/is-israel-blacklisting-these-prominent-american-orthodox-rabbis. This comes on the heels of the Chief Rabbinate refusing to accept conversions from many prominent American Orthodox rabbis.

27. Halacha is the collective body of Jewish religious laws derived from the Written and Oral Torah.

28. Gary Rosenblatt "Between a Rav and a Hard Place," *The New York Jewish Week*. RGB Media. June 26, 2009. http://jewishweek.timesofisrael.com/between-a-rav-and-a-hard-place/ October 10, 2017.

29. The term "ultra-Orthodox" is generally used to distinguish a type of Orthodoxy even more devout than what is often referred to as "Modern-Orthodox." In his short story, "What We Talk About When We Talk About Anne Frank," Nathan Englander's narrator humorously refers to the ironies of the term while describing his wife's friend and her religious transformation: ". . . Lauren met Mark and they went from Orthodox to *ultra*-Orthodox, which to me sounds like a repackaged detergent—ORTHODOX ULTRA, now with more deep-healing power" ("What We Talk About When We Talk About Anne Frank," p. 5).

30. Micah Stein, "Rallying Against the Internet," *Tablet. Superfame*. May 17, 2012. http://www.tabletmag.com/jewish-life-and-religion/99840/rallying-against-the-internet. October 10, 2017.

31. If only the Mets could fill Citi Field as quickly as a rabbinic decree.

32. Rabbi Moses ben Maimon (1135–1204) is known in Hebrew literature by his acronym Rambam and by the Western world as Maimonides. The Rambam's fourteen-volume codification of Talmudic law, *The Mishneh Torah*, is still to this day considered one of the canonical works on halacha.

33. The Babylonian Talmud, Tractate Sanhedrin 99a.

34. Rambam, Hilchot Tesuvah 3:11.

35. The term "rebbe" means teacher, "rabbeim" is the plural form of the word. In the ultra-Orthodox world, rabbinic authority means complete obedience to the halachic interpretation of the communal leaders. A further concept related to rabbinic authority is rabbinic infallibility and "Da'as Torah" (literally "Knowledge of Torah"). This idea imparts authority to rabbinic figures for all matters, not just

those relating to Judaism. For example, several ultra-Orthodox rabbis have ruled that babies should not be vaccinated and therefore numerous ultra-Orthodox children fall ill, sometimes with fatal illnesses, from preventable diseases. This concept is based upon the idea that all concepts in the world are contained in the Torah so if you are a rabbinic authority your opinion is vital on all matters.

36. Mishneh Torah, Repentance 3:7 *Mishneh Torah, Yod ha-hazakah*, trans. by Simon Glazer, 1927.

37. Menachem Kellner *Must a Jew Believe Anything?* (2nd ed. Portland, OR: Oxford, 2006), 20.

38. https://www.sefaria.org/Mishneh_Torah,_Repentance.3.7/en/Mishneh_Torah,_Yod_ha-hazakah,_trans._by_Simon_Glazer,_1927?lang=bi&p2=Hasagot_HaRaavad_on_Mishneh_Torah,_Repentance.3.7.1&lang2=bi&w2=all&lang3=en.

39. These Thirteen Principles of Faith were put into liturgical form as a summary of Maimonides's categories.

40. Isadore Twersky, *A Maimonides Reader* (Springfield, NJ: Behrman House, 1972), 402.

41. Ibid.

42. Shulem Deen, *All Who Go Do Not Return: A Memoir* (Minneapolis: Graywolf Press, 2015), 3.

43. Leah Vincent, *Cut Me Loose: Sin and Salvation after my Ultra-Orthodox Girlhood* (New York: Penguin, 2015), 43.

44. *tznius*, describes both character traits of modesty and humility.

45. Leah Vincent, *Cut Me Loose: Sin and Salvation after my Ultra-Orthodox Girlhood* (New York: Penguin, 2015), 42.

46. Ibid., 43.

47. Babylonian Talmud, Tractate *Baba Metzia* 59a.

48. Morris Dickstein, *Why Not Say What Happened: A Sentimental Education* (New York: Norton, 2015), 53.

49. Ibid., 55.

50. Ibid.

51. Leah Vincent, *Cut Me Loose: Sin and Salvation after my Ultra-Orthodox Girlhood* (New York: Penguin, 2015), 43.

52. Stephen M. Cohen, "Dramatic Orthodox Growth Is Transforming the American Jewish Community." *The Forward*, December 19, 2016.

53. A *beis din* is a halachic, religious court usually consisting of three rabbis convened to decide a legal matter.

54. Shulem Deen, *All Who Go Do Not Return: A Memoir* (Minneapolis: Graywolf Press, 2015), 11.

55. Moshe Chayim Luzzatto, *Messilat Yesharim: The Path Of The Just* (Spring Valley, NY: Feldheim, 1966), 15.

56. Yehuda Amicahi, *The Selected Poetry of Yehuda Amichai* (Los Angeles: University of California Press, 2013), 13–14.

57. Hebrew for "melody."

58. Chiune Sugihara was the Japanese consul general in Kovno, Lithuania, who between July and August of 1940 issued more than 2,000 transit visas for Jewish refugees. Among the many thousands of people Sugihara saved was the Modzitzer Rebbe.

59. The Messiah.

60. *D'veykus* means "to cleave," and a *d'veykus niggun* is a tune designed to draw the listener closer to God.

Bibliography

Amicahi, Yehuda. *The Selected Poetry of Yehuda Amichai*. Los Angeles: University of California Press, 2013.

Auslander, Shalom. *Foreskin's Lament*. New York: Riverhead, 2007.

Babylonian Talmud, *The William Davidson Talmud*, Tractate Shabbat, Folio 130, front (a) side: 1–18.

Cohen, Stephen M. "Dramatic Orthodox Growth Is Transforming the American Jewish Community." *The Forward*. December 19, 2016.

The Complete Artscroll Machzor—Yom Kippur. Mesorah Publications, New York, 1986.

Deen, Shulem. *All Who Go Do Not Return: A Memoir*. Minneapolis: Graywolf Press, 2015.

Dickstein, Morris. *Why Not Say What Happened: A Sentimental Education*. New York: Norton, 2015.

Englander, Nathan. *What We Talk About When We Talk About Anne Frank*. New York: Vintage, 2013.

Kellner, Menachem. *Must a Jew Believe Anything?* 2nd ed. Portland, OR: Oxford, 2006. Print.

Kook, Rabbi Avraham Yitzchak HaCohen. *Arpilei Tohar*. Jaffa: A. Ittin, 1914.

Luzzatto, Moshe Chayim. *Messilat Yesharim: The Path of the Just*, Spring Valley: Feldheim, 1966.

Rambam Hil. Ishut 3:4 is the Rambam on Halachot of Ishut (Marriage) Chapter 3, Section 4.

Rambam. Mishneh Torah, Repentence. 3.7https://www.sefaria.org/Mishneh_Torah, Repentance.3.7/en/Mishnah_Torah,_Yod_hahazakah,_trans._by_Simon_Glazer, 1927?lang=bi

Rosenblatt, Gary. "Between a Rav and a Hard Place." *The New York Jewish Week*. RGB Media. June 26, 2009. http://jewishweek.timesofisrael.com/between-a-rav-and-a-hard-place/October 10, 2017.

Scholem, Gershom. *Major Trends in Jewish Mysticism*. New York: Schocken, 1961.

Stein, Micah. Rallying Against the Internet," *Tablet. Superfame*. May 17, 2012. http://www.tabletmag.com/jewish-life-and-religion/99840/rallying-against-the-internet October 10, 2017.

Thoreau, Henry David, *Walden and Civil Disobedience*. New York: Penguin, 1983.

Twersky, Isadore. *A Maimonides Reader*. Springfield, NJ: Behrman House, 1972. Print.

Vincent, Leah. *Cut Me Loose: Sin and Salvation after my Ultra-Orthodox Girlhood*. New York: Penguin, 2015.

Contributors

Gabi Abramac is a linguist, anthropologist, and international affairs professional. She is currently a researcher at the Moshe David Gaon Center for Ladino Culture at Ben-Gurion University of the Negev, the director of a foreign language institute in Zagreb, Croatia, and serves as a consultant to the United Nations. She was previously a research fellow at Fordham University and New York Public Library, a lecturer at the University of Zagreb, and a Fulbright postdoctoral fellow at New York University. Dr. Abramac has twenty years of experience in applied linguistics, specializing in second-language pedagogy for adult students. She is a member of a Think Tank at the Department of Teaching and Learning at the NYU Steinhardt School of Culture, Education, and Human Development, which focuses on innovative teaching technologies and strategic leadership. In her sociolinguistic research, she focuses on the mutual relationship between language, ideology, displacement, migration, and socio-religious beliefs. As one of the last Ladino speakers in the Western Balkans she is heavily invested in language revitalization activism in the region.

Rachel Berger is an independent consultant with a background in non-profit management, philanthropy, and Jewish communal work. Rachel worked at Footsteps from 2012–2018, and in her capacity as Director of Community Engagement she led Footsteps' community building, leadership development, and public education programs as well as Footsteps' foundation relations. Prior to joining Footsteps, Rachel was the Director of Grantmaking at Bend the Arc, where she managed the organization's strategic philanthropy and grantmaking collaborations. Rachel has an MSW in Social Enterprise Administration from Columbia University, is current Wexner Field Fellows (Class 1), and was a 2011–12 Dorot Israel Fellow. Rachel lives in Philadelphia with her family.

Ezra Cappell is Professor of Jewish Studies and English and Director of the Perlmutter Fellows Program at the College of Charleston. Cappell previously served as the founding Director of the Inter-American Jewish Studies Program at the University of Texas at El Paso, and he is a recipient of the University of Texas Regents' Outstanding Teaching Award. Cappell received his BA in English from Queens College (CUNY), his MA in Creative Writing from The City College (CUNY), and his MPhil and PhD in English and American Literature from New York University. Cappell teaches and publishes in the fields of 20th-Century and Contemporary Jewish American Literature. Cappell has published numerous articles on American and Jewish-American writing, and he is the author of the book, *American Talmud: The Cultural Work of Jewish American Fiction*. Cappell is a frequent lecturer on Jewish-American culture and Holocaust writing and he serves as editor of the SUNY Press book series in Contemporary Jewish Literature and Culture.

Lynn Davidman is the Robert M. Beren Distinguished Professor of Modern Jewish Studies at Kansas University. At KU she has taught classes in Feminist Theory, Sociological Theory, and Narrative Methodology. The fundamental question that she has focused her three books upon is how people make sense of their lives after a major, unexpected biographical disruption, and how through conversations and interviews people construct narratives that establish coherence between events before and after this transformation of their lives. Her central areas of research have been gender and religion. In her books, she uses grounded theory to develop an analysis that ties the particular case study question to larger theoretical issues. Her most recent book, *Becoming Un-Orthodox* (2014) integrates her new and growing fascination with sociology of the body and the centrality of embodiment to all social interactions. Lynn also serves on the advisory board of the Center for the Study of Religion at Princeton University and is a member of the editorial board for Qualitative Sociology.

Shulem Deen is a writer and journalist, and the author of the critically-acclaimed memoir *All Who Go Do Not Return*. He is the recipient of a National Jewish Book Award, a Great Lakes College Association New

Writers Award, and a Housatonic Book Award, as well as the Prix Médicis Essai for the French edition of his memoir. A former Skverer Hasid, he first began writing the anonymous "Hasidic Rebel" blog in 2003, which received wide attention in Jewish media, and a featured profile in the *Village Voice*. More recently, he has been writing widely on the intersection of ultra-Orthodoxy and the secular world, and served for four years as editor of Unpious, an online journal focused on critiquing ultra-Orthodoxy. He is a longstanding advocate for those who have left the ultra-Orthodox community, and was listed in the Forward 50 in 2015. Since 2011, he has served on the Footsteps Board of Directors. His articles have appeared in the *New York Times*, the *New Republic*, *Salon*, the *Forward*, *Tablet* Magazine, and other publications. He is currently at work on a novel, and lives in Brooklyn, New York.

Morris Dickstein is a literary scholar, cultural historian, professor, essayist, and public intellectual. He currently holds the appointment of Distinguished Professor of English Emeritus at the City Univeristy New York Graduate Center. He is the author of numerous award-winning books including *Dancing in the Dark: A Cultural History of the Great Depression* (2009) and, most recently, a memoir, *Why Not Say What Happened: A Sentimental Education* (2015). His work has appeared in *The New York Times Book Review*; *Partisan Review*; *TriQuarterly*; *The New Republic*; *The Nation*; *Harper's*; *New York Magazine*; *Critical Inquiry*; *Dissent*; and others.

Tsivia Finman has a background in public policy and organizational management. Prior to joining Footsteps Tsivia worked at The Jewish Theological Seminary where she managed the Provosts' academic and faculty program portfolio. Tsivia was awarded a Master's in Public Administration from Wayne State University in Detroit, Michigan, in 2008, where she previously received bachelors' degrees in Public Affairs and Political Science. She grew up within the Chabad-Lubavitch community in Detroit. Tsivia joined Footsteps in 2015 to help build an operations department, overseeing key administration functions and developing systems and processes to help Footsteps grow and strengthen into its second decade. Tsivia is a current UJA Ruskay Fellow.

Frimet Goldberger is a freelance print and radio journalist. She has written widely about growing up in the Hasidic community of Kiryas Joel and ultimately leaving with her husband and children. Her radio stories have been broadcast on PRI's "The World," as well as on BBC World Service. Her story on the cover-up of sex abuse in the Hásidic enclave of New Square, New York, was awarded a 2015 Ippies Award for best investigative/in-depth story, and was also a finalist for a 2015 Deadline Club Award. Frimet graduated from Sarah Lawrence College in 2013. She now lives in the suburbs of Rockland County, New York, with her husband and two children where she runs a baking business, The Babka Lady, selling delicious babkas whose recipe originates from Hungary and was passed down for generations. She is at work on her first novel.

Joshua Halberstam was born and raised in Boro Park, continued his Talmudic studies at Kollel Chaim Berlin, and received his PhD in philosophy from NYU. He is currently Professor at Bronx Community College (BCC), City University of New York, where he teaches communication and philosophy. Before teaching at BBC, Halberstam taught at Teachers College, Columbia University, New York University, and the New School for Social Research. He has published widely in the areas of epistemology, ethics, the philosophy of religion and Jewish studies. He is also the author of a novel, *A Seat at the Table*, which traces the development of a young man raised in a contemporary Chassidic world. His most recent book (based on stories told by his father on Yiddish radio) is *The Blind Angel: New Old Chassidic Tales*, a translation of Chassidic tales from the Yiddish.

Jessica Lang is Professor of English and the founding Newman Director of the Wasserman Jewish Studies Center. A graduate of Cornell University and Brandeis University, she taught at Brandeis and The Johns Hopkins University before joining the Baruch College English department. She works on Holocaust literature and film; Jewish American literature; women's fiction; and early American fiction. Her work has appeared in *Arizona Quarterly*; *Texas Studies in Literature and Languages*; *Studies in American Jewish Literature*; *Contemporary Literature*; *Journal of Modern Literature*; *Tulsa Studies in Women's Literature*; *The Massachusetts Review*; and other newspapers and collections. Her book, *Textual Silence: Unreadability and the Holocaust*, was recently published by Rutgers University Press.

Leah Lax joined an ultra-Orthodox sect as a young teen and spent thirty years among them. *Uncovered* (2015) is her memoir of those years—as a closeted lesbian, wife, and mother of seven. Her published work includes award-winning fiction, nonfiction, and two major stage productions.

Miriam R. Moster was raised in an ultra-Orthodox family in Flatbush, Brooklyn. She pursued her BA at Baruch College and then went on to receive her MFA in creative writing from Hunter (CUNY). She currently teaches writing and literature courses at Ramapo College and Rockland Community College.

Miriam Moster is a PhD candidate in sociology at the City University of New York Graduate Center. She received her BA in philosophy from Baruch (CUNY) and her MFA in poetry from Hunter (CUNY). She has written for Jewish Telegraphic Agency, the Jewish Daily Forward, Lohud and Zeek. Miriam is currently a Wexner Graduate Fellow in Jewish studies (class 32) and a Mellon Humanities Public Fellow. She lives with her husband and son in Rockland County.

Jessica Roda is an anthropologist and ethnomusicologist serving as an assistant professor of Jewish Civilization in the Walsh School of Foreign Service at Georgetown University. She studies issues of performance, religion, gender, international cultural politics, and transnationalism. After publishing for almost ten years on the political and social implications of Judeo-Spanish music in France and Moroccan Jewish culture in Montreal, now she has undertaken an ethnography of Hasidic life in Montreal and New York City which encompasses individuals within the community, at the margins of it, in double-life, or who have left it altogether. She is working on her second book, *Performing Jewishness. Hasidic Women on Stage and on Screen in North America,* where she explores how the artistic and political performances of Hasidic women act as an agent of social and cultural empowerment within the religious world and as a space to challenge gender, race, and religious norms in the context of decolonizing feminism.

Lani Santo has dedicated her career to social justice, human rights, building inclusive and accepting communities, and supporting individuals through transformative experiences within the Jewish community and beyond. As the Executive Director of Footsteps since 2010, Lani has driven the organization's growth from a three-person start-up with a

$400,000 budget to an established 501c3 with a staff of 15, a program center in Manhattan with satellite programs in Rockland and Brooklyn, and a $2.3 million annual operating budget. Under her leadership, Footsteps' profile has expanded to reach the pages of *The New York Times* and the screen of Netflix, which debuted "One of Us," an award-winning documentary about three courageous Footsteps members. Lani is an alumna of Avodah's Jewish Service Corps and served on the Avodah board from 2004–2013. She currently sits on the UpStart Advisory Council and was named to *Forward*'s "36 Under 36" list in 2015. Lani graduated from Barnard College and holds an MPA in Public and Nonprofit Management from NYU's Wagner School. Lani lives in Brooklyn with her husband and young son.

Shira Schwartz is a PhD candidate in Comparative Literature and a graduate student at the Frankel Center for Judaic Studies at the University of Michigan, Ann Arbor. Her work focuses on the role of space and the body in the yeshiva and the production of Jewish knowledge, in both the late-antique rabbinic period and contemporary American Orthodoxies. She is a recipient of the Holstein Dissertation Fellowship, University of Michigan Institute for Humanities Graduate Fellowship, Network for Research in Jewish Education Emerging Scholar Award and a fellowship recipient and member of the New York Working Group for Jewish Orthodoxies at Fordham University. She is also a poet and an essayist.

Naomi Seidman is the Chancellor Jackman Professor of the Arts in the Department for the Study of Religion and the Centre for Diaspora and Transnational Studies at the University of Toronto, as well as a 2016 Guggenheim Fellow. Her most recent book is entitled *Sarah Schenirer and Bais Yaakov: A Revolution in the Name of Tradition* (Littman Library, 2019). Her earlier works include: *A Marriage Made in Heaven: The Sexual Politics of Hebrew and Yiddish* (University of California Press, 1997); *Faithful Renderings: Jewish—Christian Difference and the Politics of Translation* (Chicago, 2006); *The Marriage Plot, Or, How Jews Fell in Love with Love, and with Literature* (Stanford, 2016).

Moshe Shenfeld was born and raised in a Haredi family. He studied in the Hevron Yeshiva in Jerusalem until the age of 20, then he left the Haredi community and joined the Israeli Defense Forces. After his service, he went to a pre-academic program, and then pursued a Bachelor's degree in Physics, Math, and Computer Science from the Hebrew University. Today, he works as a team manager in Mobileye's algorithms department, and is studying to receive a Master's degree in Computer Science at Hebrew University. At the beginning of 2013, Moshe co-founded "Out for Change"—an NGO that is dedicated to attaining equal rights and opportunities for those who were educated in the Haredi educational system and left the community. He served as the Chairman and the Research Team Manager of the organization until 2018 and today is on the Board of Directors.

Leah Vincent is the author of *Cut Me Loose: Sin and Salvation after My Ultra-Orthodox Girlhood* (2015) and the co-author of *Legends of the Talmud: A Collection of Ancient Magical Jewish Tales* (2014). Her writing has appeared in *The New York Times, Salon, Unpious, ZEEK, Daily Beast, Jewish Daily Forward* and elsewhere. A first-generation college student, Leah earned a master's degree in public policy as a Pforzheimer Fellow at the Harvard Kennedy School. In 2014, Leah was named to both the *Jewish Week's 36 Under 36* and the *Jewish Daily Forward's Forward 50*.

Frieda Vizel grew up in the Hasidic community of Kiryas Joel and left the lifestyle with her son. She now explores contemporary Hasidic culture through creative and academic work. Frieda is a graduate student at Sarah Lawrence College and a tour guide for Hasidic Williamsburg walking tours. Her website is friedavizel.com.

Mark Zelcer is Assistant Professor of Philosophy at Queensborough Community College, CUNY and has published in various areas of philosophy including the philosophy of mathematics and ancient philosophy. He lives in Brooklyn, New York.

Index